IT'S NOT TV

THE SPECTACULAR
RISE, REVOLUTION,
AND FUTURE OF
HBO

Felix Gillette and John Koblin

VIKING

VIKING
An imprint of Penguin Random House LLC
penguinrandomhouse.com

LIBRARY OF CONGRESS CATALOGING-IN-PUBLICATION DATA
Names: Gillette, Felix, author. | Koblin, John, author.
Title: It's not tv : the spectacular rise, revolution, and future of HBO /
Felix Gillette and John Koblin.
Other titles: It is not tv
Description: New York : Viking, [2022] | Includes bibliographical references and index.
Identifiers: LCCN 2022013252 (print) | LCCN 2022013253 (ebook) |
ISBN 9780593296196 (hardcover) | ISBN 9780593296202 (ebook) |
ISBN 9780593653104 (international edition)
Subjects: LCSH: Home Box Office (Firm)—History.
Classification: LCC PN1992.92.H66 I86 2022 (print) |
LCC PN1992.92.H66 (ebook) | DDC 302.23—dc23/eng/20220405
LC record available at https://lccn.loc.gov/2022013252
LC ebook record available at https://lccn.loc.gov/2022013253

Printed in the United States of America
1st Printing

Book design by Daniel Lagin

For Jenny, Hugo, and Dexter

—Felix

For Bennett

—John

CONTENTS

PART III: BAND OF SHRUGGERS
(1998–2007)

PART IV: THE NIGHT IS DARK AND FULL OF NETFLIX
(2007–2018)

PART V: HBO TO THE MAX
(2018–2022)

IT'S NOT TV

Taking Flight

On October 1, 1975, Muhammad Ali sat in a dressing room in a sweltering coliseum in the Philippines while trainers taped his hands. In a few minutes, he would enter the ring to fight Joe Frazier for the third and final time. For weeks, Ali had been taunting Frazier in public, showing up at a press conference with a toy gorilla and saying it represented Frazier's conscience. "Come on, Gorilla, we in Manila," said Ali, jabbing the primate doll in the face. "Come on, Gorilla. This is a thriller."

The previous two fights had been dazzling. Frazier had won the first by unanimous decision. In the rematch, Ali had triumphed. This time, the winner would be crowned the heavyweight champion of the world.

Roughly nine thousand miles away, a giddy group of cable executives gathered around a TV inside a ballroom at the Holiday Inn in Vero Beach, Florida. The sun was down, the bar was open, and everyone was delirious to see the fight—that is, *if* they could see the fight. Would the technology work?

Gerald Levin, the president of HBO, a slightly rumpled man with a mop of dark hair, a caterpillar mustache, and sharp brown eyes, chatted with his colleagues in the room. What they were about to watch was more than a fight being televised live from the other side of the earth. It was the future of home entertainment. Welcome to TV's satellite age.

Among his colleagues at HBO, Levin was known as an erudite polymath. He had graduated Phi Beta Kappa from Haverford College, where he studied religion and dreamed of becoming a novelist. He possessed a wide-ranging intellect, an encyclopedic memory, and a reputation as a bit of a know-it-all.

Levin had started his career as a corporate bankruptcy lawyer in New York and then segued into consulting, hopscotching the globe. In the late 1960s, he moved to Iran to oversee the construction of a massive irrigation system. There, he came to believe that the key to business was dominating the flow of the product. "In my mind, the transmission of water and power and electrons were all the same thing," he would later say. "You just had to be in a position of controlling the conduit."

At the time, a major shift in how electrons flowed around the planet was on the verge of disrupting the entertainment business.

In early 1972, Levin met and befriended Charles Dolan, a convivial entrepreneur originally from Cleveland, Ohio, whose dad had invented an early prototype of the automatic car transmission. Together, they attended a convention in Chicago for the growing industry of cable television, which promised to use coaxial cables to deliver a clearer TV picture to the large swaths of the country that struggled, due to mountain ranges or similar impediments, to pick up broadcast TV signals.

Like his father, Dolan was driven to create new things. At the time, he was building out the first cable TV franchise in lower Manhattan, where certain neighborhoods, due to tall buildings, couldn't reliably get clear TV signals. The project was being financed by Time Inc., the magazine publishing company, which was going through a phase of corporate diversification.

Dolan's undertaking was not going well. Laying cable in New York required navigating a complex rat's nest of physical and political entanglements. Progress was slow. The operation was hemorrhaging money.

Levin came on board to help Dolan with another project that was likewise struggling. Dolan's idea—conceived on a vacation in France, months earlier—was to entice New Yorkers to sign up for his cable service by offering them an exclusive network of programming, called the Green Channel, which they wouldn't be able to see anywhere else. For a small additional monthly fee, they'd get to watch a mix of programming, which, Dolan imagined, would include local sports from Madison Square Garden and a slate of Hollywood movies, uninterrupted by ads. He planned to charge six dollars per month.

The executives at Time Inc. had serious doubts. Why would anybody pay for the Green Channel when they could get high quality shows for free from established broadcast networks?

The venture struggled to line up programming. Making an original TV series, which required payment for actors, writers, directors, producers, crew, cameras, locations, trucks, and insurance, was exorbitantly expensive. So was renting content from others. The three commercial broadcast networks, ABC, CBS, and NBC, were already paying handsomely for the rights to air major sports events. Before the advent of the VCR, Hollywood studios were wary of licensing too many of their movies to TV networks, fearing they might depress ticket sales and irritate theater owners.

In the summer of 1972, Dolan put Levin in charge of finding programming for the Green Channel. Levin met with contractors, lobbied for more resources from Time Inc., bargained with Hollywood studios, and secured a few stray TV rights from New York sports teams.

Before launching, Time Inc. executives gave the Green Channel a new name. They called it the Home Box Office, or HBO, for short. They hoped the name would convey the essence of its mission: allowing consumers to watch novel performances at home—movies, concerts, sports competitions—that had previously required buying a ticket and trekking out to a public venue.

On November 8, 1972, HBO made its debut for some 375 subscribers in the small town of Wilkes-Barre, Pennsylvania. Levin was the first executive to appear on HBO, introducing the inaugural lineup of programming, which included a New York Rangers hockey game and a year-old movie from Paramount called *Sometimes a Great Notion*, starring Paul Newman and based on the novel by Ken Kesey.

The initial test did little to stoke broader demand for the service. HBO sputtered. The network was boxed in by the emerging landscape of cable TV, which was a fragmented mess. The only way for HBO to reach cable subscribers beyond the New York region would be to cobble together a cross-country, point-to-point relay network of microwave transmission towers and existing landlines, which were controlled by the Bell Telephone Company under a broad monopoly. Doing so would cost way more than the network could afford. Much to Time's dismay, HBO was going nowhere. A year after launching, HBO had roughly ten thousand subscribers. "Very demoralizing," Levin said. "We started giving away free turkeys at Thanksgiving. Did everything we could."

In 1973, Time bought out Dolan's stake in both HBO and his Manhattan cable operation. Both were losing money, and Dolan no longer had enough resources to stay the course. He reluctantly gave up his business, took his payout, and cast an eye toward Long Island, a fertile territory for home entertainment just outside the city, largely untouched by rival cablemen. There, in the decades to come, he would go on to become a billionaire, selling cable service in the suburbs.

In December 1974, about two years into HBO's faltering life, Levin and his colleagues had an idea. They'd heard that the telecom giant RCA was scheduled to launch a commercial satellite into orbit. Called Satcon1, it was capable of transmitting moving pictures. The satellite still had unused capacity, which RCA was in the process of leasing. In a flurry of meetings, Levin convinced the Time Inc. board of directors to invest $7.5 million to rent space on RCA's "bird" for the next six years. Levin was adamant. With satellite distribution, HBO could beam shows simultaneously to cable system providers around North America. It could give the network a second chance.

The board begrudgingly conceded. Levin's sales pitch suggested that the potential upside, however remote, was enormous. "All of a sudden, these locavores, these little cable systems were going to be brought together," Levin said.

While Levin considered the best way to demonstrate the potential of the new technology, he learned that Muhammad Ali would be fighting Joe Frazier in the Philippines that fall. Given its far-flung location, none of the American broadcast networks were planning to air the fight live. The only way to see the action in the United States was to buy a ticket to one of the movie theaters or stadiums that would be carrying the fight via closed-circuit technology.

Levin saw an opportunity to deliver unique live programming, via satellite, right into people's homes. He set up a meeting with the boxing promoter Don King, a brilliant ex-bookie who was a growing force in the boxing world. He was working with Ali, orchestrating the event. Together, King and Levin hashed out a plan.

That fall, just after 10:00 a.m. in Manila, Ali and Frazier entered the ring, and the HBO satellite uplink went live. The executives in Florida gaped nervously as the screen flickered in front of them. The technology worked. "It was a thrilling moment," Levin said.

The fight was also simultaneously transmitted to a second cable TV system in Jackson, Mississippi. There, too, the method worked. "It was crystal sharp," William Hooks, an HBO sales rep, would later recall. "I remember thinking, this is really magical, this is stunning."

For the next hour, everyone watched with growing excitement as the "Thrilla in Manila" turned into one of the most memorable fights in boxing history. A new era in sports broadcasting was born, with Ali jabbing, ducking, and weaving right into the living rooms of HBO subscribers. "Could have went either way, I heard," Ali told reporters after his victory by technical knockout in the fourteenth round. "It was my rally that pulled it out."

The same could be said for HBO. The investment in satellite technology got HBO off the ropes. The successful simulcast of the fight was met with giddy excitement among the growing ranks of cable TV operators. "On came the fight from Manila, and . . . the picture quality was extraordinary," said Robert Rosencrans, the owner of the cable system in Vero Beach. "We put it on and, God, we knew we had a winner."

The following year, Time Inc. installed Nick Nicholas, a sharp-minded graduate of the Harvard Business School with a knack for operational competency, at the top of HBO to help guide the network's next phase of growth. Among Time Inc. staffers, Nicholas was known as "Nick the Knife" due to his skill at slicing budgetary fat off freewheeling magazines. While Levin moved into the role of HBO chairman, Nicholas took over the day-to-day operations of turning HBO into a functioning, profitable business.

"We had climbed on a wave we didn't even know existed, this pay-television wave," Nicholas said. "We happened to be the leading surfboard perfectly positioned on the wave, so we had a hell of a ride."

"In a very Time Inc. way, they wanted to load it up with business school graduates," says Henry McGee, who started working at the network right out of school in 1979. "Out of my Harvard Business class alone, there were five of us who joined HBO. Few of us had any experience in broadcasting. But we did know business models and were prepared to take a different look at how the industry might work."

In communities across America, scrappy entrepreneurs were hastily stringing coaxial cable through the countryside and trying to convince skeptical households to start paying for TV for the first time. To stoke HBO's growth, the network's executives made a critical decision: any cable operator who signed up a new HBO customer would get a cut of their subscription fee in perpetuity. Of the $8–$12 monthly payment, the cable operator got to keep roughly half, giving them a significant new source of income and a major incentive to talk up HBO in their sales calls to potential customers.

In the years following the Thrilla in Manila, numerous cable businesses plunked down roughly fifty thousand to one hundred thousand dollars for bulky satellite receivers, known as earth stations, with which they could catch HBO's signal from space and redirect it to paying customers. The novelty of the futuristic hardware assured plenty of free local publicity upon arrival. HBO handled the hype, storming into town with free movie posters and T-shirts, taking out ads in local publications, and blanketing nearby homes with sign-up notices in the mail.

As chairman of HBO, Levin routinely flew out to rural communities to attend ribbon-cutting festivities marking the debut of freshly set-up dishes. "When they installed the earth station, it was like the astronauts had landed," Levin said. "It was a huge attraction."

On makeshift stages, HBO representatives posed for photos with local dignitaries and gave sound bites about the wonders of HBO. One day in

Laredo, Texas, HBO executives watched in amazement as a priest stepped forward, raised a palm toward the metallic surface of a newly grounded satellite receiver, and blessed it with a prayer of gratitude.

A subscription to the "premium" network began to emerge as a kind of middlebrow status symbol, and HBO spread. To have HBO meant seeing spectacles in your home that were unavailable to your envious neighbors. "We brought the glitz of Hollywood to the plains of Kansas," an HBO salesperson would later recall. On roadside marquees, motels beckoned passersby with declarations of "Free HBO." Subscribers mushroomed. Between 1974 and 1977, HBO's customer base grew more than a hundredfold. By the end of 1977, HBO was collecting monthly fees from more than 1.6 million subscribers and was finally turning a profit.

Competitors raced to follow HBO into space, eventually giving rise to a rowdy flock of new satellite-distributed cable channels: USA, Nickelodeon, MTV, CNN, ESPN, BET. As the cable era took flight, HBO assumed the lead position.

"We didn't just build HBO," one of the network's top executives would later say. "We built the cable industry."

PART I

THE UPSTARTS

(1978–1995)

CHAPTER 1

Surviving the Premiere

One day in 1978, Sheila Nevins got a phone call from a headhunter. Did she know anybody who might want to work for the cable channel HBO? They were looking to hire someone on a temporary basis. Nevins racked her brain. What was HBO again? "Is it a dirty channel?" she asked.

Nevins was a broadcast news producer in her midthirties with a big swoop of blond hair, a wicked sense of humor, and a sly, comically exasperated manner. She grew up in a big family of Russian immigrants on New York City's Lower East Side. Her dad was a post office worker and a bookie. Her mom was a communist who thought TV rotted your brain. The family's finances were lean. But Nevins had a rich uncle who was happy to pay for her to go to expensive schools. She went to college at Barnard, where she majored in English, followed by the Yale School of Drama, where she studied directing.

After graduating, Nevins spent several years bouncing around the somber world of nonfiction programming. She did a stint in Washington, D.C., at the U.S. Information Agency, filming English lessons for foreigners. Then she returned to New York and worked as a writer for the Children's Television Workshop and a news producer for ABC and CBS.

At the time of the call, she found herself caught at a tricky impasse. Recently, she'd been freelancing for a TV news magazine on CBS called *Who's*

Who, interviewing celebrities. She was good at it, and her boss, Don Hewitt, a macho scoop-hunting newshound, was wooing her to join *60 Minutes*. Ostensibly, a great prospect. The problem was that Nevins didn't want the job. She loathed working with swaggering TV correspondents, and the highly rated Sunday-night show was a well-known hotbed of knuckle-dragging, bra-snapping newsmen. Still, she didn't want to reject Hewitt's overtures either, at least not without a good excuse.

Perhaps the opening at HBO was the answer? If she got the position, it would only be temporary, thirteen weeks, and she could avoid hurting anyone's feelings at CBS.

She applied and soon after was hired to be HBO's first "director of documentary programming," whatever that meant. HBO would pay her $8,750 for the quarter. Hewitt bid her good luck and advised her that whatever she ended up doing over there, to make sure she got her name on it.

On the morning of her first day at HBO, Nevins headed out to midtown Manhattan. The HBO offices were located on Sixth Avenue, inside the Time-Life Building, a soaring forty-eight-story skyscraper clad in limestone and green-tinted glass. Inside, there was a brightly colored Mondrianesque mural by Fritz Glarner, acres of Eames chairs, and scads of bustling, patrician men striding confidently over well-polished terrazzo floors. Standing in the maw of the magazine empire, she took it all in. "I was scared," Nevins says.

She rode the elevator up to HBO's headquarters, which were located on the sixth floor. Compared with CBS, the world of HBO wasn't all that much. There were some cluttered offices and a few dozen hectic employees: mostly young business school graduates and their secretaries, with a few film and sports geeks mixed in. Nobody looked a day over thirty. Her boss was talking loudly on the phone with his feet propped up on his desk. He was wearing tennis shorts. Everyone seemed young, unwashed, and excitable. "It was essentially what today we would call a start-up," Nevins says.

Before long, she was given an office and a vague mission. HBO, it was explained to her, was going from eight hours of programming each day to twelve. The network needed lots of extra stuff to put on the air to supplement the Hollywood movies that made up the lion's share of each day's lineup. The cheaper the better.

Nevins quickly realized that in the rush to escape CBS, she'd misunderstood the job's requirements. She wouldn't be directing the documentaries, she'd be commissioning them. She settled in and tried to figure out what might make for a good HBO documentary.

One of HBO's few contributions to American culture at the time was a ribald series of satirical comedy sketches entitled *Disco Beaver from Outer Space*, which HBO had commissioned in 1978 from *National Lampoon*. The movie featured a gay vampire in space named "Dragula" and a recurring punchline based on the word "beaver" as a euphemism for "vagina."

The bar was low.

Toward the end of her thirteen-week stint, Nevins went on an overnight work trip. On the private plane, she listened to a gaggle of male colleagues telling off-color stories. "I was very, very uncomfortable," Nevins said. "It was a lot of sex jokes. It was like being in a boys' locker room and trying to act like one of the guys. It was tough."

That night, she went back to her hotel room to get some sleep. There was a loud knock at the door. It was a drunken coworker. At first, Nevins thought that maybe he was bringing her something she needed to read for the next morning. She started to let him in, then realized the guy wanted something else. "I felt his weight against the door," she says. "I took my foot and pushed the door shut and locked it. He knocked a few times and that was it. I wasn't scared. I was annoyed."

Nevins considered quitting. But for women in the 1970s, the TV industry was full of such hazards, and she knew from experience that the broadcast networks could be even worse. HBO, at least, was hiring plenty of women. She decided to keep going. At the end of her temporary contract, Nevins stayed on. Her bosses largely left her alone. They had bigger problems to contend with.

In 1980, the four largest movie studios—20th Century Fox, Universal, Paramount, and Columbia—announced that they would team up to launch a joint venture: a subscription cable TV channel called Premiere. Getty Oil would provide the initial financing. From HBO's inception, the major studios in Hollywood viewed the company with suspicion. While HBO was paying decent fees to license their movies, the studio bosses came to believe that they'd be making a lot more money if they collectively controlled the home movie market without a middleman.

Among HBO staffers, anxiety ran high.

That fall, federal regulators intervened on HBO's behalf. The Department of Justice filed an antitrust suit, charging the Hollywood studios with illegal market fixing. Prosecutors claimed that the defendants "embarked on this venture largely out of dissatisfaction with the revenues" from HBO and that the agreement would eventually fix prices at artificially high levels. The backers of Premiere refused to fold, and the case went to trial. After weeks of contentious proceedings, the judge in the Southern District of New York ruled that the venture was a violation of the Sherman Antitrust Act. On appeal, the studios lost again. Premiere was dead.

• • •

WHILE THE STUDIOS REGROUPED, HBO executives considered how they might become less dependent on the movies that Hollywood supplied them. HBO knew that it had a short window in which to establish itself as the de facto at-home entertainment brand before other competitors followed.

The job of figuring out a viable long-term programming strategy was largely left to a macho, wisecracking executive named Michael Fuchs. Fuchs was a snappy dresser with an olive complexion, thinning black hair, and dark, caustic eyes who was determined to transform HBO into a respected creator of original programming.

Fuchs was born in the Bronx near Yankee Stadium and was raised in Mount Vernon, an inner suburb north of the city. Growing up, he loved sports, and his family called him Mickey after the Yankees slugger Mickey Mantle. But in the schoolyard, thanks to his surname "Fuchs," kids called him something else: *Fucks, Fucksface, Fuckwad, Fuckhead*. From an early age, Fuchs learned to dish it back hard on the playground. "That name has a lot to do with my personality," Fuchs says.

After high school, Fuchs studied political science at Union College in upstate New York, did a brief stint in the army, and eventually graduated from law school at New York University. By his late twenties, Fuchs was feeling listless. At the time, he was working as an entertainment lawyer for William Morris, hammering out contracts between production studios and TV networks, including a fledgling HBO.

In 1976, at the age of thirty, he joined HBO as the director of special programming. Fuchs saw an opportunity to shape a young company in its formative years, one that was striving to find its identity.

Within months of arriving at the network, Fuchs came to believe that if HBO was to thrive in the long run, it would have to focus on doing things differently than the big three commercial TV networks, ABC, CBS, and NBC. The broadcasters were too well entrenched, too strong, and too rich to compete with head-on. One study found that in 1976, of the eighty-five million Americans who owned a TV, nine out of ten viewers watched evening programming on the big three networks. Their control over popular culture felt unassailable.

HBO would have to be judicious with its limited resources and exploit programming opportunities that the networks were ignoring, Fuchs figured. Everything HBO did would have to be different. Otherwise, why would anybody keep paying?

HBO did enjoy one comparative advantage. Because it wasn't beholden to sponsors, the network could take more risks and be more provocative than the broadcasters. Without having advertisers to offend, HBO ordered up a show based on *Consumer Reports* magazine. Everyone else on TV was telling viewers what to buy; HBO could afford to tell you what *not* to buy. "Very early on I wanted us to be more candid, more open, more fresh, more experimental, more daring than the networks, who were, to me, homogenized," Fuchs said. "It was canned entertainment. It had no guts."

Fuchs set out to infuse HBO's staff with an underdog's mentality, and to build a provocative programming identity of its own. "If we're going to establish a character in this business, it's got to be through original programming," Fuchs said.

With Premiere killed off by the government and other rival services just getting off the ground, HBO continued to benefit from its head start. By 1982, the business was growing in step with the rapidly expanding industry of cable TV. In the seven years since the Ali-Frazier fight, HBO's brand name had grown nearly synonymous with cable programming. For only ten dollars a month, a family could watch dozens of newish Hollywood movies in the comfort of their own home, and HBO now had more than 13.5 million customers.

Meanwhile, the company kept pushing its technological advantage in the TV space race. In 1983, the network completed construction of a new communications center in Hauppauge, New York. It was the largest and most sophisticated satellite facility in the country. The 60,000-square-foot center featured four massive satellite dishes, which allowed HBO to beam programming into space and back to cable distributors almost anywhere on the planet. Among other flourishes, the campus included a lengthy pedestrian bridge hovering over a deep dry moat, which, according to the designers, symbolized HBO's "transition between earth and spacebound concerns." The gleaming modern design of the facility was praised by architects and conveyed the ambitions of a company leading its industry into the future.

Behind its glowing facade, however, HBO was facing continued challenges—any one of which might have ended the business. Its foremost vulnerability was that the network still had a Hollywood problem. While HBO had survived the initial attack from its suppliers, the resentment from the studio chiefs lingered.

In front of reporters, top movie executives continued to bash HBO with abandon. "If HBO and Time Inc. go on unchecked, the motion picture business, without exception, will be under total control of one company in less than five years," Hollywood executive Barry Diller, then overseeing Paramount, told *The New York Times* in 1983.

There were grumblings from customers too, including one common complaint. "The problem was we used to air the movies way too many times," recalls Quentin Schaffer, a public relations man who joined HBO in 1980. "*Jaws* would be on like forty times in a month. People said, 'God, do they not have anything else?'"

HBO needed more material, but the major Hollywood studios weren't producing enough new movies each year to satiate the demands of HBO's growing subscriber base. To help alleviate the shortage, HBO decided to team up with Columbia Pictures and CBS to form a new, jointly financed movie studio called TriStar Pictures. For an initial buy-in of tens of millions of dollars, HBO would get the exclusive cable-TV rights to all the theatrically released movies that would come out of the new studio.

Still on the hunt for more content, HBO executives also announced they would begin producing movies of their own, which would bypass theaters entirely and go direct to HBO.

Hollywood snickered. In the media, anonymous studio heads suggested HBO was poised to acquire all the lousy projects that they'd previously rejected. "They have gotten every last submission from every unproduced movie in the last ten years," one unnamed studio executive told *The New York Times*.

In 1983, the network aired its first original movie. *The Terry Fox Story* was a maudlin biographical drama, dutifully recounting the real-life saga of a Canadian runner who loses his leg to cancer—then runs across the country on a prosthetic limb to raise money for cancer awareness. Robert Duvall played a gruff press agent, brimming with can-do spirit.

Critics were not impressed. "Ralph Thomas, the director of *The Terry Fox Story*, has chosen to avoid the risk of mystery; instead, he portrays the legend at its most obvious and simplistic level," the Canadian novelist David Macfarlane wrote in *Maclean's*. "Courage is a windswept sky. Tragedy is a swirl of violins."

HBO's first forays into original TV series were no more promising. In the fall of 1983, HBO began airing a new, lascivious mystery series called *The Hitchhiker*. Each half-hour episode was introduced by a nomadic character and promised to explore the "dark shadows of the American experience, where terror and madness are found in the ordinary."

Writing in *The New York Times*, critic John O'Connor excoriated the series for its "gratuitousness" and wrote, "Judging from private comments made by some executives, the entire cable industry seems to be embarrassed by this HBO effort."

HBO staffers felt similarly appalled. Around the office, they mockingly referred to the series as *Fuck a Stranger, Then Die.*

While the studios continued to send their movies over to HBO, increasingly they had plenty of other options. By 1983, several new cable competitors were coming online, including Showtime, The Movie Channel, and the Disney Channel. Each new network was in the business of licensing movies and showing them, without commercial interruption, to paying subscribers in their homes.

HBO initially countered the surge in competition by launching a second complementary pay channel called Cinemax, catering to rabid movie fans for whom one "premium" channel wasn't enough. While HBO offered mainstream Hollywood movies, Cinemax loaded up on foreign films, karate flicks, grind-house movies, soft-core erotica, and spaghetti westerns. HBO packaged the services together at a discount, hoping to box out Showtime and the rest.

In the 1980s, prior to a coming wave of consolidation, the cable industry consisted of hundreds of independent operators, each of which controlled one patch of territory or another across the United States. In order to cozy up to the distributors, HBO set up nearly a dozen regional offices, including ones in Philadelphia, Chicago, Denver, and Dallas. Staffers used to jokingly call the HBO office in Florida "the pro shop," because everyone in the cable industry spent so much time there playing golf.

HBO's regional outposts were staffed with go-getter sales reps whose job was to talk up the pleasures of HBO to the cable companies and to wine and dine their top executives. One of the key jobs for frontline HBO workers, says Steve Davidson, a former longtime HBO affiliate sales executive, was to fend off any competing promotional offers from Showtime, which was targeting the cable operators with its own mercenary sales force. "It was hand-to-hand combat, basically," Davidson says.

One downside of HBO's business model was that the cable operators, not HBO, controlled the relationships with customers and also the information on who they were, where they lived, how often they canceled, and what else they subscribed to. HBO had minimal access to customer data. To make up for their lack of consumer insight, HBO deployed a unique and effective strategy.

Every cable company typically employed a staff of low-level workers who answered phone calls from current and potential customers, listening to their service complaints and pitching them on new subscriptions, products, discounts, or special deals. From its early days, HBO executives took a look at these regional call centers and saw an opportunity. HBO filled its satellite offices with specialists whose job was to sidle up to the cable company call centers and win over their employees.

In theory, the phone operators were supposed to be telling customers about a diverse range of offers, say, a one-time discount from the Disney Channel, or a special offer from Showtime. But HBO's specialists did everything they could to make sure that HBO, not Showtime, was at the forefront of conversations by lavishing rewards on the call center employees, ranging from cash to appliances to plane tickets to Hawaii.

"A lot of the cable companies saw it as, essentially, compensation for their employees that they didn't have to add to their payroll, because they knew HBO was coming in and offering them incentives and trips and cash and everything else," says Shelley Brindle, a former sales and marketing executive at HBO. "You could never do that today."

In the absence of data, everything for HBO was relationship based. To get a leg up, HBO also encouraged its sales people to spend lavishly entertaining their cable company clients. Every January, during the weekend of the Super Bowl, HBO would charter private jets and fly its top sales folks to someplace warm, like Hawaii, along with their most important contacts in the cable industry and their families for a week of intoxication and camaraderie. "It was a huge boondoggle," one HBO sales rep said. "There wasn't a single formal meeting, and it was just about bonding. It was as extravagant as you could imagine."

With all the new services coming to market, the cost of licensing Hollywood films was starting to get more expensive. If HBO's position in the supply chain remained static, HBO executives feared the situation would only get worse.

In the fall of 1983, HBO set up a new finance division called Silver Screen Partners, with an initial goal of investing in a dozen or so movies a year. In exchange for providing tens of millions of dollars in prefinancing, HBO would retain the cable TV rights and share in any ancillary profits.

In theory, there was nothing stopping the other premium channels like Showtime from doing the same thing. But HBO enjoyed significantly more subscribers and, thus, significantly more money to pump into the movie-making pipeline. Nobody would be able to match HBO's largesse. By the end of 1983, between its investment in TriStar, its original movies, and Silver Screen Partners, HBO was shoveling roughly $250 million a year into Hollywood. Studio bosses might still fantasize about killing off HBO, but if they did, they might be killing themselves as well.

"It's a love-hate relationship," Gerald Levin said.

• • •

WHILE HBO WAS BUSY TAMING Hollywood moguls, another headache emerged—the rapid spread of a new technology that threatened to make all the network's investment in satellites moot. With each passing month, VCRs, video cassette recorders, were growing more popular in the United States. If people could easily rent Hollywood movies at a neighborhood store with a vast selection of titles to watch on their VCRs at home whenever they wanted, why would they keep paying for HBO?

The growing threat from VCRs only exacerbated a chronic condition afflicting HBO, known in the cable business as "churn." Each month, a portion of HBO's customer base canceled their subscriptions. If, say, 5 percent of HBO's base quit, the network would need to find hundreds of thousands of new households just to stay even. A small upswing in the churn rate could translate into a heavy hit to the network's livelihood. The reasons for the turnover varied. Sometimes, it wasn't HBOs fault. People moved, died, and lost their jobs. Economic downturns happened.

But there were also plenty of customers who canceled HBO out of boredom, or dissatisfaction, or out of curiosity about a rival service. And it was these

waffling subscribers—their motivations, predilections, wants, and desires—
that HBO executives spent much of their time mulling over.

Fuchs and his colleagues needed to convince HBO's audience that if
they stuck around, something great was coming down the pipeline. Something they couldn't necessarily find at the video rental store. Each month,
HBO mailed out its bills to customers tucked inside a glossy programming
"catalogue" touting the upcoming mix of Hollywood movies, original films,
sports, and documentaries that they'd be missing if they canceled.

When it came to original programming, Fuchs believed that the key
was not to try to make shows that appealed to everybody. That was what the
broadcast networks excelled at. What HBO needed was to find niches that
worked really well for one demographic or another, something they felt so
passionate about that they'd hang on to the service, even if they ignored everything else on HBO. To try to parse out what HBO viewers cared about,
the network's small research team routinely analyzed surveys asking subscribers what programming they were watching and to rate it on a 5-point
scale.

While he occasionally glanced at the research division's data on "Total
Subscriber Satisfaction," Fuchs largely relied on his own instincts. "I tried to
make sure that HBO had something interesting for everyone," Fuchs said.

For kids, HBO snapped up a new series from Muppets creator Jim Hen-
son called *Fraggle Rock*. For young men, HBO began airing *1st & Ten*, a
bawdy football sitcom starring Delta Burke and O. J. Simpson. For fans of
topical satire, HBO offered up *Not Necessarily the News,* a sketch comedy series that riffed on topical subjects.

But most of all, Fuchs felt that HBO had one clear path to differentiate
itself from any competition. In his estimation, the broadcast networks tilted
their overall programming strategy toward female viewers in a slavish effort
to please advertisers, who were convinced that connecting with women was
the key to selling more of their consumer and household goods. Fuchs saw
an opportunity. From now on, he told staff, HBO would heavily cater to male
passions.

"I figured out that the man in the household decided whether or not to have HBO," said Fuchs. "I made sure there were things for men."

In the fall of 1983, Cinemax began airing a new documentary series called *Eros America*, which aimed to "candidly explore" various issues of human sexuality. There were segments on a Florida housewife who worked at night as a stripper; and one about college art students who paid their tuition by moonlighting as high-end escorts.

The series was being produced by Sheila Nevins, who the year before, in 1982, had left HBO's documentary department to strike out on her own and to spend more time with her young son. One afternoon, she'd been at an estate sale and happened upon an unchaste book of fiction entitled *Eros*. "Sex is a serious wound in this country," Nevins said.

Not to mention, a low-cost enticement to male viewers.

Fuchs had snapped up the show, which became an immediate hit for Cinemax. Before long, Fuchs decided to move it to HBO. The only downside, they soon realized, was the name. Many male cable subscribers were fuzzy on their Greek mythology and not properly attuned to the alluring sexual connotation of "eros." It was too subtle. "We went out and tested it somewhere in New Jersey," Nevins says. "People didn't know what the word 'Eros' meant."

Fuchs decided to rename HBO's growing fornication franchise something more to the point. *Eros America* eventually gave way to *Real Sex*, which, in turn, spawned a healthy brood of sex-related documentary series that, under Nevins's aegis, would go frolicking across HBO's late-night airtime for decades to come, including *G String Divas*, which examined the lives of the strippers working at a gentleman's club in Bristol, Pennsylvania; *Cathouse*, which documented the ups and downs of sex workers at a brothel in Mound House, Nevada; and *Sex Bytes*, a dot-com era look at cybersex. "It was an education for me," Nevins said. "I didn't know that sex was fun."

CHAPTER 2

Punch Lines

In the summer of 1984, a hit comedy almost sank HBO for good.

The amount of money that premium TV services like HBO paid to license any particular Hollywood movie was usually determined by a preset formula that adjusted the final licensing price based on the movie's performance at the box office. If a movie bombed, HBO got it for cheap. If it was a hit, they paid more. Typically, such contracts stipulated an upper and a lower limit, assuring that the final price would be kept within manageable parameters.

In June, Columbia Pictures released *Ghostbusters*, a comedy directed by Ivan Reitman and starring Bill Murray and Dan Aykroyd, about a well-timed ghost-catching start-up that hits it big. Audiences loved it. *Ghostbusters* earned some $229.2 million at the box office, making it the second-highest-grossing film of the year, trailing only *Beverly Hills Cop*. Everyone with a piece of the movie was ecstatic. Except HBO.

In a move to save costs, HBO's finance team had dreamed up a new licensing strategy that had removed the upper and lower caps on its movie deals. The new model was seen as risky by many HBO executives. But the finance team believed it would pay off in the long run. Huge hit movies, they argued, were statistical outliers. Bad, poorly performing movies were much more common. Internally, the strategy was dubbed "Monte Carlo," a reference to European roulette tables, which have no "double zeros." *Don't worry,* they assured their colleagues. *We can't lose.*

"The idea of their Monte Carlo model was that no chip would hit on double zero," recalls Henry Schleiff, a genial ex-lawyer who worked on HBO's programming team at the time. "Well, the first movie hit on double zero."

Without a cap in place, HBO suddenly found itself on the hook for roughly $40 million for the cable rights to *Ghostbusters,* an amount that threatened to wipe out HBO's profit for the entire year. Top executives at Time Inc., who increasingly relied on HBO's cash surpluses to impress investors on Wall Street, were left fuming. The subsequent blame for the screw-up was largely directed at HBO's level-headed, pragmatic chief executive officer Frank Biondi, a graduate of Princeton University, who held an MBA from the Harvard Business School.

In the fall of 1984, Time Inc. announced it was shaking up HBO's executive ranks. Biondi was let go, Fuchs was promoted to CEO, and 125 employees were laid off. Fuchs told his charges that they would overcome the setback and they should think of themselves as insurgents. It was HBO versus the entertainment establishment; HBO versus the world. "I went about my business like it was a crusade, like it was a religion," said Fuchs. "I was going to change entertainment in this country."

That fall, HBO moved out of its headquarters in the Time-Life Building and into its own space, a glassy green, fifteen-story modernist building overlooking Bryant Park, recently renovated by Kohn Pedersen Fox. In an article in *The New York Times* entitled "Mediocre Skyscrapers Dominate the Skyline," critic Paul Goldberger called HBO's new home a "faceless glass box."

Inside the new offices, Fuchs cultivated a loose atmosphere that was jocular, informal, and fiercely competitive. While most TV executives avoided taking overt political positions that could potentially alienate a particular swath of viewers, Fuchs openly flashed his progressive beliefs at every opportunity. An outspoken liberal, he liked to talk about campaigning for Bobby Kennedy in 1968 and kept a large photo prominently displayed in his office of Kennedy striding across an airport tarmac alongside his dog, Freckles. He encouraged everyone at HBO to speak their minds incautiously and to debate freely. No holding back, no bullshit.

Roughly once a month, Fuchs would host an executive lunch for key staffers inside the dining room at the top of the building. Fuchs used the occasions to pace about with a microphone, telling jokes and roasting his subordinates, who sat back and laughed a little too loudly, hoping to avoid Fuchs's festive derision. "I'm a world-class insulter," Fuchs says.

Everyone was expected to work long hours. "I used to look at people with families and say, how do they do this job and have another life?" said Fuchs.

And, for the most part, they followed him.

"I love Michael because he was so unfair and he made me so tough," Nevins said. "He was in everything—every idea. It was his personality that was the sort of founding of HBO: that maverick, irascible, intellectual, sort of primitive Jewish immigrant humor. And the certain kind of sexual license. He was, in many ways, a really important visionary of HBO."

For HBO to thrive well into the future, Fuchs told his staff, they would need to keep pushing themselves to improve the network's original programming—to make more of it, and to make it better.

"We turned up the flame," said Fuchs.

• • •

BY THE START OF 1985, HBO was still the most popular premium TV channel in the United States by a large margin. But one competitor was proving to be a true threat. Showtime, a rival cable network owned by billionaire Sumner Redstone's media conglomerate Viacom, was picking up market share, in part by ramping up its investment in stand-up comedy. HBO executives needed someone to help fight off the territorial incursion. That June, the network hired Chris Albrecht, a TV agent with a unique background in comedy, to head up HBO's nascent West Coast operations.

Albrecht was born in 1952 and grew up in Queens, New York. When he was less than a year old, his parents separated, and his father, a Yale-educated engineer who worked for Standard Oil, moved away. Albrecht attended

Stuyvesant High School, the city's top magnet school for math and science, then matriculated to Hofstra University on Long Island. One day, a drinking buddy asked if he wanted to work on the crew for an upcoming Shakespeare festival that was hosted by the college's theater department. Albrecht took the job. While hanging in the rafters over the stage, spotlighting the actors, something clicked. What he wanted to do was to become an actor.

Albrecht changed his major to dramatic literature and spent the next two years acting in school productions and reading plays. After college, a friend and fellow actor named Bob Zmuda proposed they form a comedy duo and move to New York City. Zmuda had heard that performing in comedy clubs was a great launching pad for actors looking to break into the entertainment industry. In 1974, Albrecht and Zmuda got a derelict, rat-infested apartment on the Upper West Side of Manhattan and started working as stagehands at a theater inside Riverside Church. During their time off, they sharpened their comedy routine, performing at night for a few bucks in dingy clubs around the city.

Before long, Albrecht got a job as a manager at the Improv, a storied comedy club on a squalid patch of Forty-Fourth Street, between Eighth and Ninth avenues, in Hell's Kitchen. Albrecht got to know everybody passing through the club. One day, his boss, Budd Friedman, told Albrecht that he was moving to L.A. to open a new club there. Would Albrecht like to buy 25 percent of the Improv in New York for twenty-five thousand dollars? Albrecht borrowed money from his grandmother and bought in.

He was in the right place at the right time. In 1975, *Saturday Night Live* debuted on NBC and turned into a national phenomenon. A new wave of young comedians from SNL and *National Lampoon* frequently came by the Improv to perform and party. Albrecht played the accommodating host to John Belushi, Andy Kaufman, Gilda Radner, and Garrett Morris. It was a bacchanalian, anything-goes scene, fueled by liquor and cocaine. "There used to be a slogan in the midseventies," Joe Piscopo said. "If you see something, *don't* say something."

One of Albrecht's favorite comics was a dour, gangly, intellectual kid with a big Afro who wore army fatigues and liked to tell high-concept jokes that few people understood. His name was Larry David. When things went badly, David would stop in the middle of the set and walk offstage, hurling insults out the side of his mouth. It was a total downer, the worst thing for the club. Still, fellow comedians couldn't help admiring David. In comedy, a unique point of view was the world's greatest advantage.

In 1980, Albrecht sold his stake in the Improv and parlayed his comedy connections into a job in Los Angeles as a full-time agent at ICM Partners, one of the largest agencies in Hollywood. Using his network from the Improv, Albrecht quickly amassed a deep roster of comedian clients, including Piscopo, Whoopi Goldberg, Dana Carvey, and Keenen Ivory Wayans.

A few years later, Albrecht was getting fed up with agenting when HBO came calling. Showtime, led by a shrewd young executive named Peter Chernin, was becoming a desirable destination for talented comedians. Showtime was broadcasting a "Comic of the Month" series, which showcased a twenty-six-year-old comedian named Ellen DeGeneres, whom the network dubbed "The Funniest Person in America." Showtime was also building a lot of excitement around a frequent *Tonight Show* guest host named Garry Shandling.

In 1984, Showtime aired his first comedy special, called *Garry Shandling: Alone in Vegas*, in which the comic riffed on marriage, fishing, pooper-scooper laws, breastfeeding, and all-you-can-eat buffets. "A friend of mine just got divorced," Shandling said. "He had a divorce party. They showed the wedding film in reverse with the couple walking away from each other."

In 1986, Shandling was shopping around an idea for his first TV series, a highly conceptual show in which he would play a neurotic, self-conscious stand-up comic who is aware that he's also a character on a TV sitcom. Fuchs wanted it badly and offered Shandling a chance to shoot a pilot for HBO. But before that could happen, Showtime swooped in and promised Shandling he could go straight to series, no pilot necessary. Shandling chose to go with Showtime, which went on to air *It's Garry Shandling's Show* for four critically admired seasons.

With Showtime cutting into a key part of HBO's business, Albrecht started as the network's head of West Coast programming, based in Los

Angeles. HBO's headquarters there were housed in the Century Plaza Towers. Designed by architect Minoru Yamasaki, the twin forty-four-story giants in Century City were the tallest buildings outside the city's downtown.
HBO's offices were located on one of the top floors. Except for the assistants,
everyone had an external-facing office with big windows and beautiful views
overlooking the sunny, smoggy city.

At street level, there was a strip mall, an outdoor plaza, and Harry's, a
bar and restaurant that hosted an annual Ernest Hemingway parody contest
and served as the unofficial HBO canteen. Having a boss 2,450 miles away
was something Albrecht found appealing.

Albrecht moved into a corner office and quickly became the focal point
of HBO gossip. He was funny, slick, and prone to oversharing. Every day,
he'd show up in a perfectly tailored two-thousand-dollar suit, which he called
his "coat of armor," practically zipped to his short, muscular frame. He was
a dedicated, vocal member of Alcoholics Anonymous and talked frequently
about being in couples therapy with his wife.

A caddish "dry drunk" was the office verdict.

Whatever Albrecht was into, he pursued aggressively: skiing, spin classes,
horses, sports cars—and, most prominently, women. According to former colleagues, Albrecht liked to dish to other men about the notches on his bed-
post, the more famous the conquest the better, a form of competitive jousting
that seemed to inspire a kind of fraternal awe among certain powerful men
in the business. He told one coworker that he'd slept with more than a thousand women.

He was equally prolific at collecting tight relationships with prominent
comedians and quickly proved himself peerless at wrangling talent on HBO's
behalf.

From his former clients, Albrecht knew that HBO didn't have any commercials, so comics didn't have to clean up their acts like when they did their
five minutes on Johnny Carson or David Letterman. On HBO, they could
do their full club routines. In the 1970s, George Carlin was going around
comedy clubs performing a routine called the "Seven Dirty Words You Can't
Say on Television," mocking the puritanical censorship rules in American

media. By 1977, he was doing the whole "shit, piss, fuck, cunt, cocksucker, motherfucker, tits" bit unfettered on HBO.

As he settled into his new job, Albrecht found that there was one major problem. Although it was growing, HBO's programming budget was still tiny. The network set aside roughly $35 million for the entire year—a fraction of what the big three broadcast networks were spending annually on their programming. And even that small amount, Albrecht soon realized, had to be carefully guarded internally.

There were plenty of other people inside HBO—particularly in the affiliate relations division—who thought original programming was a waste of resources. The percentage of HBO subscribers watching shows like *Not Necessarily the News*, *1st & Ten*, and *The Hitchhiker* was minuscule. In meetings, they argued that research showed the only reason people watched HBO was for the Hollywood movies. The original programming budget would be better spent on direct marketing, cable commercials, or roadside billboards. Anything besides original shows.

In a meeting once, Carmi Zlotnik, a former HBO production executive, watched in horror as a colleague proposed that the network take the entirety of its original programming budget and use it instead to buy $25 million to $30 million worth of advertising in *TV Guide*. "The whole thing could have been killed right there," Zlotnik says.

While trying to figure out how to maximize his meager budget, Albrecht heard from Bob Zmuda, his former stage partner, who had gone on to write and produce for Andy Kaufman. Zmuda had an idea: a live comedy telethon that would raise money for charity. It would be simple to film, cheap to produce, and all for a good cause. Albrecht got the project approved and with Zmuda put together *Comic Relief*, a live event hosted by comedians to combat homelessness.

On March 29, 1986, they staged *Comic Relief* at the Universal Amphitheater in Los Angeles. Billy Crystal, Whoopi Goldberg, and Robin Williams served as the hosts. For the first time, HBO made one of its events available to nonsubscribers. For one night only, anyone with cable could watch HBO for free. More than fourteen million people tuned in. Dozens of comedians stopped by to do their acts. Garry Shandling performed a routine about being single, telling the audience that the mirror over his bed reads "Objects appear larger than they really are." Paul Reubens, performing as PeeWee Herman, conducted creepy medical examinations of people in the audience.

Comic Relief raised $2.4 million for charity. It also got the sales guys off of Albrecht's back and attracted a wave of favorable press. "*Comic Relief* gave us a jolt," Albrecht said.

• • •

ONE EVENING, back in New York, Michael Fuchs made his way to the Oyster Bar in Grand Central Station to talk with Sheila Nevins about her professional future. For the past couple of years, Nevins had been working as a freelance producer, hustling from one gig to another, making documentaries and nonfiction programming, including *Real Sex*. Among the starched attendants and snappish commuters at the elegant seafood spot, Nevins told Fuchs that she wanted to come back to the network on a full-time basis. She needed the money, and HBO needed her pizzazz, she argued.

Fuchs agreed, and in 1986, Nevins rejoined HBO, taking over a corner office in the Bryant Park building. "I didn't like it because there was too much light and I couldn't see my screen," Nevins says. "But somebody said to me, *Yeah, but it's a corner office.* I said, *What does that mean?* They said, *You're moving up the chain.*"

Surveying the state of contemporary documentary filmmaking, Nevins was not impressed. "It was an elitist form," she says. "It was very pedantic."

Her main competition was PBS, a network whose work she found to be exceedingly dull. "What's wrong with the CIA? What's wrong with your heart? What's wrong with our health care?" Nevins said. "They were never people stories."

The film that Nevins loved most was *Salesman*. Made in 1969 by Albert and David Maysles, the black-and-white documentary focused on a crew of door-to-door Bible salesmen, chain-smoking cigarettes and trying to upsell poor Irish and Italian immigrants on the illustrated word of the Lord. In the particulars of the shared, grinding, Darwinian struggle was a kind of lyrical humanism. "I remember about eight years ago you were telling me this business is on the fringes," one salesman laments to another, after a grueling day of bleakly pushing Bibles.

"It's still on the fringes," he says, chuckling.

During the 1970s, while she was working as a producer on a public television show called *The Great American Dream Machine*, Nevins had spent a magical day working with the Maysles brothers. Together, they'd traversed Manhattan, going from store to store with their cameras, asking individuals to share their vision of the American dream. One man said he was shopping for the first time after becoming a widower. Another told Nevins his rules for adultery, laughing the whole way through. "I was amazed," Nevins says. "Each of them was a story."

In *Salesman*, Nevins saw what HBO Documentaries could be—a well-funded platform for filmmakers willing to explore deeply the lives of people on the fringes of society. Drug addicts. Sex workers. Circus freaks. Serial killers. Cult members. Scam artists. And because they were on HBO, it could all be R-rated.

Since few for-profit institutions were funding documentaries, Nevins could have her pick of filmmakers to commission. Nevins began assembling a constellation of independent producers, her "repertory company," as she called it, to whom she intermittently gave assignments. "You have to cast documentaries," she says. "Some films just strike certain people in my mind. You have to cast the filmmaker. Not everybody can make the same film."

With a sizable budget at her disposal, Nevins provided sustenance to scores of serious documentary makers in a lean industry. Occasionally, she even put the Maysles to work. She particularly enjoyed giving the highbrow filmmakers lucrative, lowbrow assignments. At one point, HBO's corporate siblings at *Sports Illustrated* asked her if she could produce a promotional behind-the-scenes movie about the making of the magazine's saucy swimsuit issue. "I thought, 'Aha! I'll give it to those *snobs*,'" Nevins says.

Members of the small team of HBO employees who reported to Nevins were assigned to both her highbrow and lowbrow projects. "When I was interviewing to work for Sheila, she sent me ten documentary cassettes," recalls

Kary Antholis, a former HBO development executive, who got his start working for Nevins. "She asked me to rank them two different ways on a one-to-
ten basis; which would be the most popular in the ratings and which I thought
was the most powerful, aesthetically and creatively.

"For me, that was a window into the bipolar nature of HBO's programming philosophy," Antholis continues. "Either you were doing something for
the halo of the brand by making critically acclaimed, award-winning projects.
Or you were making something that's going to get an audience. On occasion,
you'd find something that did both. But that was very rare."

Years later, Antholis would create and direct *One Survivor Remembers*,
an HBO documentary about Gerda Weissmann Klein, a survivor of the Ho-
locaust, which would win the 1996 Oscar for Best Documentary Short Subject. He also put in time at HBO tending to episodes of *Real Sex*. "You were
expected to work on both ends of the spectrum," he says.

To the press, Nevins started referring to her projects as "docutainment."
The secret, she came to believe, was to dig into the muck of individuality and
find the connective societal bonds buried within. She came up with a term
for it: *Real People Stories*.

"I saw there was a door that I could possibly open for colloquial stories
that were meaningful and that were aggressively prosocial in some way," Nevins says. "Not that I'm such a good person. But you needed an ending. And
the ending had to be: make the world a little bit better somehow. Make empathy the real reason you told that story. You'd feel for someone you wouldn't
even know and not because they are famous."

"I don't like *famous*," she continues. "I like *everyday*."

Within HBO, Nevins was aggressive about staking out and defending
her turf from any would-be interlopers. "Michael left me alone. They all left
me alone. It was a great gift," she says. "Stories are all around you if you have
the freedom to grab them."

CHAPTER 3

The Unsweet Science

HBO was getting nibbled on by pirates.

With each passing year in the 1980s, satellite receivers were getting smaller and cheaper. What was once a capital-intensive investment limited to major companies was now something that any middle-class enthusiast could buy from a retail specialty store and install on a roof. Once a dish was up and running, they could pull down any TV signal without paying. They could get HBO for free.

Studies suggested the industry could be losing hundreds of millions of dollars a year to the free riders. Some cable executives wanted to push Congress for new regulation outlawing the piracy. But the environment in D.C. would be tricky. Ronald Reagan was just starting his second term as president, and fervent belief in deregulation was ascendant in Washington. Getting the government to crack down on recreational satellite usage was going to be a tough sell.

In the hallways at HBO's satellite center, they had a better idea. Beat the pirates with technology. In the weeks before Christmas, a team of HBO engineers put the finishing touches on an encryption software system, which they'd licensed from a military contractor. On January 15, 1986, the new system went live, and HBO became the first TV network in the world to scramble its signal. Moving forward, every transmission originating from HBO's satellite hub would first be encrypted. Only authorized cable companies or lawful, paying HBO subscribers would be given the codes to decipher the signals. The free ride was over.

Howls rose up from around the country. Suddenly, legions of people who'd gone out and spent hundreds of dollars on a backyard dish could no longer see HBO. They would have to pay. And they were furious. One of the reasons they were so upset is that they would no longer be able to watch boxing on HBO.

Going back to the early days of the Thrilla in Manila, HBO had included boxing in its mix of sports programming, along with gymnastics, tennis, swim meets, college basketball contests, and Rangers and Knicks games from Madison Square Garden. But as HBO grew into a national network, executives pared down the range of live sports programming. They phased out the New York–centric events and focused on boxing, which appealed to audiences across the country, regardless of geographical affiliations. It was also cheap to broadcast, compared to baseball, basketball, football, or hockey—the TV rights for which were escalating in price and would only get more expensive with each passing year.

The world of televised boxing, by contrast, was a buyer's market. While its mainstream popularity was as strong as ever, the broadcast networks were having some trouble marketing the sport to blue-chip, commercial sponsors, who'd grown wary of being associated with its violence ever since an appalling tragedy had gone down on live television.

On November 13, 1982, in a ring outside Caesars Palace in Las Vegas, the lightweight champion Ray Mancini was fighting a longshot challenger named Kim Duk-Koo. In the fourteenth round of a fiercely contested fight—which was being broadcast live on CBS—Mancini caught Kim with a series of hard right hands, sending the dazed fighter tumbling into the ropes, where he lost his balance, fell over, and slammed his head on the canvas. The referee called the fight. But the damage was done. Kim's brain was bleeding internally. Minutes later he fell into a coma and was rushed to a nearby hospital, where he underwent brain surgery to relieve the pressure. Kim died days later from the injuries.

A few weeks later, Howard Cosell, the dean of American sports broadcasters, sat ringside in the Houston Astrodome calling a heavyweight fight for ABC between the titleholder Larry Holmes and an underqualified challenger, a former kickboxer named Randall Cobb.

By the start of the thirteenth round, the bout was turning ugly. Holmes was battering Cobb ferociously. Cobb was bleeding from his nose and his face was swelling badly. Yet somehow he kept fighting. Cosell grew increasingly agitated. With each blow, he expressed his growing disgust in his inimitable nasally voice, as familiar to most American TV viewers as the voice of their father, their priest, or their president. "Nose bleed again," Cosell said. "One feels almost a concussion from the mere thud of Holmes's left on Cobb's head. Obviously this referee has no intention of stopping this fight."

"The blood is all over Cobb's face now," Cosell continued. "I wonder if that referee understands that he is constructing an advertisement for the abolition of the very sport that he's a part of?"

Cobb survived to the final bell, losing to Holmes in a unanimous decision. (Years later, thanks to his mangled mug, he went on to enjoy a second career playing goonish bad guys in Hollywood films, including *Raising Arizona*, *Fletch Lives*, and *Ace Ventura: Pet Detective*.) But the spectacle of Cosell, Mr. Boxing himself, denouncing the sport on national TV left televised boxing badly bruised. Mainstream advertisers backpedaled away cautiously.

With no nervous sponsors looking over their shoulders, HBO executives once again saw an opportunity to do the opposite of the broadcast networks. HBO rushed in. "The funny thing about the networks is that they chose the wrong time to get out," said Ross Greenburg, a top executive at HBO Sports. "Because the eighties were probably the greatest decade in boxing history."

Greenburg was a loyal and lowkey HBO stalwart. He grew up in the Westchester suburbs of New York and went to college at Brown University, graduating in the late 1970s. Afterward, he landed an entry-level job at ABC

Sports under its charismatic leader Roone Arledge, a producer who saw the sports world through a journalistic, storytelling lens.

Greenburg joined HBO in 1978, the same year as Sheila Nevins, during the network's start-up days inside the Time-Life Building. Just twenty-three years old at the time, Greenburg imported Arledge's sports philosophy into his new job at HBO: in short, find the most compelling athletes and chronicle their life's tale. "I had a vision of what ABC Sports was and I just changed the letters and carried it over to HBO Sports," Greenburg says. "*Stories.* Telling it like it is."

In the years to come, Greenburg would help oversee a small but prestigious stable of sports-related programming that would feature a mix of erudite newsmagazine and analysis shows, including *Inside the NFL, On the Record with Bob Costas, Real Sports with Bryant Gumbel*, and a smattering of sports documentaries.

The documentaries, which were conceived and produced independently of Sheila Nevins's group, often delved into sports history. In style and manner, the productions were reminiscent of what Ken Burns was doing at PBS with sound effects, music, and extensive narration. "I was heavily influenced, I'd have to say, by Ken Burns and his *Civil War* miniseries," Greenburg says.

The overarching goal of HBO Sports, he says, was to differentiate itself from the bigger, richer broadcast networks by focusing on the quality of the storytelling and the drama of the athletes on and off the field.

At the start of 1985, the boxing world was buzzing about an eighteen-year-old heavyweight fighter who was living with a Spartan-like trainer named Cus D'Amato on a country property in rural New York and who was demolishing any amateur who dared step in the ring with him. In March, Mike Tyson signed on for his first professional fight, squaring off against Hector Mercedes in a small arena in Albany, New York. Tyson knocked him out in the first round.

Back in their offices overlooking Bryant Park, Greenburg and his colleagues had taken note of the young phenom and were drawing up a strategy to get him on the air. For years, the world of professional boxing had been a fragmented mess, with three different organizations, the World Boxing Association (WBA), the World Boxing Federation (WBF), and International Boxing Federation (IBF), each staging their own fights and declaring their own champions. In the fall of 1985, HBO executives met with promoter Don King and together mapped out a plan for the Heavyweight World Series, a tournament designed to bring together the top fighters from all three divisions and, by its end, to crown a single champion.

On November 22, 1986, in a fight at the Las Vegas Hilton billed as "Judgment Day," a twenty-year-old Tyson knocked out Trevor Berbick in the second round, becoming the youngest heavyweight champion in the history of the sport. The fight was seen live on HBO and, thanks to the new scrambling technology, by paying subscribers only.

With each passing month, Tyson grew more famous. The national media was filled with profiles of the stout, thick-necked fighter with the lisping soprano voice. People couldn't get enough of him. Tyson was a rarity in American sports life, an unapologetic bad guy, happy to play the role of the brooding, violent outlaw. He came into the ring in silence, no music, no dancing. He wore black trunks and black shoes with no socks. Unlike most professional fighters, he talked openly and gleefully about his love of violence. In 1986, after knocking out Jess Ferguson, Tyson told reporters, "I wanted to drive his nose bone into his brain."

Outside the ring, he regaled journalists with tales of his wild teenage years growing up in Brownsville, Brooklyn. He told them about how he used to pick pockets, mug strangers, rob stores, and steal from his neighbors.

Yet what made Tyson particularly compelling was that beneath his effervescent savagery lurked a quiet, gentle streak that he could never fully stifle. He was prone to impulsive bouts of kindness, handing wads of cash to poor people or rushing into traffic to help an old person cross a street. It was the same softness of heart that had gotten him picked on as a child, the thing he had learned so forcefully to repress. "Everyone was afraid of him," his sister once told Gary Smith of *Sports Illustrated*. "He was very mean. And the sweetest, most compassionate boy you ever saw."

"I did evil things," Tyson said. "But my heart was always pure."

Even after he became the most feared fighter in the world, he couldn't quite snuff out his inner softy. It was there in every profile, frequently illustrated by his lifelong love of pigeons, which he raised, first on rooftops of abandoned tenements, then in backyard coops in the Catskills. He bred the birds, watched them take flight, and defended them from all manner of predators: slobbering Labradors, cruel neighborhood kids, circling falcons. "They're my brothers and babies," Tyson said in 1986.

Tyson's peculiar mix of profanity, violence, and tenderness stoked people's appetite to see him in the ring, read about him in magazines, and watch him on TV. It was a mesmerizing formula. Fuchs gave Seth Abraham, the head of HBO Sports, wide leeway to spend whatever it took to woo Tyson's team and to strengthen HBO's grip on the boxing world. "People used to say that Michael gave me an unlimited budget," Abraham says. "I always exceeded it."

In late 1987, HBO signed Tyson to a deal that would pay him $26.5 million for seven fights over the next two years. It was a significant chunk of HBO's spending on programming. But every time Tyson stepped into the ring, droves of new subscribers signed up for HBO and an unusually high percentage of the network's existing customers would tune in to watch him fight. Over the previous year, the five highest-rated telecasts on HBO were boxing matches. Four featured Tyson.

"Mike Tyson is our Arnold Schwarzenegger. He's our Sly Stallone. He's box office appeal to our subscribers," Greenburg said. "Mike Tyson is our franchise."

HBO's audience, it turned out, loved a charismatic villain. Mike Tyson was the first in a long series of HBO antiheroes to come.

• • •

FOR YEARS, many top Hollywood writers, directors, and showrunners had treated HBO's paltry, scripted programming department like a pack of vulgarians, best avoided. In the late 1980s, that began to change, thanks, in part, to Bridget Potter, one of HBO's top creative executives in New York. Potter grew up in the suburbs of London and moved to New York with her parents as a teenager, spending the 1960s immersed in the avant-garde Greenwich Village art scene, hanging out with a politically active, antiwar group of hippies.

At HBO, she reported to Fuchs and kept on the prowl for projects that could earn HBO more respect within the broader industry. All the tensions between HBO and the entertainment establishment had hurt its prospects in finding rich original programming. Series like *The Hitchhiker* weren't launched just because of the poor taste among HBO executives—it was also due to lack of opportunity. "All these stories about how HBO was going to eat Hollywood, that was very destructive to us in our work with the creative community," she said.

Potter also kept an eye out for promising, politically charged projects. In 1988, she found one. That January, HBO announced a new limited series from the Pulitzer Prize–winning "Doonesbury" cartoonist Garry Trudeau and the director Robert Altman. Following early success with movies like *McCabe & Mrs. Miller* (1971) and *Nashville* (1975), Altman's career had slowed down. Even so, by HBO standards, Altman was a huge get.

With Ronald Reagan's second term in office winding down, the United States was deep in the throes of a fierce presidential campaign. The Democratic and Republican fields were crowded with hopeful candidates. *Tanner '88* added one more into the mix.

The series, shot in the style of a pseudo-documentary, followed the fictional candidacy of Jack Tanner (Michael Murphy), a former Michigan congressman, stumping on the campaign trail in step with events unfolding in the real election.

The first hour-long episode aired in February, on the eve of the New Hampshire primary. To add a sense of authenticity, Altman shot the scenes in the field using videotape and featured several appearances by real candidates playing themselves, including Bob Dole, Gary Hart, and Pat Robertson.

"The idea is take a repertoire of fictional characters and have them rub up against reality and be buffeted by real events, as I do in the comic strip," Trudeau said.

Critics applauded the ingenuity of *Tanner '88,* which quickly caught on with the real-world political operatives the show was satirizing.

Even three decades after the series came and went, the show was still celebrated by critics—in 2020, *New York* magazine called it the second-best HBO limited series ever made and credited it with creating a blueprint for future Christopher Guest movies like *Best in Show* and *Waiting for Guffman*.

But at the time, few HBO subscribers bothered tuning in. HBO ended the series in August, following the eleventh episode, which was set at the Democratic National Convention in Atlanta.

Reviews hinted at a potential turnoff to HBO viewers: the show's earnest, do-gooder protagonist Jack Tanner. "Is Tanner, who marched in Selma, who holds a doctorate in history, who left Congress to spend time with his young daughter when she had Hodgkin's disease, too likable?" Judith Michaelson wrote in the *Los Angeles Times*.

"Jack Tanner is too good to be true," Harry Waters wrote in *Newsweek*.

For an HBO audience that was otherwise enthralled with the latest theatrics of Mike Tyson, the show's pious protagonist may have been too blandly drawn. It was not a mistake HBO would make again.

•   •   •

IN EARLY 1989, shortly after George H. W. Bush was sworn in as president, HBO suddenly found itself drawn into the biggest story in the business world. That March, HBO's parent company announced it was merging with Warner Communications—a vast, publicly traded colossus, which among other assets owned the Warner Bros. movie studio, the Atlantic record label, and DC Comics, home to Superman, Batman, and Wonder Woman. The deal, valued at upwards of $18 billion, would create a new giant called Time Warner. If the merger passed regulatory scrutiny, the new company would emerge as the world's largest entertainment conglomerate, with more than thirty-five thousand employees.

"The fact is, unless a company becomes really aggressive on this world stage, they're not going to be a major player in the future," said Gerald Levin, the recondite former head of HBO with the caterpillar mustache, who was now set to become the vice chairman of Time Warner.

The proposed merger quickly came under fire from competitors. In May,

Viacom filed a $2.4 billion antitrust lawsuit on behalf of its pay-TV channels Showtime and The Movie Channel seeking to scuttle the deal. The lawsuit alleged that for decades HBO had been engaging in anticompetitive practices, in part by colluding with distributors to make it more difficult for Showtime to acquire films, and that the merger with Warner would make the situation worse for consumers. Time Inc. officials responded that the suit was without merit.

Beneath the heated courtroom machinations, a personal feud was boiling over. At the time, Viacom was run by Frank Biondi, the former CEO of HBO, who had lost his job to Fuchs six years earlier in the wake of the *Ghostbusters* debacle and, in his new capacity, was now overseeing Showtime.

Biondi and Fuchs had once been nearly inseparable. They'd been close friends, and regular tennis partners. Fuchs was godfather to Biondi's daughter. But over time their relationship had soured. The lawsuit made it worse, and the bitterness spilled into the press. "If Michael wants to take it personally I can't do anything about it," Biondi told *The New York Times*. "It's not like a godfather is really a significant relationship."

While the antitrust suit was eventually settled by their parent companies, the rivalry between Showtime and HBO—and between Biondi and Fuchs—would only get more heated in the coming years, as the premium networks took turns raiding each other's executives and on-screen talent.

In the summer of 1989, after swatting back a hostile bid from Paramount, Time and Warner completed the deal and began merging assets. Under its flashy chief executive officer, Steve Ross, Warner was known for its gold-plated executive culture and its puckish, robber-baron spirit. Those at the top of the company lived like pot-bellied kings. Following the merger, Time Warner execs got their first taste of Ross's regal perks, which included a fleet of private jets and a lavish private villa in Acapulco, Mexico, where leaders would periodically retreat for rowdy get-togethers far away from the prying eyes of New York media watchers.

At the time, HBO was starting to find other ways, besides boxing, to capitalize on the bloodlust of American viewers. The 1980s were a golden era of slasher films. Masked mega-killers like Michael Myers from the *Halloween* series and Jason from the *Friday the 13th* franchise ruled the multiplex, racking up profits and spawning gory imitators.

In June 1989, HBO began airing *Tales from the Crypt*, a limited horror series from producer Joel Silver (*Commando, Lethal Weapon, Die Hard*) based on the 1950s comic books from William M. Gaines, better known as the publisher of *MAD Magazine*. "There's a good reason these comics were essentially banned in 1954," supervising producer Bill Teitler said at the time. "They're ghoulish, nightmarish, perverse stories."

The HBO series was narrated by the Crypt Keeper, a grisly animatronic puppet created by a twenty-six-year-old special-effects prodigy named Kevin Yagher, whose résumé already included the terrifying Chucky Doll from *Child's Play*.

The plan was for each new episode of *Tales from the Crypt* to feature the imprimatur of a different director. Just a few years earlier, top Hollywood talent would have run away from HBO screaming. But now the barrier felt increasingly permeable. Thanks to *Tanner '88*, HBO's creative stigma was slowly disappearing. Robert Zemeckis (*Who Framed Roger Rabbit*) signed on to create one of the first episodes of *Tales from the Crypt*. Later, Tom Hanks and Arnold Schwarzenegger would likewise direct episodes.

HBO chose to debut the horror series in June, a time of year when the networks filled their schedules with reruns. Once again, Fuchs's counter-programming strategy was effective. The series got the attention of critics desperate for something fresh to write about.

Critics tended to be impressed by the show's high production values and special effects but were taken aback at the adult anthology's rampant nudity and violence, particularly in its striking treatment of women. In one of the premiere episodes, a suburban mom kills her husband with a fire poker and then is terrorized at length by a serial killer dressed up as Santa Claus. In another one, a prison executioner loses his job when his state bans the death penalty but continues to electrocute criminals on a freelance basis. He later reveals his philosophy on women: "If you treat whores like queens and queens like whores, you got no problem."

The first handful of episodes did well enough that HBO decided to turn

Tales from the Crypt into a regularly recurring anthology series—albeit with much smaller production budgets than the original batch. It would go on to become a staple of HBO's lineup and a fan favorite, running for seven seasons until 1996.

A review in *Variety* later noted that an episode of *Tales from the Crypt* about "crazed punkers" featured "full frontal nudity, simulated sex, the brutal and bloody murder of a young woman, demonism, profanity, and a general odiousness."

"It is also very well executed," wrote the critic.

Confronted with such critiques, HBO executives were developing a standard line. Nobody received HBO in their home involuntarily. The network was an invited guest. Anyone who was offended could cancel. "We strive to bring the best TV that is not available on the commercial networks that is worth paying for," Albrecht said. "You'd never see anything like this on a network."

CHAPTER 4

That "Cable Edge"

By the late 1980s, HBO's programming team in Los Angeles was growing increasingly frustrated with their bosses back in New York. The big craze in network TV was building half-hour sitcoms around rising comics. Thanks to its surfeit of stand-up specials, HBO seemed perfectly positioned to capitalize on the trend. And yet, back at the Bryant Park headquarters, Michael Fuchs remained reluctant to invest major money in the kind of traditional TV series at which the broadcast networks excelled and gave away for free to anyone with an antenna.

The team in L.A. watched with dismay as one potential project after another went out the door. Roseanne Barr did a comedy special for HBO. Afterward, the show's director, Rocco Urbisci, said she wanted to do a series with the cable network. But Fuchs said no. Instead, Barr's groundbreaking series went to ABC. Peter Locke, an executive producer of *1st & Ten*, approached HBO about making a show around comedian Tim Allen. Again, Fuchs shot it down.

Albrecht's former client Keenen Ivory Wayans asked if HBO would produce a new sketch comedy show he was doing for Fox called *In Living Color*. The West Coast team began working on the pilot. But when Fuchs found out that HBO would be responsible for putting up fifty thousand dollars an episode in deficit financing—a pittance in TV terms—he stepped in and made HBO abandon the project. The show would go on to become a hit for Fox and make several of its cast members into stars, including the Wayans brothers, David Alan Grier, and Jim Carrey.

To Albrecht, the process of what series got made at HBO felt increasingly arbitrary. "It was basically, 'We're not really in the television business,'" Albrecht says. "We were kind of in the boutique 'what Michael likes' world and 'what we could convince him to do' world."

By 1990, Albrecht was set to quit and return to life as an agent, this time at the Hollywood agency CAA. But when he tried to give notice, Fuchs refused to let him out of his contract. Instead, they worked out a compromise. HBO would start a division that would package comedy shows and sell them to other networks.

At the offices in Los Angeles, a bright and industrious thirty-year-old programming executive named Sasha Emerson got to work writing a memo, illustrating how HBO would go about forming its own mini-TV studio.

Emerson grew up in Manhattan in the 1960s and '70s. Her mom was a former school teacher. Her dad was an international lawyer, who loved flea markets and enjoyed a side gig writing theater reviews for an Indian American newspaper in exchange for free tickets. Sasha was his precocious sidekick. Together, they combed through flea markets and theaters, assessing everything on display, looking for gems. The theater scene in New York at the time was going through a period of experimental resurgence, and they took it all in, seeing LeRoi Jones, La Mama, Mabou Mines, Harold Pinter, and Sam Shepard.

For college, Emerson went to Brown, where she majored in English. At twenty, she entered the dramaturgy program at the Yale School of Drama, intent on a career producing plays and working alongside playwrights.

Then Hollywood came knocking. During her final year, the dean of the school recommended her for a highly selective executive training program at CBS. Emerson applied, interviewed, and was accepted. Hers was a class of three.

CBS moved Emerson to Los Angeles, gave her a salary, and put her through the paces, immersing her for rotating stints in the network's various departments, from drama to comedy to promotions. After a year, CBS hired her full time as a manager in the movies-for-television division, a high volume unit that was putting out dozens of features a year. "We would joke that there was a list of words we could use to make up any title: *Mommy. Scream. Nightmare. Innocence*," Emerson says. "The movies would be like *Mommy's Nightmare Is a Scream*. Most of them were kind of pulpy stuff. But there were also a number of prestige projects with big stars. It was a great learning experience."

Emerson soon jumped to Disney, and then in the fall of 1986 to HBO, where she joined the small team charged with developing original programming. At HBO, her colleagues quickly recognized Emerson as someone who loved to meet new people and connect them to other members of her ever-expanding constellation of friends, artists, and associates.

"She has a huge collection of people she knows," says Dean Parisot, a filmmaker (*Galaxy Quest*) who in 1990 directed the HBO original movie *Framed*, starring Jeff Goldblum as a painter. Somewhere along the way he got pulled into Emerson's orbit. "It's like a big soup that she's constantly adding ingredients to."

Emerson's skill set meshed well with HBO's needs in the mid-1980s. She was a prodigious reader and possessed an encyclopedic knowledge of up-and-coming playwrights, directors, and stage actors—anyone from the theater world who ought to be working with HBO. Among other projects, Emerson went to work on several anthology series, including *Tales from the Crypt* and *Vietnam War Story*, which was a collection of freestanding half-hour dramas loosely organized around the topic of the Vietnam War.

Each new episode in an anthology series typically features a new cast, a new director, and a new set of creative needs. It was a genre of storytelling that required a lot of bodies, and Emerson with her deep network of creative friends could reliably provide them. At the time, she also helped develop *Prison Stories: Women on the Inside*, a dramatic trilogy of films about incarceration, each by a different female director. On that project, in particular, Emerson began tapping into the American theater scene to find talented, as yet unknown writers, directors, and actors—frequently women and people of color—who could deliver quality performances for HBO.

A number of promotions followed. By the time she turned thirty, Emerson was a senior and executive vice president at HBO, on the fast track, bound for great things. So it was no surprise when in 1990 the network tapped her to be the head of development and creative leader of HBO Independent Productions, the newly formed boutique production studio.

Emerson got to work scouting potential projects that could be packaged and sold to the broadcast networks. Before long, she and her colleagues were racking up sales. One early, successful project grew out of Emerson's friendship with Charles Dutton.

Dutton was an actor who'd grown up in Baltimore, got arrested as a teenager on a range of charges including manslaughter, and spent more than seven years in prison. While incarcerated, he discovered a love of theater. After his release, he went back to school, threw himself into acting, and eventually matriculated to the Yale School of Drama, where he first crossed paths with Emerson.

Around the time that Emerson started working on HBO Independent Productions, Dutton was performing a leading role in August Wilson's *The Piano Lesson*. "People don't realize this but he is really funny," Emerson told her colleagues. She saw comedic potential.

In summer of 1991, Fox began airing the resulting show from HBO Independent Productions, which was entitled *Roc*. The sitcom, set in a predominantly Black neighborhood in Baltimore, starred Charles Dutton as Roc Emerson, a curmudgeonly garbage collector, and Ella Joyce as his no-nonsense wife, Eleanor Emerson, a registered nurse. The reviews were solid, and the series would continue for seventy-two episodes across three successful seasons, earning HBO a significant payday. The Emersons soon joined the Cosbys as one of the few stable Black families on American prime-time TV. Their last name, Emerson, was a nod to the series' energetic catalyzer back at HBO.

● ● ●

WITH HBO INDEPENDENT PRODUCTIONS TAKING FLIGHT, Fuchs's resistance to making more scripted series was wearing down. At the time, one idea he actually liked arrived at HBO's doorstep courtesy of John Landis, the comedy director behind such hit movies as *The Blues Brothers* and *Trading Places*. Even by the convoluted standards of Hollywood, Landis's project had sprung from an unusual source of inspiration.

More than a decade earlier, back when Landis had been directing *Animal House*, Universal had given him a spacious, rent-free office on the studio's lot. The lavish bungalow, reminiscent of Hollywood's Golden Era, had a living area, three bathrooms, four offices, a kitchen, a personal shower, and a secretary.

By the late 1980s, Landis's perk was starting to attract some unwanted scrutiny. He had been making a bunch of movies for other studios like Warner Bros. and Paramount. Finally, the bosses at Universal made clear to Landis that if he wanted to hang on to his coveted pad, he needed to start earning his keep. Sid Sheinberg, the studio's imperious head, gave Landis a peculiar assignment. Find a way, he said, for MCA/Universal to monetize a collection of old, dusty, black-and-white TV series and films dating back to the 1950s and 1960s. Landis felt he had little choice but to say yes.

It would not be an easy task. The shows, like *General Electric Theater, Schlitz Playhouse,* and *Heinz Studio 57,* felt jarringly outdated and were impossible to sell into syndication. But the footage did have something going for it. It featured some of the era's most recognizable actors, some long in the tooth, and some just getting their start, including Ronald Reagan, Groucho Marx, Zsa Zsa Gabor, and Joan Crawford. It could be worth something, if someone had the right idea.

For several months, Landis met with writers and tossed around potential concepts. Nothing clicked. Finally, Landis and Universal executives came upon Marta Kauffman and David Crane, a pair of struggling writers, who were doing menial jobs at a New York law firm while writing plays and musical theater on the side. At a meeting in Los Angeles, the duo was shown three minutes of black-and-white footage and asked if they had any ideas.

On the flight back to New York, Kauffman and Crane started sketching something out. Within a day, they'd developed a long-shot pitch to use the clips in a situational comedy about a middle-aged guy whose subconscious is filled with images from old television shows, the result of watching too much crummy TV as a kid.

They pitched it. Get writing, they were told.

Before long, Landis found a willing buyer in HBO, which ordered a pilot. Susie Fitzgerald, a key programming executive for HBO at the time, recalls that Albrecht and Fuchs found the idea appealing for a simple reason. "It was low budget, and it had nudity in it," Fitzgerald says.

Fitzgerald grew up in Pasadena, California, and went to college at Smith, where she majored in biology. After graduating, she moved to Northern California and eventually landed a temporary gig as an assistant to a pair of staffers in the production department at HBO in Los Angeles. When a production coordinator abruptly quit, Fitzgerald got her job.

Soon, she was working for Chris Albrecht, bolstering HBO's lineup of comedians. In 1986, she worked on Robin Williams's HBO comedy special *An Evening at the Met*, which was widely hailed as a manic masterpiece by the supersonic joke teller. Over time, Fitzgerald helped to recruit a growing number of up-and-coming female comedians to HBO, including Whoopi Goldberg, Roseanne Barr, and Ellen DeGeneres.

After several years of late nights at the comedy clubs and early mornings back in the Century City offices, Fitzgerald asked to switch roles. She was reassigned to work alongside Sasha Emerson, developing HBO's scripted series, such as *Tales from the Crypt* and the forthcoming *Dream On*.

For mentorship, Fitzgerald increasingly turned to Bridget Potter, who was overseeing original programming from back in New York. "I was a biology major," Fitzgerald says. "I was not an English major, I was not a humanities major. So me moving from production into stand-up specials and into scripted—like, what the hell did I know?"

A Potter mantra became ingrained in Fitzgerald's mind: "She was always like, 'What is it? What is it *about*?'"

In 1990, HBO began airing *Dream On*, starring Brian Benben as Martin Tupper, a book editor in New York who is going through a divorce, raising a pubescent son, and throwing himself headlong into New York's dating scene. Throughout each episode, the directors made abundant usage of the old MCA footage to illustrate Tupper's interior monologue. The effect was deeply Freudian—one part *All in the Family*, one part *The Interpretation of Dreams*. In an early episode, Tupper realizes his blind date is a college undergraduate who is roughly half his age, and his mind flashes to a scene, in black-and-white, of a man bending over a crib and gingerly picking up a baby.

While Fuchs had signed off on the sitcom, he was hardly throwing Mike Tyson money at it. HBO's initial budget for *Dream On* was minuscule: $350,000 per each half-hour episode, recalls Kevin Bright, an executive producer on the series. It was too little, Bright says, to even shoot on a real sound stage. Instead, the producers set up shop in a North Hollywood warehouse, surrounded by razor wire and next door to a sketchy dive bar, just a couple of miles outside of Burbank Airport. The roar of jet engines frequently interrupted takes. "We got some soundproofing in the second season, but the whole first year when a plane came we had to shout *CUT*," Bright says.

"We used to call it guerrilla television," Kauffman says.

From the start, the writing on the show was witty and the scripts were sharp enough to attract a series of notable guests, including David Bowie and Jason Alexander, as well as promising newcomers like Matthew Perry. But unlike any network sitcom, *Dream On* also featured a steady procession of topless women, plus a plethora of sex-driven plotlines. Often, early drafts of scripts came back with a note from HBO executives: *It doesn't really have that cable edge to it.*

"Cable edge was code for it didn't have any nudity in the script," Bright says. "We definitely received pressure from HBO to try to have nudity in every episode."

The critical reception, while largely positive, homed in on the incessant undressing. "The show has its weak spots, most notably in a pointless tendency to be smarmy," John J. O'Connor wrote in *The New York Times*. "This may be the first series to proclaim publicly almost every week that it has a breast fetish."

In interviews, Landis noted that *Dream On* offered a more explicit, uncensored version of sexuality in place of the winking innuendo that was the lifeblood of network sitcoms. "It means we have breasts in the script just for the sake of seeing breasts," Landis said. "Excuse me, but what's so bad about that?" HBO's marketing team proudly promoted the show as a "sexy new comedy for grown-ups."

HBO viewers lapped it up, and the ratings for *Dream On* quickly surpassed anything previously achieved by an HBO original series.

The high quotient of strong language and topless women, says Kauffman, was a concession to the desires of the network—one that happened to be pandering to the male viewers that Fuchs insisted were HBO's core audience. "For me, as a feminist, I had a really hard time with everything from how do you audition people to what was the set going to look like when women were naked?" she says. "And how much of it is stuff that we absolutely needed and how much of it is are we doing this for HBO? Those are things I struggled with all the time."

She wasn't alone. Inside of her HBO office in Century City, Susie Fitzgerald blanched when she saw all the nudity in the early episodes. "I was like, 'Oh my god, like, what would my parents say?'" she says. "I felt like I was working on a soft-core porn thing at the beginning."

As the series progressed, *Dream On* took on a range of serious topics, including safe sex and AIDS. Eventually, HBO executives realized that viewers were growing attached to the characters, and the pressure for 'cable edge' tapered off. "I feel like we had the opportunity to tell some really good stories," Kauffman says. "I don't feel like it was a deal with the devil."

●　●　●

MICHAEL FUCHS LOVED PRACTICAL JOKES and quips of all manner. He took pride in never holding a meeting without telling at least one knee-slapper. "Business and humor, I'm a big believer in that," Fuchs says. "If you want to wake up a crowd, tell them a joke."

After a brief engagement to the actress Brooke Adams (*Invasion of the Body Snatchers*, *The Dead Zone*) Fuchs was single again in the early 1990s. He was living in a triplex apartment in lower Manhattan and dating around town with Martin Tupper–like zeal. Every year, Fuchs hosted a star-studded Oscar night party. During the summer, he routinely threw glitzy premieres for HBO movies in the Hamptons.

Fuchs surrounded himself with a tight-knit pack of male colleagues who liked to play tennis together, go shopping, and travel to HBO's boxing matches, where they mingled ringside with politicians and celebrities.

At least once a year, the whole management team went away together on a camaraderie-building company retreat to someplace warm. On the trips, everybody cut loose. Whatever resort they were staying at, Fuchs made sure it had plenty of tennis courts so they could squeeze in some matches between strategy meetings. "It was a band of brothers," says one former HBO executive.

Back in the corporate offices, Gerald Levin, HBO's founding father, now overseeing all of Time Warner's investments in video programming, was keeping a watchful eye on HBO's growth and evolution. "It was probably a male-dominated culture," Levin said. "A lot of horseplay in the meeting environment. Kind of a, *can you top this joke, jokester?* You had to be really sharp witted. But a very strong collective spirit, I thought."

To build camaraderie within the broader company, Fuchs also organized annual retreats for the members of HBO's regional sales and marketing teams. Once a year, HBO's frontline workers would fly in from the provincial offices to a tropical resort for four raucous days of networking, panels, and Q&A sessions with celebrity guests.

Each retreat had a theme. One year, HBO threw a "prom night," in which the men were required to wear tuxedos, and the women, in evening dresses, filled out "dance cards," dividing up their time on the dance floor with various male colleagues. Another year, the sales retreat had a circus motif. At night, everyone gathered in a big tent to watch a procession of jugglers, animal trainers, and sword swallowers. At a high point in the festivities, HBO's head of sales rode in triumphantly mounted on top of an elephant.

"If you were a young dude in your twenties or thirties, you'd have thought you had died and gone to heaven," says Dave Baldwin, a boisterous, bearded ex–school librarian who for years ran HBO's scheduling department. "People back then were either single or about to become single again."

Decades before tech companies in Silicon Valley adopted the technique of throwing over-the-top, celebrity-infused company parties to brand themselves, HBO used its fun-loving reputation to gain a competitive edge recruiting new employees fresh out of the country's top business schools. For Linda Frankenbach, a graduate of Columbia University's Business School, choosing between HBO and a traditional job in banking or finance was an easy call—she joined HBO and stayed there for a dozen years, working primarily in affiliate sales and marketing.

"I used to say to folks when they ask me how did I get to HBO, 'Well, I had a decent background, but mostly, I could drink and dance.' I think that's what got me in," Frankenbach would later recall. "It was way more fun than college."

Every summer, Fuchs and his inner circle flew to London to attend Wimbledon. Next to boxing, tennis was the most important element in HBO's slight package of live sports programming. In 1975, the network had made a novel deal with the All England Club to air the early round, weekday matches, which were previously unavailable to American audiences. For decades, HBO's daily Wimbledon coverage—taken from a BBC feed, and without any broadcaster commentary—served as a staple of the network's summer lineup, beloved by fervent tennis fans, if few others. "The Wimbledon numbers were almost invisible," says Quentin Schaffer, HBO's former communications executive. "It was for pure tennis aficionados. But it was nice to have in the portfolio of sports because we could not afford to own a portion of a major sport."

"I treated HBO like it was camp," Fuchs says.

Some members of the team found the constant rah-rah of the retreats numbing. "These outings were just a chance to go somewhere for a few days and let Michael talk," Albrecht says. "They were useless in terms of any decisions really getting made."

For female executives, HBO continued to be a challenging place to work. It wasn't just the "prom night" retreat parties and constant calls for more "cable edge." It was also the internal resistance to creating shows about women. Susie Fitzgerald, the former biology major, was struck by the preponderance of Y chromosomes in the gene pool of HBO talent. "I was like, why can't we have a female lead?" she says. "And we would go to research meetings, and they were like, 'The man controls the remote control, and the women will watch what they watch.'"

Still, she kept pushing for more female-driven scripted programming. Fitzgerald pointed out that HBO's lineup of comedians had expanded to include more female comics. Why couldn't one of them—or some other qualified woman—be the lead of a series? Years later, Fitzgerald says, she still remembers the dismissive reply that Albrecht gave her. "But they're not going to take their tops off," she recalls him saying.

* * *

BY THE EARLY 1990s, HBO's investment in Mike Tyson was starting to look dicey. Tyson's personal life was in disarray. His marriage to the actress Robin Givens was falling apart. The media was filled with disturbing details from their messy divorce, including reports of a miscarriage and allegations that Tyson had physically assaulted Givens. Once, after their split, a reporter asked Givens, a cultured, polished graduate of Sarah Lawrence College, how she could fall for such a rough, violent man. What was she attracted to? "The danger," Givens said.

The chaos enveloping Tyson's life took its toll. On February 11, 1990, in front of a riveted crowd inside the Tokyo Dome, Tyson stepped into an uppercut from Buster Douglas. Tyson's head snapped backward. As he fell, Douglas hit him again. It was the tenth round of a fight everyone expected Tyson to dominate. Las Vegas bookies had put Douglas's chance of victory at 42–1. Back in the United States, HBO subscribers huddled around their televisions, watching the incredible spectacle live. It was hard to believe what they were seeing. Tyson, the most dominant athlete in the world, fell to the mat, got up on one knee, and struggled and failed to jam his mouthguard back in. The referee called the fight.

"I would be willing to say it's the greatest upset in boxing history," HBO's Larry Merchant announced from ringside. A few minutes later, Merchant was in the ring, interviewing the euphoric, if shell-shocked, victor. "Why did you win this fight that no one on the planet gave you a shot at?" he asked. Douglas could barely speak. "Mother," he said. "My mother."

Afterward, the broadcast networks tried to buy the rights from HBO to rebroadcast the fight in prime time. But HBO executives turned down the quick cash, announcing instead that the subscription network would be re-airing Tyson's defeat in its entirety the following Friday night, giving everybody a few days to sign up for HBO.

For Seth Abraham, the dapper, free-spending head of HBO Sports to whom Ross Greenburg reported, Tyson's stunning defeat came at an awkward time. For months, he had been in talks with Don King, trying to work out a huge new deal with Tyson, whose contract with HBO would soon be expiring. The loss to Douglas complicated the equation.

Abraham was confident that Fuchs would back him no matter how much he spent. But he was less sure about how Jeffrey Bewkes, HBO's assiduous chief financial officer, would react. Bewkes was not a fan of boxing. Abraham had an idea.

One morning that July, five months after Tyson's shocking loss, HBO's managers gathered in a conference room on the eighth floor for a network-wide budget meeting. Bewkes sat at the head of the long table, presiding over the dry proceedings.

Just after 10:00 a.m., the swinging door between the conference room and an adjacent galley kitchen suddenly burst open. A muscular figure, dressed in black leather pants, a black turtleneck, and a black beret charged into the room. Everyone watched in shock as Mike Tyson strode over, reached down, and grabbed Bewkes by his lapels.

"'You better give Seth whatever the fuck he wants,' Tyson snarled, 'or you'll have to answer to me.' The color drained from Jeff's face," recalls Abraham. "Then we all started laughing."

Tyson let go and smiled. Just kidding. Earlier that morning, Abraham explained to the group, he'd snuck Tyson into the building through a back service entrance. For the past hour, Tyson had been hiding in the kitchen waiting for his cue to pounce. While the color returned to Bewkes's ashen face, Tyson stood around amiably chatting with the charmed HBO executives.

The prank was a resounding success. Even so, Tyson's time with HBO was fast coming to a close. Six months later, following a first-round technical knockout of Alex "The Destroyer" Stewart in Atlantic City, Tyson announced he was jumping to HBO's competitors at Showtime. Don King told reporters the eight- to ten-fight deal would pay Tyson roughly $120 million. It was a major coup for HBO's rivals. But, as it turned out, their gloating was short-lived.

In July 1991, Tyson was arrested and accused of raping an eighteen-year-old beauty pageant queen in a hotel room in Indiana. During the subsequent trial, Desiree Washington, Miss Black Rhode Island, testified about sitting on the bed inside Tyson's room at the Canterbury Hotel, listening to him talk sweetly about his pet pigeons. "I thought that was neat because I love animals," she testified. Then he attacked her.

After several weeks of testimony, the jury convicted Tyson on one count of rape and two counts of criminal deviate conduct. He was sentenced to six years in prison. Afterward, in a series of interviews, casino owner Donald Trump loudly defended Tyson, arguing that incarceration was an unjust punishment and seeming to blame the victim, pointing out to NBC News that the young woman had been seen "dancing with a big smile on her face" on the evening of her attack.

• • •

ONE AFTERNOON in the late summer of 1991, Chris Albrecht entered Sasha Emerson's spacious office with its sweeping city views in HBO's Los Angeles headquarters and shut the door. There was plenty of HBO business to talk over. In addition to *Roc*, HBO Independent Productions had sold a number of other series, including *Down the Shore,* a sitcom on Fox about a bunch of childhood friends cohabitating in a beach house, and *The Ben Stiller Show*, a short-lived sketch comedy show cocreated by Stiller and a young writer named Judd Apatow. Also, an initial deal had just been struck for *Martin*, a sitcom starring comedian Martin Lawrence, which would eventually turn into a prime-time hit for Fox. Under Emerson's creative leadership, the unit was thriving.

A few minutes later, inside the office, there was a loud thump. Afterward, according to former HBO staffers, rumors began ricocheting around the office. This was no prank. Something horrible had happened.

The next day, the staffers learned that Emerson had been summoned to New York. While she was gone, her office was packed up and moved to another floor, a strange development that was left unexplained.

Meanwhile, in L.A., word quickly spread among Emerson's many friends in the industry about what had transpired. Emerson and Albrecht, both married at the time, had been having an affair, which had ended a few months earlier. According to a source who spoke about the incident with Emerson in the immediate aftermath, that afternoon in the office, Emerson told Albrecht she was seeing someone new; in an apparent fit of jealous rage, Albrecht had attacked Emerson, charging at her from across the room, grabbing her by the neck, knocking over her executive chair, and strangling her down to the floor.* Before she could lose consciousness, he let go.

Afterward, Emerson hurriedly left the building, got in her car, and drove off. Before making it home, she pulled over, called Michael Fuchs in New York, and told him exactly what had happened.

Though it sounded to Emerson's friend like a clear-cut assault, no police report was made. Instead, back in New York, Fuchs and his chief financial officer, Jeffrey Bewkes, were coming up with a plan for how to handle the situation without in any way getting law enforcement involved.

Weeks later, with the festering situation still unresolved and Emerson cut off physically and bureaucratically from her typical professional duties, her lawyers requested a mediation. On September 20 and 21, Albrecht and Emerson sat down for an extended mediation session led by two outside lawyers hired by HBO from a group called the Center for Dispute Resolution. Over the course of two long days, inside a conference room on the seventh floor of an office building overlooking the Avenue of the Stars, Emerson proceeded to explain to them in no uncertain terms what Albrecht had done to her.

---

* Through his lawyer, Albrecht says "he rejects and disagrees with the characterization of what occurred" in Sasha Emerson's office in the summer of 1991. He declined to comment further.

A short while later, the Center for Dispute Resolution presented a confidential assessment of their findings to HBO executives. Afterward, Emerson left the network, sent packing with a settlement, undisclosed to company shareholders. Albrecht was allowed to stay. As far as anyone could tell, his only penalty for strangling a colleague was that he would now report to Bridget Potter in New York instead of directly to Michael Fuchs, losing a slight modicum of his independence.

There was no official explanation from Fuchs, Bewkes, Albrecht, or any of HBO's bosses. The strategy, apparently, was to get everyone to sign nondisclosure agreements and then pretend that nothing untoward had happened. There was an agreement that there would be no press about Emerson's departure.

On November 11, 1991, however, an unsourced item appeared in *The Hollywood Reporter*, erroneously noting that "in an executive shuffle," Emerson had exited HBO "over differences of opinion with management."

"That was a violation," Emerson said to her friends.

It would not be the last.

For the next sixteen years, Albrecht, Bewkes, and Fuchs would succeed in keeping knowledge of the violent, disturbing event out of the press. Their secret would remain covered up, buried, and selectively forgotten. Until one night, years later, amid a dark Las Vegas gale, when the truth at last would wriggle free.

CHAPTER 5

Quality Noise

With each passing year, HBO's original film department was growing darker, more Tyson-like in its delivery. From its inception, HBO had made a bunch of uplifting movies about men of high moral character, including biopics of Nelson Mandela, Edward R. Murrow, and Simon Wiesenthal. With time, HBO's choice of historic figures grew more violent and misanthropic. "In the beginning, I wanted to make movies about heroes," Michael Fuchs said. "We ran out of heroes very quickly. We started doing villains."

HBO subscribers reacted favorably to the darker material. Dramatic depictions of menacing real-life figures started filling HBO's Saturday nights. *Stalin* provided a closeup look at the Russian dictator and his atrocities. *Citizen Cohn* offered a blistering portrait of Roy Cohn, the manipulative, power-obsessed adviser to Senator Joseph McCarthy (and, later, Donald Trump). *One Man's War* told the story of the Paraguayan despot Alfredo Stroessner and the heinous acts of his secret police.

Eventually, HBO dialed up an original movie about the rise and inglorious fall of Mike Tyson. "The American public, for some reason, was captivated by his transgressions as much as they were by his boxing," says HBO's Ross Greenburg, who produced the film, which starred Michael Jai White as Tyson. "He became a larger-than-life figure because of the violent incidents, not in spite of them."

Overseeing the original movie division in L.A. was an executive named Bob Cooper, a former independent film director from Montreal who had joined HBO in 1988.

Under Cooper, HBO Pictures sought out controversial cultural topics like abortion, racial injustice, and gun control—subjects that the broadcast networks were unlikely to touch out of fear of upsetting sponsors. HBO did so with an openly liberal, pugilistic point of view. "As long as we're accurate, we can be offensive," Cooper said.

In 1992, Cooper made a call to the prolific TV producer Aaron Spelling, whose past hits included *Charlie's Angels* and *The Love Boat*. A few years earlier, Spelling had signed on with NBC to produce a film adaptation of *And the Band Played On*, the bestselling book by journalist Randy Shilts that investigated America's early, inept response to the AIDS crisis.

For several years, NBC sat on the project, and Spelling grew frustrated, eventually concluding that a story about gay activists struggling against the indifference of the political and medical establishment was too controversial for NBC, and perhaps for all of network TV.

Cooper heard of Spelling's predicament and reached out with a suggestion. Bring it to HBO. The cable network, he told Spelling, wasn't afraid of stirring up controversy. Months later, when NBC's option on the film finally expired, Spelling sold it to HBO. Cooper quickly ushered the film into production.

During casting, several well-known Hollywood actors, including Richard Gere, Steve Martin, Anjelica Huston, and Lily Tomlin signed on to play minor roles. The actors arranged to work for reduced salaries of roughly ten thousand dollars per week—much less than they were accustomed to earning on theatrical projects—and to donate half of their paychecks to AIDS charities. "I wanted to do this because maybe other people won't do it," Tomlin said.

The making of the movie soon hit several snags. A number of prominent activists accused HBO of unfairly blaming the gay community for the spread of AIDS; and several scientists alleged that HBO was twisting the historical record and spreading bad science. During postproduction, Cooper got into a spat with the film's director, who publicly accused him of "arbitrary and censorious behavior."

As the controversies mounted, Cooper worried that he'd be pulled off the movie. As he scrambled to wrap up the project, he got a call from Fuchs. Don't worry, Fuchs told him, he would defend Cooper in the press. Just don't start playing it safe.

When HBO broadcast *And the Band Played On* on September 11, 1993, it was hailed as a major moment in the struggle for AIDS awareness and was credited with being the first major movie to confront the AIDS crisis (*Philadelphia*, a legal drama starring Tom Hanks as a gay lawyer with AIDS, would arrive in theaters months later). "At a time when most made-for-TV movies have gone tabloid crazy, here is a rare one that tackles a big subject, raises the right issues, fights the good fight," Richard Zoglin wrote in *Time* magazine.

"People thought I was fearless," Cooper says. "It wasn't me. Michael Fuchs made me fearless."

HBO basked in the adulation. Just a few years earlier, the studio chiefs had ridiculed HBO for sifting through their rejected projects. Now, HBO executives turned the tables, telling the press that they were proud to be making the movies that the entertainment establishment was too cautious, too hidebound, to produce themselves. "The primary part of our decision is to ask, 'Could anyone else do it?'" Bridget Potter said. "If the answer is yes, then it's not for HBO."

With each new cinematic exposé, HBO executives further embraced the network's identity as a vigilantes' den of fearless storytellers shedding light on difficult social truths. "There is no modern Dickens," Fuchs told reporters. "So I sent a note out and said, 'let us be Dickens,' let us look at contemporary society like no one else in the country."

Back in New York, the network was plowing additional money into HBO Showcase, its East Coast programming unit, which was headed by Colin Callender, an erudite British producer who'd grown up in a Jewish family in

London and spent his early professional years working in the theater. He joined HBO in 1987. Like his West Coast counterparts, Callender's team in New York gravitated toward dramatic movies that filtered real-world events through a prism of progressive righteousness.

In *Dead Ahead: The Exxon Valdez Disaster*, HBO provided a withering portrayal of the events surrounding the massive oil spill of 1989. The film, starring John Heard as a scrupulous Alaskan wildlife officer, mixed the drama with real archival footage from the environmental disaster, showing coastlines rimmed with black sludge and dying seabirds, their wings smothered in oil.

Critics were impressed, and HBO executives distilled their new movie strategy into a pithy slogan. The network's goal, they told reporters, was to create movies that felt like cultural events, that inspired editorials, and provoked outrage. Their mission, in short, was to create "quality noise." "The value of quality noise is that we believe it helps give meaning to the word HBO," Cooper said.

To generate as much quality noise as possible, HBO hit on an effective tactic. Before an original movie first appeared on HBO, the network would stage an elaborate premiere at a movie theater for a strategically selected group of guests, often in exotic locations. It was a great way, they quickly discovered, to generate loads of free media attention.

In November 1992, on the seventy-fifth anniversary of the Russian Revolution, HBO hosted a premiere of *Stalin* at a theater in Moscow. The screening was attended by the film's cast, HBO executives, and a collection of Russian dignitaries.

The movie, which starred Robert Duvall and featured the cinematography of American New Wave legend Vilmos Zsigmond, had been shot during the tumultuous dissolution of the Soviet Union. "We filmed in all those recesses of the Kremlin," says former HBO executive and *Stalin* producer Ilene Kahn Power. "It will never be done again. It would be like the Russians coming and filming in the Lincoln Bedroom."

When the production had finished shooting, Kahn Power and her team held the wrap party at one of Stalin's former homes in the city. There, the producers dished out some two thousand Big Macs, procured from Russia's first McDonald's, which had recently opened in Pushkin Square. "All of these guys on our crew kept stuffing the hamburgers in their jackets," Kahn Power says.

On the night of the film's premiere in Moscow, a row of sorts erupted in the theater. During the screening, says Kahn Power, many of the Russian officials in the audience took offense at the film's depiction of Lenin's wife. The Americans, they believed, had made her overly unattractive, an intolerable slight. "So half of them walked out," Kahn Power says. "It was a wild, wild night."

The commotion aligned perfectly with HBO's overarching goal for the event, which was to stir up some "quality noise" in front of the foreign correspondents who were stationed in Moscow, covering the Kremlin for major American newspapers. "It worked," said Quentin Schaffer. "Every outlet there covered this. We got a tremendous amount of international attention."

* * *

WITH HBO THROWING OFF PROFITS and accumulating awards, Fuchs felt it was time for HBO's corporate parents to give him more power. Following the merger, Time Warner now controlled Warner Bros., one of the biggest movie studios in Hollywood. Having made inroads in the world of made-for-TV movies, Fuchs wanted HBO to set up a new comedy pipeline at the studio that would create a handful of movies every year for theatrical release.

But Hollywood's distaste for HBO hadn't entirely dissipated, particularly at the management level. The two top executives at Warner Bros., Terry Semel and Bob Daly, had spent the past decade listening to every grandiose pronouncement uttered by the self-satisfied Michael *Fuckheads* in New York. They weren't about to make things easy for Team Fuchs now. They fiercely resisted every effort by HBO to grab a piece of Warner Bros.' moviemaking resources. When Fuchs proposed that HBO should pay less to license Warner Bros. movies following the merger, they shot down that idea too.

Once, they even raided HBO's talent. Since its debut, the success of *Dream On* had catapulted Marta Kauffman and David Crane from unknown musical theater writers into cable TV wunderkinds. A few seasons into *Dream On*, Leslie Moonves, then the head of Lorimar Television, a division of Warner Bros., began pursuing Kauffman, Crane, and Bright, the show's executive producer, to leave HBO and sign new long-term development contracts with him. When Fuchs put up little resistance, Kauffman and Crane walked away from HBO and signed with Lorimar, becoming Warner Bros.' marquee writers.

Shortly into their new deal, Kauffman and Crane came up with an idea for a sitcom about six friends living in New York, sharing romantic and professional adventures. *Friends* would go on to become one of the most popular and lucrative sitcoms in the history of television, making a fortune for Warner Bros.

Fuchs's continued ambivalence toward scripted programming was not absolute. There was one person, in particular, he desperately wanted to corral for the network—namely, Garry Shandling. Fuchs was still smarting over losing *It's Garry Shandling's Show* to Showtime a few years earlier. So when Shandling's run on Showtime ended in 1990, Fuchs rushed in and scooped up the comedian's next idea for a series: a behind-the-scenes office comedy about a late-night talk-show host that would be informed by Shandling's years of guest hosting *The Tonight Show*. Fuchs loved the idea and ordered it straight to series at thirteen episodes.

Back in Los Angeles, the development team was aghast. They'd been told repeatedly that television series were not a priority.

"It was all very much a personal playground for Michael," Albrecht says.

In the summer of 1992, HBO began airing *The Larry Sanders Show*, a satire of a late-night talk show, starring Shandling as a thin-skinned, egomaniacal host and the actor Jeffrey Tambor as his dopey sidekick, Hank.

Each episode toggled between two styles: the show within the show, which was often filmed in front of a live audience and mimicked the feel of NBC's *The Tonight Show*, and the "off-camera," behind-the-scenes moments, shot to look like a documentary. The setup allowed Shandling to draw a sharp contrast between the characters' behavior in public, where they tended to be warm, charming, and emotionally intelligent, versus in private, where they were reliably paranoid and manipulative. "The show is a metaphor for the two-faced quality people have in their lives," Shandling said.

From the start, HBO subscribers showed minimal interest. But critics loved it. Shandling's send-up of traditional TV was informed by experience. Long before he lampooned its conventions, Shandling had spent decades mastering them. Shandling grew up in Tucson, Arizona. His father was an entrepreneur, his mother ran a pet store. In 1975, after a stint at the University of Arizona studying electrical engineering, he dropped out of school and moved to L.A. to become a TV writer.

He broke into the industry as a script writer for shows like *Sanford and Son* and *Welcome Back, Kotter.* One rainy day, while driving to get a haircut, Shandling got into a bad car accident and was rushed into surgery. When he recovered, he vowed to begin chasing his long-shot dream of becoming a successful stand-up comedian.

He started doing sets during amateur night at the Comedy Store and telling jokes for a living. "You don't know what it was like being an unwanted child," he said onstage his first night. "My mother had tried to talk her doctor into performing an abortion. But he said he wouldn't do it because it was illegal to perform an abortion once a child had reached the age of fifteen." From there he rose through the ranks, eventually becoming a recurring guest host on *The Tonight Show.*

By the time *Larry Sanders* made it to air, the real world of the late-night talk shows was in a state of flux. In May 1992, Johnny Carson hosted his final episode of *The Tonight Show.* His retirement set off a fierce battle for succession. The drama of the late-night power struggle was splashed across the pages of Hollywood trade publications and in newspapers around the country. It was the perfect backdrop for a show like *Larry Sanders,* which mined the fragile insecurities of the industry.

To add to the sense of verisimilitude, *Larry Sanders* featured a steady stream of Hollywood celebrities playing themselves, including Sharon Stone, Dave Chappelle, and Dana Carvey. It was the same effective trick that HBO had first deployed four years earlier during the production of *Tanner '88*—and one that would continue to pop up regularly in HBO shows for decades to come.

An early theme of *Larry Sanders* was the inherent inauthenticity of ad-supported television. In the first episode, the network's cutthroat head of late-night programming tells Larry and his colleagues that the climate of broadcast television is "getting kicked in the balls." "What do we do to keep our advertisers happy, other than giving them free handjobs?" she says. "It's come back to us this way. They want you to do live commercials as part of the show."

When Larry is later asked to promote a product called the Garden Weasel even though he's never gardened, he gets upset. Eventually, he musters up the courage to tell Artie (Rip Torn), his brusque, no-nonsense producer, that doing the promotional spots might be a "little bit unethical."

"Larry, don't start pulling at that thread," Artie says incredulously. "The whole world will unravel."

Like *Dream On*, the budget for *Larry Sanders* was tiny compared to broadcast sitcoms. Todd Holland, who would go on to direct more than fifty episodes of the series, says that among other cost-saving oddities, the show lacked a full-time production designer. Also, the set was missing certain key elements. "We always had trouble with Larry's home as a set," Holland says. "They built the living room, the front door, and the bedroom. But they didn't build a kitchen. I kept saying that the heart of a house is the kitchen. But there just wasn't the money or the will to add one."

Throughout the series, the crew was constantly running around trying to cannibalize set pieces and props from previous, failed shows made by its production company, Brillstein-Grey Entertainment. "It was like a student film," Holland says.

The critical success of *The Larry Sanders Show* proved to be a tipping point in how HBO would finance its original programming in the future. Nearly all of HBO's early series—*Tales from the Crypt, Dream On*—were either coproductions or licensed from other studios entirely. The setup allowed HBO to defray costs while sharing the risk of the investment with another company. With *Sanders*, the downside of the arrangement became increasingly clear.

"It wasn't until *Larry Sanders* came along, when they kind of realized, 'Oh god, I wish we owned that show,'" says Quentin Schaffer. "It's so definitive HBO, and yet we don't own it. There's a value to owning them and putting them on again and again."

Even with a skimpy budget, the production worked, in large part, because of some mesmerizing performances. The show relentlessly probed the shadows of the human ego—how people truly behave when they think nobody is watching. "*Larry Sanders* taught me that flawed human behavior is ten times more interesting than correct human behavior," Holland said.

In the years to come, a baroque procession of dysfunctional, yet beloved, HBO characters would follow.

• • •

BY 1992, Michael Fuchs was often seen around the offices in the company of Richard Plepler, a convivial, thirty-three-year-old public relations whiz who'd recently joined HBO. Plepler, who'd spent several formative years after college soaking up the lessons of political persuasion on Capitol Hill in Washington, D.C., was a fervent believer in the power of personal relationships to advance one's cause. He was a preternatural networker who seemed to know just about everyone in Democratic politics and journalism, despite his young age.

At HBO, Plepler became an advocate for a strategy that he sometimes called the "permanent campaign." The basic idea was that you didn't wait until the feverish onset of a crisis to figure out who you needed to court and win over to defend you publicly in your moment of need. It was much more effective to have already invested the time and energy, under cooler circumstances, in courting those influential members of public opinion, much better to have already forged a bond.

Every lunch, every dinner, every film premiere was an opportunity to sit down with someone of note in public office or the press and start building a foundation of mutual understanding and respect. The goal of the permanent campaign was to build an ever-expanding bank of goodwill that might be called upon for the network's advantage at some later date.

Plepler would tell his colleagues that, unlike the free broadcast networks, HBO couldn't afford to take a single day off from advancing its cause. There was no off-season for HBO. If a customer wasn't satisfied with the network, they could cancel the service just like that. HBO, Plepler would say, "needed to be elected every month."

Before long, Fuchs was regularly taking counsel from Plepler, who quickly became known inside the company as much more than a public relations guy. He was a key HBO strategist and Fuchs's esteemed consigliere.

"I saw myself in those early days as a campaign manager," Plepler says. "And Michael was the candidate."

During cable TV's infancy, many customers lived in rural areas, where broadcast TV reception was lousy. As a result, for years HBO's audience had skewed heavily white. With time, however, cable television was growing increasingly popular in dense urban areas. In the mid-1980s, Nielsen introduced a new way of measuring the audiences of TV shows that, among other things, allowed the company to gather and share with its clients much richer and more detailed information on what Black households were watching. The change inspired some TV executives to start rethinking their strategies for appealing to minority audiences. HBO executives eventually realized that they might be able to grow their subscriber base faster if they did a better job of catering to a broader array of customers.

"Suddenly, Black viewership of television became quantified," said Don Anderson, one of the few Black executives to work at HBO.

In the early '90s, HBO's lineup grew noticeably more diverse, thanks to original movies like *The Josephine Baker Story*, a biopic starring Lynn Whitfield as the pioneering Black entertainer, and a Forest Whitaker–directed social crime drama called *Strapped*, which starred Bokeem Woodbine as a troubled teenager.

On Friday nights in 1992, HBO started airing a new comedy series called *Russell Simmons's Def Comedy Jam*, hosted by comedian Martin Lawrence and taped in front of a raucous audience at the Academy Theatre in New

York. Each episode featured a monologue by Lawrence followed by a series of four brief stand-up acts by Black comedians. The material was pointed and profane. It was also popular.

"Once you were worried about wiring, not West Virginia, but west L.A., the demographics of cable customers you focus on changes tremendously," says Henry McGee, a former longtime HBO executive who is Black.

Meanwhile, HBO's documentary division continued to roam around the fringes of American society, looking for individuals with unusual stories to tell. One morning in June 1993, Sheila Nevins read a wire-service article in the *New York Times* about three teenage boys in West Memphis, Arkansas, who'd just been arrested for allegedly murdering three eight-year-old kids. The small town of twenty-eight thousand people on the western bank of the Mississippi River, opposite Memphis, Tennessee, was in an uproar. The murders were grotesque. The bodies of the three second graders had been found in a drainage ditch in a patch of woods off a highway.

Police were charging the three teenage suspects with capital murder. As they were taken away from the local courthouse, an angry crowd of onlookers shouted at them, calling them "baby killers" and "freaks."

Police weren't commenting on the possible motive. But the town was filled with rumors about Satanism, devil worship, and the occult. The article quoted several local residents who suggested that at least two of the boys were known as weirdo outsiders who wore dark clothing. One kid from the local high school said the defendants were known to draw things like pentagrams, skulls, and snakes, and had once shown up at a football game with black tears painted on their faces.

Nevins was intrigued. She knew that ABC's newsmagazine, *20/20*, had done a feature on Satanism and that it had rated well. A documentary touching on devil worship, she suspected, might draw a big audience to HBO.

After reading the article, she reached out to Joe Berlinger and Bruce Sinofsky, a pair of filmmakers who had recently released *Brother's Keeper*, a highly acclaimed documentary about a murder in a farming community in rural New York.

Nevins had met Berlinger years earlier, when he'd been working for the

Maysles brothers, handling tasks like marketing and publicity. At the time, he'd told Nevins that he wanted to be a filmmaker himself. And eventually, Nevins gave Berlinger one of his first real production gigs, overseeing an episode of *Real Sex*. "I was the guy on the street asking people about their sex lives," Berlinger says.

Now, Nevins wanted Berlinger and Sinofsky to look into the murders in Arkansas. The filmmakers liked the idea of a film exploring Satanism run amok in America. A few weeks later, they headed out to the Mississippi River town and, for the next several months, throughout the summer of 1993, embedded with the grieving families of the victims.

When they got there, the local media was filled with stories pointing to the guilt of the arrested teenagers. On a scale of one to ten, the lead detective in the case was telling everybody, the evidence was an eleven. A slam dunk. One of the boys, Jessie Lloyd Misskelley Jr., a soft-spoken, compliant sixteen-year-old, had confessed to committing the crime in cahoots with the two other boys.

"I hate them for it," a mom of one of the victims told the filmmakers. "I never hated anyone in my life. And I hate these three—and the mothers that bore them."

That fall, Berlinger and Sinofsky began interviewing the three defendants, who were locked up in a county correctional facility awaiting trial. The more they talked with the boys, the more their doubts started to grow. Nothing added up. "It wasn't like a light bulb went off and Bruce and I were, like, these kids are innocent," Berlinger says. "But something wasn't right."

They checked in with Nevins back at HBO. She advised the filmmakers to follow the story wherever it led them.

A few weeks later, with the criminal trials approaching fast, things grew weirder. On Christmas Eve 1993, Berlinger, Sinofsky, and their cameraman spent a freezing afternoon filming the parents of Christopher Byers, one of the murdered children, grieving at his gravestone. Afterward, they all went back to the Byerses' house to decompress.

Feeling exhausted, the cameraman excused himself and repaired to another room to take a nap. When he woke up a short while later, the adoptive father, Mark Byers, a gangly Satan-cursing man, was sitting next to him rubbing his arm. Byers thanked the cameraman for all his hard work on the movie and then offered him a gift of appreciation, a folding hunting knife.

On the ride away from the house, the cameraman recounted the story to the filmmakers. Something about the gift seemed odd, they all agreed. Back at the hotel, they examined the knife. Unfolding it, something caught their eyes. It looked like a dried clump of human blood. Christ, they thought. What should we do now? The prosecutors' theory of the crime posited that the three murdered boys had been cut up with some sort of knife.

The filmmakers called Nevins, who summoned them back to New York. Back at HBO headquarters, they met with Nevins, Richard Plepler, and some lawyers to decide how to proceed. Berlinger and Sinofsky came from a school of documentary filmmaking that valued objectivity in story gathering. "We really didn't want to become part of the story," Berlinger says.

Still, they couldn't exactly bury the bloody knife in a riverbed. It was their civic duty, they all agreed, to share the potential evidence with investigators in Arkansas—which they soon did.

Afterward, they got back to making their movie. Three years later, when it finally aired on HBO, *Paradise Lost* would join the American pantheon of true-crime storytelling—and set off a national outcry.

• • •

LOOKING TO EXPAND on the growing success of *Def Comedy Jam*, HBO turned to one of Albrecht's former clients, a young comedian named Chris Rock. In June 1994, Rock did his first comedy special for HBO, called "Big Ass Jokes." Shot in front of a live audience in Atlanta, the half-hour show delved into Rock's childhood, interracial relationships, and celebrity. "Michael Jackson," said Rock, pacing back and forth on stage. "People are like, 'No, he ain't do it.' Well? Let him babysit your kids."

Rock grew up in the 1970s in a middle-class family in Brooklyn, bused into schools in white neighborhoods where Black students were few and far between. There, he was frequently picked on, giving him a refined sense of racial dynamics that would shape his life's work. Rock dropped out of school in tenth grade and took a series of jobs at fast-food restaurants. In between shifts, Rock did walk-on sets at comedy clubs in Manhattan. He had a boyish face, which made it that much funnier when he dug into mature subjects with knowing precision. He spent much of his time onstage talking about his family and where he grew up. "I talk about my father a lot because I have one," Rock would say onstage. "Fathers are very rare in my neighborhood. I remember I won my eighth-grade science fair just by bringing my father in."

In 1988, Rock's father died suddenly from a ruptured ulcer. The last thing Rock felt like doing was getting up onstage and telling jokes. Albrecht reached out to Rock and offered his condolences. To help him get back on his feet, HBO signed the comedian to a development contract, which paid the comedian "somewhere between fifteen thousand and twenty-five thousand dollars," according to Albrecht. Rock returned to the clubs and kept refining his material.

In 1990, Rock was invited to join the cast of *Saturday Night Live*, his biggest job yet. But SNL was just entering a boorish phase, one that would be dominated for the next several years by blunt physical comics like Chris Farley and Adam Sandler playing loutish, thickheaded simpletons. The things that made Rock a growing legend in comedy clubs—brutally honest dissections of race, and gender, and money—had little place on the show, and he was largely relegated to the sidelines.

HBO quickly proved to be a much better forum for Rock's particular talents. For viewers and critics who mainly knew him for his brief goofy segments on *Saturday Night Live*, Rock's 1994 stand-up performance on HBO was a revelation.

For Rock and HBO, it was just the start of big things to come.

• • •

IN THE SPRING OF 1995, Michael Fuchs received a big promotion at Time Warner. Gerald Levin, now the chairman of the entire mega-conglomerate, announced that Fuchs would be taking over as the new head of Warner Music, by far the largest record company in the world. With a huge stable of artists, ranging from Madonna to Dr. Dre to Hootie & the Blowfish, Warner Music was more than twice the size of HBO, generating nearly $4 billion of annual revenue.

As he transitioned into the music business, Fuchs insisted that he maintain his role as chairman, overseeing HBO. His deputy, Jeffrey Bewkes, would become HBO's new CEO. Bridget Potter, who declined to relocate to Los Angeles, would lose her job. Albrecht—a mere four years after his desk-side strangulation of an esteemed coworker—would be bumped up to president of original productions.

At forty-nine years old, Fuchs had ascended into the stratosphere of cultural influence at Time Warner and looked perfectly positioned to someday rule over the largest entertainment company on earth.

Instead, Fuchs's career rapidly imploded.

The music division that Fuchs walked into proved to be an alligator pit of internecine rivalries and feuds. He struggled to exert control, elbowing out top executives and promising to muscle the organization into submission. But along the way, he managed to alienate himself from many factions of the music business, which largely viewed him as a novice and an outsider.

Facing an uproar among conservative culture warriors over the explicit lyrics in rap songs, Fuchs announced in September that Warner Music would be selling off its $115 million stake in Interscope Records, home to artists like Snoop Dogg and Tupac Shakur. Conservative pundits declared victory and gloated in the press. To some observers in the industry, it looked like Fuchs, a self-styled champion of free speech, had failed to stand up for his artists. "It's a sad day for Warner," said Ice-T.

Behind the scenes, Time Warner's CEO Levin began negotiating a $7.5 billion acquisition of Turner Broadcasting System, Ted Turner's Atlanta-based media conglomerate, which owned several major cable networks, including TNT, TBS, the Cartoon Network, and CNN. Rumors began circulating that Levin might give control of HBO to Turner and perhaps even strip Fuchs of the music division. Suddenly, Fuchs's future at the company looked uncertain.

In November, as part of a corporate restructuring, Levin unceremoniously ousted Fuchs and handed the reins of Warner Music to Robert Daly and Terry Semel, the cochairs of Warner Bros., who had been feuding with

Fuchs for months. In the struggle for power, Fuchs's rivals in Hollywood had finally bested him. Media reports of his dismissal were filled with anonymous gloating.

"He was an arrogant and vindictive bully who tried to intimidate grown men into subservience," an unnamed Warner Music executive told the *Los Angeles Times*. "In my opinion, he got what he deserved."

Back at the HBO offices in New York, there was a mixture of sadness and shock. Many at the network owed their career to Fuchs. Now, they were losing their boisterous head counselor. "Michael was an extraordinary talent and will land on his feet, but I find this very distressing for him," Bewkes said.

In the end, however, it was hard for anyone to feel too bad for Fuchs, who walked away with a settlement package from Time Warner worth tens of millions of dollars.

Some industry observers speculated that for his next act Fuchs might sign on with one of the other big Hollywood studios and begin exacting revenge on his enemies at Time Warner. But no such job was forthcoming, not then, not ever. Fuchs, it seemed, had alienated too many powerful people in Hollywood for too long. His career in show business was kaput.

Decades later, self-employed and wholly forgotten in the entertainment industry, Fuchs would still be bitterly keening over his downfall at Time Warner and what might have been for him and for HBO. "Honestly, what I thought I could become was the anti–Rupert Murdoch," Fuchs says.

PART II

HE SHADOWS

(1995–1999)

CHAPTER 6

The Land of Oz

In the fall of 1995, Jeffrey Bewkes, HBO's lanky, square-jawed executive, took full control of HBO for the first time. Though Bewkes had been at the network for more than a decade and a half, he was largely unknown outside the company. He preferred to spend his downtime sailing and skiing and spent much less time schmoozing at industry parties than his volcanic mentor Michael Fuchs.

Taxonomically, Bewkes was an endemic specimen of the East Coast Wasp establishment. He grew up in the affluent suburb of Darien, Connecticut. His father was a powerful business executive. Bewkes went to boarding school at Deerfield, college at Yale, and business school at Stanford. He seemed destined for a comfy career in finance. But in 1979, after a brief stint at Citibank, Bewkes passed up an opportunity to work for the bank in Hong Kong and instead took a twenty-thousand-dollar-a-year job at HBO, then little more than a speck in the vast Time Inc. empire.

At HBO, Bewkes worked briefly on the network's ongoing campaign to get hotels to sign up for HBO. He then became an assistant manager at Take 2, Time Inc.'s cheap and experimental alternative to HBO, which would eventually serve as a precursor to Cinemax. One day, Bewkes was in the bathroom when Gerald Levin strolled over to the urinal next to him and started quizzing Bewkes on the Take 2 expansion into Iowa. Fuzzy on the details, Bewkes thought to himself, "Oh man, I'm in trouble."

On the spot, Bewkes ad-libbed, explaining to the chairman how the economics of the cheap four-dollar-a-month network made no sense. "And he looked at me—I won't say that he turned to pee on me, but he almost did," Bewkes recalled. "And he said, 'Why do you say that?'"

Afterward, Levin summoned Bewkes and his superiors to a meeting to go over the numbers. As a result of the chance encounter in the men's room— at Time Warner such things only happened in the men's room—an employee in his late twenties was given the rapt attention of company leaders, even if his bosses were quietly stewing that they were being undermined. Bewkes was on his way to big things.

"I was there for twenty minutes, and they were listening to me," he said. "HBO's biggest strength has always been that culture."

Over the years, as HBO's fortunes soared, so too did Bewkes's. In the rapidly evolving world of cable TV, he proved to be a smooth salesperson for HBO. He was well liked by colleagues, widely regarded for his geniality and dry wit.

Bewkes took control of HBO at a good moment for the network. Following the mild recession of the early 1990s, the U.S. economy was enjoying a major upswing under President Bill Clinton. Families who had canceled their cable subscriptions during the downturn were resubscribing.

Additionally, a new service called DirecTV had started to deliver bundles of TV programming via satellite to millions of paying subscribers in the United States, Latin America, and the Caribbean. It began to drive loads of additional customers into the laps of HBO.

In 1994, HBO and Cinemax had added 2.3 million subscribers, the best gain since the early 1980s, while generating a hefty $257 million of profits on revenue of $1.5 billion. HBO would only keep growing, and Bewkes brought a different sensibility to the job than his predecessor.

"Michael was not a traditional CEO in the sense that Michael had a founder's kind of mentality—it was his vision to branch off into original programming," says Richard Plepler, the HBO's communications chief. "And

Jeff came in and had trained as a COO, and as a CFO. He ran the company in a more traditional fashion than Michael did."

The network was flush with cash, and Bewkes was confronted with the same question that Fuchs consistently did not want to entertain: whether to invest in ongoing television series. Unlike his predecessor, Bewkes had a different point of view.

"I just said to everybody, 'We don't have a choice,'" Bewkes said. "'If we don't develop good original series that are unique and identifiable, we're not going to have a business if all we've got is movies.'"

Bewkes gave Chris Albrecht the go-ahead to start investing in high-quality, dramatic TV series. The question was where to begin. Too many of HBO's original series had been superficially clever, at best. In 1996, HBO had begun airing *Arli$$*, a half-hour comedy series about a cheerfully sleazy sports agent, Arliss Michaels (Robert Wuhl), who will do anything for his roster of clients—including, in one case, selling an aging superstar's frozen semen on a home shopping channel.

The male-centric comedy, which was proving popular with a small but devoted group of HBO subscribers, was typical of the network's efforts to date. It could be acerbically funny, and it featured a constant parade of real-life sports celebrities playing themselves within the show, including Shaquille O'Neal, John McEnroe, and Al Michaels. *Arli$$* also served up plenty of "cable edge." Yet few critics credited the series with anything resembling sophistication.

"Don't be fooled by appearances—or HBO's promotions. Arliss Michaels is not the Larry Sanders of sports," Mark Lorando wrote in the New Orleans *Times-Picayune*. "*Arli$$* is essentially a cartoon, a broad comedy willing to sacrifice realism for laughs."

To differentiate itself from network TV shows, HBO would need to go deeper. Too many people came into meetings at HBO asking what kind of show the network was hoping to make—precisely the wrong question. HBO was looking for writers who knew what they wanted to create and were willing to approach a topic with a strong point of view.

Albrecht eventually zeroed in on an idea from a seasoned TV writer named Tom Fontana. For the past several years, since January 1993, Fontana had been writing and running *Homicide*, an hour-long police procedural that aired on NBC. The show was based on a nonfiction book by David Simon, a crime reporter for *The Baltimore Sun*.

For his next show, Fontana wanted to create a dramatic series that was set in a prison. For years, he'd been thinking about the Attica Prison riots of 1971, a national tragedy that had unfolded not far from Buffalo, New York, where Fontana had grown up.

Fontana envisioned a show where the incarcerated characters would all be packed closely together, with no easy road to redemption, no exit. The problem was that, as a rule, American TV networks didn't do dramatic series about prisons. It was too dark and confining, went the thinking, the opposite of the kind of escapism that viewers craved.

There were cautionary tales. In the spring of 1987, ABC aired a series called *Mariah*, an hour-long drama about the lives of correctional officers and inmates at a maximum security prison on the outskirts of a small country town. The ratings were horrid, and *Mariah* was quickly canceled.

Still, Fontana believed in the idea. His agent set up a meeting with each of the four networks, and Fontana made the rounds. Everyone passed.

Then one morning, he got a phone call from a friend, a TV agent who knew about Fontana's quandary. The agent said he'd just come from a meeting in Los Angeles with Chris Albrecht of HBO. During their conversation, Albrecht had casually mentioned that HBO had made a couple of prison documentaries that had done pretty well. "There may be somebody stupid enough to do your show," the agent told Fontana.

Fontana flew out to Los Angeles and pitched his idea to the West Coast development team. The essence of it, he explained, was the timeless human struggle between retribution and rehabilitation. The HBO executives were intrigued. The fact that the broadcast networks wouldn't touch the subject made it that much more enticing.

HBO wasn't ready to fully commit to the series quite yet. But Albrecht told Fontana to do some more research. To get things rolling, HBO cut a modest check to Fontana and his production partner, Barry Levinson, a Baltimore-born producer best known for directing movies like *Diner* and *Rain Man*.

To learn more about prison life, Fontana took a tour of a state penitentiary in New Jersey, accompanied by Bridget Potter, who after stepping down from her job at HBO had stayed on the project as a supervising producer. Over several hours, the inmates regaled them with all sorts of disturbing stories. One guy told Fontana about how he'd used his job in the prison cafeteria to get revenge on a rival inmate. Day after day, the prisoner said, he would secretly slip small, imperceptible bits of broken glass into the inmate's plate of food. Eventually, the accumulated glass particles ate away at his rival's stomach lining, destroying his guts from the inside out.

"Didn't that take forever?" Fontana asked.

The inmate shrugged. "I'm in prison," he said. "I had the time."

Fontana banked away the anecdote for future use on his series.

For months, Fontana revised his script with feedback from Potter, who kept giving him more or less the same advice. *Looks great. Just make it a little darker.* When the writing felt ready, Fontana took the cameras and production equipment from the Baltimore sets of *Homicide* and shot a fifteen-minute mini-pilot for HBO. "I sort of borrowed a little bit from NBC, which I never told them," Fontana says.

Afterward, Levinson and Fontana took the footage to Los Angeles and screened it for HBO's development team. In the past, the project might have ended there. But now with Fuchs out of the way and the money rolling in from DirecTV, HBO's West Coast team was free to pursue the kind of big, splashy dramatic series they had long envisioned.

Fontana recalls that during the development process, Albrecht once pressed him on a single question. "What's the one thing you never got to do in a pilot on broadcast television?" he had asked.

"Kill the lead character," Fontana responded.

"Well, then do it," Albrecht said.

HBO went on to order up a dozen episodes of the prison series, entitled *Oz*.

• • •

Sheila Nevins was putting
the finishing touches on another project exploring the dark crevices of the
American justice system and the twisted fate of those who inadvertently fall
into it.

In the summer of 1996, HBO aired *Paradise Lost: The Child Murders at
Robin Hood Hills*, Joe Berlinger and Bruce Sinofsky's long-simmering documentary about the slaying of the children in Arkansas. The film opens with
graphic crime-scene footage, showing the bodies of the three murdered kids,
lying naked, soiled, and stiffened on the muddy banks of a forested drainage
ditch. Shocked by the horrifying act of violence, the surrounding community is in an uproar and calling for vengeance.

The police have arrested three angst-ridden teenagers and charged them
with orchestrating the heinous crimes. At the ensuing trials, prosecutors present, at length and with absolute certitude, a series of disjointed, speculative
arguments about how the crimes allegedly took place. Much of their theory
is built on what seems to be an error-ridden, illogical, and seemingly coerced
confession by Jessie Misskelley, the diffident, learning-impaired boy. During
an interview, Misskelley tells the filmmakers that he made up his confession
in its entirety in order to get the police to let him go after a long day of inter-
rogation. All of it, he says, was fabricated.

Lacking physical evidence connecting the accused teenagers to the crime
scene, the prosecutors focus instead on their dark gothic stylings. Damien
Echols and Jason Baldwin, jurors are told, like to dress in black clothing,
make artwork of pentagrams, and listen to heavy metal music. Echols admits
in court that he is a member of the Wicca religion, a form of paganism that
believes in a female deity.

On the witness stand, an expert on the occult testifies for the prosecution that Satanic worship is on the rise in America. The darkly clothed defendants, he says, fit the bill of people who dabble in such dark arts.

During the trial, the police discuss the knife that was given as a gift to
the filmmakers by Mark Byers, the erratically behaving stepfather of one of

the murdered boys. Subsequent lab tests show that the blood on the blade could possibly have come from Byers, or from his murdered stepson. But the evidence is inconclusive, adding yet another layer of doubt to the already muddled proceedings.

When the prosecution rests, their overall case looks remarkably weak. Even so, the jury finds the defendants guilty. Misskelley and Baldwin are sentenced to life in prison. Echols is sentenced to die by lethal injection. He is shackled, placed in a bulletproof vest, and escorted out of the courtroom, headed for death row.

The debut of the HBO documentary touched off a firestorm. Critics recoiled at the hideousness of the crime and the community's seemingly unjust rush to judgment.

It was the early days of the World Wide Web, and outraged viewers congregated online to vent over the case, share court documents, and raise money for appeals. A number of celebrities, including the actor Johnny Depp, Eddie Vedder of Pearl Jam, and Natalie Maines of the Dixie Chicks, would later join the cause. The teenagers became known as the "West Memphis Three."

At film festivals, viewers jammed into Q&A sessions to pepper Sinofsky and Berlinger for more details about the prosecution and what could be done to help the teenagers get a new trial. Berlinger was floored by the response. "People taking time out of their lives to advocate for somebody they'd never met, who they'd only learned about in a movie, is incredible," Berlinger says.

On the awards circuit, *Paradise Lost* racked up honors. The film included several stylistic novelties, including a haunting soundtrack by the band Metallica, which had never previously licensed its music for TV, and many beautiful aerial shots of the leafy Mississippi River town. Years later, following the advent of cheap commercial drones, such footage would become de rigueur in documentaries. But to get their shots, Berlinger and Sinofsky had to hire a helicopter service in Memphis. One day while they were out shooting, they landed at a barbecue festival to take a break and get some lunch. Afterward, they got back in the helicopter and kept shooting. Along the way, somebody on the crew neglected to wipe off their hands sufficiently. To this day, says Berlinger, you can see a slight smudge in the corner of the aerial shots, possibly the most watched barbecue imperfection in the history of film.

Despite the outraged cacophony from viewers, critics, and celebrities, the three young men at the center of *Paradise Lost* continued to languish in prison well after the film's release. Rather than reversing course, the state of Arkansas tried to discredit *Paradise Lost*, portraying the HBO film as a flash of sensationalized entertainment, not to be taken seriously.

But Berlinger, Sinofsky, and Nevins would not go away so easily. Their commitment to the story was just getting started. Over the next decade and a half, Nevins would commission two follow-up sequels from the filmmakers, chronicling the legal fights to try to free the West Memphis Three. "I did really think they were there by mistake," Nevins says. "And I really felt that nobody was stopping me. I just said, I'm going to do two. And now I'm going to do three. It was a gift. I wasn't a dope. You put the two things together, you get a certain kind of success."

"We felt like we had to keep going," Berlinger says.

• • •

IN THE 1980s, the network had billed itself as "Nobody Brings It Home Like HBO," a slogan banging away at the point that with HBO you could watch theatrical releases from the comfort of your own living room. Later, when Showtime became a serious threat, HBO changed its tagline to "Simply the Best." But by the mid-1990s, HBO's place atop the premium cable heap was no longer in dispute. They needed some way of telling everyone that HBO wasn't just better than cable. It was also better than broadcast TV. It was one of a kind.

Eric Kessler, HBO's head of marketing, tapped the network advertising agency, BBDO Worldwide, to dream up something new. The agency got to work. Eventually, mock-ups of potential ads and slogans started circulating among HBO executives and consultants. Before leaving HBO, Bridget Potter had taken a look and wasn't impressed. The tone of the material was too safe, too conventional. She felt that the ad agency didn't really get what HBO was about. To help make her point, Potter says she helped to put together a sizzle reel, compiling some of the most outlandish, off-color, violent, and profane moments from HBO's recent programming history.

Once during the campaign's development, a handful of folks from HBO trekked over to the BBDO offices for a meeting. On a screen at the front of the room, the HBO team fired up the reel of clips for everyone to consume while they nibbled on cookies. For several minutes, they quietly watched the montage of comedians telling wildly inappropriate jokes, gory scenes from *Tales from the Crypt*, and shocking footage from various HBO crime documentaries.

When it was over, Potter recalls, a member of BBDO's crew broke the silence. Whatever that is, he said, it's not television. Exactly, Potter remembers thinking. *Now you get it.*

In the fall of 1996, the first spot in the resulting campaign hit the air. It was titled "Chimps." In it, a group of chimpanzees swing back and forth from trees in the wild, and then, suddenly start quoting lines from movies like *The Godfather, Network,* and *The Empire Strikes Back.* Jane Goodall, the famous primatologist, watches from nearby, jotting down observations of the animals' "inexplicable behavior." "Got to go now," she says to herself. *"Braveheart* is on." Inside her field cabin she settles in to watch the Hollywood movie starring Mel Gibson. Behind her, several chimps peek in through the windows. The sun sets, the movie plays, the chimps applaud happily.

The scene cuts to black, and HBO rolled out the new tagline: "It's Not TV. It's HBO."

HBO steered some $60 million into a campaign to blitz the viewing public with the "It's Not TV" mantra. A few months later, the ad won the first-ever Emmy for a TV commercial.

In October 1996, just as "It's Not TV" commercials began circulating, HBO premiered a new original movie called *If These Walls Could Talk*, created by and starring Demi Moore. At the time, Moore was at the height of her powers in Hollywood. She was the star of several box-office blockbusters like *Ghost* and *A Few Good Men*, and was the highest paid actress in the industry, receiving up to $12 million per movie.

Like many successful actors, Moore wanted to expand into producing.

Four years earlier, in 1992, she had struck a deal with TNT, the cable network owned by Turner Broadcasting, to develop a three-part film about abortion in America over three different eras: the 1950s, the 1970s, and the 1990s. Moore planned to star in the project, and producers were initially confident they could have cameras rolling by the spring of 1993.

Instead, TNT executives, ever mindful of what might upset sponsors, grew skittish. Moore called them "restrictive." Communication broke down. "For a long time, we couldn't get anyone at Turner on the phone," Moore later recalled. "We had to beg for a meeting—beg!"

Eventually, TNT dropped it, and HBO darted in. "The idea of Demi Moore—who at that point was a mega-star—doing something for television was a pretty extraordinary idea," says Colin Callender, the former HBO executive. "We basically agreed to do it pretty instantaneously."

It also was the kind of project validating HBO's ongoing desire to serve as a kind of modern-day Charles Dickens. The movie was socially relevant and could potentially bring viewers to a topic mostly left untouched in American entertainment.

Cher joined the cast, as did Sissy Spacek. "The script was beautifully written, and I believe in what it was saying," Spacek said. "I have two daughters, and it concerns me that a woman's right to choose is being threatened now."

Though some critics found it heavy handed, *If These Walls Could Talk* earned several Emmy and Golden Globe nominations and was met with generally positive reviews. The movie was unapologetically pro-choice and unflinching. One scene graphically depicts Moore's character in 1952 getting an abortion from a careless doctor. Afterward, she bleeds out on her kitchen floor. "It was essential because of what's being asked from the other side, who are pro-life, what they're trying to bring us back to," Moore says of the scene. "It is exactly what that experience would be—this back-alley abortion that left so many women scarred or dead."

If These Walls Could Talk proved HBO could attract major star power. And it spawned a memorable sequel four years later about gay women in America, which starred Sharon Stone, Ellen DeGeneres, Vanessa Redgrave, Chloë Sevigny, and Michelle Williams. But the most enduring legacy of this otherwise mostly forgotten movie might be how HBO executives reacted when the Nielsen ratings came in.

"The numbers were astounding," Callender says.

Richard Plepler, the network's public relations strategist, remembers being at the Four Seasons Hotel in Washington when the ratings came in. At around 7:00 a.m., his phone rang. It was the new head of the network practically screaming as he rattled off the ratings. "It's unbelievable!" Bewkes hollered into the phone.

It was the highest rating ever for an HBO original production. Nearly twenty million people watched at least one part of the film and seven million watched the whole thing through. The record would hold for another four years until it was eventually toppled by the second-season finale of *The Sopranos*.

The reaction from viewers floored HBO executives. They had figured that HBO's male audience would not exactly stampede to watch a movie about abortion. But the surge of viewers made HBO's leaders rethink their assumptions. For years, they'd been going out of their way to tailor programming decisions to the tastes and interests of men. Perhaps the network's core constituency could be broader?

Afterward, in a series of meetings, Callender, Albrecht, and other executives discussed how they might alter their programming strategy. "What we've just learned is that there's probably a real appetite among female viewers on HBO to see programming about themselves that is real," Callender says. "And if we are going to do a woman's story, then the way to do it is to tell it with the voice and with authenticity that is different from what you would see with other women's programming."

Albrecht added, "It was the beginning of the dawning for me on a lot of things."

CHAPTER 7

A Glamorous Playground

In the fall of 1996, HBO's development team began scouring the literary scene, looking for compelling source material that might be adapted into something appealing to female viewers. Soon, they were in hot pursuit of a book by Candace Bushnell, a socially omnivorous newspaper columnist who wrote about the lives of single women in New York City.

Just a few years earlier, in 1990, Bushnell had gotten her first break, writing a recurring segment called "The Human Cartoon" for *Hamptons Magazine*, a glossy periodical devoted to the passions of rich New Yorkers who summered in luxurious second homes.

Every day, Bushnell planted herself on Gibson Beach in Sagaponack, a sun-kissed stretch of sand known as "media beach" because it was usually packed with Condé Nast editors, television producers, and literary figures like George Plimpton. There, Bushnell began chronicling the scene under the guise of journalism. "But it really was fiction," she recalls. The Hamptons in-crowd savored her every byline.

Soon Bushnell caught the attention of editors at *The New York Observer*, a small weekly newspaper that closely chronicled New York's power players. Though the *Observer*'s circulation was minuscule, its rollicking, well-reported stories and quirky, charming headlines made it an essential read for both aspirational up-and-comers and the city's establishment. In 1994, the *Observer*'s new editor, Peter Kaplan, wondered if Bushnell would write a column for the paper. A sex column, of sorts. But also, not a sex column.

"Kaplan said, 'We have to have one foot in sex, and one foot in society,'" Bushnell says.

They named the column "Sex and the City," a nod to Helen Gurley Brown's seminal advice book *Sex and the Single Girl*. Therein, Bushnell played a steely anthropologist, recording notes on her dating adventures and those of her friends while describing the various archetypes of New York men.

While writing the increasingly popular column, which ran from 1994 to 1996, Bushnell freelanced for other publications. *Vogue* assigned her to write a profile of Darren Star, a thirty-four-year-old television hitmaker. Star had recently created two of the biggest melodramatic successes in broadcast television for Fox, *Beverly Hills, 90210* and *Melrose Place*.

Both shows catered to teens and young adults, then an underserved demographic on television. Both series were rooted in the west side of Los Angeles. After just three seasons on *Melrose Place*, Star left the show, intent on putting some distance between himself and Aaron Spelling, the TV megalodon who had produced both Fox hits. Star decided to set his third show in New York. The CBS drama, entitled *Central Park West*, would star Mariel Hemingway as the editor of a Condé Nast–like magazine.

Star's escape from Los Angeles put him in good company. He was part of a wave of Hollywood talent that was getting fed up with Los Angeles in the mid-1990s, thanks to the region's earthquakes, floods, and fires. "Goodbye, L.A. Hello, N.Y.C.," blared the cover of *New York* magazine in February 1995, teasing a story about the sudden creative migration.

Star grew up in Potomac, Maryland, the son of an orthodontist and a freelance writer. In his entire life, he'd spent a mere three months living in New York. But inspired by the midcentury glamour of *All About Eve*, he felt confident that he could capture a romantic vision of the city. Whereas network shows like *Law & Order* portrayed New York as an urban jungle, *Central Park West* would treat it as a glamorous playground.

"I felt like New York and L.A. had sort of flipped," Star said. "L.A. was still reeling from the riots and O. J. Simpson. It didn't feel like a happy place to me. New York, I felt like, was about to explode."

While working on the *Vogue* profile, Bushnell offered to introduce Star to the city and its nightlife. Together, they visited an S&M club and spent a weekend in the Hamptons, bonding. "We were both middle-class kids from the suburbs who weren't supposed to be artists," Bushnell says. "Usually if you're an artist, really terrible things have happened to you. But Darren's parents were really nice, and *my* parents were really nice."

In the fall of 1995, *Central Park West* debuted on CBS and promptly tanked. After one listless season, CBS canceled it. Afterward, intent on staying in New York, Star needed a new project to develop. He realized Bushnell could be the inspiration for a perfect TV character. "She was socially a popular girl," Star says. "A lot of fun and really smart and really beautiful. You know, she is one of a kind."

Star scooped up the movie and TV rights to Bushnell's book, a collection of her *New York Observer* columns, which was about to be published by Warner Books. "I wanted to do a show that felt more like an independent film made for TV—R-rated and adult, very frank and honest about sexual relationships," he says.

But who would buy it?

One day, while Bushnell was rollerblading on Ocean Road in Bridge-hampton, Jamie Tarses, the thirty-two-year-old head of ABC's entertainment division, drove by in a red Mercedes convertible with her boyfriend, Robert Morton, an executive producer of David Letterman's late-night show.

"Candace!" Tarses shouted as the car slowed down. "We really want to buy this at ABC. We really do. Who's your agent?"

At the same time, HBO's team was poring over Bushnell's book and feeling similarly gung-ho. The essays were funny and dark, complex and romantic. "Welcome to the age of Un-Innocence," Bushnell wrote. "The glittering lights of Manhattan that served as backdrops for Edith Wharton's bodice-heaving trysts are still glowing—but the stage is empty. No one has breakfast at Tiffany's, and no one has affairs to remember—instead, we have breakfast at seven a.m. and affairs we try to forget as quickly as possible. How did we get into this mess?"

HBO executives were all in. "They really pursued it hard," says Bushnell, recalling HBO's interest. "Like, they wanted it. They *really* wanted it."

Under normal circumstances, Star and Bushnell would have chosen Tarses and ABC. In 1996, the broadcast network was purchased by the Walt Disney Company and featured a solid lineup of multicamera sitcoms, including *The Drew Carey Show*, *Ellen*, and *Home Improvement*, and dramas like *NYPD Blue* and *The Practice*. But Star had lost interest in doing a standard comedy in front of a live studio audience with canned punch lines and an aggressive laugh track. He also felt embittered over the cancellation of *Central Park West*.

"He was pissed off at network television," Bushnell says. "He was angry."

Star was also skeptical about Disney's ABC actually embracing a show about sex. In his experience, network executives were stunningly squeamish about carnal affairs, even in the 1990s. Star was still fuming over the repeated fights he had gotten into years earlier with Fox executives. When he was writing *90210* episodes, his minders at Fox pushed back on anodyne plotlines about teen sexuality, such as when high-school heartthrob Brenda (Shannen Doherty) lost her virginity or when she had a pregnancy scare. "It was a traumatic experience dealing with sex on *90210*," Star said.

Likewise, when he wrote *Melrose Place*, Star felt it was preposterous to do a show that took place in West Hollywood without a gay character—a plan that continuously ran into strong opposition from the network.

Star assumed the experience would be similar if they went with ABC. "I asked them, 'Are you even going to be able to call the show *Sex and the City*?'" Star recalls. "I do feel like it would have become *Love, American Style* over there."

By contrast, Star had a soft spot for HBO. When he was growing up in the late 1970s, his family subscribed. Each month, as a kid, he'd devoured its programming catalogue, taking notes on what films he could watch in the weeks ahead. More recently, he'd become an admirer of *The Larry Sanders*

Show and thought the network would be the sort of place that would leave him alone to make his art project. He wanted to be free from the tyranny of Nielsen ratings, and he did not expect *Sex and the City* to be any sort of commercial success.

When they sat down with Star, HBO executives were impressed. Carolyn Strauss, a top member of the development team, had never watched *90210* or *Melrose Place*, but she liked that Star had spent so much time in the trenches of network television and was yearning to be liberated from its rigid conventions. At the time, the pages of Tom Fontana's early *Oz* scripts were rolling in, and he appeared to be thriving in his newfound freedom away from network TV. Also, Strauss just really liked Star's pitch. *Sex and the City*, Star said, would be *That Girl*, the 1960s ABC sitcom starring Marlo Thomas, for the 1990s. "The characters in the book were fantastic," Strauss recalls. "And it was that kind of aspirational thing. It was irreverent. It was funny."

On the question of which network to go with, Bushnell was indifferent. In a few short years, an offer from HBO to make a TV series would become the ultimate status symbol among New York writers. But at the time, it meant almost nothing in Bushnell's peer group. "I didn't even own a TV," she says. "The literary world wasn't even keen on movie adaptations. There was a feeling that they didn't want to sully the work."

In the quest for New York status, HBO was not even on the map.

"The HBO guys were part of the world socially, but not creatively," she says. "It was books. It was literature. It was going to Elaine's."

In the end, based largely on Star's preferences, they picked the ad-free cable network over ABC. Eight weeks after the premiere of *If These Walls Could Talk*, HBO had a deal to make *Sex and the City* into a series.

• • •

IN FEBRUARY 1997, *The Chris Rock Show* debuted on HBO. Each episode of the weekly program included taped sketches, a musical performance, and a lengthy interview with someone in the news. Grandmaster Flash was its musical director. Comedian Louis C.K. was one of its writers.

On the first night, which coincided with Rock's thirty-second birthday, the comedian interviewed lawyer Johnnie Cochran about the aftermath of the O. J. Simpson trial, Prince sang his single "Face Down," and Rock did a skit in which he wandered around a predominantly white neighborhood in Queens asking people to sign a petition that would rename one of the streets "Tupac Shakur Boulevard." A later episode featured fake commercials touting Mike Tyson's candidacy for president of the United States.

If Rock was a poor match for the oafish SNL humor of the 1990s, he was the perfect fit for HBO. The show would run on the network for the next three years and establish Rock as the grinning visage of HBO comedy.

"He was authentic but not threatening," Albrecht says. "The whole package was appealing, and his mind was unique and brilliant. He could bring everybody into the tent."

Meanwhile, Albrecht's development team was continuing its hunt for a distinctive HBO drama. Before long, their paths intersected with a gnomic, imaginative, frustrated TV writer named David Chase.

Chase grew up in the 1950s in the New Jersey suburbs of Clifton and North Caldwell, west of Manhattan, north of Newark. His father owned a hardware store. His mother was a telephone-book proofreader, who was, in Chase's view, high strung and dramatic. The area's residential developments were studded with car repair shops, luncheonettes, dry cleaners, schoolyards, and delicatessens, and crisscrossed by patches of wilderness, which clung to the low ridges of the nearby Watchung Mountains and tumbled down haphazardly into the populous valleys below. As a kid, Chase would frequently seek out the breezy shade of the bordering forests to play beneath the sugar maples and black birch, the sounds and smells of northern New Jersey leaving a mark somewhere deep in his brain. "Lots of my childhood consisted really of playing in the woods," Chase says.

Like most middle-class Italian American kids of the era, Chase was entranced by the area's gang activity. He and his father were devoted viewers of *The Untouchables*, a series centering around the FBI's hunt for Prohibition-era Italian mobsters. At fourteen, he gave a presentation about organized crime to his sophomore speech class at West Essex High School.

For college, Chase went to Wake Forest for two years then transferred to New York University. Afterward, he attended film school at Stanford, graduating in 1971. It was the era of New Hollywood. A wave of young American directors were making distinctive, eccentric, powerfully original films, and Chase, who loved the baroque, surreal, penetrating work of filmmakers like Federico Fellini and Luis Buñuel, aimed to join their ranks. In the meantime, he got a paying job in television.

In the years that followed, as his movie work went nowhere, his career in TV took off. He became a writer and producer for a number of popular broadcast dramas, including NBC's *The Rockford Files* and later CBS's *Northern Exposure*. He wrote a made-for-TV movie, *Off the Minnesota Strip*, about runaway teenagers who become prostitutes, which won an Emmy, and then created a prime-time TV series for CBS called *Almost Grown*. The family drama got canceled after a single season.

On the side, Chase wrote several scripts for feature films, none of which ever got made. At the urging of his wife, Denise, Chase started seeing a therapist.

In the spring of 1990, Chase watched the early, mysterious, campy, surreal episodes of David Lynch's drama *Twin Peaks* on ABC. He marveled at its dream sequences. To stylize the cryptic scenes, Lynch would use tape-recorder devices to teach his actors how to speak their lines backward. Chase had done similar exercises in film school, though he had never put the odd-sounding language to any practical use. "That blew me away," Chase says.

But the experimentalism and originality of *Twin Peaks* would prove to be an anomalous event in American broadcast television, not indicative of any kind of paradigm shift in the industry. *Twin Peaks* was canceled after two seasons. To Chase, TV felt more like an intellectual dead end with each passing year.

In the mid-'90s, Chase's entertainment lawyer, Lloyd Braun, joined Brillstein-Grey, the powerful management-production company that produced and co-owned HBO's *Larry Sanders*—one of the rare shows that Chase admired. "*The Larry Sanders Show* was very influential on me," Chase says. "Not in the particulars, but in spirit."

In June 1995, Chase signed a development deal with the agency. One day, following a meet-and-greet with the partners, Braun walked Chase to the elevator. On the way out, he gave his client a pep talk. Everyone at the agency, he said, believed that Chase had a great TV series in him. Maybe something like *The Godfather*? Not a comedy. It had to be an hour-long drama. "That was the last thing I wanted to hear," Chase says. "Because I wanted to be in motion pictures. But also, it stunned me and made me feel warm inside. I was surprised, and it motivated me."

He told Braun he'd think about it. Chase knew *The Godfather* idea was wrong. He conjured up images of a show set in the 1940s with guys in long coats, driving old cars and carrying machine guns. Not a chance, he thought. It'd be an inferior version of what everyone had already seen. But he did have another idea involving gangsters that he had sat on for a while.

In the 1980s, Chase's wife had often encouraged him to write about his rocky relationship with his eccentric mother. At parties, whenever Chase told anecdotes about his mom, it always got laughs. At the same time, one of his colleagues from *The Rockford Files* had suggested he write about his years in therapy. What if he combined the two ideas into a comedy and added a mob element? A mobster at battle with his kooky, manipulative mother and his own inner demons.

Chase had once pitched a similar idea to his agents at the United Talent Agency. They were not impressed. Mob movies were dead, they told him, and it would never sell.

But Braun's suggestion of *The Godfather* got Chase thinking about putting his mobster-in-therapy idea back together. Television would offer one benefit: he could explore the lives of the women surrounding the mobsters. In most mob movies, *Goodfellas* aside, women were bit players. Chase knew from his network television experience that drawing a large female audience was critical to the success of a television series. Maybe in an episodic format he could create rich characters out of the mobster's mother, wife, daughter, and therapist.

Within two months of signing the Brillstein-Grey deal, Chase was in a room pitching the idea to executives at Fox. They said they loved it and made a three-hundred-thousand-dollar commitment to do six episodes. By the time Chase submitted a script in December 1995, he did so with some ambivalence at the prospect of being stuck writing more television. In the end, it didn't matter. During the intervening weeks, the Fox executives had soured on the idea after it finally dawned on them that the Fox standards and practices team and the network sales executives who sold commercial time to advertisers would balk at the gritty material.

"Fox was a network that was governed by sales," says Bob Greenblatt, a top Fox executive in the 1990s, who had made the deal with Chase. When Fox got cold feet, Brillstein-Grey executives made a last-ditch pitch to the network: They promised that one of their clients, Jim Belushi, could be cast as Chase's mobster, Greenblatt recalls. Fox formally passed.

Chase spent the next year pitching the show to the other broadcast networks. It went nowhere. Too dark, the network executives insisted. The therapy angle would make the mobster seem weak. Maybe something tidier, suggested Leslie Moonves, who was running CBS's entertainment division. "I don't really have a problem with the robbing and murdering and all that, but does he have to be seeing a shrink?" Chase recalls Moonves saying. "I said, yeah. Then he said, does he have to be on Prozac? I said, yeah. And that was the end of that."

But Moonves and CBS were interested in another Chase project. They hired him to put together a script about the Witness Protection Program for the actress Marg Helgenberger, an Emmy winner from ABC's *China Beach*. As Chase wrote the script for his new show, he liberally took ideas and characters (Big Pussy, for instance) straight from *The Sopranos* script. "Everybody had passed on the script," recalls Kevin Reilly, an executive at Brillstein-Grey who worked closely with Chase. "I thought it was dead, and I was like, 'It was good, let's just use that.'"

If CBS had opted to make the pilot for the Helgenberger show, *The Sopranos* would have been effectively finished. But CBS passed on the chance to make the Witness Protection idea into a show in early 1997. Chase was beside himself. "I thought David was going to have a stroke," Reilly says.

• • •

CHASE'S DEVELOPMENT DEAL with Brillstein-Grey was about to end, and now they were running 0 for 2 in getting a network to commit to an idea. But Brad Grey, the energetic cohead of Brillstein-Grey—who was the long-time manager of Garry Shandling and an executive producer of *The Larry Sanders Show*—had one other idea. Maybe they should take a meeting with HBO and try to resurrect *The Sopranos*? HBO executives were running around town talking about investing in hour-long series, and the network had a prison drama that was set to premiere later that year.

In February 1997, inside HBO's offices high above Century City, Chris Albrecht and his deputy, Carolyn Strauss, sat down with Chase to hear the idea. Albrecht took the meeting, in part, because it was his friend Grey calling. The two had been tight for years, dating back to the 1970s, when Grey was first starting out managing comedians and Albrecht was running the Improv. "Brad didn't pitch me on a lot of stuff," Albrecht remembers. "So I took the meeting seriously."

Chase made his pitch half expecting to receive the same, dispiriting response that he'd gotten from the broadcast networks. But Albrecht and Strauss listened attentively and afterward they said something surprising—they loved the therapy angle. It would take viewers inside the gangster's mind and make them feel complicit in his subsequent thuggery. "If anything I would do more therapy stuff," Albrecht told Chase.

"They just seemed different," Chase says. "They were smarter. They got it."

And unlike the executives at the broadcast networks, Albrecht and Strauss were enthusiastic about another key aspect of Chase's pitch. "Everybody else had said, well, you're not going to shoot it in New Jersey, are you?" Chase recalls. "What you mean is that you're going to do what *NYPD Blue* does. You'll shoot it in California and every month go back to New York and shoot a couple exteriors. Because, why shoot in New Jersey? I would always say, kind of stupidly, or maybe naively, no, no, no, I want to shoot it in New Jersey. To them, it just meant they'd have to spend more money."

But the HBO executives were pro-Jersey, just as they were pro–New

York for *Sex and the City*. "That was my big beef about *Moonstruck*: phony Italians, phony New York," says Albrecht, referring to the Oscar-winning 1987 romantic comedy that took place in New York but was mostly shot in Toronto. "We always knew it would be more money. But we wanted to make sure that we weren't full of shit. And making those kinds of commitments would tell people that we were for real."

The extra cost of shooting on location, they all agreed, would be well worth the resulting authenticity they were seeking: the look, the sound, the smell of the organized "waste management" industry. Albrecht told Chase a story about how he'd once crossed paths with the organized crime racket while running the Improv in Hell's Kitchen. "We talked about how the mob pressured him to continue to use their garbage service," Chase says.

On the surface, Albrecht and Chase couldn't have seemed more different. Albrecht was a baluster of optimism—tan, cocksure, his bald head closely shorn. Chase was splenetic and tight-lipped. "Too dark for Hollywood," Chase sometimes grumbled to his friends. "Curmudgeonly," says Reilly. At the meeting, he wore a striking outfit, a black shirt and lawn green pants like an Italian wiseguy who'd just strolled in from the early bird greyhound races at the Palm Beach Kennel Club.

"They were Italian, and I loved those pants," Chase recalls. The green beauties, which he'd picked up from among the baubles, three-hundred-dollar-flip-flops, and taxidermied chickens at Maxfield, the ornately beatnik Los Angeles boutique, would carry Chase at least partway through all the good fortune to come before eventually petering out, sometime mid-*Sopranos*. "They became my lucky pants," he says. "But then, I don't know, I couldn't fit into them anymore."

Although they didn't discuss it at the meeting, Albrecht and Chase had some things in common. Both men had Sicilian roots, had spent much time in therapy, and had difficult relationships with their mothers.

Decades earlier, growing up without his father around, Albrecht had largely relied on his mom for emotional sustenance. For much of his childhood, she had been a devotee of Edgar Cayce, an American mystic who traveled the country giving his followers psychic readings, purporting to uncover their past lives, predict their futures, and interpret their dreams. The answer to many of life's big questions, he told his followers, was latent in their subconscious minds, waiting to be uncovered. Cayce did so for them while immersed in a self-induced unconscious state. He was known as "the sleeping prophet."

From a young age, Albrecht was fascinated with the potential power of the subconscious mind. Throughout his adolescence, he kept a dream journal and grabbed ahold of anything that attempted to explain how art connected to people through subconscious means.

By the time he got to the top of HBO, Albrecht was an admirer of Joseph Campbell, a literature professor at Sarah Lawrence College who specialized in the archetypal, cross-cultural nature of mythological storytelling. Albrecht was hardly alone in his fascination. Ever since George Lucas began citing Campbell's work as an inspiration for the movie *Star Wars,* the professor's book *The Hero with a Thousand Faces* had become a well-worn touchstone among Hollywood executives.

With Fuchs out the door, HBO's development team was looking for storytellers who could push deep into what Jung might call the shadows of the American mind, the parts of our collective brain that were typically repressed on TV. Albrecht routinely gave a DVD collection of interviews with Campbell, which Bill Moyers conducted for PBS, to other HBO executives. Great storytelling, Albrecht liked to tell subordinates, came from the unconscious. HBO wanted writers who could intuitively communicate in mythological terms.

Chase seemed like he fit the bill.

When he was young, Chase had suffered from nightmares about nuclear apocalypse. Occasionally, he would wake up and jot down his dreams. In real life, you could never quite make sense of the messages from your unconscious. But in the movies, you could. Maybe you could also do that on HBO. "I love dreams," Chase says. "Dreams and films are so similar."

Chase wanted to direct the pilot himself. At first HBO resisted. But Chase argued he was the best choice to harvest something meaningful from the rich downer soil of New Jersey where the bodies get buried and the spec houses grow. Eventually, Albrecht agreed, and HBO gave Chase the go-ahead to do the pilot.

In the spring of 1997, Chase got started. The previous year, he'd seen the movie *Trees Lounge*, written and directed by the actor Steve Buscemi, which he'd enjoyed. On the basis of the film, Chase decided to hire its casting directors, Sheila Jaffe and Georgianne Walken. They began sifting through the ranks of Italian American actors and holding auditions for *The Sopranos* in a cramped walk-up studio on the Upper West Side of Manhattan.

One of the hardest parts to cast was the most important: the role of the lead male, Tommy Soprano, the boss of the crime family (later, renamed Tony). Chase was initially intrigued by Steven Van Zandt, the scowly guitarist of Bruce Springsteen's E Street Band who would end up playing Soprano's colleague, the strip club proprietor Silvio Dante. Also weighing in on the casting was Susie Fitzgerald, the former HBO development executive who had since left for Brillstein-Grey, in part, over her frustration at HBO's resistance to making female-centric series. Fitzgerald was now pushing for a Jersey-born character actor named James Gandolfini. There wasn't much tape on Gandolfini, who'd spent his time onscreen playing supporting roles as goons and henchmen, including small parts in *True Romance* and *Get Shorty*. But when Fitzgerald and Jaffe looked at Gandolfini, they felt they were seeing Tony Soprano in the flesh.

At first, however, the audition process did not go smoothly. For whatever reason—nerves, or self-sabotage, or indecision—Gandolfini kept flaking out in front of Chase. According to Fitzgerald, the initial blundering gave Chase pause, concerned that Gandolfini would be difficult to work with on set. But eventually, after several misfires, something clicked.

"When he finally settled down and really did a reading, it was just obvious," Chase says. "There was just not any question about it. He was the guy."

The casting of Tony Soprano's wife, Carmela, was even more difficult. Months went by, and one actress after the next read for the part. Nobody felt right. A few days before the cameras would start rolling on the pilot, Albrecht and Chase had no one. Finally, Carolyn Strauss offered a suggestion, inspired by the casting on a different HBO production. "Did you read Edie Falco yet?" Strauss said to Albrecht. "The prison guard on *Oz*."

Albrecht was desperate. "I can always get another prison guard on *Oz*," he recalls saying. "If we don't cast Carmela in a couple of days, we're not going to be able to shoot the pilot."

Falco, who'd spent roughly two decades as a journeyman actress while waitressing on the side, was summoned to the Mayflower Hotel on Central Park West to meet with Chase and Albrecht. "I just did exactly what I knew this character should be in my mind," she later said. "Also knowing that there's no way I would get cast because I was not the stereotypical Italian American–looking actress."

Falco was blond, and the actresses cast for such roles were typically dark-haired. Falco suspected the role would go to someone like Marisa Tomei. But Chase and Albrecht saw something else as she read her lines with John Ventimiglia (who would go on to play Artie Bucco, the mercurial chef) standing in as Tony. "As soon as the words came out of her mouth," Albrecht says, "I was like, 'I know this lady.'"

Falco was offered the job the next day.

CHAPTER 8

Shooting the Moon

On a Saturday night in July 1997, *Oz* made its debut on HBO. The series revolved around the cloistered, violent lives of the inmates and officers at the Oswald State Correctional Facility, nicknamed Oz. From the start, Fontana kept his word and pulled off an unorthodox plot maneuver, killing one of his main characters straight out of the gate.

In the first episode, a cocksure Italian American gangster named Dino (John Seda) swaggers through the prison, flirting with the prison nurses and picking fights with other inmates. As punishment, correctional officers shoot him up with a sedative and throw him into solitary confinement. In the final scene, a rival sneaks into the cell, douses Dino in gasoline, and lights him on fire with a match.

The spectacle left reviewers slack-jawed. Many were impressed by the writing, if astounded by the show's level of brutality. "It is neither the acting nor the direction that is going to have viewers buzzing. It's the in-your-face intensity, graphic subject matter, anger, rage, sadism, fear and the way Fontana burns it all into your brain until you feel as if you have just spent an hour in hell," David Zurawik wrote in *The Baltimore Sun*. "You will see things Saturday night in *Oz* that you will not see anywhere else on television."

Just like the HBO ads said.

To shoot *Oz*, Fontana and his colleagues took over a single sprawling floor of the Chelsea Market, a former Nabisco cookie factory on the West Side of Manhattan. The show featured a cast with far more Black and brown faces than the typical network drama, including major roles by Ernie Hudson, B. D. Wong, Harold Perrineau, and Eamonn Walker. The show's diversity, says Fontana, was driven by the reality of prison demographics in the United States.

Several cast members came from theatrical backgrounds. Fontana had once seen J. K. Simmons playing Captain Hook in a Broadway production of *Peter Pan*. On *Oz*, Fontana cast him as Vern Schillinger, a sadistic white supremacist who welcomes his new cellmate to life in prison by forcibly branding a swastika onto his buttocks while cheerfully humming a lullaby by Brahms.

After years of writing for commercial television, Fontana realized that on HBO the lack of ad breaks would allow him to design the narrative in a completely different manner. He threw out the conventions of network structure and experimented with new cadences. Often he found himself writing sequences that stuck to characters longer, building tension in the viewers, not allowing for any emotional sense of escape. "I wanted the audience to be as off balance as any man who was in prison," Fontana says.

During the first season, the ratings for the series were unspectacular. But, as far as Fontana could tell, HBO executives didn't seem to mind. After years of fending off insipid notes from network executives, Fontana was amazed by how little HBO interfered with his vision for the show. *Oz* would go on to run for six seasons and fifty-six episodes. During that time, Fontana says he got approximately five notes from HBO executives—all of which he enthusiastically accepted. Most of the feedback, says Fontana, was encouraging. "It was just, tell the truth," Fontana says. "Be as accurate and authentic as you possibly can."

Fontana's barbarous depiction of prison life eventually caught the attention of one former HBO contributor turned ex-con. Fontana says that, out of the blue, he was contacted by representatives of Mike Tyson, who after spending three years in an Indiana prison, was out on parole, looking for work, and watching *Oz*. They asked if Fontana would consider writing Tyson

into the show. Fontana told the boxer's people he'd think it over. But ultimately, Tyson's HBO homecoming was not to be. Fontana passed.

Before *Oz*'s debut, various people in the industry told Fontana that he
must be loony to abandon the gilded land of prime-time network television
for the obscurity of HBO. But as the reviews of *Oz* rolled in, says Fontana,
such conversations reversed course. "The naysayers, who told me I was killing
my career by doing *Oz*, once they saw the show, they were like, 'Oh fuck, we
get it,'" he says. "I went from looking like an idiot to looking like a genius for
doing a show on HBO."

HBO's development team watched *Oz* with a growing sense of what the
network might become. "When people looked at that show, it kind of blew
the doors off: Holy shit look what they can do on television," Albrecht said.
"*Oz* showed what was possible."

One writer who was closely studying the series was David Simon, a newspaper reporter from *The Baltimore Sun* whose first nonfiction book Fontana
had turned into NBC's *Homicide*. Fontana had mentored Simon in the ways
of TV, assigning him to write a number of scripts for the crime procedural
and teaching him the basics of the craft.

Simon watched *Oz* with awe. The stuff that Fontana was pulling off on
HBO was something on another level. At the time, Simon was on the verge
of publishing his second nonfiction book, *The Corner: A Year in the Life of
an Inner-City Neighborhood*, which chronicled the impact of the drug trade
and the city's ineffective war on drugs on one block in West Baltimore. Simon
reported and wrote the book with Ed Burns, a former city homicide officer.

Having watched up close as NBC turned his first book into a prime-
time drama, Simon initially believed there was no way anybody in TV would
touch *The Corner*. He suspected its depiction of drug addiction and urban
decay would be both too cerebral and too grim for broadcast television. But
seeing what Fontana was doing with *Oz* got Simon thinking. Maybe HBO
would be interested? "*Oz* was a revelation to me," says Simon.

Simon reached out to Fontana to see if he and Barry Levinson might want
to team up again to work on *The Corner*. But after several years of shooting

Homicide, they'd apparently had their fill of Baltimore street crime. Instead, Fontana put Simon in touch directly with HBO.

At the subsequent meeting in Los Angeles, Simon pitched his idea for a dramatic series that would look at the decline of a postindustrial American city from all angles—from the point of view of the cops, the drug dealers, the addicts, the politicians. Albrecht interjected. Just do the book, he said. HBO wanted *The Corner* as a six-part miniseries.

It wasn't exactly what Simon had envisioned. But perhaps there'd be another opportunity to pitch his bigger series about Baltimore down the road. At the very least, he thought, the miniseries would help him sell more books.

Meanwhile, HBO had a difficult decision to make on *The Sopranos*. After David Chase finished the pilot episode, HBO set up a test screening with an audience chosen to satisfy certain demographic criteria. When the results came back, HBO executives faced a difficult dilemma. The pilot had scored poorly, suggesting they ought to cancel the project.

For months, HBO dithered. There were plenty of reasons not to go forward with *The Sopranos*. It would cost a fortune to make and market. Chase's cast featured a bunch of actors who were largely unknown. Centering a show around a murdering mobster was also a huge risk. "Can we do this? Will people watch this?" HBO executives kept asking themselves, recalls Carolyn Strauss. "It wasn't like someone said, 'No, this will never work.' It was more like, '*Can* this work?'" she says. Also, the HBO executives didn't like the name. To their ear, *The Sopranos* sounded like a show about opera.

But Albrecht had enjoyed the first hour of *The Sopranos*. He felt he could relate to Tony Soprano, a middle-aged boss struggling to find the meaning of his own life while dealing with the usual pressures of running a business, being a husband and a father, occasionally erupting in violence against his rivals, coworkers, and girlfriends. "The only difference between Tony Soprano and every guy that I know is that he's the don of New Jersey," he would say repeatedly.

That the head of the network so readily identified with the impulses of a violent mobster didn't give anyone pause at the time—only later would it seem like another overlooked warning sign. In the end, Albrecht decided to toss aside the unfavorable data and to trust his gut instinct. HBO ordered an additional twelve episodes of *The Sopranos*.

• • •

IN THE SPRING OF 1998, HBO was getting ready to air *From the Earth to the Moon*, an ambitious twelve-part miniseries produced by Tom Hanks, Brian Grazer, and Ron Howard, chronicling America's Apollo space program in the 1960s and '70s. Its production would prove to be an important inflection point in the network's history.

Early in the development process, Carmi Zlotnik, HBO's then-director of production, got a phone call from Grazer, who had recently finished making *Apollo 13*, a big-budget Hollywood space adventure starring Tom Hanks and Kevin Bacon. The movie had grossed over $350 million at the global box office for Universal Pictures.

HBO's tendency to skimp on its productions—from the lack of a proper sound stage on *Dream On* to the missing kitchen on the set of *Larry Sanders*—was well known in the industry. Zlotnik, a former freelance producer who joined the network in 1987, was the executive in charge of maintaining the tight budgets. "The beginnings of HBO were very, very frugal," Zlotnik says. "That's what I was originally brought in for."

On the call, Grazer made the case to Zlotnik that HBO's miserly ways wouldn't cut it this time around. *From the Earth to the Moon* would only reach its full potential, he argued, if HBO was willing to think bigger and spend more than it was accustomed to. When it came to space adventures, special effects mattered immensely. "Tom Hanks wants to go to the moon," Grazer told Zlotnik. "Your job is to take him there."

Afterward, Zlotnik relayed the conversation to Albrecht. To do all the special effects that Grazer and Hanks wanted—to make space travel look like it did in *Apollo 13*—the production would need more than the $50 million originally budgeted for the miniseries. Zlotnik said an extra $15 million should probably suffice. Back in New York, Jeffrey Bewkes considered Zlotnik's request and decided to approve the extra spending. This time around, HBO would spare no expense.

The result, Zlotnik says, was the beginning of a major shift in HBO's fundamental strategy. Rather than pinching production budgets as in the past, HBO would begin to expand them—while trying to figure out new ways to recoup the extra costs beyond simply selling more subscriptions. It was a mindset the film industry had been using effectively for half a century. "It was nothing new," Zlotnik says. "We just started applying it to television in a different way."

When the miniseries was ready to go, HBO uncorked a massive marketing campaign, costing upward of $8 million, to blast the series into the American zeitgeist. In the run-up to the premiere, ads for the series flooded the pages of glossy magazines and aired repeatedly on broadcast and cable TV. HBO ran an extended ninety-second ad for the series during the closing ceremonies of the Olympic Games on CBS. The network painted a thirty-story rocket on the side of a building in Los Angeles. Toy stores sold a bunch of tie-in products, including telescopes and miniature lunar landers. Some thirty thousand educational kits went out to schools around the country.

The promotional blitz culminated on March 5, 1998, with a party inside the White House hosted by Bill and Hillary Clinton. For Richard Plepler's "permanent campaign," it was a major moment of validation. Plepler worked his connections: he met with Capricia Marshall, the White House social secretary, and quickly made her into a champion. And he convinced his friend John F. Kennedy Jr., then one of New York's biggest socialites and the founder of *George* magazine, to come to the White House for it, where he got to visit the private residence for the first time since he was a child living there in the 1960s.

Here was HBO, a few years removed from being the pariah of Hollywood, being publicly feted by the leader of the free world. "We wanted the people in Washington, the opinion makers, to know that HBO isn't just sex and violence—that HBO does some smart, prestigious shows," Quentin Schaffer recalls.

"That was the kind of thing where people began to say, 'You know, HBO has a different gear,'" Plepler says.

The guests at the White House reception included a mix of space program veterans, top figures in the Democratic Party, and HBO executives. Following a screening of the miniseries in the East Room, President Clinton, John F. Kennedy Jr., and Bewkes all gave speeches.

"Thank you, Jeff Bewkes, for taking a chance on this project," President Clinton said. "I hope all of you who are part of this project will be able to look back ten, twenty, thirty, forty years from now with immense pride that you have once again sparked the imagination, the dreams, the hopes, and the courage of the American people to follow our astronauts into space and to follow our imaginations wherever they lead."

Afterward, everyone walked over to the State Dining Room to celebrate, recalls Kary Antholis, the HBO development executive. "It was in the middle of the Lewinsky stuff, so there was a weird vibe with the president," he says. "But everybody was very elegant. It was a very nice, informal party."

"We had all the astronauts there who had walked on the moon, and Walter Cronkite, John Kennedy, Tom Hanks, and Steven Spielberg," Plepler recalls. "I can remember Jeff looking at me and saying, *How the fuck did you do this?*"

All of the hoopla in the media surrounding HBO's big bet on original programming was already impacting how people saw the network, sometimes with unlikely consequences. Antholis recalls that once during the rollout of *From the Earth to the Moon*, astronaut Buzz Aldrin buttonholed him outside an event and pressed into his hands a script for a sci-fi movie that Aldrin, the famed moonwalker, wanted to make for HBO. (The network passed.)

• • •

IN JANUARY 1998, Garry Shandling sued Brad Grey in Los Angeles Superior Court, alleging that his longtime friend and manager had taken advantage of him financially and seeking $100 million in damages. A lawyer for Grey responded that the accusations were "sheer lunacy."

Two months later, Grey filed a $10 million countersuit, accusing Shandling of behaving erratically on the set of *Larry Sanders*, mistreating numerous writers, and arbitrarily firing staff, thereby creating unnecessary costs for the show.

The spat escalated in the press, with each side accusing the other of disloyalty, dishonesty, and deception. All of which put HBO in an unusual bind. Shandling was the creator of the network's most prominent comedic series, the final season of which was set to air in a few short months. At the same time, Grey was an important power player in Hollywood. Not only was he the co-owner of *Larry Sanders*, but he also represented many top screenwriters, and he was deeply involved in HBO's ongoing development of *The Sopranos*.

HBO struggled to stay neutral in the dispute. So, too, did Susie Fitzgerald. While working year after year on *Larry Sanders*, she had grown close to Shandling. She was by his side when the show's budget was a meager $550,000 an episode. And she was there with Shandling as he went through his habitual cycle of hiring writers, firing writers, and needing help to find new writers.

Shortly after he filed the lawsuit against Grey, Shandling explained to Fitzgerald that it would not blemish their sterling relationship. "Look, the lawsuit's over here, and you and I are over here. We're not gonna mix them," she recalls him saying.

Like many creative prodigies, Shandling could be irascible. He was chronically disenchanted with something related to the show and would often complain of exhaustion. At the end of the show's previous season, its fifth, Shandling had abruptly left the set before filming had even concluded. He told a producer to write him out of the season's last three scenes. "I'm tired, I'm gone," Shandling said, before jetting off to Hawaii and Fiji.

But the lawsuit and countersuit, both of which would eventually be settled out of court on undisclosed terms, seemed to give Shandling a shot of adrenaline, and he approached the series' denouement with renewed gusto. "There was something about the lawsuit that really gave him a lot of focus and energy," Fitzgerald says.

In the final season, which aired from March to May 1998, *Larry Sanders* offered a grimly dark portrait of show-business succession. In between lines of cocaine, Larry's avaricious agent Stevie (Bob Odenkirk) double-crosses his client, ultimately helping a bunch of mouth-breathing network executives to replace Larry with a younger comedian, Jon Stewart, playing himself.

In addition to Stewart, the future influential host of *The Daily Show* on Comedy Central, *Larry Sanders* had showcased an impressive array of young, comedic talent over the course of its six seasons. Among others, the series included memorable performances from Janeane Garofalo, Sarah Silverman, and Mary Lynn Rajskub. But the greatest legacy of *Larry Sanders* might have been the comedy-writing process that it instilled in Shandling's mentees, including a young comedian named Judd Apatow, who joined the writer's room in the second season.

Apatow was no stranger to HBO. During the 1980s, while attending college at the University of Southern California, Apatow had volunteered on HBO's *Comic Relief*. In 1992, he performed onstage as part of HBO's *15th Annual Young Comedians Special*. Around the same time, he cocreated and executive produced *The Ben Stiller Show*, a sketch comedy series that HBO Independent Productions sold to Fox, and that ran for thirteen episodes before being canceled in January 1993.

Afterward, Shandling hired Apatow to write for *Larry Sanders*. While the turnover in the writer's room was frequent, Apatow stayed with the series through its final season. Along the way, he got to work as a director for the first time, and he absorbed Shandling's approach to crafting meaningful scripts and performances.

"In terms of the writing, it was all about truth, and having the courage to tell the truth, just getting to the core of people's essence," Apatow would later explain. "All the lessons about writing, all came from *The Larry Sanders Show*. When I did *Freaks and Geeks* with Paul Feig, in my head, all I thought was, oh, this is just *The Larry Sanders Show* if it was different people in high school. And so, I would just think what would Garry do in this situation? What question would Garry ask to figure out this problem? It was like having, almost like, a program in my head of Garry's approach to breaking things down."

At a crucial juncture in the third season of the series, Larry quits his job and moves to Montana. But his flight from show biz quickly proves to be unsatisfying. Outside of his professional obligations, Larry has no interests, no hobbies, no life. Instead of fly-fishing, Larry sits around watching old tapes of himself working. Eventually, his producer Artie travels out to Montana to convince him to return to his natural habitat and to reclaim his seat at the office. "C'mon, Larry, I knew you wouldn't be happy here," Artie says. "You're a talk-show animal. You're like one of those goddamn creatures out of Greek mythology: half man, half desk."

The influence of the series—its improvisational air, naturalistic acting, and its strong conviction that the office place is the grating, inescapable center of the modern universe—would be far reaching, serving as the primary inspiration for the next generation of workplace comedies like *The Office*, *Parks and Recreation*, and *30 Rock*. Thanks to Larry Sanders, half-deskified humans would come to rule American TV comedy.

On May 31, 1998, HBO aired the final episode of the series. At the outset, Larry gets up onstage, thanks his crew, and delivers one last monologue, which is heavy on jokes about President Bill Clinton's sex life, then all the rage in late-night television. Then came the onslaught of valedictory goodbyes from the likes of Jim Carrey, Tom Petty, Jerry Seinfeld, Warren Beatty, Carol Burnett, Ellen DeGeneres, and Sean Penn.

In reality, Shandling's own goodbye to his cast and crew on the HBO show had been less than gracious. When they had finished shooting the last scene of the final episode—a bittersweet moment of personal reckoning between Larry, Hank, and Artie in the shadowed bleachers of the shuttered stage—Shandling stormed off.

"Before anyone could have a glass of champagne, Garry just walked off that sound stage and was gone," recalls the director Todd Holland. "He didn't say goodbye. He didn't say thank you. He didn't say anything to anybody. It was disappointing. We had all worked so hard to manifest his vision for so long. It was a very strange, very un-Buddhist reaction."

Susie Fitzgerald had a bitter farewell too.

Days before the final episode was going to be shot, Shandling called her and abruptly demanded to know what she had been telling Brad Grey about him. What secrets had she revealed? He blasted her with one question after the next. It was a loyalty test, Fitzgerald realized, which left her feeling blindsided.

On the final day of shooting, Fitzgerald arrived on set, eager to be there for the end of a six-year journey. But apparently Shandling didn't want her there. He told Holland to have Fitzgerald moved from the front of the stage to a location well behind the monitors. Actually, that's too close, he clarified. Move her even farther back. Fitzgerald walked off the stage and burst into tears. Jon Stewart saw her crying and consoled her.

Years later, when Fitzgerald was a programming executive at AMC in the 2010s, she wanted to reconnect with Shandling and left him several messages. She thought he should be a producer and a mentor of sorts to young comedians in the mold of what Judd Apatow was doing.

She never heard back. "He had some demons," she says.

CHAPTER 9

The Ground Floor

You think people will come?" asked Richard Plepler.

Quentin Schaffer mulled it over. He wasn't sure if anyone would bother showing up for a premiere party for *Sex and the City* but thought it was worth a try.

For years, HBO had been staging lavish premiere events for its original movies. But to date the network had never done anything similar for its original series. Nobody had. Premiere screenings for new TV series were practically unheard of. Anybody could watch a new TV series from the comfort of their own home, and the actors starring in new TV shows were rarely famous. More often than not, they were of zero interest to the paparazzi and celebrity press. Whereas a movie could tell a complete story in two hours, what would you show at the premiere of a TV show? One episode? Two? Three?

The four lead actors on *Sex and the City* were hardly established stars. "They were all B-talent," recalls Schaffer. But perhaps Candace Bushnell could be a selling point. She was a magnet for attention within a certain crowd and her column was popular among some New York power players. Maybe HBO could entice a few of them to show up.

In the spring of 1998, Schaffer rented out the Sony Loews on Thirteenth Street, just south of Union Square Park. The screening would be followed by

an after party at Lot 61, an Amy Sacco nightclub in West Chelsea that specialized in sixty-one different flavors of martinis and featured a signature cosmopolitan. There would be no red carpet and few frills. If the whole thing
was a disaster, at least it wouldn't be an expensive disaster. Schaffer estimated
that the entire night cost HBO about thirty-five thousand dollars. "Bupkus,"
he says.

When the night of the premiere arrived, Schaffer watched curiously as
the guests descended on the theater. It wasn't the most glittery crowd, but it
was a distinctly New York one. Ron Galotti, the publisher of *Vogue* and inspiration for the character Mr. Big, mingled alongside book editors (Morgan
Entrekin of Grove/Atlantic), writers (Bret Easton Ellis, Brad Gooch), art dealers (Mary Boone, Larry Gagosian), tabloid reporters (Page Six), and New
York fixtures who could be counted on to show up to literally anything (Anthony Haden-Guest).

It turned out not to be the starriest New York event of the night. That
same evening, *Harper's Bazaar* editor Liz Tilberis hosted a dinner downtown
for Miuccia Prada, Calvin Klein, Sigourney Weaver, and Martha Stewart.
But the excitement felt well worth the effort. You could feel the anticipation
building around *Sex and the City*, the show coming to life.

Seven months later, HBO would try it again, throwing a screening of *The
Sopranos* in the four-hundred-seat basement theater of a Virgin Megastore.
Bruce Springsteen attended, and from there, the experiment mushroomed
into a tradition.

In the years that followed, the network would do it so often and with
such enthusiasm that HBO premieres would soon grow into a boozy fixture
of cultural life in Manhattan, jostling with book parties and fashion shows
for the top guests and the most attention from the press. "It was a huge moment," Schaffer says, looking back at the initial *Sex and the City* martinifest.
"It became like *the* thing. People couldn't wait to go to the premiere of a new
series."

While the expectations for *Sex and the City* were growing, HBO was
getting bogged down elsewhere in the press. At the time, HBO was preparing to air *A Bright Shining Lie*, a docudrama about the failures of the Viet-

nam War, based on Neil Sheehan's 1988 book of the same title, which won the National Book Award and the Pulitzer Prize for nonfiction.

The movie told the story of John Paul Vann (Bill Paxton), a righteous colonel in the U.S. Army who begins covertly warning American reporters about their government's many policy blunders in the war. With a hefty $14 million production budget, the film possessed all the hallmarks of a classic HBO original movie, set against the poignant backdrop of American history.

But for once, HBO's trusty docudrama format backfired on the network.

It started during the run-up to the movie's May 30 release when somebody leaked a copy of the movie's script to Daniel Ellsberg, the former military analyst who in 1971 hastened the end of the Vietnam War by releasing the damning Pentagon Papers to American news reporters.

During the war, Ellsberg had worked closely with the real-life Colonel Vann—and he'd featured prominently in Sheehan's book. Reading through the leaked script, he realized that HBO's movie also included a character with his name and likeness, though nobody had bothered to tell him ahead of time. The more he read, the more irate he became at the movie's characterization of the events he had lived through. Everything seemed warped and off base.

Aghast, Ellsberg sent the script to David Halberstam, the revered journalist, who had covered the war for the *New York Times*. Like Ellsberg, Halberstam appeared as a prominent character in both the original book and, now, the HBO screenplay. He too balked at the accuracy of the adaptation, and the two famous journalists went public with their complaints.

"You are safe from a libel suit from a dead man," Ellsberg wrote in an open letter to HBO. "But if you persist in presenting this false and defamatory impression of John Vann, you can be sure of eliciting feelings of rage and contempt from many living people who knew him, starting with me."

HBO executives raced to control the damage. The movie's writer and director Terry George quickly tweaked the script, removing both Ellsberg and Halberstam and cutting out some scenes to which they had objected. But ultimately, it wasn't enough to defuse the controversy. The film's debut was met with another round of public criticism. Pressed for his reaction to the movie, Sheehan told reporters he respected the filmmaker's efforts but was disappointed by the final result. The *Los Angeles Times* took to calling the whole brouhaha the "HBO Papers."

The episode left a stinging mark on HBO's carefully cultivated reputation as fearless truth tellers. It was fine, even expected, for conservative cultural critics to attack the liberal values underlying an HBO original movie. But it was much more uncomfortable for HBO to have the accuracy of their docudrama called into question by progressive heroes famous for telling difficult truths to the American public.

Afterward, HBO executives vowed not to make the same mistake ever again. In the future—particularly when delving into politically charged subjects—HBO would make extensive use of consulting contracts, giving prominent experts on the subject an early financial relationship to the film. The last thing HBO ever wanted to do was alienate people like Halberstam or Sheehan, paragons of secular American culture.

"Let's say you do a project with Neil Sheehan, who would never come to HBO before," Schaffer says. "If it goes well, he's part of your family, and then he comes with his next project, and over time, it's like a snowball. So you want to keep them happy. But if you don't and then it blows up, you get this— people saying, 'HBO doesn't know what they're doing, they fucked this up.' After this incident? It was a real lesson."

• • •

IN JUNE 1998, HBO began airing *Sex and the City* on Sunday nights. The jaunty comedy revolved around the madcap romantic life of Carrie (Sarah Jessica Parker), a sly New York dating columnist, and her three professionally accomplished, romantically challenged best friends, Samantha (Kim Cattrall), Charlotte (Kristin Davis), and Miranda (Cynthia Nixon).

The series treated New York with a deeply romantic gaze, which Parker would later compare to a Jeff Koons version of Gotham, a blown-up fantasy highlighting its shiniest angles. Parker liked to call New York City the show's "fifth lady."

In the first season, the heroines set off into a lush jungle of velvet-roped nightclubs and thousand-dollar purses on a journey of self-discovery. While contemplating a column on women's self-empowerment through sex, Carrie walks into Dolce & Gabbana to try on shoes she can't afford. "I decided to investigate this theory I have about shopping as a way to unleash the creative subconscious," Carrie says.

Patricia Field, a downtown stylist with a boutique in Greenwich Village, served as the show's costume designer, creating a striking and authentic look for the series' leading ladies: no miniskirts, no hair scrunchies. The sensibility earned *Sex and the City* instant credibility in New York fashion circles and would make a mark on the wardrobes of American women for years to come.

Beneath the show's lustrous surface was an unshakable ambiguity. For Carrie and her friends, there was nothing certain about the value of love and marriage, friendship and professional independence, promiscuity and safe sex. All of it was shrouded in a thick, unsettling fog of moral ambivalence, particularly around the show's central question: whether you can be satisfied in life without a reliable long-term romantic partner.

Darren Star, the show's creator, was intent on writing a series about sex that wasn't moralistic or grim. He'd grown up on movies like *Shampoo* and *Bob & Carol & Ted & Alice*, which were released in the throes of the sexual revolution and gleefully addressed love and lust. "Those sorts of adult films just weren't around in the eighties and nineties anymore," he says. "Part of that has to do with AIDS. AIDS made people really scared about sex and people weren't able to laugh about sex and take sex lightly."

The initial reviews were mixed. The series' frank discussions about sexual performance from a female perspective seemed to make some male critics deeply uncomfortable. "Worse still, they're sexual bores—four beautiful women in the most electric city on the planet, and not an ounce of passion among them," wrote Mark Lorando in the *Times-Picayune*. "In fact, they may be getting TOO MUCH sex. Their affairs aren't so much casual as they are mindless. Which raises another problem: You can't keep calling it a comedy if they all get AIDS."

Darren Star marveled at the tone of the male critics. "Men wrote about this show like it was the most offensive thing they'd ever seen," he says. "There were a lot of reviews that were so nasty and demeaning—so misogynistic."

Despite the squeamishness of critics, the series immediately pulled in large numbers of HBO viewers. The initial ratings for *Sex and the City* were about 50 percent higher than those of *Larry Sanders*, and the show's popularity kept growing from there, particularly with women.

Prior to its debut, some HBO executives had worried that the Manhattan-centric series wouldn't resonate with residents in large swaths of the country. But its aspirational tone quickly caught on throughout the American heartland. Before long, HBO was boasting in the press that the series was developing a cult following, not only in big coastal cities, but also in places like Cleveland and Baton Rouge. By the end of its first season, it was the highest-rated comedy in all of cable.

HBO started throwing *Sex and the City* promotional events at shopping malls around the country. "I love that on the show they talk about men the way that men talk about women," Pat Khan, a forty-year-old media company executive in Atlanta told the *New York Times*. "It turns the tables, and I try to think of how I can do that in my own life."

Before long, the series was being hailed as an important barometer on the state of womanhood in American culture. Its central quartet would appear on the cover of *Time* magazine, coupled with a classic jab of newsweekly provocation: "Who needs a husband?"

• • •

ON MAY 14, 1998, NBC aired the final episode of TV's most popular comedy, *Seinfeld*. The finale, though largely panned by fans and critics, drew an enormous audience of more than seventy-six million viewers. It was the kind of mass cultural event that broadcast TV once enjoyed regularly, but was becoming increasingly rare as cable TV programming improved and audiences splintered.

That summer, Jerry Seinfeld announced that for his follow-up act, he would be performing his well-worn stand-up material one final time, and he would be doing it on HBO.

On the night of Sunday, August 9, HBO aired the resulting production, entitled *I'm Telling You for the Last Time*. The show began with a taped skit, shot at a graveyard, in which a tearful Seinfeld stands by a coffin and prepares to bury his jokes in the ground while a conga line of comedians, including George Carlin, Jay Leno, and Garry Shandling, look on.

Following the skit, Seinfeld launched into his trademark comedy routine. For a little over an hour, standing on the stage at the Broadhurst Theatre in Manhattan, Seinfeld told jokes about cows, cereal, pharmacists, flight attendants, seedless watermelons, and New York taxi drivers.

The special pulled in good ratings for HBO, and publicly the network declared victory. But behind the scenes, executives were left wondering if the price they had paid was worth it. The performance had cost HBO a fortune to acquire, produce, and promote. Compared with a popular, recurring series like *Sex and the City*, any one-time product—be it a stand-up act, a music concert, a boxing match, or an original movie—looked like a rather inefficient way to attract and retain subscribers, no matter how buzzy. All of which added to the growing belief inside the network that original series, not original specials, were the key to the network's future.

Stand-up and musical acts had long been a hallmark of the network. Going back to the early 1980s, the belief within HBO was that the bigger the spectacle the better. There was Dolly Parton, live in concert from London. Madonna in Sydney. Billy Joel in Leningrad. Michael Jackson in Bucharest. Tina Turner in Rio de Janeiro.

"When we did it in the eighties, it was such a hot idea to see a performer in that kind of setting," says Betty Bitterman, HBO's vice president of programming, who oversaw comedy and music specials from 1980 until her retirement in the mid-1990s. "We took a different approach in how it was shot. We wanted to make a subscriber feel like we were giving you a ticket, that you were there."

When she started at HBO, she drew up a list of every performer she wanted to have on HBO's airwaves. Bitterman says the network tried to stage an enormous live performance featuring a giant comic or a major music star roughly once a month. Over the years, HBO cycled through the comedy legends, as well as the rock and pop stars. Many appeared multiple times.

Though HBO would never completely abandon big events, things gradually began to shift.

"It wasn't as novel as it had been," Bitterman says. "And there was a desire on the part of HBO to stretch out, to get into more scripted comedies, and then it went from there to scripted dramas. The big events, we had done it. In fact, when I left HBO I looked at my list and noticed I had checked them all off. I said, okay, I can go now."

• • •

HBO WAS NOT YET FINISHED mining the aftermath of *Seinfeld*. At the time, Chris Albrecht was busy rekindling his longtime friendship with Larry David, the cocreator of *Seinfeld,* who Albrecht had first befriended back at the Improv in the 1970s. David was now looking around for something to do next.

Not long after *Seinfeld*'s conclusion, David decided to get back into stand-up comedy and began preparing for a series of surprise appearances at clubs in New York and Los Angeles. His friend, the comedian Jeff Garlin, suggested David film the comeback and turn the whole thing into a documentary. David liked the idea but worried that the bits in between his performances would be boring. He had a better idea. He'd make a mockumentary, in which he would play a lightly fictionalized version of himself and a bunch of actors would play the people in his life, including his wife, his friends, and his neighbors. His performances in clubs would be real footage. Everything else would be loosely scripted and improvised on the spot.

He called Chris Albrecht to see if HBO might be interested. Albrecht loved the idea. It would be weird and experimental and continue in HBO's growing tradition, starting with *Tanner '88* and continuing through *The Larry Sanders Show,* of mashing together real-world and fictional events to comic effect.

David hired Robert B. Weide, a filmmaker who'd made several documentaries about comedians, including Lenny Bruce, to direct the mockumentary. The resulting hour-long special, *Larry David: Curb Your Enthusiasm*, aired in the fall of 1999 and featured a reality-bending plotline in which David's alter ego is preparing for an HBO stand-up special, which he eventually bails out on at the last moment. The special featured several guest appearances by *Seinfeld* alumni playing themselves, including Jason Alexander and Jerry Seinfeld.

The mockumentary earned enthusiastic reviews from TV critics who appreciated the experimental format and the plethora of inside jokes about the entertainment industry. It also left HBO wanting more.

David proposed turning the project into a recurring series—an idea that gelled perfectly with HBO's evolving strategy. Series, not specials, were the network's new main event. HBO ordered a first season of ten episodes.

• • •

WHILE INVESTING MORE IN ITS ORIGINAL SERIES, HBO was busy reviewing some of the network's historical programming commitments. In particular, Jeffrey Bewkes had soured on one of Fuchs's favorite HBO traditions: tennis. HBO had been airing the early rounds of Wimbledon since 1975. But the production was getting more expensive, growing from about $50,000 per year initially to $8 million a year. The viewership was minuscule. Bewkes was having a hard time seeing much value for HBO.

When Seth Abraham, the head of HBO Sports, heard that HBO's Wimbledon coverage was potentially in jeopardy, he snapped into action. He wrote a lengthy memo to Bewkes laying out the various reasons (prestige! tradition!) why the network should continue its coverage. When that didn't sway Bewkes, Abraham decided to try one last, long-shot gambit.

Although Bewkes wasn't a big sports fan, Abraham knew that Bewkes's then wife, Margaret Brim, who had once worked for Roone Arledge, the legendary sports producer for ABC, loved sports. Abraham decided to invite Bewkes to an upcoming boxing match at Madison Square Garden, anticipating that he would beg off—at which point, Abraham would invite Margaret. Sure enough, says Abraham, his plan proceeded exactly as he had hoped.

A few weeks later, at the big fight, Abraham got to work. "So Peg is sitting with me," he recalls. "I spent the entire night lobbying her to keep Wimbledon."

She seemed receptive enough. But the next day, a Sunday, Abraham got a phone call from Bewkes, who was not only unmoved about Wimbledon but also annoyed by his colleague's effort to win over his wife. "Don't ever do that again," Bewkes told him, according to Abraham.

HBO's airing of Wimbledon in the summer of 1999 would be the network's last.

* * *

IN EARLY 1999, the first season of *The Sopranos* made its debut on HBO, running on Sunday nights from January through April. At the start, Tony Soprano, a burly, balding wiseguy, married and living in suburban New Jersey, is trying to cope with a growing slew of vexations.

The acting boss of his crime family, Jackie Aprile (Michael Rispoli), is dying of cancer. Tension is building between him and his uncle, Corrado "Junior" Soprano (Dominic Chianese). His cousin-apprentice, Christopher Moltisanti (Michael Imperioli), is an impatient hothead with authority issues. Tony spends much of his working life at the Bada Bing strip club in tense side-room meetings, trying to solve the many grievances of his violent, petty crew and eating the occasional lobster.

His home life is also full of irritations. His son, Anthony Jr. (Robert Iler), is getting in fights at school, his daughter, Meadow (Jamie-Lynn Sigler), is stressed out about getting into college, his wife, Carmela (Edie Falco), is spiritually and romantically unfulfilled, and his mother (Nancy Marchand) is resisting Tony's effort to move her into an assisted-living home. Also, she may be secretly trying to orchestrate his murder.

Tony's one innocent pleasure is looking after some ducks that have nested in his backyard pool and given birth. Tony feeds the baby birds and builds them a ramp, which makes it easier to waddle in and out of the pool. Then one day, the ducklings take flight, soaring high into the sky, and disappearing beyond his yard's protection. The sight of the birds' departure causes

Tony's mind to short-circuit, triggering the first of many fainting spells to come. Later, he heads off to work, cradling a field guide to North American birds on his lap, as if it were a Bible.

Following the blackout, he starts seeing Dr. Jennifer Melfi (Lorraine Bracco), who begins to root out the subconscious source of his panic attack. To manage his stress, Tony has been self-medicating with large amounts of alcohol, gunplay, bowls of ice cream, extramarital sex, and the History Channel. Dr. Melfi adds Prozac to the mix.

Soon, Tony is making progress. During a session, he tells Dr. Melfi about a dream in which he turns his bellybutton with a screwdriver, and his penis falls off. He picks it up and starts looking for a mechanic to put it back on. A seagull swoops down, grabs his dismembered equipment, and flies away.

"What else is a waterbird?" Dr. Melfi asks.

"Those goddamn ducks," Tony says.

He tears up, discerning at last a painful parallel—his own, vulnerable brood. "That's the link," he says. "That's the connection. I'm afraid I'm going to lose my family like I lost the ducks. That's what I'm full of dread about."

The Sopranos was shot at Silvercup Studios, a former bakery in Long Island City, Queens, and on location in and around Chase's old stomping grounds in New Jersey. The dynamics of the family and the quirks of the various characters, Chase says, were based not just on his nutty family members but also on some of the egomaniacal, ball-busting TV executives he'd had the ill fortune to cross paths with in Hollywood.

In many ways, Chase's portrait of Tony Soprano called to mind HBO's first violent, melancholy, pigeon-coddling antihero with mother issues. In many ways, Tony Soprano was like Mike Tyson. But Chase says that any parallels between the two specimens of HBO megafauna were inadvertent. "It's a total coincidence," he says.

Pieces of the story came to him from all over. "Anything that comes into my consciousness, I'll use it if it seems to apply," he says.

Tony's ducks were inspired by a family of real-life waterfowl that Chase had seen years earlier, relaxing in the backyard pool of a CBS executive in Los Angeles and making use of a ramp she'd constructed for them. "I just thought immediately, I'm going to put that in a show," Chase says. "I don't know why."

None of it was entirely planned. Castration dreams are a bedrock of Freudian analysis. But Chase says the dream with the screwdriver and the lost penis was based not on any book about dream logic, but rather on something John Patterson, a director on the series and a friend of Chase's since film school, had woken up with one day and conveyed to him. Only later, during the writing process, did Chase recognize the subconscious flight path he could take between Tony's fainting spells and his dread of arrest, death, and general extinction—only then did he connect the ducks. "That dream was like a found object," Chase says.

One thing that was intentional, says Chase, was his desire to show how Tony's anxiety about the looming obsolescence of his chosen profession was part of something much bigger in the country. "I was very concerned about America," Chase says.

During a therapy session in the pilot episode, Tony tells Melfi that his ideal of America, the land of freedom and opportunity, loyalty and standards, is slipping away. "The morning of the day I got sick, I've been thinking. It's good to be in something from the ground floor," Tony says. "I came too late for that, I know. But lately I'm getting the feeling that I came in at the end. The best is over."

"Many Americans, I think, feel that way," Melfi says.

Prior to its debut, enthusiasm for *The Sopranos* was muted. Part of the problem was that *Analyze This*, a feature film from Warner Bros. starring Robert De Niro as a mafioso crime figure seeing a therapist, played by Billy Crystal, was about to open in theaters. Ads for the film were already in heavy rotation. The confluence of mob-boss-in-therapy storylines made *The Sopranos* sound unoriginal.

Even so, it didn't take long for *The Sopranos* to catch on. The series landed in a country with a booming stock market but that was also suffering through a record number of layoffs thanks to a spree of mega-mergers and corporate consolidations. While CEO pay was skyrocketing, the median family income in America was dropping. Everywhere you looked in America, the middle class was being squeezed. Professional anxiety was running high—and for good reason. It wasn't just organized crime in New Jersey that felt endangered.

"In 1998, we saw the advent of e-commerce," an economist told CNN a few days before *The Sopranos* premiered. "That's going to wreak havoc on how we buy our goods and services. Jobs like retail clerks, travel agents, stockbrokers, even grocery store personnel—all those jobs are at risk of becoming more and more obsolete as we change."

Almost immediately, *The Sopranos* seemed to touch a nerve. Some 3.5 million viewers watched the premiere. The buzz kept growing.

Critics were effusive. With each passing month, the volume of praise grew louder. "*The Sopranos,* more than any American television in memory, looks, feels and sounds like real life," Stephen Holden wrote in *The New York Times.* "*The Sopranos* sustains its hyper-realism with an eye and ear so perfectly attuned to geographic details and cultural and social nuances that it just may be the greatest work of American popular culture of the last quarter century."

By the end of the first season, the cumulative audience between new episodes on Sunday nights and the multiple repeats during the week had grown to more than ten million viewers, making it the most popular drama in HBO's history and the highest-rated show in all of cable TV over the previous three years. "I get more recognition out of *Sopranos* on the street than any of the movies I've made," Lorraine Bracco said that spring. "Even *Goodfellas.*"

For the most part, HBO executives left Chase alone to pursue his vision for the show with minimal creative interference. But there was one moment during the production of the first season when Chris Albrecht attempted to intervene.

In the fifth episode, Tony takes his daughter on a road trip to Maine to look at colleges. While there, he happens upon a former wiseguy who is in the witness protection program after becoming a police informant. Tony spends the rest of the trip hunting down the snitch, eventually catching him, dragging the smaller man to the ground, and strangling him to death.

When the script came in, Albrecht raised an objection. The strangulation scene, he adamantly told Chase, was too much. In the first several episodes,

Tony had already driven a car into a guy who owed him money, bashed a dopey bartender at the Bada Bing in the head with a telephone, and mangled a rival gangster with a staple gun. All perfectly fine. But showing the protagonist strangle someone to death, Albrecht argued, would disgust viewers. They'd no longer be able to look past Tony's dark, abusive side and see his humor and charm. He'd be ruined.

Chase—who at the time knew nothing of Albrecht's strangulation of Sasha Emerson in HBO's West Coast offices—took the executive's concern at face value and disagreed. He told Albrecht that if Tony doesn't strangle to death that particular character, the squealer, then the authenticity of the show would suffer. "I'm sure the actual method didn't make it better. Maybe that's why it struck him," Chase says. "I'm not going to speculate."

Ultimately, after a few tweaks to make the mafia turncoat come across as even more loathsome, the strangulation scene stayed in the episode. Albrecht's own violent incident—the real one, which to date HBO had successfully managed to edit out of the network's own narrative—would stay hidden from public view for several more years.

By the end of the first season, *The Sopranos* was the talk of the entire TV industry. Soon, there was lots of chatter about the broadcast networks commissioning *Sopranos*-like shows of their own. HBO executives responded by pointing out that ABC, NBC, CBS, and Fox had all previously passed over *The Sopranos*. They were temperamentally incapable of doing anything similar. Never mind the nudity, the language, and the violence. The networks, HBO argued, were too hidebound by tradition. They wouldn't have let David Chase direct the pilot episode himself or let him shoot the series on location in New Jersey, instead of, say, Los Angeles or Vancouver. And there was absolutely no chance that they would have cast James Gandolfini, a heavyset, balding actor with a scant history of leading roles, as the protagonist of an entire series.

It's not TV. It's HBO.

At more than $2 million per episode, *The Sopranos* was HBO's most expensive show yet. But splurging on original series, as opposed to original movies, was well worth it, the network's executives explained to reporters, because the serialized format helped HBO pull in and retain subscribers much better than one-off events.

"A movie comes and goes, and you know it will be on video six months later," Albrecht said. "But, as far as audience retention goes, if you want to know what happens to Tony Soprano next week, you've got to have HBO."

PART III

BAND OF SHRUGGERS

(1998–2007)

CHAPTER 10

Sunday Is HBO

By the mid-1990s, a new gold rush was sweeping through California. Everywhere you looked, wild-eyed entrepreneurs and venture capitalists were eagerly setting up digital storefronts and touting new prospects alongside the gushing new stream of commerce known as the World Wide Web. It was a vast, unconquered territory where huge fortunes would soon be made.

In the spring of 1997, a pair of colleagues at a software company in Sunnyvale, California, began tossing around ideas, in the spirit of the time, on how to capitalize on the dot-com boom inflating around them. Marc Randolph, an excitable direct-marketing entrepreneur, and Reed Hastings, a cerebral software engineer, could see the web's huge potential for ecommerce. But what would be their angle? They considered selling a range of different products: custom dog food, baseball bats, surfboards, and shampoo. Eventually, they turned their attention to the movie rental business.

"Amazon was having good luck with books," Hastings later said. "Why not films?"

For nearly two decades, since triumphing over Betamax in the 1980s, VHS tapes had ruled over the multibillion-dollar movie rental market in the United States, largely unchallenged. But by 1997, electronics manufacturers and movie studios were just beginning to roll out a new technology called DVDs. The thin, round disks, which looked exactly like CDs, promised more storage, better sound quality, and higher picture resolution than VHS tapes. The disks never had to be rewound, and studios could load them up with add-on features like behind-the-scenes interviews with actors and directors, potentially opening up a new and lucrative market for DVD collectibles.

Randolph and Hastings sensed an opportunity. The timing felt perfect. The first DVD players were just arriving in U.S. stores, and so far nobody in American retail had yet seized control of the emerging market. Blockbuster, the king of American home movie rentals, was deeply invested in the existing VHS ecosystem. In all likelihood, the chain of more than four thousand retail outlets would be slow to adapt.

Together, Randolph and Hastings decided to create the first online DVD store in America. They'd build a website, where people would be able to browse a selection of DVDs without ever leaving their home or setting foot in a store. Because DVDs were small and lightweight, they could cheaply send out whatever disks the customers chose via the U.S. Postal Service.

Thanks to a previous venture, Hastings was well positioned to invest in something new. He'd recently sold off his first software development company, Pure Atria, in a deal ultimately worth upward of $500 million. To start their new cyberbusiness, he put up $1.9 million of his own money, while Randolph raised a hundred thousand dollars or so from his friends, his former coworkers, and his mother.

The entrepreneurs set up Netflix's first bare-bones headquarters inside an office park in Santa Cruz, California, across from a Wendy's, in a musty space formerly home to a neighborhood bank. With a small team of employees, they started to amass a collection of DVDs, snapping up anything and everything available on the new format. While they built the company's first website and designed a customized red sleeve for mailing the disks, they stored their growing DVD selection on makeshift shelves inside the bank vault they'd inherited from the previous tenant.

In April 1998, on the eve of Netflix's launch, the founders didn't know what to expect. Neither had any experience in the movie business. As they prepared to open, they kept reminding themselves of a famous quote about the entertainment industry. "Nobody knows anything," the Hollywood screenwriter William Goldman once wrote. "Not one person in the entire motion picture field *knows* for a certainty what's going to work. Every time out it's a guess—and, if you're lucky, an educated one."

The quote gave the inexperienced Netflix founders hope. If everybody else was going on instinct, they would go on evidence. While the internet was still in its infancy, it was already clear that websites were fantastic machines for capturing data on customer choices. Did people watch more comedies or thrillers? Were documentaries more popular in the winter or summer? They had no idea. But they suspected that given enough time, their website would provide the answers.

As Randolph would later recount in his memoir, *That Will Never Work*, a methodology quickly took root at Netflix that was highly empirical. Before they made any decision about design, or strategy, or inventory, the Netflix founders would first run a series of tests on their website. Then they would collect the resulting data and pore over the evidence, looking for patterns in how people had reacted.

The quickest way to go out of business in the internet age, they believed, was to make decisions based on your own instincts, preferences, political beliefs, desires, and tastes. They vowed to follow the data wherever it took them.

"It was a huge advantage for us," Randolph says. "There was this view in Hollywood that certain people were the gifted tastemakers. You'd see it in the movies. They'd sit in the big office and greenlight things: 'This is *Pretty Woman* meets *Out of Africa*. Gold!' They'd fight for years to get to the point where they can greenlight the movie. They know what people want."

"We never pretended that's how decision making should work," he adds. "For us, it was always very data driven."

· · ·

IN THE LATE 1990s, with the business world going increasingly bonkers over the dot-com craze, and the Nasdaq Composite Index hitting new heights, HBO staffers heard some unsettling news. HBO's parent company, Time Warner, was on the verge of selling itself to an internet start-up in the suburbs of Washington, D.C.

HBO executives were surprised. The thought of AOL.com owning Time Warner was hard to imagine. HBO's rank and file typically had little love for their corporate overseers at Time Warner. In the years since the merger with Warner, the company's broader culture had grown famously dyspeptic. It was hard to talk about the place without invoking metaphors about feuding European monarchies.

"We didn't care who was in the corporate office," says Dave Baldwin, then a top HBO scheduling executive. "Most of us thought they were idiots who were spending too much money anyways. But as long as we met our finance numbers and targets, they would leave us alone."

What would life be like for HBO under new ownership? To judge by recent press coverage, AOL seemed unbearably cocky. The company's youngish CEO, Steve Case, was being celebrated as a genius of the new digital economy. No longer limited to magazine covers, he'd recently appeared in an ad campaign for the Gap, donning a pair of business-casual khakis, photographed by fashion icon Richard Avedon. Case was apparently a new kind of American celebrity—a promethean tech god, delivering the spark of dial-up internet access to the mortals.

While many Time Warner division heads were outwardly supportive of the deal, HBO's chief executive Jeffrey Bewkes was vocally opposing the merger. He found the rationale being advanced by AOL boosters—namely, that Time Warner was a bloated, slow-moving, hidebound colossus in need of reinvention—to be not only wrong but also insulting. But for the time being, his concerns went unheeded.

Gerald Levin, the CEO of Time Warner and original head of HBO, had clearly lost faith in the company's ability to determine its own future. The dawn of the internet had rattled Levin's belief in pay-TV. The Net was ascendant, and the satellite age, which he had helped launch, felt like it might fall to earth. To keep growing, Levin wanted to pair up with someone who could help Time Warner make the next technological leap forward. The khaki-clad cyber visionary in Virginia seemed to fit the bill. AOL was the future.

In the summer of 2000, with the AOL merger still pending, Jeffrey Bewkes got into a chauffeured car next to Chris Albrecht. On this particular afternoon, Bewkes and Albrecht were on their way to a high-stakes meeting. They were deep in negotiations with director Steven Spielberg and actor Tom Hanks to produce a miniseries based on the book *Band of Brothers* by the historian Stephen Ambrose. The details of the contract needed to be finalized. On the drive over, according to a later account in *GQ*, Albrecht and Bewkes agreed not to go a penny over $90 million for the budget.

A few hours later, they were back in the car, returning from the sit-down with a finalized contract, stipulating a $120 million budget for the ten-episode series. *Band of Brothers* would be the most expensive miniseries ever made. At an average of $12 million per episode, the figure would represent a roughly five times increase over the cost of typical prestige drama like *The Sopranos*.

Albrecht was incredulous. Why, he asked Bewkes, did he ditch the $90-million limit they'd agreed to? Bewkes shrugged. His decision hadn't been made based on any market research, revenue calculations, or subscriber projections. It just felt right, he explained. Ever since *From the Earth to the Moon*, HBO had been on a roll in part by investing whatever it took to produce distinctive programming. They'd figure out how to make up the money on the back end. In later retellings, Albrecht would dub this "the HBO Shrug."

In October 2000, HBO introduced a new series into its growing Sunday-night rotation. Following the finale of the third season of *Sex and the City*, HBO aired the first episode of *Curb Your Enthusiasm*.

Like Larry David's earlier mockumentary, *Curb Your Enthusiasm*, the series, starred David, playing his alter ego alongside a set of fictionalized characters, including his wife, Cheryl (played by Cheryl Hines), his manager, Jeff Greene (Jeff Garlin), and various actors and comedians playing themselves, including Ted Danson, Richard Lewis, and Kathy Griffin. Most of the dialogue was improvised. For each episode, cast members were given roughly sketched outlines rather than a polished script. Their comedic instincts took it from there. The heavy reliance on spontaneity gave the show a loose, cinema-verité vibe.

Early on, the show revolved around David's inability to assimilate to the easygoing professional and social life of his post-*Seinfeld* semiretirement in Los Angeles. David is a fish out of water in the sunny climate of Southern California, who can't help but trample over the basic social etiquette of his well-off peer group of successful actors and comedians.

In the early episodes, he is constantly running into reminders of former New York institutions, like Paul Simon and Barney's, that have managed to adapt to the West Coast environment. Yet, David, for his part, can't help but rub everybody the wrong way, whether he's golfing at his country club or attending a dinner party thrown by a former porn star.

Critics tended to focus on the ways *Curb Your Enthusiasm* extended or diverged from the Seinfeldian traditions. "Instead of moving over to the sunny side of the street, David has decided to share his rather bleak vision of the human existence once again with television viewers," Charlie McCollum noted in the *San Jose Mercury News*. "But instead of limiting it to one character in an ensemble—George Costanza was the David voice in *Seinfeld*—he has created a comedy that falls totally within that vision."

Within the HBO comedic universe, the series seemed like a direct evolutionary leap forward from *The Larry Sanders Show*. Like Garry Shandling's creation, *Curb* worked on two levels, simultaneously offering a sly, self-aware critique of a high-strung comedic performer delving into his own bouts of odious behavior, while also sending up a city and an industry that is prone to vapidity.

The series added to a growing trend at HBO. Twenty years after the network arrived as an outsider in Hollywood only to face hostility, ridicule, and ostracization by the entertainment establishment, HBO was solidifying its reputation as the go-to place in American entertainment for incisive, insidery critiques of life in Hollywood.

In the months and years to follow, HBO continued to snap up media-centric series with a relish unmatched by any other network. HBO's oeuvre of entertainment industry critiques would ultimately come to include *Project Greenlight*, a reality series about newcomers breaking into the movie business, produced by Matt Damon and Ben Affleck; *Entourage*, a fratty comedy-drama about the high-flying, lascivious lifestyle of a young, newly minted movie star and his pack of buddies from Queens, New York, enjoying the fruits of Hollywood; and *The Comeback*, a mockumentary set in the television industry.

• • •

IN 2000, Chris Albrecht got a divorce from his wife of nineteen years. Newly single, he spent his nights out on the town, carousing with celebrities and dating much younger women. He could transfix any room with wild tales about the debauchery of the New York comedy scene in the 1970s.

By comparison, Carolyn Strauss was a steady, serene presence. Strauss, who has sharp hazel-green eyes and short, choppy back hair, was reserved and inscrutable. At Time Warner, a company groaning under the collective weight of so many paunchy, middle-aged, straight white men, Strauss stood out as the rare gay female executive. In meetings with actors and agents, she typically listened intently while Albrecht did most of the kibitzing.

Often when a showrunner received specific feedback from the network on a particular episode or script, it was Strauss who delivered the message. By the late 1990s, she was playing a major, if publicly unheralded, role in shaping the network's ascendant slate of programming.

Strauss grew up in Scarsdale, New York, a suburb just north of New York City. Her dad worked in the tobacco business. Her mom worked in publishing. In high school, she was a standout varsity softball player. After graduating from Harvard in the mid-1980s, Strauss moved to the city and got a temp job at HBO, which eventually grew into a full-time position. After a stint in promotions, Strauss started working as an assistant to Betty Bitterman, who'd come to HBO with decades of experience in show business, including a run as the top producer on *The Merv Griffin Show*.

Strauss was terrible at secretarial work, but the job had a perk: she was in charge of the cassette library, which meant she could stay at the office late into the night familiarizing herself with all of HBO's original programming efforts to date. Bitterman, a high-ranking programming executive in charge of comedy and musical specials, worked late hours, too, and liked what she saw.

"She was just so smart," Bitterman says. "And so aware. She could size things up real fast. She got the essence of things."

In 1990, Strauss moved to HBO's office in Los Angeles, which was less corporate and was gaining more power with each passing year as more of the TV industry continued to shift from New York to L.A. There, Strauss became Albrecht's closest adviser.

For years, during meetings with writers and agents, Strauss kept encountering a frustrating problem that she felt was holding HBO back. They'd talk over a great idea, get excited, and then run into a wall. Why should the writers and agents do it for HBO? A broadcast network would pay more money and give them more exposure, a bigger audience, better ratings. For a long time, Strauss had struggled to provide a convincing answer. But by the late 1990s, Strauss felt confident that they'd solved the issue.

For experienced creators, tired of network TV's restrictions, HBO could offer them the promise of more creative freedom. They could learn the traditional limitations on broadcast, then push beyond them on HBO. That would be the network's calling card. It was HBO's job, in Strauss's view, to bring them in and show them that they could do what they hadn't done before. "We could offer something really different," Strauss says.

Which was why, over time, HBO's creative ranks were filling up with veterans of broadcast television: Tom Fontana, Garry Shandling, Darren Star, Larry David, David Chase. "They knew what the rules were and they knew the rules they wanted to break," Strauss says. "And for the people who wanted to do something other than for the network back end—which had been very, very lucrative, and which we couldn't offer them—here was a place."

As Albrecht puts it, "We were good enablers."

In early 1999, Strauss came up with an idea she thought would make for a good HBO series. Strauss had just finished reading *The American Way of Death* by Jessica Mitford, an investigative account, first published in 1963, that shed light on what went on inside the shadowy U.S. funeral industry. The book revealed how Americans had become estranged from the realities of death to their emotional and financial peril, leaving them vulnerable to a rapacious mortuary industry, upselling so many empty solaces, like luxury coffins.

"In the funeral home, the man of prudence is completely at sea, without a recognizable landmark or bearing to guide him," Mitford wrote. "For those who have the stomach for it, let us part the formaldehyde curtain."

Strauss was struck by the parallels with the American TV industry. On TV, death was aseptic, fleeting, distant, unreal. It was always wrapped up in neat and tidy packages or hidden behind a barrage of misleading gimmicks. What if HBO did a drama set inside a funeral home that brought death to life in all its emotional dishevelment? She knew the perfect person for the job.

Alan Ball was a versatile screenwriter with a round, owlish face, a frayed graying beard, and a playfully dark sense of humor. He'd spent much of his late twenties creating off-Broadway plays in New York while supporting himself as a graphic designer in the art department of *Adweek*, a trade publication about the advertising industry.

In the early 1990s, he moved to Los Angeles, where he worked as a writer on a pair of network sitcoms, ABC's *Grace Under Fire* and CBS's *Cybill*— jobs he came to loathe. On set, he spent much of his time learning horrible hackneyed writing tricks, dealing with capricious stars, and second-guessing what the network executives would want from a script, which was always the same thing. Make everybody nicer and spell out the subtext. "It was kind of soul deadening," Ball said.

At night, Ball would work on his passion project, a screenplay about a writer who has lost his ardor for life and then, suddenly, snaps out of his lethargy. In the late 1990s, DreamWorks Pictures bought the script. In September 1999, the studio released *American Beauty*, Ball's tale of a suburban copywriter caught in a thankless job and a sexless marriage, who starts smoking weed and lusting after his teenage daughter's best friend. The movie was a surprise hit, pulling in $130 million at the box office and winning Ball an Academy Award for Best Original Screenplay.

Around the time that *American Beauty* landed in theaters, Ball got together for lunch with Strauss, who pitched him on the idea of doing a series for HBO set in a family-run funeral home. Ball was intrigued. He'd spent time in such a venue at an impressionable point in his life. When he was thirteen years old, growing up in Georgia, his older sister, Mary Ann, was driving him to a piano lesson when a car crashed into their Ford Pinto, injuring Ball's leg and killing his sister. The accident cast a long shadow over the rest of his childhood.

Death, he agreed, was one of the most inhibited areas of modern TV. It was ripe for a less sanitized treatment. But at the time, he told Strauss, he was already committed to do a TV sitcom for ABC. Good luck with the project, he told her.

That fall, ABC began airing Ball's sitcom, *Oh, Grow Up*, a *Friends*-like series about a bunch of attractive, wisecracking roommates living together in Brooklyn. At the time, reality-TV shows were eating up all the prime-time attention on broadcast TV. Compared with the giant audience of ABC's hit show *Who Wants to Be a Millionaire*, the ratings for Ball's sitcom were paltry. In December, ABC abruptly canceled the series, leaving Ball crestfallen and pondering what to do next.

Thanks to the success of *American Beauty*, Ball was flooded with offers. "People were calling me and saying, we have this hacky stand-up comedian we'd love to build a show around, or we have this washed-up movie actor who wants to do TV, or the president of this network has an idea about a man who is reincarnated as his wife's dog," Ball said. "I was like, oh, Jesus. I can't go back into that gulag."

Maybe the opportunity at HBO was worth revisiting? That year, he'd been watching the first season of *The Sopranos* and marveling at its quality.

Over Christmas, Ball wrote the pilot for *Six Feet Under*, a dramatic series about a heavily repressed family who runs a funeral home. When a car accident suddenly kills the father, his widow and children struggle to get over the loss while running a business sustained by death's omnipresence. Ball decided to set *Six Feet Under* in L.A. He would later describe the city as "the capital of the denial of death."

Before long, Ball was at HBO discussing the pilot script with Albrecht and Strauss. "Their notes were, 'It feels a little safe. It feels a little networky.

Can you just make the whole thing a little more fucked up,'" Ball said. He got to work on making the whole thing darker.

"I had to sort of unlearn a lot of habits," Ball says. "You do year after year of network TV and you learn to anticipate the notes."

· · ·

ON JANUARY 11, 2001, AOL completed its mega-merger with Time Warner, the largest in U.S. history.

Not long after the deal was completed, HBO staffers learned that everyone at the company would be required to start using AOL's email platform for their official work communication. The change did not go over well. Although the newcomers arrived with reputations as digital savants, HBO employees were dumbfounded when they discovered AOL's system was archaic, functionally limited, and extremely buggy.

David Roofthooft, who was working on HBO marketing promos at the time, recalls that the compression was horrendous, making it nearly impossible for anyone to share large video files with their coworkers. "We were a video company and you couldn't even share video through their system," he recalls. "It was absolute garbage, and it crashed all the time. If you wanted to share anything of any size or resolution, it was a train wreck."

Not to mention an ominous sign of things to come.

Soon, emissaries of the new internet-minded regime began showing up at HBO's offices and taking stock of their new asset.

One day, a top AOL manager came to HBO to address the troops. In a conference room inside HBO's Bryant Park headquarters, the cybervisionary launched into a lecture about HBO's finances. Ross Greenburg of HBO Sports recalls feeling a growing sense of discombobulation listening to the dire importance of HBO hitting its quarterly profit numbers. *Quarterly profits?* An emphasis on such short-term metrics was unheard of at HBO. The whole tenor of the speech, Greenburg says, felt anathema to the network's creative culture. "I'll never forget his line," Greenburg recalls. "He was like, 'If we start to see that you're not going to make the quarterly earnings, we're throwing the furniture out of this window.'"

"Good lord, it was horrible," says Andrew Goldman, an HBO scheduling executive at the time. "It felt like we were being punished on some level. It was our first taste of people who didn't get us. They acted like, okay, we'll sprinkle a little AOL magic on this and we'll change HBO—and HBO didn't need changing."

Shelley Brindle, then a rising executive with HBO's subscriber marketing group, remembers the first visit from her new AOL bosses. The executives, she says, arrived from Virginia on private jets, sat down at their first big meeting with her team, and asked the HBO staffers to turn over all their subscriber data. The intent, they explained, was to begin comarketing AOL services to existing and former HBO customers. There was an awkward pause. "We were like, um, what subscriber data?" Brindle says. "This was after the deal was closed!"

It was left to the HBO staffers to explain that the network didn't deal directly with their customers and that it was the cable companies who collected, retained, and controlled all of the information on HBO subscribers. The network itself had zilch. "There was nothing we could do to help them," Brindle says. "We didn't have access to the customers. Unfortunately, they didn't realize until after the acquisition that there was really no additive value for either side."

For as long as anyone could remember, executives at HBO, Time Inc., and Time Warner had dressed formally. The women wore conservative attire: pantsuits, blouses, dresses, heels. The men donned suits, tailored button-down shirts, well-appointed cuff links, and designer ties. While the AOL deal would ultimately fail to disrupt the future of media, it did succeed briefly at disrupting the prevailing wardrobe at Time Warner.

Styles in the C-suite changed overnight. Longtime HBO staffers watched with some dismay as members of the company's senior management team began adopting the khaki-infused style of the AOL tribe. A smattering of business casual could be seen blooming in every AOL Time Warner conference room.

Gerald Levin, a reliable suit-and-tie man for decades, started showing up in public wearing denim shirts and suede shoes that looked like slippers. Other go-getters followed his lead. Neckties all but disappeared.

One of the sartorial holdouts was Jeffrey Bewkes, who continued to wear suits to the HBO offices every day. At one point, another executive at the company confronted Bewkes, Dave Baldwin recalls. In front of a group of onlookers, the executive made note of Bewkes's suit and tie and asked if he was planning to reinstate the Time Inc. dress code of days past.

"Jeff just looked at him and said, 'No. If you want to look like an internet asshole, be my guest,'" Baldwin says.

The more time they spent familiarizing themselves with AOL products, the more alarmed many HBO staffers felt. For all the talk about AOL's futuristic prowess, to their eyes AOL's actual engineering and technology looked painfully rudimentary. By 2001, it was already clear to everybody that high-speed internet delivered over fiber-optic cables would play a major role in distributing topical programming of all sorts. And yet, somewhat astonishingly, the AOL team seemed entirely wedded to an earlier generation of dial-up telephone access. "They didn't have a high-speed product," Baldwin recalls. "It was like, okay, these guys are fakers, at best."

Among his HBO brethren, Bewkes was doing little to hide his disdain for the internet gurus they reported to. One night, the network's executives gathered on the top floor of the HBO headquarters for a going-away party for John Billock, a longtime marketing and sales executive at HBO who was heading off to Connecticut to lead their parent company's cable distribution business, Time Warner Cable. With the party in full swing, Bewkes got up to deliver a speech. "We were all sitting there and he got the mic," recalls Carmi Zlotnik. "The first thing he said was, 'Let me tell you something. *Fuck AOL*.'"

While HBO executives were figuring out how to fend off their new corporate overlords, Alan Ball was putting the finishing touches on *Six Feet Under*. The series debuted on Sunday, June 3, 2001, and ran through August. Over the course of thirteen episodes, the series showed off many of the new hallmarks of HBO original programming under Strauss's meticulous guidance.

In the pilot episode, the patriarch of the Fisher family (Richard Jenkins) is killed in a car accident, leaving his mortuary business, Fisher & Sons Funeral Home, to his prodigal elder son, Nate Fisher (Peter Krause), and his gay, duty-bound brother, David Fisher (Michael C. Hall). The sudden loss touches off a messy existential crisis for the entire clan, including the family matriarch, Ruth Fisher (Frances Conroy), a fretful, regimented worrier, and her angsty teenage daughter, Claire Fisher (Lauren Ambrose). "I understand, you know, feeling like you've got this shadow over you all the time," Claire says to her high school guidance counselor in an early episode.

"What's your shadow?" he asks.

"Death, I guess," she replies. "Death and silence. Is that crazy?"

It was the kind of story that Joseph Campbell and his acolytes would have no difficulty interpreting in mythological terms. "The TV part here is *death:* holy shit, Dad died," Albrecht said. "The death of an archetypal figure— death of a king."

Whereas network TV shows shied away from the emotional consequences of death, each episode of *Six Feet Under* began with somebody's dramatic, often ghoulish demise, then followed the emotional ripples as they spread outward from the embalming table of the Fisher & Sons Funeral Home. Throughout the series, the writers on *Six Feet Under* kept a bank of newspaper clippings filled with stories about unusual deaths, which they could later use for creative inspiration.

As in *Larry Sanders*, one of the early themes is the grotesquery of commercial advertising. The pilot is interspersed with several fake, off-putting commercials for mortuary products, including tricked-out hearses and "wound filler." "We put the fun back in funeral," boasts one ad.

Over time, the series developed a warmer, less cynical take on the funeral business, thanks, in part, to several books by Thomas Lynch, a poet and undertaker, which Ball read while doing research for the series. "There's a beautiful, beautiful essay about him and his brother washing their father's dead body," Ball said. "I started seeing the poetry and the beauty. I felt like that's where I wanted to go with the show."

Reviewers were overwhelmingly impressed. Not only did they praise the series on its own merits, but many critics held up *Six Feet Under* as yet additional evidence of the growing superiority of the entire HBO storytelling brand.

The warm reviews were important to Albrecht and Strauss. Some critics had groused that HBO simply had fallen into incredible beginners' luck with the success of *The Sopranos* and *Sex and the City*. To the programming executives, *Six Feet Under* offered definitive proof that the HBO way of doing business worked.

By the early 2000s, HBO was pursuing a new strategy for marketing its original series. HBO set out to own Sunday nights. "I had this idea that came from the artillery world called 'fire for effect,'" Zlotnik says. "Which is to concentrate everything in one place, rather than dispersing it."

Zlotnik consulted with Dave Baldwin, the network's top scheduler, to see which night of the week made the most sense competitively. Baldwin thought it over. Thursdays were out of the question. That was the biggest, most competitive night for the broadcast networks, in part because many advertisers believed it was the best time to target consumers in the run-up to the weekend. Why not claim Sunday night, Baldwin suggested. The commercial networks had largely given up on the time period, often running licensed movies that were long past their prime.

HBO didn't have enough original series to fill Sunday nights with fresh episodes fifty-two weeks a year. But if they piled on everything, including documentaries, music and comedy specials, original movies, and sports, they could get pretty close. "Let's just load up whatever we got on Sunday nights," Baldwin said. "We went to marketing and got them behind it."

To support the programming strategy, HBO conceived of a new advertising campaign. The idea was to emphasize HBO's Sunday-night lineup by featuring characters from across HBO's slate of shows all mingling with one another. The goal was to create a shock-and-awe premium-cable show of force.

HBO's promotion team did a search online to see if they could find some music that fit the theme. What they found was a melancholy anthem entitled "Always on Sunday" by Tammany Hall, a little-known indie-rock band.

HBO optioned the song and set out to create some accompanying

imagery. But there was a problem. While broadcast networks typically man-
dated the stars in their shows to do a certain number of promos for the network, HBO's creator-empowering model was comparatively laissez-faire.
Whether the actors in a series were asked to appear in HBO promotions was
largely left up to the showrunners. Often, they declined to make it a priority.
As a result, HBO's marketing team knew it would be logistically and politically impossible to get all the actors from all the series to show up for an
original shoot for their campaign.

Eventually, they found a work-around solution. HBO acquired some
beautiful, slow-speed footage that had been shot at the Golden Globes, which
captured a number of HBO stars, including James Gandolfini, Edie Falco,
and Frances Conroy mingling in evening wear and looking elegant at the
awards show.

In the promo that followed, HBO set the images of their glamorous
ensemble of stars to the Tammany Hall soundtrack. Then a message filled
the screen: "The Stars of Sunday Night. All in One Place."

Soon variations of the ad were playing routinely on and off HBO. "The
song is fairly melancholy," says David Roofthooft, who worked with HBO's
marketing team. "But that was very much part of the tone of the network at
the time from a branding standpoint."

Again and again, spots from the campaign hammered away at TV viewers with its memorable tagline: "Sunday is . . . HBO."

CHAPTER 11

Cable Envy

In January 2001, the network announced that its new epic World War II miniseries *Band of Brothers* would premiere in September, right at the start of the traditional fall TV season—a make or break time for broadcast network shows. It was a part of the year that HBO had historically avoided. No longer.

"Just as soldiers formed a beachhead in World War II, this can be a beachhead for us in terms of fall programming," Albrecht said. "We're pretty confident; we're not going to say, 'Here, it's September, go watch NBC.'"

Such quotes, along with HBO's growing success in TV series, were starting to rankle its competitors in broadcast TV who were watching their audiences splinter and migrate to the edgier programming on cable. HBO's decision to make a big splash in the fall TV season didn't go over particularly well in some corners of the industry.

Just a few months later, in April, Bob Wright, the president of NBC, did something unusual. He made a couple hundred copies of a particularly violent portion of the third season of *The Sopranos*. In the episode, entitled "University," one of Tony's captains, Ralph Cifaretto (Joe Pantoliano), beats to death a young woman he's impregnated, who has been working as a stripper at the Bada Bing.

Wright sent the tapes to dozens of executives at NBC, at other studios, and at production companies. In a letter accompanying the package, Wright expressed his alarm over the violence on the hit series and asked what lessons NBC might learn from it. "It is a show which we could not air on NBC because of the violence, language, and nudity," he wrote.

Word of Wright's contemptuous letter spread quickly. Wright told reporters that he hadn't meant to insult *The Sopranos* and was only interested in starting a dialogue on the shifting ethical standards of television.

The letter soon made its way to David Chase. "I was furious," says the creator of *The Sopranos*. "I was getting out of network television, which had always been my dream. And it felt like it was shadowing me."

The letter, Chase says, was full of shameless hypocrisy. "He was talking about how disgusting the whole thing was and then said, *Is there anything here we can use?* All in one little letter," Chase says. "How intelligent is that person? He was the head of the network. He probably didn't understand why it was appealing to people and sent the tapes around so that maybe someone else would figure it out."

The episode in question had been cowritten by Terence Winter, a key member of *The Sopranos* staff, who would go on to create two original series for HBO in the years to come. At the time, he brushed off the criticism from NBC. "It was jealousy," Winter says. "It was a way of picking at the show. People would say, 'Oh, they can do cursing and language and we can't.' Well, that's not why your show is shitty. It's because the way you tell stories is ridiculous. It doesn't feel real. It's the writing."

Winter was an affable, knockabout screenwriter with a bald head and a wide, barrel-of-monkeys smile. He grew up in the 1960s, the youngest of five siblings, in a working-class Irish Catholic family in Marine Park, Brooklyn. When he was seven, his father, a public relations employee at Texaco, died of cancer, and his mom went back to work as a secretary, leaving him to run wild around the frenetic neighborhood and to pick up part-time work at the neighborhood butcher shop.

After graduating from a vocational high school, Winter tried to break into Brooklyn's delicatessen industry, only to get swindled by his partners.

He went back to school, eventually paying his way through college at New York University and law school at St. John's University with a string of grinding jobs. Cab driver. Hospital security guard. Doorman. He had no real interest in the law but wanted its air of respectability and the approval of his hypercritical mom. "A lot of this was trying to win the respect of my mother," he says.

Winter slogged his way through graduate school, landed a job in corporate law in the late 1980s, and soon realized he had a problem. He hated being a lawyer. To the shock of his family, he quit his well-paying job and moved to Los Angeles to pursue his dream of becoming a TV sitcom writer.

Rejections piled up. Winter took a day job as a paralegal, lived like a monk, and for several years spent his nights and weekends writing spec scripts. Eventually, he got an agent and was accepted into a sitcom writers' workshop hosted annually by Warner Bros.

Before long, he was getting actual writing jobs on real shows. It didn't matter how formulaic or simpleminded the series were, Winter couldn't believe he was getting paid to write. His worst day as a TV writer was ten times better than his best day as a lawyer. He got his union card and was ecstatic. He wrote scripts for a string of largely forgettable shows: *The Cosby Mysteries*, *Xena: Warrior Princess*, and *Flipper: The New Adventures*.

The latter was a 1995 revival of a classic dolphin-centric series, and it proved to be a real challenge. "I don't think most people realize that there are, organically, only ten stories in the world that involve a dolphin," Winter said. "When you figure out what those ten stories are and then you've still got twelve more episodes to do—there's nothing like the sound of those crickets in the writers room. *Flipper . . . has to be involved in a murder?* It's really impossible."

Around that time, Winter's friend Frank Renzulli got hired to write on a new HBO series about wiseguys in New Jersey. Winter desperately wanted to join the show. He'd grown up around blue-collar Italian American families in Brooklyn and brushed up against real-life mobsters during his time at the butcher shop. He knew how they talked, how they thought. But it was too late. Chase was done hiring.

Throughout the first season, Winter read Renzulli's scripts and offered feedback and suggestions. Before the start of the second season, Renzulli got Winter an audience with Chase. Winter gave him a script he'd written for a feature film. Chase hated it. But based on Renzulli's recommendation, he agreed to hire Winter anyway for the second season. "Almost any other show-runner would have looked at my résumé and said, *Are you fucking kidding me?*" Winter says. "But David said, okay, if you're vouching for him, I'll give him a shot."

The writers room for *The Sopranos* was located in a big conference room on the second floor of Silvercup Studios, with windows looking back over the 59th Street Bridge, an incredible view of the city. The mood was loose. Each day, Winter would sit around telling stories with fellow writers like Renzulli, Robin Green, Mitch Burgess, Todd Kessler, and David Chase. Everyone shared a kind of grating, East Coast sense of humor. People razzed on each other constantly, and there were a lot of digressions.

"If you were a fly on the wall in *The Sopranos* writers room, you'd be asking yourself when are they going to talk about the show?" Winter says. "The answer is: it's all part of the show. It was literally everything from what I ate for dinner last night to one time this guy in my neighborhood did such and such to . . . one time I dated a woman and she threw a piece of meat at me. All of this stuff would somehow find its way into the show."

Soon, they realized that one thing they all seemed to have in common, weirdly, was difficult relationships with their moms. "My mother was an incredibly negative person, at least toward me, for whatever reason. So, I totally got it," Winter says. "We all had Livia Soprano for a mother."

The writers who weren't in sync with Chase were quickly let go. But Winter stuck around and thrived. The writing rules, he says, were canonical though largely unspoken. Chase hated exposition. Do it deftly, or not at all. No spoon-feeding the viewer plot points. No mob clichés. No gangsters saying, "Fuggedaboutit!" Chase liked when characters didn't say what they meant. He liked when they spoke in broken sentences. He liked when they lied.

"In network TV, it's almost a rule that things wrap up neatly," Winter says. "David loved loose ends."

For days following NBC's criticism of Winter's episode of *The Sopranos*, HBO executives took turns publicly mocking the broadcasters' false piety. "All you have to do is look at the ratings on Sunday nights to understand what was behind that letter," Albrecht said. "With the XFL, NBC injected big breasts and four-letter words in the hopes of selling more young men more beer."

Others in Hollywood saw Wright's action as a spasm of jealousy, more evidence that the networks felt increasingly disadvantaged in the competition with cable networks for viewers' attention. Brad Grey told the *New York Times* that reps for every network, including NBC, had approached him "asking me to give them the next *Sopranos*."

Sure enough, two years later, in the fall of 2003, NBC would air *Kingpin*, a series about the brooding violent leader of a Mexican drug cartel and his dysfunctional family, which critics widely viewed as a feeble, *Sopranos*-lite knock-off. Around the country, headlines would dismiss NBC's attempt to muscle in on HBO's turf. The *San Francisco Chronicle*: "*Sopranos* has nothing to fear from NBC's mob drama *Kingpin*." The *Arizona Republic*: "Close but no *Sopranos*." The *Fort Worth Star-Telegram*: "Second Soprano; *Kingpin* druglord can't hold a cannoli to Tony." Ratings would prove lousy, and NBC would quickly give up on *Kingpin* after only six episodes.

Unlike their counterparts in broadcast television, HBO executives didn't have to live every waking moment with one eye scanning the Nielsen ratings. "The network executives were all jealous about that because they were basically looking every night: 'How's the show doing? Do I have a job tomorrow?'" Quentin Shaffer says.

In the months after Bob Wright's mealymouthed critique of *The Sopranos*, the tension between HBO and the broadcast networks continued to flare up. "A company that uses the slogan 'It's Not TV. It's HBO.' shouldn't be winning Emmy Awards," Leslie Moonves, the head of CBS, who'd personally whiffed on *The Sopranos*, told the *New Yorker*. "They should be winning something else."

"It's a tagline," HBO's Richard Plepler responded. "Get a life. Jesus."

In HBO's increasingly head-on challenge to the predominance of broadcast network series, HBO soon found a keen ally in David Simon, the former *Baltimore Sun* crime reporter and creator of the HBO miniseries *The Corner.* In June 2001, Simon wrote a lengthy memo to Albrecht and Strauss explaining how, with their blessing, his next project could serve as a direct attack on the heart of broadcast television.

Much of HBO's recent success, Simon noted in the letter, had come by counterprogramming against the networks—that is, by intentionally creating the types of shows that the broadcasters simply wouldn't touch. A gritty prison drama. A show exploring the subconscious tar pits of a violent mobster. A series in which female friends openly debated the merits of oral sex. But, Simon observed, HBO had steered clear of the one genre that served as the broadcast networks' bread and butter. HBO had never done a cop show.

Simon explained that on the surface his proposed series, *The Wire*, would look like a standard-issue broadcast police procedural. But it would quickly become obvious to viewers that they were watching something more subversive. Instead of wondering "whether the bad guys will get caught," Simon wrote, they would soon find themselves questioning "who the bad guys are and whether catching them means anything at all."

"You will not be stealing market share from the networks only by venturing into worlds where they can't, you will be stealing it by taking their worlds and transforming them with honesty and wit and a darker, cynical, and more piercing viewpoint than they would undertake," he added.

HBO's programming team agreed with Simon's assessment. It was time for HBO to do its first cop show.

* * *

IN THE SUMMER OF 2001, HBO commenced a huge, $10-million promotional campaign for *Band of Brothers*, the largest in the network's history.

To kick things off, HBO flew more than forty surviving D-Day veterans and their families to France for the premiere screening, which HBO staged at Utah Beach in Normandy on the fifty-seventh anniversary of the Allied landings there. For the occasion, HBO erected a massive thousand-seat structure on the beach. A line of French children, waving American flags, greeted HBO's visitors as they arrived. The crowd included Tom Hanks, Stephen Ambrose, hundreds of aging veterans, a number of European heads of state, and the children and grandchildren of Winston Churchill, Dwight D. Eisenhower, and Franklin D. Roosevelt. Fighter jets flew overhead in salute.

Back in the United States, HBO hosted a series of screenings for veteran groups and schools throughout the summer. Other AOL Time Warner cable networks featured extensive tie-in promotions. Ads for the series flooded newspapers and magazines. Jeep shot a series of *Band of Brothers* TV commercials, celebrating the Allies' use of the vehicles in the war. Through cable and satellite operators, HBO sent out *Band of Brothers*–themed mailings to the more than fifty million homes that weren't currently subscribing to the premium network. "Give the Gift of HBO to the Greatest Generation," read the mailers.

On Sunday, September 9, 2001, HBO aired the first two hours of the ten-part series. Like the book, the miniseries told the story of an elite group of soldiers in the U.S. Army as they train in Georgia, parachute into France on D-Day, and capture Hitler's Eagle's Nest compound.

The spoils of "the HBO shrug" were on full display. *Band of Brothers* was shot, in part, at Hatfield Studios, a former aerospace factory north of London where Spielberg and Hanks made much of *Saving Private Ryan*, and, in part, in the mountains, towns, and resorts of Switzerland. The huge ensemble cast included some five hundred speaking roles and more than ten thousand extras.

The reviews were positive.

Then, just two days after the debut, on September 11, 2001, terrorists attacked the United States, knocking down the Twin Towers in Manhattan and setting the Pentagon ablaze. With the nation suddenly at war, HBO hastily decided to shut down all its advertising for *Band of Brothers*. Ratings for subsequent episodes of the miniseries fell off precipitously.

"It was always going to be an emotional and difficult show to watch," Albrecht said in November. The terrorist attack, he added, "just increased that feeling."

• • •

IF THERE WAS A DOWNSIDE to the growing renown of HBO's original programming, it was that the network could no longer serve up the kind of crass, mediocre series that periodically slipped into its original lineup in the 1980s and expect it to be ignored. Critics and viewers had raised their expectations.

In the fall of 2001, HBO debuted a new series, written and starring comedian Mike Binder, a longtime comedy club pal of Albrecht's, called *The Mind of the Married Man*. Carolyn Strauss and others at the network had resisted putting the show on the air. But Albrecht overruled them. He thought the show was hilarious.

Originally entitled *My Dirty Little Mind*, the series revolved around the relentlessly lurid conversations between three middle-aged newspapermen in Chicago as they struggle with their marriages, bellyache about their sexual frustrations, and occasionally indulge in extramarital fantasies and infidelities. In one early scene, Micky, the show's protagonist, takes his wife to task at the family dinner table over her resistance to anal sex, while their nanny stands nearby looking horrified. In another, Micky visits an illicit massage parlor but ultimately declines the topless masseuse from giving him "the happy ending."

Throughout the series, the "cable edge" was strong. The writing was not.

Critics greeted the series as HBO's ham-fisted, retrograde attempt to create a male version of *Sex and the City*. The reviews were vicious.

"It's not possible in a family newspaper to describe most of the sexual content," David Zurawik wrote in *The Baltimore Sun*. "But there is something to be learned from it: how unexciting and even deadening the extra amount of sex allowed on premium cable can be when it's not tied to any artistic vision."

After two painful seasons, HBO canceled the series.

Meanwhile, more changes were roiling HBO's parent company. In early December 2001, Gerald Levin stunned Wall Street by announcing that he was retiring as the head of AOL Time Warner, to be replaced by his deputy,

Richard Parsons. Levin's big move, the sale to AOL, was looking iffy. The dot-com bubble had recently burst. Online advertising was drying up. And AOL subscribers had plateaued.

But Levin told reporters that he had other, more personal reasons for leaving. The recent September 11 terrorist attacks—as well as a tragic event in his own family—had left him feeling emotionally drained. Several years earlier, in 1997, Levin's thirty-one-year-old son, Jonathan, an English teacher at a public high school in the Bronx, had been gruesomely robbed and murdered inside his Manhattan apartment by one of his former students and an accomplice. Afterward, in a state of mourning, Levin had inserted a clause in his corporate contract that would allow him, with six months' notice, to exit the company well before the contract's 2003 expiration.

Now, at the age of sixty-two, some three decades after he'd first accepted a job from Time Inc. to work on HBO, Levin said he was resigning. He felt it was time to work on himself. He wanted to show the business world that it was possible for the top executive at the most powerful media conglomerate on the planet to relinquish control of the company without dying or being fired. His existence, he told reporters, was about more than just AOL Time Warner earnings. "I need to reclaim my identity," he said. "I'm about to demonstrate the real me."

After leaving AOL Time Warner, Levin would soon divorce his wife, leave New York City, marry a clairvoyant healer, grow a beard, and become the director of the Moonview Sanctuary, a holistic wellness institute in Santa Monica, California, with a yoga room, a collection of hand drums, a marble statue of Buddha, and an outsize gong.

At Moonview, Levin spent his days participating in ceremonial drum circles with his male clients and helping them let go of their egos and cope with their own mortality. "Instead of a male hierarchy, it becomes almost feminine in its openness," he would later tell *New York* magazine. "Normally, you're defended, calculating, with an agenda. Here, it melts away. Each session is particular to the individual and to the group, depending on what's needed. Does somebody need a rite of passage? Does somebody need an understanding of love? Ultimately, we're trying to break down male culture."

• • •

IN THE SUMMER OF 2002, HBO began airing the first season of *The Wire*, David Simon's attempt to remake and subvert the great American cop show.

At the start of the series, Jimmy McNulty (Dominic West), a righteous, self-destructive homicide detective, tells a politically connected judge that a bunch of murder investigations have recently fallen apart in court because a group of dealers in West Baltimore are intimidating state witnesses. The judge goes ballistic, calls McNulty's superiors, and demands action.

Furious at McNulty for going behind their backs, the heads of the police department assign him, along with a bunch of their misfit officers, to a special task force. Soon, McNulty and his cohorts home in on D'Angelo Barksdale (Larry Gilliard, Jr.), a midlevel dealer, who is the cousin of Avon Barksdale (Wood Harris), the current king of the Baltimore drug trade. As part of the operation, they soon get a wiretap on the Barksdale organization.

As the ensuing investigation unfolds, *The Wire* follows the story from the alternating perspectives of the cops, the dealers, and the addicts. With each passing episode, the universe of the surrounding Baltimore community keeps expanding outward, eventually pulling in every layer of the city: church leaders, politicians, business owners, dock laborers, schoolteachers, recovery counselors, metro journalists, and social workers.

Much of the series was shot on location in the streets, housing projects, and municipal buildings of Baltimore. The plot revolved around a diverse, sprawling group of morally complex characters, including a doleful, streetwise drug addict named Bubbles (Andre Royo), a gay, stash-robbing vigilante named Omar Little (Michael K. Williams), and an upwardly mobile drug lieutenant, Stringer Bell (Idris Elba), who in his free time studies business administration at a community college.

To the press, Simon called it a "visual novel." In place of the typical cop-show paradigm of good versus evil, *The Wire* dug into the conflict of the individual versus the system. There were no tidy moments of personal redemption—not for the cops, not for the street crew, and not for the addicts. Just a crush of hardened individuals trying to survive in the face of dispiriting civic decay.

It was a story, says Simon, about the dysfunction of the postindustrial American city and how it got left behind. "I never looked at *The Wire* as being a story about Baltimore," says Simon. "We obviously wrote the specifics of Baltimore into the piece because we knew them. But we could have done that with Pittsburgh, or Cleveland, or St. Louis. I looked at it as a story about postindustrial urbanity—the postmodern problems of city living and self-governance."

The initial reviews of *The Wire* were lukewarm. While some reviewers appreciated the series' authenticity and attention to detail, others were turned off by its meandering pace, impenetrable dialogue, overabundance of characters, and the multivariable complexity of its plot.

In early episodes, Avon Barksdale, the powerful Baltimorean drug mogul, is often seen conducting business in the back room of a strip club called Orlando's. After the first season aired, a couple of viewers reached out to Simon and asked if the setup was a homage to HBO's big hit show on which Tony Soprano and his gang often work out of the Bada Bing strip club. Surely that couldn't have been a coincidence?

Simon was initially confused. *The Bada what?* The setup in *The Wire*, he explained, was based on a real Baltimore drug legend who'd run things out of a strip club called the Eldorado Lounge. Unlike seemingly everyone else in the TV industry, Simon wasn't obsessing over *The Sopranos*. After seeing fifteen minutes or so of the pilot, he had turned it off and stopped watching altogether. He didn't want it in his head while he was writing.

"That affirmed it for me: I can't watch that show until I finish the run of this show," says Simon. "And I never did. I watched *The Sopranos* after *The Wire* was well over."

Others at HBO were keeping an eye out for any inadvertent crossovers. Toward the end of filming the first season, Simon and his colleagues were preparing to shoot the opening scene of the penultimate episode: an elaborate dream sequence in which Detective McNulty would find himself naked on stage performing in front of an audience of his colleagues and drug dealers.

But at the last minute, before shooting started, Simon got a note from Carolyn Strauss, encouraging him to kill the dream. Simon accepted her suggestion and went back to his trailer to churn out a new opening scene for episode 12. On *The Wire*, there would be no flights of fancy into the subconscious of its characters.

"At the time, Carolyn Strauss just said, you don't need it. We already know where McNulty's damage is," Simon recalls. "Later on she told me that nobody has made a better meal of protagonist dream sequences than David Chase. She said that was part of her decision."

Strauss was quietly shaping the evolution of the storyline in other meaningful ways as well. Initially, when Simon and his colleagues sketched out the arc of the first season, they planned for Shakima Greggs (Sonja Sohn), an ethical, right-minded detective, to be shot and killed toward its end. But before that could happen, Strauss intervened.

She convinced the creators of *The Wire* that Greggs should survive the shooting. In an entertainment world chock-full of heterosexual white male cops, Detective Greggs was a Black lesbian police officer. She was unique, Strauss argued, and worth keeping around. Ultimately, Simon agreed, and Detective Greggs would go on to become one of the series' most intriguing and revered characters.

During the first season, few viewers tuned in to *The Wire*, particularly compared with *The Sopranos* and *Sex and the City*. Simon worried that HBO would quickly cancel the series.

Feeling anxious, he called Strauss to talk over the low ratings. She reassured him not to freak out. "I said, well, it's a pretty shitty number, isn't it?" recalls Simon. "She said, oh, it's a cute little number. Don't worry. It's not how we do things here."

In November 2002, HBO renewed *The Wire* for a second season.

* * *

BY 2002, the benefits of HBO's decision—made during the shooting of *From the Earth to the Moon*—to shift toward a more theatrical model of spending on its shows were becoming more apparent. The HBO shrug was good not just for morale but also for the network's bottom line.

HBO's slickly produced, popular series were no longer just attracting new subscribers to the network, they were also generating significant additional streams of income for HBO, fueling sales of related merchandise like *The Sopranos Family Cookbook*, *Sex and the City* tote bags, and *The Tao of Bada Bing*. In particular, DVD collections were proving to be a gold mine.

While elsewhere on the internet Netflix was busy winning over the DVD-rental business, HBO was aggressively moving into DVD sales. By the early 2000s, HBO was selling hundreds of thousands of the pricey DVD sets. *The Sopranos*, *Sex and the City*, and *Band of Brothers* were particularly strong sellers. For the first season of *The Sopranos*, HBO's box set retailed for $99.98. HBO marketed *Band of Brothers* as the perfect gift for veterans of the armed services. The suggested retail price: $120.

In addition to padding HBO's profits, the collectable DVD sets served as great advertisements and incentives for nonsubscribers to sign up for the premium network in order to catch new seasons. "It would also help with the marketing because retailers like Walmart would have a dedicated HBO DVD section," says former HBO executive Henry McGee.

According to McGee, by the mid-2000s—between DVDs, syndication deals, overseas licensing, production fees, and merchandise—ancillary sales were accounting for roughly 20 percent of HBO's overall revenues. The new strategy of spending more to make more was paying off handsomely.

With each passing month, though, the union between Time Warner and AOL was looking more rocky. Wall Street's strong initial support for the deal was disappearing. By the summer of 2002, AOL Time Warner shares were trading near an all-time low, having lost more than 80 percent of their value over the past year, erasing billions of dollars in value. Analysts and investors were apoplectic. HBO staffers, many of whom had large amounts of their personal nest eggs tied up in company stock, were also growing deeply embittered.

From day one, staffers were free to sell off their newly converted AOL

Time Warner stock, but were discouraged from doing so. Word circulated around the offices that if you cashed in a lot of AOL Time Warner stock at one time, you were likely to get a stern note from the bosses in corporate.

"We were brainwashed into thinking that the stock was going to go into the ozone," recalls Dave Baldwin, the former HBO scheduling chief. "Everyone was talked into holding the stock. They actually had these big conferences where they showed the math. I held all the way down. It left an awful lot of bad blood."

In July, Robert Pittman, the conglomerate's embattled chief operating officer, quit. A few days later, word got out that the Securities and Exchange Commission was investigating AOL Time Warner's accounting practices.

To help quiet the concerns on Wall Street, the company announced that Don Logan, a veteran of Time Inc., and Jeffrey Bewkes, HBO's CEO, would be taking over as co-COOs. All along, Logan and Bewkes had been two of the most vehement internal critics of the merger with AOL. Moving forward, Bewkes would oversee the company's entertainment divisions, including not just HBO, but also CNN and Turner Networks. After all the turmoil, the traditional media crew had won out over the cyberspace squad. "We reject foreign bodies, just like in an operation," Baldwin says. "AOL was a foreign body."

As a parting gift, Bewkes's colleagues at HBO gave him a Sharper Image air purifier. It was a nod both to Bewkes's mild germophobia and also the unhealthy environment in AOL Time Warner corporate offices. "Jeff protected HBO at what could have been a very vulnerable time," Carmi Zlotnik says.

Following his promotion, Bewkes announced that his friend Chris Albrecht would be stepping up into the role of HBO's chairman and chief executive officer. Never mind what appalling secret lurked in his past. "The company has really grown toward Chris," Bewkes told reporters.

Supporters inside of HBO believed Albrecht's education in comedy clubs would help him navigate the growing business challenges facing the company, as the internet continued to grow in importance. If comedy taught you anything, it was how to take deliberate risks repeatedly, when others were hanging back.

"In business and creativity there is no safety in the pack," says Zlotnik. "The value creation is in doing things differently. I picked something up from the comedy world, which I call 'calculated boundary transgressions.' If you fall below the margin in comedy, you're banal, commonplace. You're not funny. If you go too far, you're avant garde or overly intellectual. That's not funny either. Comedians acquire a sense of how to target that commercial range effectively. It takes a certain kind of intrepid personality to be able to break the bonds of conventionality."

Not long after Albrecht took over, HBO found itself coping with an unpleasant attack from its top star. That spring, *The Sopranos* was about to start shooting new episodes for its coming fifth season, a huge undertaking with thousands of moving pieces and a lot at stake.

On March 6, 2003, just three weeks before filming was scheduled to begin, James Gandolfini filed a lawsuit against HBO in California Superior Court, seeking to nullify his employment contract with the network. Gandolfini's lawyer, Martin Singer, suggested to reporters that unless HBO gave Gandolfini a significant raise, he was done playing Tony Soprano.

Executives at HBO were floored. In the fall of 2000, Gandolfini had signed a contract that would pay him $10 million for two seasons of work, at roughly $400,000 per episode, and HBO was preparing to give their star actor another bump up in pay. The lawsuit, filed in the middle of active negotiations, took them by surprise.

Suddenly, HBO's hit show was hanging in limbo.

In truth, it wasn't the first time that Gandolfini had held up production of the show. Since first slipping behind the wheel of Tony Soprano's Chevy Suburban and donning his signature bathrobe four years earlier, Gandolfini had occasionally struggled with the pressure of playing such a gloomy, exasperated, barbaric human. It was a taxing role. When the series was shooting, the days and nights on set were long, intense, and emotional. To channel Tony's incandescent rage and resentments, Gandolfini would have to work himself up into an emotionally agitated state. Coming back down wasn't easy.

Off set, the job was taking a toll. The popularity of the show had made Gandolfini famous. Wherever he went, strangers took the opportunity to cat-call *Tony effing Soprano! Yo, Mr. Bada Bing!* In 2002, Gandolfini and his wife filed for divorce. It was a messy split, and unsavory details of his personal life had leaked into the press, including news that several years earlier he had undergone treatment for cocaine and alcohol abuse.

Several times during the first four seasons of *The Sopranos*, Gandolfini had gone unexpectedly missing from the set, disrupting the complex choreography of a series in which every extra hour in production cost large sums of money. Once, in 2002, Gandolfini had disappeared with no warning for nearly four days, causing a panic among his friends and colleagues, before finally showing up at a random beauty salon in Brooklyn.

Now, Gandolfini was threatening to wander off again—maybe, this time, for good.

Lawyers for HBO responded to Gandolfini's suit by calling it "frivolous, preposterous, and insane" and filing a $100 million countersuit. About a week later, Gandolfini backed down, ending his litigation and allowing production to begin on the fifth season of *The Sopranos*.

David Chase says that in retrospect he'd been concerned, in his role as the show's executive producer, that Gandolfini's holdout might bring about a sudden, premature end to *The Sopranos*. But at the same time, he'd felt at peace with his creation's possible demise. His ambivalence, Chase recalls, was something he'd cultivated since the beginning for strategic purposes.

"The reason I maintained that attitude was so that I could not be bullied or coerced into doing artistic things that I didn't want to do," Chase said. "And if anybody wanted to cancel the show, that was okay with me. That's how I felt. If it goes, then finally, finally I can get on with my movie career, which like an idiot I'd been postponing for decades."

CHAPTER 12

Novel Reckonings

In the early 2000s, HBO began developing an original movie about Donald Trump. The project came to HBO via Jeffrey Auerbach, a media executive who had done stints working for the Philadelphia Eagles, Hearst Entertainment, and Sony Entertainment Pictures.

The idea was to focus on the epic battle that Trump had waged in the 1990s against rival casino owner Steve Wynn over control of an undeveloped property in Atlantic City. Wynn wanted to turn the site, formerly occupied by the city's dump, into a resort. Trump wanted it for a golf course. Much litigation, backstabbing, and name-calling ensued.

At HBO, Kary Antholis, a programming executive on the West Coast, began actively shepherding the project, to be entitled *Trump vs. Wynn*, toward production. In late 2003, Danny DeVito signed on to direct the movie, and a script written by Rick Cleveland, the supervising producer of *Six Feet Under,* took shape. To conduct research, DeVito and Antholis took a trip together to Atlantic City, staying at the Borgata and catching some shows.

When Donald Trump found out about the movie and its unflattering portrait of him as a shoddy businessman, his lawyers sent a letter to HBO threatening to sue. "HBO, to my wonderment and pleasure, nicely said, 'fuck off,'" Auerbach recalls.

The movie went into preproduction. The producers hired a crew, set up offices, and started making casting decisions. In addition to directing, De-Vito would play the role of a crooked private detective who gets caught with a wiretap hidden in his jockstrap. DeVito's then wife, Rhea Perlman, signed on to play a supporting role as well. The biggest debate was over who would play Trump.

"I want to be played by a very handsome, very brilliant person," Trump told the *New York Post*, while continuing behind the scenes to try to get the movie killed.

Before long, HBO homed in on Christopher Walken to play Trump and Harvey Keitel to play Wynn. Each would be paid $1 million—a hefty payday by the standards of TV movies. Antholis recalls that on the morning HBO was set to make the offers, he called DeVito to talk things over. But DeVito had some bad news. The night before, he and Perlman had broken bread with Trump. At some point during the dinner, DeVito had decided to back out.

"You know, Kary, I'd love to work with you," Antholis recalls DeVito telling him. "Call me the next time you need a director for a movie that's about dead people."

"Trump did his thing," Auerbach says.

Without DeVito, the project fell apart. "Kary and I always laugh," Auerbach says. "We realize we could have saved America if we'd just made that fucking movie and people saw who Donald really was."

In the fall of 2003, HBO executives watched closely as one of their rivals in network television got caught in a political melee. That November, CBS was scheduled to air *The Reagans*, an original docudrama starring James Brolin as President Ronald Reagan and Judy Davis as his wife, Nancy.

But before the made-for-TV movie could air, conservative cultural critics got their hands on the script and went berserk. The movie's portrayal of the Reagan family, they insisted, was biased and unfair. They took particular issue with the film's portrayal of President Reagan's uncaring response to the AIDS crisis, zeroing in on one scene, in particular, in which Reagan responds to the public health threat by saying, "They that live in sin shall die in sin." Never happened, the conservatives hollered. Total liberal fabrication.

In response, the film's producers acknowledged that Reagan had never said those exact words but insisted it was beside the point. The line, they argued, accurately captured the spirit of Reagan's dismissive reaction to the AIDS crisis and was well within the rules of the docudrama format.

In the face of the criticism, Les Moonves, the chairman of CBS, buckled. He ordered a last-minute reworking of the script, which removed the controversial line. On November 4, he announced that CBS was pulling the movie entirely. In a statement, CBS noted that the movie "does not present a balanced portrayal of the Reagans."

Later, CBS sold the rights to the movie to its corporate siblings at Showtime.

The entertainment industry watched Moonves's capitulation play out with a mix of embarrassment, horror, and resignation. The unwillingness to support a strong point of view was exactly why programming about politically and socially charged issues was so maddeningly rare on broadcast TV—and why such material had almost entirely migrated to HBO. To air such projects you needed a backbone.

The timing of CBS's debacle couldn't have been any better for HBO.

Following a grueling year of production, the network was just getting ready to premiere a $62 million adaptation of Tony Kushner's Pulitzer Prize–winning play, *Angels in America*. The six-part miniseries was directed by film and theater luminary Mike Nichols and featured an all-star cast, including Meryl Streep, Mary-Louise Parker, Emma Thompson, Patrick Wilson, and Jeffrey Wright. Al Pacino was cast as Roy Cohn, the closeted, gay Republican strategist (and recurring fixture in various HBO productions).

The miniseries, just like its source material, offered a searing portrait of the Reagan administration's response to the plight of AIDS. But unlike CBS, HBO was well prepared to deal with any preemptive attacks on the veracity of its program. The network was eager to move on from the earlier embarrassing imbroglio over *A Bright Shining Lie*. This time, in the weeks leading up to the premiere, prominent liberal voices in the media came out early touting the authenticity of HBO's adaptation.

"How much of this really happened and how much is fantasy?" Frank

Rich, the venerated progressive political columnist and theater critic, wrote in the *New York Times*. "Mr. Kushner is not making a historical documentary, or practicing journalism, any more than those behind *The Reagans* were. Whatever his script's fictions, it accurately conveys the rancid hypocrisy among powerful closeted gay Republicans in Washington as AIDS spiraled."

"*Angels* is the most powerful screen adaptation of a major American play since Elia Kazan's *Streetcar Named Desire* more than a half-century ago," Rich added. "Threats of a boycott against a channel soon to unveil a new season of *The Sopranos* will go nowhere."

In December, HBO began airing *Angels in America*, a transfixing blend of biblical metaphors, social commentary, and psychological surrealism. With a plague sweeping the land, Prior Walter (Justin Kirk), a thirty-one-year-old gay man from a Waspy, aristocratic family, is dying of AIDS. His suffering is exacerbated by loneliness and heartache. His boyfriend, Louis Ironson (Ben Shenkman), can't cope with the specter of death and has abandoned him.

Later, Roy Cohn is lying in a hospital, dying of AIDS. He has used his clout with the Reagan administration to cut in line and secure a large batch of the experimental drug azidothymidine. Cohn keeps his voluminous stash of the drug locked in a refrigerator next to his bed. His nurse, Belize (Jeffrey Wright), admonishes him for corralling more of the drug than he can possibly use while thousands of others are dying in need of it. "Look at you, the dragon, atop the golden hoard," he says. "It isn't fair, is it?"

"No," Cohn says. "But as Jimmy Carter said, neither is life."

Angels in America became a significant moment for the network. Before the idea was scrapped, the adaptation was originally supposed to be a two-part Robert Altman film for New Line Cinema. When it fell apart, HBO Films chief Colin Callender snatched it up and convinced Nichols to direct his first movie for television.

Bringing in Mike Nichols, says Richard Plepler, was a "major inflection point" for the network. "To me, that was an apotheosis," he says. "It was a moment when perhaps the greatest legendary auteur put his imprimatur on HBO just as we were already leaning into being a talent-friendly environment. Just by Mike being there, it said HBO was a special place. It was a crucial moment."

• • •

IN THE SIX YEARS SINCE ITS DEBUT, *Sex and the City* had grown into a cultural phenomenon, altering women's fashion in America, transforming brands like Manolo Blahnik and Jimmy Choo into household names, spawning bus tours of Manhattan, touching off an urban cupcake revival, rousing the cosmopolitan from the cocktail graveyard, and giving rise to a cottage industry of academic papers dissecting what the series revealed about the state of American feminism.

On the night of February 22, 2004, *Sex and the City* aired its final episode. Carrie has quit her job, left her friends, and moved to Paris to be with her boyfriend, Aleksandr Petrovsky (Mikhail Baryshnikov), a renowned Russian artist. Samantha is undergoing chemotherapy for breast cancer and has lost her legendary sex drive. Charlotte and her husband, Harry (Evan Handler), are struggling through fertility issues. And Miranda is worrying about her boyfriend Steve's mother, who is showing signs of dementia.

Just as it seems their lives are spinning away from each other in the hollow doldrums of middle age, the heroines are pulled back together to share their latest triumphs and sorrows one more time over brunch. In the end, Charlotte adopts a baby from China, Miranda rescues Steve's mother from eating moldy pizza out of a garbage can in Brooklyn, and the thundering horsepower of Samantha's libido is restored to good health. With a vase of flowers at her bedside table, she rides off into the sunset, straddled atop her fashion model boyfriend, Smith, randily ever after.

Across the Atlantic, following a lover's quarrel in a Parisian hotel room, Carrie breaks up with Petrovsky. Moments later, she stumbles into her commitment-phobic ex-boyfriend, Big (Chris Noth), in the lobby. After years of yo-yoing back and forth, the couple reconciles again, this time for good. Then Carrie makes one last defining life choice. She decides to get back together with the show's other true love. "I miss New York," she tells Big. "Take me home."

Some 10.6 million people watched the episode, the most in *Sex and the City*'s history, setting a new record for an HBO season finale. Among eighteen-to-thirty-four-year-old women, HBO beat out everything on broadcast television during the time slot, despite being in only 30 percent of the nation's homes.

Afterward, members of the series took a victory lap. Sarah Jessica Parker appeared on CNN's *Larry King Live* and explained to viewers that they'd actually shot two other possible endings for the series. One, in which Carrie reconciles with Petrovsky, not Big; and another, in which she ends the series estranged from all her suitors, single yet again for television eternity. Parker said she was happy with how things turned out. "I feel like Carrie and Big triumphed on Sunday," she said.

Not everyone was thrilled. To some viewers, it felt like an oddly conventional denouement for a show about independent women not looking to define themselves by a man. Among the detractors was Darren Star, the show's creator. By the final season, he was no longer writing episodes—years earlier, he had left the show, vowing not to interfere with the writers he had turned it over to. But given the opportunity, he says, he would have done it differently.

"I think the show ultimately betrayed what it was about, which was that women don't ultimately find happiness from marriage," he said years later. "Not that they can't. But the show initially was going off script from the romantic comedies that had come before it. That's what had made women so attached. At the end, it became a conventional romantic comedy."

The series proved to be an unfortunate throwback in another way too. While *Sex and the City* would become one of the most lucrative franchises in HBO's history, its vast financial windfalls largely eluded the woman who conceived it. Candace Bushnell's original deal with Star was for roughly one hundred thousand dollars. In retrospect, she says, the contractual language was vague and her equity on the back end, where *Sex and the City* raked in millions of dollars in merchandising and licensing fees, was minimal. HBO's coffers were rewarded handsomely. She was not. "It was a bad deal," Bushnell says.

On its way out, *Sex and the City* and HBO enjoyed one more moment in the limelight. On the night of Sunday, September 19, 2004, HBO ruled over the Primetime Emmy Awards like never before. Garry Shandling, the former face of HBO comedy, hosted the ceremonies inside the Shrine Auditorium in Los Angeles.

With more than ten million viewers watching from home, Shandling made fun of the brutes and sluggards in the TV industry for their growing reliance on reality television competitions to the detriment of scripted narratives. "When I see a television commercial come on, I think, thank God, professional actors in a story," he said.

By the end of the night, HBO had grabbed sixteen awards, more than double the haul of any other network. For the first time, *The Sopranos* won for Best Drama. Terence Winter—just a few years after crafting lines for Flipper—picked up a trophy for his savage, funny writing on the HBO show. Two of its cast members, Michael Imperioli, who plays Tony's wastrel cousin, Christopher Moltisanti, and Drea de Matteo, who plays Christopher's ill-treated girlfriend, Adriana La Cerva, were awarded for their supporting roles.

The night's biggest winner was *Angels in America*, which received the most accolades, winning eleven total Emmys, a record, including best miniseries; Lead Actor (Al Pacino), Lead Actress (Meryl Streep), Supporting Actor (Jeffrey Wright), Supporting Actress (Mary-Louise Parker), and Outstanding Directing (Mike Nichols).

And, finally, after several past nominations, Sarah Jessica Parker won for Outstanding Lead Actress in a Comedy Series. Parker smooched her husband, Matthew Broderick, climbed onstage, and rattled off a long list of thanks to her colleagues on *Sex and the City*, including Michael Patrick King, a veteran writer who had assumed showrunning duties after Star backed away. "It's a glorious finish to a journey of a lifetime," Parker said.

For those who had been with the network since the beginning, it was an amazing spectacle. HBO had come a long way from *Disco Beaver from Outer Space* and "*Fuck a Stranger, Then Die.*"

"It sort of was like, okay, we can run with the big boys," Carolyn Strauss recalls. "It was just so amazing in terms of the television landscape, where the networks were so dominant. And it was sort of barging into the castle. It was a major, major thing."

The one HBO show that continued to be overlooked by the Television Academy, in spite of its critical acclaim, was *The Wire*. Since its debut, the series had attracted a slim but impassioned fan base. It was particularly popular with critics, journalists, and academics who generated a considerable amount of free press for HBO and routinely referred to the show by its prevailing epithet: *Dickensian*. More than a decade after Michael Fuchs had proclaimed that HBO would become the Charles Dickens of cable TV, it was *The Wire* that, in the eyes of many reviewers, had come closest to achieving the goal.

Even so, over the course of its six-year run, the series would pick up no major Emmy Awards for acting, directing, or writing—a snub that would go on to rankle supporters of the show and raise questions about potential racial bias against *The Wire*'s majority Black cast. "It's like them never giving a Nobel Prize to Tolstoy," Jacob Weisberg, the former editor of *Slate* would later say. "It doesn't make Tolstoy look bad, it makes the Nobel Prize look bad."

• • •

IN DECEMBER 2004, David Simon's crime series wrapped up its third season, which culminated with the dramatic death of a much-adored character. In the season finale, Stringer Bell, the scrupulous drug dealer, who is on the cusp of transforming into a legitimate real estate developer, is shot to death. The ultimate Baltimorean renovation project would go unfinished.

To help build out the chapters of his "visual novel" and try to avoid some of the clichés and bad habits of network TV, Simon had stacked his writers' room with other ex-journalists from the *Baltimore Sun* and with accomplished, literary crime novelists, including George Pelecanos (*The Sweet Forever*), Richard Price (*Clockers*), and Dennis Lehane (*Mystic River*).

Over time, the fresh perspectives had helped Simon keep true to his promise in his original memo to Albrecht and Strauss. *The Wire* was a cop show that broke with many of the genre's conventions. But in spite of the novelty, only a small number of people were tuning in.

Throughout its third season in the fall of 2004, *The Wire* was getting clobbered on Sunday nights, in part by ABC's *Desperate Housewives*, a soapish, serialized drama featuring an ensemble cast of dysfunctional characters. Having watched HBO's aggressive move into Sunday nights, the broadcast networks had eventually counterattacked. Marc Cherry, the creator of *Desperate Housewives*, said the show was heavily influenced by *Sex and the City* and *Six Feet Under*. Before selling it to ABC, Cherry had even pitched the idea to Albrecht and Strauss, who had passed. "It's the network version of what an HBO show is," Cherry said.

Losing to a broadcast version of an HBO reject was not a comfortable position, and following Stringer Bell's dramatic demise, the future of *The Wire* looked uncertain. In January 2005, at the annual Television Critics Association meeting in Los Angeles, reporters pressed Albrecht on whether the series would be renewed for additional seasons. Albrecht shrugged. "I have received a telegram from every viewer of *The Wire*," he told the audience. "All 250 of them."

Shortly thereafter, Albrecht made up his mind. He told Simon that the show was over. Whatever Simon wanted to do next, HBO would happily take it.

But Simon didn't want to let go of *The Wire* just yet. He asked Albrecht and Strauss for one final opportunity to make his case about why the show should keep going. They agreed to hear him out. Simon went to Los Angeles and explained in the meeting how in the fourth season, the series would follow a group of middle-school students as they are pulled into life on the street. The fifth season would introduce characters from *The Baltimore Sun* while focusing on the media's complicity in America's postindustrial decline.

As Simon excitedly pored over the potential storylines, Albrecht came around. Why not? *The Wire* could have two more seasons, he decided. Afterward, Strauss told Simon she was amazed. His un-cop show had been uncanceled. "I've never seen that happen," she told him.

That so many critics loved *The Wire* was a crucial factor in HBO's final calculus—it always was. Up close, watching this with amazement, was Casey Bloys, a placid, fresh-faced HBO staffer with an easygoing manner, who was new to the network and still astounded by how different the HBO mindset was from that of broadcast television. Bloys, who hailed from a Quaker-rich region of pastoral Pennsylvania, had joined HBO the previous year, 2004, from a production studio owned by Disney that supplied series to ABC. There, his colleagues had been completely indifferent to reviewers. "If we got, like, a B in *Entertainment Weekly*, we would go, 'Oh my God, that's great,'" Bloys says.

Now at HBO, Bloys was struck by his bosses' near obsession with critics.

"What was crazy was, I remember when I got to HBO, in meetings, they would talk about the critics, they knew all the critics, and they would say, 'Oh, Alessandra Stanley at the *New York Times*, she's not going to like this' or 'Robert Bianco from *USA Today*, this is the kind of show he's going to hate,'" he says. "I remember thinking, wow, how do they know all these critics and their rhythms and what they like and what they don't like?"

As he rose through the ranks, Bloys assimilated such lessons. In just a few years' time, his own taste would come to have a major impact not just on HBO, but on the entire television industry.

While HBO was breathing new life into *The Wire*, another strongly reviewed HBO series was drawing to a close. In the summer of 2005, HBO began airing the fifth and final season of *Six Feet Under*. As always, the inescapability of death remained the show's foremost theme. With a handful of episodes left to go, Nate Fisher, the family's charming elder son, drops dead after a rousing bout of adulterous sex, leaving the Fisher tribe once again bereaved.

In the final scene of the series, Claire Fisher gets behind the wheel of a blue Prius and heads east, toward New York City, embarking on her career as an artist, her whole life in front of her. With the ghostly image of her brother Nate disappearing in her side mirror, she pulls onto the highway. As the roadside landscape flies by her, the show spins forward into the future, showing snippets of the lives of the Fisher clan as they continue to age, ma-

ture, marry, love, prosper and, ultimately, die: in a hospital bed, in the back
of an armored truck, at a picnic, on a cruise ship, on a couch, on a bed.

Ball's juxtaposition of the open road at the start of adulthood and the
closing eulogies at its end, the simultaneous feeling of life's expansiveness
and brevity, of one's fate expanding and slamming shut, made for the most
memorable final chapter in HBO's canon to date. "It just felt right," Ball
says. "This is a show about the fact that everybody is going to die. But at the
same time, people live and embark on new adventures. They both exist. Those
are both truths."

The emotional ending generated a deluge of attention. "The whole overwrought montage was at least half ludicrous, and almost half lovely," Virginia Heffernan wrote in the *New York Times*. "But that precious ratio—which
recalls the balance of silliness and beauty in Trollope and some of Hardy—
has always been the show's strong suit, a 19th-century tone ingeniously invented and confidently maintained over five seasons."

Ball was hardly the only HBO creator being judged by critics in literary terms and sized up against great novelists from the past. By the mid-
2000s, HBO had successfully ushered in a distinctly new epoch of American
storytelling—the era of the cable TV auteur. Like nineteenth century British novelists or 1970s New Hollywood directors, the cable TV auteur became
in the 2000s a revered figure in popular culture, lionized by the press, piled
into syllabi by academia, and readily identifiable by certain distinguishing
traits. He was brilliant, garrulous, irascible, literary, foul-mouthed, impassioned, lyrical, excessive, vengeful, self-righteous, and brimming with arcana.
He was not just exquisitely good at making TV, but also at talking about it.
And, though it was never explicitly stated, he was always a *he*.

HBO's executive ranks were overwhelmingly white and male, and the
network would not air a major drama from a female creator for several more
years. Series by persons of color were even more rare. In 2014, the *Huffington
Post* conducted a study that found that across HBO's entire history "just
under 8 percent of HBO's original dramas and miniseries came from women,
and 2.6 percent came from people of color."

HBO's press team went out of its way to play up the authorship of its new shows, orchestrating extensive profiles of its series' creators by a select group of top magazine and newspaper writers. Gradually, HBO came to be known not just as a network or a business, or an entertainment brand, but as a club of auteurs whose names any reasonably cultured person could rattle off at a cocktail party with the ease of naming NFL quarterbacks or celebrity chefs. Tom Fontana. David Chase. David Simon. Alan Ball. David Milch.

• • •

MILCH WAS THE CREATOR OF *DEADWOOD,* a character-driven western which would run on HBO for thirty-six episodes from 2004 to 2006. Initially, Milch had conceived the show as something else entirely. When he'd first met with Albrecht and Strauss, he pitched them not on a western but rather on a series about ancient Rome at the time of Jesus, and how the symbol of the Cross came to be "the organizing principle for that society." The HBO executives told him terrific, but unfortunately they already had a Roman series in development. "I said, 'don't go anywhere, I've got an even better idea,'" Milch later recalled. "I made up essentially the same show except set in the Dakota territory. And instead of it being about the Cross it was about gold. They liked that."

Early on, *Deadwood* was hailed as HBO's next great contender for pop-culture predominance, potentially its next *Sopranos.* Although *Deadwood* would never achieve mass appeal at that level, it did attract a vehement following among a fair number of HBO subscribers and critics. Whereas *The Wire* was frequently tagged as Dickensian, *Deadwood* came to be commonly known as HBO's *Shakespearean* drama, thanks to its highly stylized language, elaborate soliloquies, and ornate, oratorical cursing.

"Oftentimes profanity is used to complete the metrics of a speech," Milch said. "It's a different thing to say, 'prick,' and to say 'fucking prick.' It has to do with rhythm. The audience will incorporate that intuition without it ever rising to the level of consciousness. . . . If the metrics of the profanity aren't right, it sounds stupid."

Set in 1876 in a mining camp in former Lakota territory that is not yet part of the United States, *Deadwood* tells the story of a fringe community in the shadows of the Black Hills, which is caught in the early, giddy days of a gold rush. Al Swearengen (Ian McShane), the ruthless owner of the Gem saloon and brothel, is the town's de facto boss. At the outset, Swearengen is profiting nicely by providing credit, whisky, card games, and prostitutes to the miners who are pouring in from around the country, hoping to get rich quick. The town has no sheriff, no official laws, and plenty of inebriated gunplay. Those who get killed are fed to the hogs. Soon, Swearengen is butting heads with Seth Bullock (Timothy Olyphant), a righteous former marshal from Montana who has arrived in Deadwood to open a hardware store. In addition to pickaxes and chamber pots, Bullock brings with him a muscular demand for basic morality and fair play. Much perturbation and bloodshed follow.

"The idea of how people comport themselves in the absence of any governing principle is fundamental," Milch told reporters on the eve of the series' debut. "For me, it was an opportunity to reenact original sin in the American experience."

Over time, thanks to a bunch of beguiling profiles, Milch emerged as the ur-specimen of the HBO type. He was an auteur's auteur. A literary prodigy at Yale University, a mentee of Robert Penn Warren, the Pulitzer Prize–winning author of *All the King's Men*, Milch attended the Iowa Writers' Workshop, where he studied under the novelist Richard Yates, got sozzled with Kurt Vonnegut, and began publishing works of fiction and literary criticism. In the 1980s, he abandoned academia for commercial television.

"There was a tremendous appeal to making a living," Milch said.

Within a few years, he grew into one of the most coveted, temperamental, and highly paid TV writers in the industry, penning numerous award-winning episodes for *Hill Street Blues* and *NYPD Blue*. He was also a voracious addict, prone to binges of gambling, alcohol, and heroin. He had a knack for crafting memorably loathsome, fundamentally abusive characters who also suffered from occasional bouts of charitability and humanity. "Even a shitbird is capable of isolated, constructive gestures," Milch said. "None of us has a clean journey."

His creation of *Deadwood* for HBO solidified Milch's standing in the new canon of serialized TV virtuosos—TV writers capable of diving into primordial undercurrents of humanity and reemerging with spellbinding tales of penitence and debauchery. "Any show which is ambitious is meant to transcend itself, to transcend its own conventions," Milch said. "To transcend—as opposed to negate or refute. So, although a show has a marshal, and the bartender, and so on, there's always the feeling that something else and more is going on."

Years later, Milch would strike an exclusive deal with the estate of William Faulkner to turn the Nobel laureate's work into film and television projects.

In a 2005 profile in the *New Yorker*, Mark Singer described the highly ritualized process by which Milch composed scripts for HBO. Inside a trailer at the Melody Ranch Studios in Santa Clarita, Milch would recline on the floor surrounded by a group of interns and staff writers. Then without laying so much as a finger on a computer, Milch would hold forth on the *Deadwood* universe, its historical context, characters, narrative subtext, and plot, while his hushed staff would listen to and transcribe his every word.

"Milch has a prodigious memory, which means that these densely layered observations are at the disposal of his consciousness, as well as his unconscious, when he finally sits down, or lies down, to write," Singer noted. "After witnessing this process on several occasions—the ambience in the room seems equal parts master class and séance—the comparison that strikes me as most apt is channelling. The only sounds are the hum of an air-conditioner and Milch's voice, or, more precisely, the voices of his characters speaking through him."

Milch could rhapsodize about writing for cable TV like a mystic inviting disciples into a sacred liturgy. "You know, the chemist Friedrich August Kekule worked for twenty years trying to figure out the structure of the benzene ring, and he couldn't do it," said Milch. "And then one night he was sleeping and he had a vision of a snake swallowing its tail. So he told his students about it and they said, 'Not bad, you go to sleep and you wake up with that.' And he said, 'Visions come to prepared spirits.'"

On Sunday nights in the fall of 2006, HBO began airing the fourth season of *The Wire*. In one early scene, a group of adolescent boys crouch in an alleyway and use a cardboard box and some bread crumbs to try to capture a white homing pigeon. They've heard that the worker bird could fetch three to four hundred dollars from the new king of the Baltimore drug trade, Marlo Stanfield (Jamie Hector), who collects such prized specimens.

Stanfield is a ruthlessly efficient, cold-minded, scar-faced leader who is quick to knock off his rivals and grab territory from weaker crews. His only apparent sign of humanity is his coop full of pigeons, which he cares for and looks after lovingly.

Throughout the fourth season, the group of boys find themselves pulled between typical childhood pursuits, like going to middle school and playing video games, and the lure of starting their careers in the drug trade. Stanfield's rival for their attention is a former police detective turned middle-school teacher named Roland Pryzbylewski (Jim True-Frost), who is earnestly trying to keep the youngsters in school and off the streets.

The arrival of yet another ultraviolent villain with a weak spot for birds called to mind HBO's other beloved antiheroes, Mike Tyson and Tony Soprano. But Simon says the connection was unintentional—just another thematic coincidence.

The scene of the boys trying to trap a valuable worker pigeon, says Simon, was a nod to the broader conflict about to play out over the season's thirteen episodes, setting up Marlo to be the competing mentor to Pryzbylewski. "It was deliberate and thematic," says Simon. "The idea is that lessons are taught. Season four is about people being educated for their role in a fucked-up, neoliberal, unbridled capitalistic world."

While Emmy Awards would continue to elude *The Wire*, a few years later, in 2010, Simon would be honored with a prestigious MacArthur Fellowship. Over the years, the so-called genius awards had been conferred on a pantheon of esteemed poets, essayists, novelists, literary critics, linguists, playwrights—and, with Simon, for the first time, a writer for HBO.

Thanks to its growing renown, by the mid-2000s, HBO had emerged as a prestigious beacon in American culture, the kind of place which could have its pick of the many young, aspirational go-getters throwing themselves at HBO's doorstep, hungry to leave their mark. But the days of twentysomething executives joining HBO right out of college or graduate school and suddenly being thrust into high-flying, fast-paced managerial roles were long gone. HBO's formative days as a happy-go-lucky start-up were, by now, a distant memory.

Instead, newcomers found themselves navigating something entirely different—a rigid environment in which the power structure could feel ancient, immovable, and set in stone. Seemingly all of HBO's top leaders in sports, in marketing, in programming, in sales, were middle-aged folks who'd spent the bulk of their careers fighting on behalf of HBO and were now basking in the comforts and rewards of their success.

Some new arrivals to HBO looked around and feared there wasn't much room left to grow at the network. "No one ever got promoted because no one ever went anywhere," says a former HBO staffer. "HR had a term for anyone who had been there for over ten years: The Elders. You had to get along with the Elders. Otherwise, you were never going to get anything done."

CHAPTER 13

Internet PTSD

In early 2006, a group of executives in HBO's Los Angeles office had an idea. Clearly, HBO should buy Netflix.

In the eight years since launching, Reed Hastings and Marc Randolph's bet on internet-optimized DVD rentals was looking increasingly prescient. From next to nothing, the DVD industry had since ballooned into a thriving market with more than $12 billion in annual rentals and sales in the United States. Netflix had grown in tandem, going public on the Nasdaq exchange in 2002, turning its first annual profit the following year, and continuously refining its algorithms to better match customers with movies to watch based on their prior choices. The company ended 2005 with 4.2 million paying subscribers.

Along the way, Hastings had taken over as CEO, and the expanding company had moved into new, more spacious offices in Los Gatos, California, a town in the temperate foothills of the Santa Cruz Mountains. Hastings, who had spent two formative years in the 1980s volunteering with the Peace Corps in Swaziland, saw Netflix's future through a missionary lens. It was not just an online DVD rental store, in his eyes, but also a laboratory of twenty-first-century modes of production, one that ought to be studied, codified, and taught to future business leaders.

Hastings would go on several years later, in 2009, to distill his philosophy into something called the "Netflix Culture Deck." The widely circulated presentation, consisting of over 120 slides, offered readers a series of earnest slogans ("Values are what we value") and orotund prescriptions ("Be wary of efficiency optimizations that increase complexity and rigidity"). Tech boosters would hail it as an "impactful" treatise, a kind of slideshow *Das Kapital* for the algorithmic age.

Workplace revolutions aside, Netflix still faced plenty of more immediate challenges. At the start of 2006, the company was busy fending off a territorial incursion from Blockbuster, the formidable, saber-toothed ruler of the VHS-rental industry. Two years earlier, Blockbuster had launched its own DVD-by-mail subscription service, one that was remarkably similar to Netflix's, only cheaper. Since then, the competition between the two companies had grown fiercer. With other large tech companies including Amazon and Apple preparing to enter the TV and movie downloading business, investors were growing fretful. Netflix looked vulnerable.

HBO's West Coast business team watched all this with growing interest. By 2006, they were convinced there might be an opportunity to jump in and buy the California upstart. On paper, the acquisition made perfect sense. HBO was the dominant player in delivering popular movies, ad free, over cable and satellite, while Netflix remained the market leader in DVDs selected via the internet and distributed by mail. Together, HBO and Netflix would control a huge swath of how consumers saw Hollywood movies following their initial release in theaters, giving HBO even greater leverage over movie studios in the secondary markets.

The deal would give Netflix more muscle to wrestle Blockbuster into submission. It would also help HBO build a direct relationship with customers that, for once, didn't depend on the cable and satellite distributors.

Following a promotion, Carmi Zlotnik was now overseeing a newly formed business development team in Los Angeles that was devoted to figuring out how HBO could prosper on the web. Obviously, AOL wasn't the answer. There had to be a better way to position HBO's business for the future.

"We'd been toying with how to do that," Zlotnik recalls. "The first proposal was: *Let's just go buy Netflix.* Eventually our paths are going to converge. We need to get to the internet and so do they."

In September 2006, John Penney, a business development executive who'd recently come on board at HBO, joining Zlotnik's team in L.A., put the finishing touches on a 35-page pitch deck, explaining why HBO should make the acquisition. The proposal was entitled "Project 'Sneaker Net' HBO + Netflix." It laid out a straightforward rationale for the deal.

The combination of HBO with Netflix, the document explained, would help "overcome strategic threats" to both companies from a rapidly changing and increasingly cluttered home entertainment market. It would generate "many strategic and financial benefits" by creating a service uniquely positioned to provide "content delivery across all DVD and subscription TV windows." And it would "vault Time Warner to a new level of direct-to-consumer engagement" via a "stickier," more robust subscription product.

In big prominent type, the first page of the document was marked "CONFIDENTIAL."

At the time of Penney's proposal, Netflix was valued at roughly $1.4 billion—a reasonable-size company for Time Warner to target. Despite all its problems, HBO's parent company, which had officially dropped AOL from its name 2003, was still valued at roughly $70 billion, and there was an investment fund already set up within Time Warner for the specific goal of targeting next-generation entertainment and technology businesses: companies just like Netflix. An acquisition seemed well within reason.

That fall, Penney and Zlotnik went to New York to present the idea to a contingent of East Coast HBO leaders. Inside the company boardroom, they sat down with a group that included HBO's chief operating officer, Bill Nelson, head of marketing, Eric Kessler, and Harold Akselrad, HBO's general counsel.

Penney began explaining how the acquisition of Netflix would benefit HBO and Time Warner. But he was quickly cut off. Nelson, Kessler, and Akselrad were not impressed. For years, they'd heard about the supposed wonders of AOL and the Shangri-la synergies of the web. It was all a bunch of claptrap.

Netflix, they argued, was a flash in the pan. It would likely implode under the pressure of its own rapid growth. Besides, investing in such a prominent tech company would be sure to upset their partners in cable and satellite distribution. It was too risky and not worth the inevitable headaches it would trigger.

"I didn't even get through the presentation," Penney says.

"It just felt like there were a bunch of people who were trying to manage for retirement," Zlotnik says. *"Let's not rock the boat."*

Penney and Zlotnik were disappointed. They believed Netflix's rapid growth, low subscriber churn, and high customer satisfaction were no fluke. With time, it would become clear that they were onto something. Over the next decade and a half, between 2006 and the fall of 2021, Netflix's market cap would soar from $1.4 billion to over $300 billion.

With Netflix off the table, the team in Los Angeles put their hope in plan B: going direct to consumer with an HBO-branded internet service of their own design. For years, HBO's in-house information technology team, under the leadership of chief information officer Michael Gabriel, had been working quietly and diligently to build a working prototype of an internet-delivered service that would be ready to flip on whenever the moment was right. Whatever HBO's business executives decided to do, Gabriel's team was ready to deliver.

Now, Jim Moloshok, a former Warner Bros. and Yahoo executive, working with Albrecht and Zlotnik in Los Angeles, wanted to turn the system on. At the time, Myspace was the biggest thing on the internet, and initially HBO's business team began referring to the nascent project as My HBO. Moloshok says the basic idea for My HBO was to make HBO feel as distinctive online as it did on TV—and to do so independently of the cable companies.

Moloshok and his team were already exploring different ways that HBO could distribute My HBO with a new set of partners outside the cable TV universe. They had begun talks with Amazon, which was in the process of building its own online home entertainment hub and was eager to include HBO's rich library of programming in the mix. Around the same time, according to Moloshok, HBO also reached an initial agreement with SanDisk, a large hardware manufacturer. Under the arrangement, says Moloshok, SanDisk's USB memory devices, which were then big sellers, would come preloaded with HBO software. It would be a fast and easy way of getting an HBO software application loaded onto people's home computers.

"You'd buy the USB stick and boom," Moloshok says. "You put it in your machine. It autoloads. For the first month, you get the service for free and we get your credit card number."

Underlying the strategy, he says, was Albrecht's growing wariness of HBO's historic distribution partners, particularly Comcast, the giant, voracious cable conglomerate based in Philadelphia. For decades, in order to pad their profits, cable companies had relied on selling HBO subscriptions to their customers. Every time a sale was made, HBO got its cut and so, too, did the cable company. But in recent years, those same companies had come up with other things to upsell to their customers: particularly phone lines and high-speed internet access. On those sales, the Comcasts of the world kept the whole fee. HBO took nothing.

It was just a matter of time, Albrecht believed, before the big cable companies started going out and buying content, sports, and movies. Eventually, they wouldn't need HBO at all. "In this business, nobody is our friend," Moloshok remembers Albrecht telling him. "But Comcast is our enemy."

The assessment was not commonly held elsewhere at HBO. Moloshok says that there was a growing schism between Albrecht's team in Los Angeles and the affiliate sales and marketing executives back in New York, who were wary of overly aggressive streaming ideas that might upset HBO's traditional partners in cable TV. By any measure, Comcast was HBO's biggest and richest client, accounting for nearly a quarter of HBO's total domestic subscription revenue.

Throughout 2006, meetings between the East and West Coast factions of HBO grew increasingly hostile. Among themselves, the West Coasters started jokingly calling their visits to the New York offices "sock parties." It was a reference to a type of hazing ritual in which a group of fraternity brothers would ambush a wayward member of their tribe and pummel them with

bars of soap stuffed in socks. It was a safe way of sending a painful message—
Get in line, bro—without leaving any outward signs of the beatdown.

Moloshok felt that the disastrous experience with AOL had left many
HBO business leaders suffering from a kind of internet PTSD. They'd been
told that the internet was the future, and instead they'd watched as their email
crashed, their stock in the company plummeted, and their savings shriveled.
Instead of retiring to Florida, they were still commuting into the HBO offices from their homes in the New York suburbs, staring down who knows
how many more bitter winters in the northeast. All because of the internet
assholes.

Among HBO sales and marketing folks, bashing the web had become a
kind of self-soothing. "A lot of people got very hurt," Moloshok says. "As a
result, there was a great resentment about AOL and the internet."

Not everybody's incentive was to think long term. The annual year-end
bonuses for many top executives at the network were tied, in part, to the number of HBO subscribers at big cable companies like Comcast. If those numbers went up, so did their compensation. Moloshok and others believed that
the sales and marketing folks in New York were protecting the status quo, in
part to protect their own personal compensation. "All they wanted to know
is what does this do for me?" Moloshok says. "And how long is it before I can
return to Boca Raton."

That fall, after months of simmering disputes, the dueling visions of
HBO's streaming future—going it alone on the internet versus going through
cable partners—finally came to a head. In late 2006, members of HBO's West
Coast team gathered in a conference room on the eighth floor of HBO's headquarters in New York to present a prototype of their new direct-to-consumer
streaming product, which thanks to the input of a focus group, had been
rechristened from My HBO to HBO GO.

What transpired was a sock party to remember.

At the meeting, division heads sat around a long central table, while
their deputies crowded around the edges of the room. Moloshok began his
presentation, but before he could get very far, all hell broke loose. Members
of HBO's affiliate sales division met his proposal with a forceful rebuttal.

Releasing a streaming product into the market without input from their distribution partners, they argued, would kneecap HBO's all-important relationship with cable and satellite companies. If a big company like Comcast got upset, they could immediately stop promoting HBO to their millions of customers. HBO's churn rate would soar, and subs would plummet overnight. Going "over the top" via the internet would jeopardize everything.

Moloshok kept trying to win over the room. The moment had come, he said, for HBO to establish a direct relationship with its consumers. HBO could control its own destiny. "Everybody in the so-called 'old guard' started yelling at me. *We can't do that. It's terrible. The internet is going to ruin us. Look at AOL!*" Moloshok recalls.

"I thought they were just going to riot," Zlotnik says. "They were convinced we were going to sink the entire business."

The discussion kept raging. Finally, Chris Albrecht had seen enough. He banged his hands loudly on the conference room table to silence the room. "*Listen,*" he said, "Jim Moloshok did not invent the internet. You can't blame him for its existence."

After the meeting ended, the skirmishes continued. "We fought it," recalls Steve Davidson, then head of sales for HBO, who'd spent many of his early years at the company handling its all-important relationship with Comcast. "We weren't ready to do it. It was premature by a few years. There wasn't any pathway. You're either in or you're out. We had four or five billion dollars' worth of domestic revenues on the table. If you want to put that at risk you'd better be sure if you go over the top what it's going to do to that subscription business. We weren't really sure."

HBO was, in a sense, caught in a trap of its own success. Its position in cable was just too strong and too lucrative to jeopardize by chasing the technology of an uncertain future. "We were in a classic innovator's dilemma," says Shelley Brindle, then a top sales and marketing executive at HBO.

On November 2, 2006, Moloshok and Albrecht were sitting at the Teterboro Airport in New Jersey waiting to board the HBO jet for a flight back to Los Angeles when news of their pending plans for HBO GO broke prematurely in *Businessweek*.

"If HBO takes on the internet presence expected in the coming months, it could cause no small dustup with some of HBO's biggest customers—namely the cable and satellite companies," the article reported. "HBO executives have been hashing out the details of what they will offer online, and a spokesman says no formal decision has been made."

Moloshok and the West Coast crew read the article with a sinking sense of betrayal. They felt sandbagged. They were hardly ready to discuss their plans with anyone outside the company. Now, everyone in the cable industry would lurch into high alert. "It was leaked because they wanted to kill it," Moloshok says.

Sure enough, when word got out, HBO's partners in the cable industry were not amused by HBO's secret effort to make an end run around them. A few weeks later, Moloshok recalls, he was curtly summoned to Philadelphia to make a presentation about HBO GO in front of top executives at Comcast. It was another tense, hostile affair. "It was like *show me what you're doing or we are going to shoot you,*" Moloshok says.

• • •

AS THE DEBATE over HBO's digital future raged inside of HBO, Netflix was charging forward with its own streaming plans. In January 2007, Netflix announced it would be launching a new product, called Watch Now, that would allow subscribers to stream movies and TV episodes instantly on their personal computers via the internet. At the start, the choices would be limited to about a thousand movies, a tiny selection compared with Netflix's DVD-by-mail catalogue, which included more than seventy thousand titles.

Reed Hastings noted that Netflix's DVD business, which was on the verge of delivering its billionth DVD by mail, would continue to dominate in the short term. Even so, Hastings was convinced that the instant gratification of streaming would eventually reshape the industry. In a demonstration for reporters, Hastings used the service to stream an obscure 2005 movie from New Zealand called *The World's Fastest Indian*, starring Anthony Hopkins as a heroic designer of experimental motorbikes. "This is a big moment for us," Hastings said.

While HBO was struggling internally to mount a viable streaming strategy for the future, the network was facing more immediate challenges. Many of the network's hit series were now either over—*Sex and the City*, *Oz*, *Deadwood*—or would soon be coming to an end: *The Sopranos*, *The Wire*.

The network's hot streak in developing new series had cooled considerably. Recently, several had premiered with lots of HBO-caliber hype only to fizzle. *Lucky Louie*, a sitcom created by and starring the comedian Louis C.K., as a mechanic at a muffler shop, lasted for a single, disappointing season. *The Comeback*, yet another HBO send-up of the entertainment industry, starring Lisa Kudrow, would eventually become a cult favorite but was a ratings disaster in 2005. It also was canceled after one season.

A handful of other HBO series, including *Big Love*, a drama starring Bill Paxton as the head of a polygamist Mormon family, and *Entourage* were connecting with fans—but the audiences were nothing in size compared to *The Sopranos*. There were ambitious series like *Rome* and *Carnivàle*, which cost a fortune and were expected to last at least five seasons. Both were canceled after two.

Where HBO's next blockbuster series might come from was unclear. As the final season of *The Sopranos* crept closer on the calendar, the need for HBO to come up with a new Zeitgeist-rattling series kept growing. But throughout pockets of the company, an air of midlife malaise had settled in, sapping away some of the urgency of HBO's formative years. "We were first to market. We had a first mover advantage. We were making money hand over foot," says a former HBO executive. "Quite frankly, we didn't have to try that hard."

Around Hollywood, there were growing murmurs that HBO was beginning to lose its competitive edge over its rivals. Showtime was airing buzzy series like *Weeds*, from an up-and-coming writer named Jenji Kohan, and *Dexter*, a series about a vigilante serial killer starring *Six Feet Under* alumnus Michael C. Hall. And FX, a network owned by Rupert Murdoch's media empire that was explicitly aiming to be the "HBO of basic cable," was building itself into a force with shows like *The Shield*, *Rescue Me*, and *Nip/Tuck*, a provocative drama from a writer named Ryan Murphy.

"They ran into a fallow period," says Bob Greenblatt, who ran Showtime from 2003 through 2010, speaking about HBO. "Each show seemed a little bit grander than the last. *Rome*, to me, was the ultimate overproduced, over-conceptualized idea. Before, there was no Showtime and no FX, who were now directly in the business of, 'Give us your HBO shows. We want those too.' There were suddenly more competitors, and I think they got a little too big for their britches just in terms of wanting to continue to top themselves."

HBO executives acknowledged that due to their recent success, the network's standing in Hollywood had inverted. No longer the upstarts, HBO was now the defending champion of home entertainment. "It's people hating the Yankees," Carolyn Strauss said. "It's human nature to root for the underdog."

In January 2007, HBO executives appeared at the annual Television Critics Association gathering in Pasadena, California. They talked up a bunch of new series that were in production and would be airing soon, including two promising dramas from female creators. Cynthia Mort, a former writer on *Roseanne*, would be delivering *Tell Me You Love Me,* a series about three couples seeking relationship help from a therapist. And Linda Bloodworth-Thomason, the creator of the hit CBS sitcom *Designing Women*, would be overseeing *12 Miles of Bad Road*, a drama set in Dallas, starring Lily Tomlin.

HBO also played up the potential of a new dramatic series, entitled *John from Cincinnati*, by its uberauteur, David Milch. A few months earlier, following the finale of its third season in August 2006, HBO had canceled Milch's *Deadwood*. Afterward, facing a shelling from its die-hard fan base, HBO quickly signed off on Milch's next project.

At the press conference in Pasadena, Milch described *John from Cincinnati*, which would be set in a Southern California beach town and revolve around a dysfunctional family of supremely talented, addiction-prone surfers. In front of the assembled reporters, Milch dropped references to Einstein, Stephen Hawking, William James, and Sigmund Freud. Though he had never surfed, Milch explained, he'd spent much of his life riding various waves of addiction to drugs, alcohol, and gambling. Addiction was a topic he knew intimately.

In order to get *John* ready to debut immediately after the final episode of *The Sopranos*, later that summer, the network was rushing it through production at warp speed. When reporters asked if that could potentially cause any issues, Milch acknowledged that it was going to be a big challenge to have the series ready in time.

"I've had seven angioplasties," Milch said. "There's plenty that can go wrong."

CHAPTER 14

A Desert Gale

Boxing euphoria was back.

In the spring of 2007, HBO was lining up a fight that rivaled the excitement of the network's 1980s boxing heyday. On May 5, at the MGM Grand in Las Vegas, Oscar De La Hoya, the handsome, sunny, thirty-four-year-old light-middleweight champion, would defend his WBC title against Floyd Mayweather Jr., a fierce competitor, on the rise and undefeated. When tickets first went on sale, they were gobbled up within three hours, generating some $19 million in revenue, a Las Vegas record. HBO would be carrying it live on pay-per-view.

To stoke the excitement, HBO announced that in the run-up to the showdown, it would be airing a four-part, all-access documentary series entitled *De La Hoya/Mayweather 24/7*. Since its early days, HBO Sports had previewed big fights with so-called countdown shows, which introduced the fighters with few frills and little in the way of narrative suspense. But this time around, the network decided to do something more adventurous.

HBO announced it would be giving *24/7* a prime slot in HBO's schedule. Three of the four episodes would air on successive Sunday nights, following *The Sopranos* and *Entourage*—essentially guaranteeing a large audience.

The final episode of the preview series would air on HBO on a Friday night, the day before the fight in Las Vegas.

To make *24/7*, HBO executives tapped Jason Hehir, a thirty-year-old producer for HBO Sports. Hehir was excited by the opportunity but also wary of the assignment. Since joining the network in 2005 as an entry-level producer with *On the Record with Bob Costas*, he found a creative environment that felt surprisingly inflexible. For years, HBO Sports had been cranking out award-winning Ken Burns–like documentaries. But to Hehir, the style of the films looked increasingly stale. He was not a huge admirer of how the Elders were running the division.

"HBO Sports internally was kind of the antithesis of HBO as a brand," Hehir says. "HBO as a brand was seen as edgy and progressive and at the forefront of creative and technological innovation. Whereas HBO Sports was pretty stodgy and stuck in its own ways."

But perhaps this time would be different, Hehir hoped. The setup looked promising. The actor Liev Schreiber, who provided the mesmerizing voice-over on several other HBO Sports programs, including *Hard Knocks*, the network's popular all-access series about life inside an NFL training camp, would serve as the narrator for *24/7*. "He was the ace up our sleeve," Hehir says. "We could have Liev read the phone book and it would sound like the Gettysburg Address."

With the fight approaching fast, HBO sent production crews to De La Hoya's training camp in Puerto Rico and Mayweather's facility in Las Vegas. Nothing went smoothly. Neither boxer was accustomed to being filmed so intimately, so close to a big fight. And Mayweather's world, in particular, was filled with acrimonious drama. A bitter family feud was playing out between Mayweather's father and his uncle, both former boxers, who were intent on training Mayweather junior but were not speaking with each other.

Several times, according to Hehir, members of Mayweather's team told the HBO filmmakers to turn off their cameras and hand over their tapes. Hehir resisted. If they had a problem, he told them, they could call his bosses at HBO Sports. Pretty soon, Hehir was summoned to a meeting with Ross

Greenburg, the head of the department, and given a stern talking-to. "Floyd was essentially an employee of HBO because they had just signed a multi-fight deal with him," Hehir says. "I was the expendable one in the equation. I learned that pretty fast."

Adding to the tensions, the turnaround time for 24/7 would be much faster than on typical HBO Sports documentaries. With the multimillion-dollar fight looming, the stakes were high. As the early footage poured in, says Hehir, he often didn't see eye to eye with his bosses on how they should tell the story.

One night in Las Vegas, during the run-up to the fight, HBO's crew was hanging out while Mayweather got his hair cut in his cavernous Las Vegas mansion. Suddenly, the rapper 50 Cent, wearing a custom hooded sweatshirt with his own face on it, rode into the room on a Segway. "He's the villain in rap music," said Mayweather, glancing over at 50 Cent puttering around in his 50 Cent outfit. "I'm the villain in boxing."

It was a surreal moment, perfectly encapsulating the celebrity-centric Las Vegas milieu that Mayweather inhabited. Hehir and his colleagues were excited about the clip, which they planned to use in the first episode. But Hehir says that when his boss, Rick Bernstein, a longtime veteran of the network, saw the first draft, there was a problem. According to Hehir, Bernstein didn't know who 50 Cent was and instructed Hehir to cut the scene. Hehir was flabbergasted. His team hastily compiled a dossier of magazine stories featuring the top-selling artist. Eventually, Bernstein relented. The Segway-riding rapper could stay in.

But the disagreements in the editing room didn't end there.

To quickly establish for viewers the fierce animosity that had been brewing for months between the two boxers, Hehir wanted to include a flurry of clips at the beginning of the first episode, in which Mayweather insulted De La Hoya. Again, his bosses told him to tone it down and remove several insults. Hehir protested. Finally, hours before the first episode aired, they reached a compromise. Hehir was allowed to restore one clip of Mayweather calling De La Hoya a "pussy."

When the ratings came in the following morning, everyone felt relieved.

Some 1.4 million households had watched *24/7*, and critics were buzzing about HBO's slick new reality show. "It's Mayweather's relationship with his family that makes the most compelling TV," the Associated Press reported. "They're the first family of boxing, but this family is more dysfunctional than the one run by Tony Soprano."

In the weeks that followed, stylistic clashes between Hehir and his supervisors kept recurring. Hehir says he was trying to tell a serialized story with an arc. His bosses, he felt, were simply trying to maximize pay-per-view customers. "I didn't really feel like I had a champion or a rabbi in that office who was going to defend me," Hehir says. "I was on my own."

• • •

ON THE EVE OF THE SHOWDOWN, Chris Albrecht packed his bags, boarded the HBO jet, and headed to Las Vegas. Albrecht's date for the fight was his new girlfriend, Karla Jensen, a tall TV correspondent. Jensen, who spoke Spanish fluently, first got to know Albrecht through her freelance work for the network, covering HBO's red-carpet premieres in promotional videos, which were often distributed to HBO's partner networks in Latin America. Recently, the pair had been seen together attending a handful of movie premieres and award shows, posing for photos.

On Saturday night, more than sixteen thousand giddy fans, including Albrecht, Jensen, and Time Warner CEO Dick Parsons, packed into the MGM arena to watch the fight. It was Cinco de Mayo, and the crowd was lit. The seats closest to the ring were filled with celebrities, including Jim Carrey, Eddie Murphy, Jack Nicholson, Denzel Washington, Charlie Sheen, Michael Jordan, Magic Johnson, and Mike Tyson, along with a congregation of HBO executives.

Marc Anthony sang the national anthem, and Mayweather arrived in the ring sporting a giant sombrero and a pair of red-white-and-green trunks—a tribute, or perhaps a mockery—of De La Hoya's Mexican heritage.

Just after 8:25 p.m., the fighters touched gloves and began throwing punches.

The fight went on for twelve intense rounds. It was a tight, technical showdown, which could have gone either way. But in the end, when the split decision was announced, it was Mayweather who triumphed. Afterward, the heavily pro–De La Hoya crowd booed. Chants of "Bullshit, bullshit," filled the arena.

The night's clearest victor was HBO. Some 2.4 million households had paid in the ballpark of fifty-five dollars each to see the fight. It was an all-time record for the sport, beating the previous high mark set a decade earlier, when 1.99 million had tuned in to see Mike Tyson fight Evander Holyfield—an infamous fight in which Tyson bit off a piece of Holyfield's ear in the ring.

It was time to party.

After the fight, many of the well-connected members of the sell-out crowd headed to the hottest soiree in town: an epicurean bash that HBO was throwing outdoors, under the desert stars, on the expanse of poolside decks that stretch out behind the MGM Grand. With everyone jacked up on the adrenaline from the fight, the Cinco de Mayo revelry pushed deep into the night.

At 3:05 a.m., near the valet stand outside the MGM Grand, a couple of Las Vegas cops spotted something horrific going down. According to the subsequent police report, they saw a "white male grabbing a white female by the throat with both hands" and then "dragging her" toward the entrance of the hotel. The officers rushed in, pried the man's hands off her throat, put him in a submission hold, and pinned him to the asphalt.

While being placed into custody, Chris Albrecht, who according to the police report smelled of alcohol and was slurring his speech, told the arresting officer that he was the CEO of HBO. He explained that the victim was his girlfriend. They'd been out celebrating with friends at nightclubs after the bout, then bickering on the drive back to the hotel. She "pissed me off," Albrecht told the police.

Karla Jensen had red marks on her neck. But her windpipe did not appear severely damaged from the strangling. She was conscious and speaking. When the police asked her if she needed medical attention, she declined. The cops arrested Albrecht and took him to the Clark County Detention Center where he was deposited among the stuporous predawn crowd of drunks and grifters.

The next afternoon, Albrecht was released from jail. Soon, news of his arrest was ricocheting across the internet. Thanks to posts on the Smoking Gun and TMZ, his mug shot was everywhere: his eyes steady, brow furled, lips curled in a faint snarl. The overall impression was menacing. The head of HBO looked like a capo from *The Sopranos* following a rough night at the Bada Bing.

At the time of Albrecht's release, Dick Parsons, the CEO of Time Warner, was still in Las Vegas on the heels of the boxing match. He was preparing to attend the Cable Show, an annual gathering thrown by the National Cable & Telecommunications Association, which would be kicking off the next day just down the Strip from the MGM Grand, at the Mandalay Bay Convention Center.

It was Time Warner spokesperson Ed Adler, inbound for the convention, who delivered the bad news to Parsons: Albrecht had been arrested. It was bad. How should the company respond?

Parsons dispatched Jeffrey Bewkes, the Time Warner chief operating officer, to handle the situation, which made sense. Albrecht reported directly to Bewkes. But for Bewkes, the timing of such a thorny assignment could hardly be worse. At the moment, his long, painstaking ascent up the Time Warner corporate ladder, decades in the making, had finally reached a momentous juncture. With Parsons set to retire the following year in 2008, the company's board of directors was deep in the process of evaluating Bewkes as the company's next CEO. Bewkes was on the verge of becoming the head of the biggest media company on the planet, a job that would pay him tens of millions of dollars a year and lavish him with the kinds of perks that could make the robber barons of yore blush. He could almost taste it. But it was not a done deal yet. Things could still fall apart.

Now this.

After getting out of jail on Sunday afternoon, Albrecht met up with Jensen, who was declining to press charges. They headed to the airport, where a company jet was waiting. Back in Los Angeles, Albrecht called Bewkes, who was conferring with his communications advisers, including HBO's Richard Plepler and Steven Rubenstein, the head of a public relations firm that did work for the network. By now, the news media was swarming around the story, trying to figure out how the company would handle the explosive situation.

Though it seemed far-fetched that Albrecht could hang on to his job following such a conspicuous and despicable act of domestic abuse, there were a few factors working in his favor. Bewkes, now in charge of Albrecht's fate, was also his close friend. And though few people in the media knew it, HBO had already helped to bury the story of Albrecht strangling one woman. Perhaps the company could be convinced to look past another.

There was one potential complication. A security camera at the MGM casino had captured the scene of Albrecht strangling Jensen on video. If the footage of the brutal attack got out, if the press got ahold of it, if somebody posted it online, there would be mayhem. Already, the media attention was at a fever pitch.

As everyone figured out what to do next, Albrecht hired Allan Mayer, a crisis communications expert with the company 42 West in Los Angeles. The best move, they eventually decided, was to tell the press that Albrecht was a recovering alcoholic who had recently fallen off the wagon and lost all control in Las Vegas, as people are wont to do. The booze was to blame.

On Tuesday morning, Albrecht announced that he would be taking a "temporary leave of absence" as CEO, effective immediately, to get professional treatment. In a short statement to his HBO colleagues, Albrecht apologized for his behavior, vowed to seek professional help, and thanked them for their "understanding" at such a "difficult" time. "This weekend was a wakeup call to me of a weakness I thought I had overcome long ago," Albrecht said. "I had been a sober member of Alcoholics Anonymous for 13 years. Two years ago, I decided that I could handle drinking again. Clearly, I was wrong."

Inside of Time Warner, many employees were outraged that the company appeared to be on the verge of preserving Albrecht's job. Evidently, if you were Jeffrey Bewkes's friend, strangling a woman in public wasn't cause for immediate dismissal?

Less than a year earlier, a high-end escort had been arrested in New York, and afterward named Time Warner's chief financial officer as one of her best clients, a guy who not only routinely paid for sex but also used his lavish Time Warner salary to shower her with luxury gifts. The revelation had set off a tabloid frenzy. Now, Albrecht's arrest added to the sense that the wildly compensated leading men of Time Warner were running amok.

Many women at the company were furious, including Shelley Brindle, one of the top-ranking female executives at HBO. "I went and talked to our head of HR," Brindle says. "I said, if he doesn't go, I'm going. And there's going to be a hell of a lot of women who will be leaving too."

But before HR could do much of anything, a leak forced the company's hand.

The following day, the *Los Angeles Times* published an article by reporter Claudia Eller revealing for the first time publicly that sixteen years earlier Albrecht had physically assaulted Sasha Emerson in the HBO offices in L.A. HBO CHIEF ACCUSED OF ASSAULT IN 1991, read the headline. The newspaper reported that the resulting confidential settlement paid to Emerson had been overseen by none other than Jeffrey Bewkes.

With the Time Warner board of directors watching, the pressure on Bewkes to take action now ratcheted up even higher.

The story in the *Los Angeles Times* also touched off a new string of articles attempting to piece together Albrecht's apparent pattern of abusive behavior. Within Los Angeles's creative community, Emerson's many friends watched the news with a mix of elation over Albrecht's downfall and empathy for his latest victim.

During the years since 1991, they'd witnessed the toll that the workplace assault had taken on Emerson, which turned out to be worse than some of them had initially imagined. Given her young age, track record of accomplishment, and obvious talent, they had assumed that her career trajectory would continue to soar.

But overcoming what had happened at HBO proved to be no simple matter. In the weeks after leaving the network in the fall of 1991, Emerson had started looking for a new job. At one point, in an effort to help, a friend had connected her with his agent, who was a powerful, well-connected rainmaker in the industry. Emerson went in and met with the guy. No sooner had she sat down than he delivered the sage advice for which she had been summoned. "I'm gonna give you a bite of the reality sandwich," the agent said. "No woman ever wins."

A number of promising job leads ended abruptly with little explanation. It was almost as if the stigma of being battered at the HBO offices had attached to Emerson rather than to her attacker.

Meanwhile, inside of HBO, Albrecht was using his position to shape the narrative in Hollywood's creative community of what had happened. According to a former HBO employee, in the period following Emerson's departure, Albrecht would disparage her in business meetings with prominent TV writers and producers who came in to pitch ideas to the network. The staffer recalls watching firsthand as Albrecht made up all sorts of false things about Emerson, saying that she was unhinged, unprofessional, and worse. "It was so disgusting what he would say," says the former employee, who was in the room when Albrecht made these remarks. "It was really vile."

Eventually, after a few months, Emerson landed a job as the West Coast head of television for New Line Cinema, a Hollywood production company. There she worked successfully developing TV shows, films, and animated series based on New Line movies such as *Dumb and Dumber* and *The Mask*. If it was less prestigious than HBO, it was still a happy professional home. Even so, according to her friends, the whisper campaign against Emerson continued apace. In an industry town, it was all but inescapable. After six years at New Line—now remarried and raising three children—Emerson left the entertainment business and embarked on a new career as an interior designer.

Over the years, Emerson's time at HBO and her contributions to shows like *Tales from the Crypt* and projects like HBO Independent Productions all but disappeared from the network's public narrative. "There was a real campaign to blacken her out and make it seem that what had happened there was a corporation dealing with a chaotic, problematic person—rather than someone who took a very unfair settlement and a very arbitrary, sexist, misogynistic expulsion," says one TV writer who worked with HBO and was friends with Emerson. "The company rewrote the narrative so that they looked like they hadn't done anything wrong."

Now, sixteen years later, the news was finally out, the secret unburied. This time around, it would be all but impossible for Albrecht or his allies to portray him as the victim. Not only was there a police report circulating, but there was also the MGM security video—which, in the grand Las Vegas tradition, would somehow manage to stay entirely hidden from public view in the weeks, months, and decades that followed.

As details of the earlier event spread in the media, current and former Time Warner and HBO executives declined to say anything about their role in the original financial settlement with Emerson, which they'd never disclosed to shareholders, or their decision to retain Albrecht. An anonymous source told the *New York Post* that in 1991 there just wasn't "as much sensitivity" to "the issue of violence against women."

"I think it's a blatant abuse of shareholder funds," Susan Shultz, a corporate governance expert with the Board Institute, a better-business advocacy group, told the *Los Angeles Times*. "It impugns the integrity of a company and tarnishes the brand."

On Wednesday, May 9, 2007, in the hours following the revelation of Albrecht's prior attack on Emerson, Bewkes spoke with Albrecht. In an emotional conversation, Bewkes got all choked up and told his friend he had to go. That afternoon, Albrecht resigned from HBO.

Two days later, via his lawyer in a Las Vegas courtroom, Albrecht pleaded no contest to a misdemeanor charge of battery. He agreed to pay a thousand-dollar fine and attend domestic violence counseling.

Afterward, Albrecht released a statement via his publicist. "My behavior was clearly inappropriate," Albrecht said.

PART IV

THE NIGHT IS DARK AND FULL OF NETFLIX

(2007-2018)

CHAPTER 15

HBOver

HBO was adrift.

The media, already churning with speculation on how HBO could survive the coming end of *The Sopranos*, escalated into a frenzy over the network's uncertain future in the wake of Albrecht's Las Vegas arrest. With the network at a risky crossroads, Dick Parsons and Jeffrey Bewkes turned to HBO's in-house risk manager. In June, they announced that Bill Nelson, the network's chief operating officer, would be replacing Albrecht as the new CEO.

Nelson was a military veteran who had fought in Vietnam as a member of the U.S. Army's 101st Airborne Division, the Screaming Eagles. He had wavy gray hair, a solid white mustache, and held a CPA in accounting. During his early professional years, he performed risk assessment and regulatory compliance for Time Inc. In 1984, he joined HBO. In style and manner, he came across as the un-Albrecht, stolid and inflammable. And he inherited a crisis.

"The whole company is in shock," Nelson says. "First off, we can't believe what we're reading or hearing. And then you say to yourself, 'Oh my God, what's going to happen?'"

Nelson got to work trying to steady the troops. "I said to them, 'This company is really more than any one person, no matter who the person is, no matter what position, including CEO," Nelson says.

Beneath Nelson, HBO appointed a troika of co-presidents: Eric Kessler, the head of marketing and sales, Harold Akselrad, the network's general counsel, and Richard Plepler, the architect of HBO's permanent campaign. For now, they would run the network collectively in a power-sharing arrangement. Each would report to Nelson.

Not long after his promotion, Nelson summoned the West Coast digital business team to New York and revealed that their go-it-alone vision for HBO's streaming future had lost out. He told them that Kessler, the newly appointed co-president, would be taking over the development of HBO GO. Instead of going direct to consumers, HBO would roll out its new streaming service through its cable partners like Comcast, who in the future, as in the past, would be responsible for administering HBO's relationships with its customers. "It was the safe thing to do," Moloshok says. "It handed over the responsibility to the cable companies once again."

That summer, Moloshok, Penney, and Zlotnik all left HBO.

Years later, they would look back on 2006 and 2007 as the time when HBO failed to seize control of the streaming era of home entertainment, ultimately giving Netflix a huge head start. "It was a major wasted opportunity," Moloshok says.

"HBO probably would have destroyed Netflix, which is what big companies do when they buy disruptive innovators," Penney says. "But on the other hand, who knows?"

Of HBO's three new co-presidents, it was Richard Plepler whose job description was changing the most. In addition to running HBO's communications, he would now be overseeing HBO's programming decisions. He would be helped on the West Coast by Michael Lombardo, a lawyer who had joined HBO in the 1980s and spent much of his career working on business affairs. Moving forward, Lombardo would manage HBO's operations in Los Angeles while reporting back to Plepler, who would remain in New York. Carolyn Strauss would now report to both men.

Tall and gregarious, Plepler was always described in the press, without fail, as perma-tanned, an apt description, which he hated. Plepler grew up in Manchester, Connecticut, just outside of Hartford, the elder brother in a liberal family that was active in Democratic politics. His father was a trial lawyer—"The Jewish Atticus Finch," Plepler says—and his passion for politics and public affairs came from both parents. "At our dinner table, even when I was a young teenager, you were expected to have read the *Times*," he says. "My dad would say, 'Did you read Safire? Did you read Reston? Did you read Russell Baker?'"

Plepler attended Franklin & Marshall, a small liberal arts college in Lancaster, Pennsylvania, where he studied government and played on the tennis team. After graduating in 1981, he moved to Washington, D.C., to work for Christopher Dodd, the U.S. senator for Connecticut.

Plepler moved to New York in 1984 where Esther Newberg, a family friend who was well on her way to becoming a major literary agent, helped guide him. Newberg had known Plepler since he was ten years old. "When I came to New York, I didn't know anybody, and Esther was kind of like a big sister to me," he says.

Newberg recommended he meet with John Scanlon, a charming, well-read publicist with a bottomless appetite for networking. Scanlon seemed to know everybody in media, entertainment, and journalism. His electric group of close friends included the Irish poet Seamus Heaney, the newspaper columnist Pete Hamill, and ABC Evening News anchor Peter Jennings. Scanlon met with Plepler and hired him to work in his boutique PR shop.

"John played a huge role in my inauguration to the city," Plepler says. "He introduced me to a lot of people. He took me seriously. All the people who I met as a little pisher in New York at twenty-four years old were because of John. He was unbelievably generous to me."

Working under Scanlon, Plepler gained an orientation toward the news profession that would guide his future career. "From John, I really learned the tenets of the communications business," Plepler says. "Like me, John loved journalists. And his secret was that he loved journalists. He loved being in the conversation about what was going on, and he saw journalism as a sacred craft."

Some of Scanlon's competitors were merely publicists, says Plepler. Scanlon was a *strategist*.

Within two years, Plepler branched out on his own, opening a public relations firm with a fairly grandiose name belying his relative inexperience: RLP International. At the beginning, Plepler was its sole employee. With time, his clients grew to include a wonky mix of Democratic politicians and highbrow media outlets like Mort Zuckerman's *Atlantic Monthly* and HBO. In 1990, Plepler raised money for and produced *A Search for Solid Ground: The Intifada Through Israeli Eyes*, a documentary about the Israel-Palestinian conflict that aired on PBS.

Plepler joined Time Warner as a full-time public relations executive in 1992 and began working closely with Michael Fuchs, implementing the strategy he had learned from Scanlon. So began HBO's permanent campaign. Plepler had keen political reflexes and strong media marketing instincts, but he knew next to nothing about the cable television business or the creative process. "Michael really took a chance on a thirty-three-year-old kid who basically really didn't deserve a seat on the executive committee of the HBO table," Plepler says. Fuchs showed him the ropes, and Plepler grew into his closest adviser.

Following Fuchs's firing in 1995, Jeffrey Bewkes had a decision to make about Plepler. Should he cut him loose? Gerald Levin, Ted Turner, and Terry Semel at Warner Bros. warned Bewkes that Plepler would be a spy on Fuchs's behalf. But Plepler pledged his devotion, and Bewkes decided to keep him on.

In the years that followed, Plepler put his ever-growing network of cultural and political power players to work for HBO, frequently inviting writers to lunches with Bewkes at midtown restaurants and managing the guest lists for HBO's various parties and premieres.

In the spring of 2007, Plepler's promotion to co-president, charged with overseeing programming, put him in an enviable position. Because HBO was traditionally a creative-led company, the move set him up to possibly take over the network for good—that is, if HBO's lineup didn't flop miserably.

Which was no sure thing. For the first time in forever, the network's slate of future shows looked dreary.

"There was nothing coming out in 2007 that was stunning," Nelson says.

• • •

ON JUNE 10, 2007, HBO aired the final episode of *The Sopranos*. After years of strife, Tony's empire is teetering. His crew is fighting a murderous battle against the Lupertazzi crime family. His brother-in-law, Bobby Baccalieri, (Steven Schirripa) has been shot to death. His consiglieri, Silvio Dante (Steven Van Zandt), is in a coma. One of the family's capos has gone missing and may be testifying for the government. A grand jury has been impaneled. Subpoenas are flying. "You can take 2007," says Paulie Gualtieri, "and give it back to the Indians."

In the ultimate scene, Tony takes a seat in a booth at Holsten's luncheonette in Bloomfield, New Jersey. While he waits for his wife, his son, and his daughter, he slips a few quarters in the jukebox and chooses Journey's "Don't Stop Believin'." Carmela arrives. Then A.J. Then the onion rings. Each time a patron enters the front door, a bell jingles, and Tony's weathered mug looks up expectantly, until suddenly, midsong—with a massive audience watching raptly at home—the scene cut to blackness and silence.

Seconds passed. Eons, in TV time. There was nothing more. The credits rolled.

Around the country, there arose a berserker's shriek. Confused viewers demanded to know what the hell had just happened. Had their cable connection been cut off? Was Tony whacked? Arrested? Had he blacked out?

Everybody wanted answers, and there was nobody to provide them. *Sopranos* writer Terence Winter and his wife—who at the time were visiting New York from their home in California—were watching the final episode with a big group of relatives while their newborn baby slept soundly upstairs. As they settled in excitedly for the final chapter of the show, Winter refused to reveal any details about how it would end, but assured everybody it was going to be great and special: They would love it!

"As soon as it cut to black, my brother and sister, everyone, were like *what the fuck was that?*" says Winter. "I said, 'We got to go, the baby needs to go.' We got in the car, and I was like, 'Well, *that* was not the reaction I thought we would get.'"

David Chase and his wife were at their vacation home in France. Chase tried to follow the reaction from afar, but the geographic distance and the language barrier made it difficult, at first, to gauge the level of mania that he had stirred up. Only later, when his buddy Steven Van Zandt told Chase about his harrowing experience on talk radio standing up for the ending, did the creator of *The Sopranos* begin to appreciate what he'd done.

Much of the tooth gnashing soon devolved into an irrational, cryptozoological-like debate about whether Tony had survived the final dinner unscathed. Was he alive or dead, or alive, or dead? The delirium raged on for weeks, then months, then years. "I didn't realize all of it until it kept on happening, year after year," Chase says.

One thing was certain. Before walking away from the wilds of New Jersey, Chase had given such a vigorous curb-stomping to the conventions of traditional TV that its form would be forever altered. "Paradox, moral relativism, internality. All the stuff that network television has battled and ejected in the past 60 years—except in a very few instances—is the essence that David Chase brought to his 86 hours," wrote Peter Kaplan in the *New York Observer*. "David Chase fought for and won a strange moment of pure insight into the American process. It was romantic, bleary, filthy, piercing. It was as much a comedy of American sobering up after 9/11 as *Dallas* was a comedy of America getting drunk on the Reagan years."

Following *The Sopranos* finale, hoping to hold on to a chunk of the large, gobsmacked audience, HBO premiered *John from Cincinnati*, the new supernatural beach-bumming drama from David Milch.

In the first episode, an aging surfer named Mitch Yost (Bruce Greenwood) and his wife, Cissy (Rebecca De Mornay), are bickering with their son, Butchie (Brian Van Holt), a former surfing champion turned heroin addict.

Amid the cacophony of intergenerational cussing, strange things are afoot. Much to his surprise, Mitch keeps mysteriously floating a foot or so off the ground like a hovercraft at a middle-school science fair. A neighbor's pet bird dies and then is reborn at the touch of Butchie's fourteen-year-old son, Shaun (Greyson Fletcher), a budding phenom in the waves.

All the while, an oddball named John Monad (Austin Nichols) is tagging along, following around members of the Yost tribe. "The end is near," he keeps saying. "The end is near."

Critics were baffled. For many reviewers, Milch's stabs at magical realism felt more absurd than mystical. In the *Orlando Sentinel*, Hal Boedeker called it a "pretentious and talky botch," that "won't fill the void left by *The Sopranos*." In the *Boston Globe*, Matthew Gilbert knocked the "auto-eroticism of the writing" and noted that "sitting through three episodes made me feel sad for HBO."

The ratings were likewise horrid and did little to temper the growing concern that in terms of HBO's golden age, the dim-witted prophet guy from *John from Cincinnati* might be onto something.

The end is near.

A few days after the unsettling surf drama premiere, the mood inside HBO grew even more tense thanks to a haunting visit from a phantom of HBO's past. In the dozen years since his ouster from Warner Music, Michael Fuchs's career had fizzled. Despite his formative role at HBO, he had failed to secure another job at a rival entertainment company and gradually slid into a kind of semiretirement, investing in a series of dubious ventures, including an ill-fated real-estate boondoggle in Hawaii that would ultimately devolve into lawsuits and bankruptcy. With each passing year, his once incandescent reputation grew fainter.

By 2007, many newcomers to the network had never even heard of the guy. To restore his name to prominence, or something vaguely resembling it, Fuchs began lobbying HBO's management to rename its internal theater on the fifteenth floor of its Bryant Park headquarters after him. Eventually, his badgering worked.

One afternoon in mid-June, a crowd of HBO staffers and invited guests gathered in the small theater for the renaming ceremony. Fuchs, slightly handsome and slightly jowly, got up onstage and faced the crowd. For several, awkward, profanity-filled minutes, Fuchs mocked and belittled his former boss, Gerald Levin, who was not in attendance.

"It's nice that HBO thinks so much of me that the sign on the men's room is bigger than the sign on my theater," Fuchs said.

With an air of theatricality, Fuchs pulled out what looked like the forty-thousand-dollar watch that he'd been given as a going away present twelve years earlier. Fuchs placed the timepiece on the floor and stomped on it feverishly.

The crowd watched Fuchs's performance uncomfortably. It couldn't end quickly enough.

Days later, Fuchs told the *New York Post* that the watch was just a prop. He was only kidding around. "I'm a great roast-master," he said. "HBO is an irreverent place. I established that culture, so I couldn't show up and not have a little bit of fun."

To some HBO folks in the audience, the stunt came across as little more than a pathetic, self-pitying tantrum. "This wasn't like David Geffen having Lincoln Center named after him," Quentin Schaffer says. "This is like a tiny little theater in the HBO building that the general public doesn't even have access to."

At the same time, the network was facing other, more pressing concerns. That summer, taking a page out of HBO's playbook, several basic-cable networks were rolling out new high-quality serialized dramas while the broadcast networks were in reruns. A handful were getting the kind of critical attention typically showered on HBO.

Critics were particularly impressed by *Mad Men*, a stylish new drama about a troubled advertising executive on Madison Avenue navigating the bedlam of the 1960s. The series was airing on AMC, a basic-cable channel that replayed classic movies. As each rave duly noted, the creator of the series was Matthew Weiner, a former writer for *The Sopranos*, who had originally pitched *Mad Men* to HBO.

That the buzziest new series of the summer ended up on AMC, not HBO, seemed to suggest something momentous was happening in home entertainment. Maybe HBO wasn't so special after all.

"We have the best movie library on TV," said Charlie Collier, an AMC executive. "Our goal is to make cinematic-quality scripted series that can stand side by side with these great movies. It's a strategy that worked very well for HBO."

"AMC said they wanted to do an HBO kind of series," Weiner said.

They weren't alone. For the first time in years, Showtime was challenging HBO's cultural dominance in premium cable. Under the leadership of its entertainment president, Bob Greenblatt, a former executive producer on HBO's *Six Feet Under*, Showtime was gaining critical acclaim thanks to a slate of quality series, which included *Dexter, Californication*, and *Weeds*.

As the summer progressed, HBO's cable supremacy felt increasingly imperiled. In August, after only ten episodes, Plepler canceled *John from Cincinnati*. The show's failure set off another round of critical stories on the state of HBO. Why, everyone wondered, was a public relations strategist now running HBO's programming decisions? Had HBO lost its touch?

Rival executives took turns sniping at the network. "What they were was unassailable," said John Landgraf, the head of FX. "And they aren't that anymore." At Showtime, executives were casually tossing around a gleeful nickname: "HBOver."

HBO badly needed a breakout new show. But there was another problem brewing. A large chunk of Hollywood's creative community was on the verge of shutting down. For months, the writers unions and the major studios had been going back and forth on a range of contentious issues such as how writers would be compensated for future work appearing on new, digital platforms.

On November 5, 2007, unable to reach an agreement, the Writers Guild of America East and West, representing more than ten thousand TV and movie writers, announced they were going on strike. Overnight, the industry ground to a halt. The strike would last for the next one hundred days, further exacerbating HBO's struggle to find a new hit series.

In the meantime, the annoyances kept multiplying. Shortly after his arrest in Las Vegas and dismissal from HBO, Chris Albrecht had landed a job at IMG, an international talent management company. In December,

Albrecht announced his first deal: he'd sold the American rights to the British series *Secret Diary of a Call Girl* to HBO's rivals at Showtime. The tart half-hour comedy was an adaptation of a racy 2005 nonfiction book chronicling the illicit activities of an anonymous, high-end U.K. sex worker.

At the time, HBO already had a similar project in development: *Diary of a Manhattan Call Girl*, based on the saucy novel by Tracy Quan to be written by *Sex and the City* creator Darren Star.

Now, thanks to Albrecht, the two escort-related projects were in open competition.

Albrecht assured reporters that Showtime's take on prostitution was a winner. He'd long wanted to develop a series about upscale escorts, he told *Variety*, but had only now found the perfect version. "This was exactly what I had always wished we had found," Albrecht said. "Like *Sex and the City*, it's got the glitz, but it's got real emotion, too." Shortly thereafter, HBO shelved its *Diary* for good.

Like everyone in the industry, executives at Netflix were keeping their eyes on the tumult at HBO. Not long after leaving the network, Albrecht sat down for dinner with Netflix's chief executive officer Reed Hastings at Valentino, an upscale Italian restaurant in Santa Monica, which served lamb chops with fava beans, smoked quail, and lasagna with duck ragu. John Penney, the former business development executive for HBO who had followed Albrecht to IMG, also attended the meeting.

According to Penney, the conversation eventually got around to the thirty-five-page deck he'd written up and presented to HBO management a few months earlier, proposing to buy Netflix. Hastings was intrigued. How much, he asked, would you guys have offered? Around $2 billion, they responded.

"Hastings said that at that price he would have done it," Penney recalls.

• • •

OVER THE SUMMER, Plepler and Lombardo met with skeptical TV critics and reporters at a press conference for the first time.

"I can remember sitting up onstage with Lombardo and somebody essentially saying, 'Hey, your big shows are off the air, what do you got?' And the implicit question was: 'Who are you guys? What do you know?'" Plepler says. "I said, look, there's not a Bewkes philosophy or a Chris Albrecht philosophy, or, for that matter, a Richard Plepler or Lombardo philosophy. There's an HBO philosophy. And that philosophy is to bet on great writers and great talent and to have a shared vision of what constitutes an original voice."

While HBO's programming department continued its hunt for original artists, Plepler turned his ear to the network of brainy New Yorkers who routinely gathered in his dining room to drink wine and swap stories. If his mentor John Scanlon's secret weapon was to love the journalists he courted, Plepler would go a step further and start collecting them.

"HBO was doing the kind of work which was of interest to serious cultural aficionados and columnists, and so it was always clear to me that that was a pretty organic link between the brand and the interpreters who wrote about culture," Plepler says.

In late 2007, Plepler recruited Tina Brown, the former editor of *Tatler*, *Vanity Fair*, and the *New Yorker* to join HBO as a "creative consultant." "If I collide with some interesting material, I'll call or email them," Brown said of the arrangement. "Richard wants to encourage people who have good relationships with the creative community to simply be thinking about HBO when they're out and about."

A few months later, the network announced that Frank Rich, the influential columnist for the *New York Times*, would likewise start moonlighting for HBO as a consultant. Plepler had known Rich since 1995. At the time, the columnist had taken an interest in writing about the rap lyrics controversy then swirling around Time Warner and called Plepler in his PR capacity. Afterward, they'd grown close.

"I thought Frank—and I proved correct on this—just had an unbelievable ear for cultural talent and for artists," Plepler says. "And I knew that he would be a great ally to Mike and me just as a sounding board, which is how this all started: reading things, giving us a reaction."

Rich explained that since giving up theater criticism for politics, people had occasionally asked him to look over their play or manuscript and "to try and tweak it or whatever." It was a process he enjoyed. "I love this stuff so much," he said. "This is a way to kind of do it in a less amateur fashion and on a more regular basis. It's a way to satisfy this craving I have had."

Few people in the industry thought the arrangement would bear fruit. Time would soon prove them wrong.

While Rich and Brown were figuring out the network, some HBO staffers were getting ready to flee. Following the success of *De La Hoya/ Mayweather 24/7*, HBO announced it was expanding the docuseries brand. The second iteration of the show would provide an all-access look at the lead-up to Floyd Mayweather's defense of his title in an upcoming bout against Ricky Hatton. The fight would take place at the MGM Grand.

Once again, HBO tapped Jason Hehir to produce the series. Hehir accepted the assignment with some ambivalence. In the wake of the Mayweather versus De La Hoya fight—and the $136 million it had generated via pay-per-view—his bosses had recognized his contribution, all those sleepless nights and tense moments, with a slice of the spoils. A very small slice. They gave him a fifteen-hundred-dollar bonus. "Before taxes," Hehir says. "That was seen as really, really gracious."

Despite his misgivings, Hehir again threw himself into the high-pressure, quick turnaround series. On December 8, Mayweather defeated Hatton in a technical knockout in the tenth round. Again, critics were impressed by HBO's *24/7* series leading up to the bout.

Not long afterward, according to Hehir, he was summoned to a meeting in New York with his boss, Rick Bernstein, to discuss a new project. There was a rumor around the offices that HBO Sports was interested in doing a documentary about Ted Williams, the legendary slugger for the Boston Red Sox. Hehir had grown up in the suburbs of Boston and long dreamed of doing a full-length documentary for HBO Sports. Hehir felt confident that this would be his big shot.

But at the meeting, according to Hehir, Bernstein proposed something entirely different for the producer's next big assignment: making a video of his son's upcoming Bar Mitzvah.

Shortly thereafter, Hehir quit HBO.

In the years that followed, Hehir would go on to direct a series of award-winning sport documentaries for ESPN's 30 for 30 franchise. And in 2020, he would create *The Last Dance*, a multipart series about the Chicago Bulls for ESPN and Netflix, which would become the most watched documentary in ESPN's history—and one of the biggest cultural hits in America during the early months of the coronavirus pandemic.

For years, first under Bewkes, then Albrecht, HBO Sports had grown less and less central to the network's mission. Now, thoroughly marginalized, HBO Sports was driving a budding star into the arms of a rival. "HBO Sports was at the time the antithesis of forward-thinking HBO," Hehir says. "It was tweed-jacket-wearing, old-school, do-things-by-the-book HBO Sports. It was kind of like this antiquated annex within that building."

* * *

IN MARCH 2008, HBO announced that Carolyn Strauss would be stepping aside as the president of entertainment and shifting into some less central, unspecified role. In the twenty-two years since graduating from Harvard, Strauss had never worked at another company. Though few HBO subscribers knew Strauss's name, her creative insights had shaped HBO's programming renaissance, one scrupulously considered note at a time.

The reason for the change, HBO's new management team suggested, had more to do with hospitality than sensibility. Word circulated in the press that in the months following Albrecht's departure, Strauss had snubbed Matthew Weiner, the former writer for *The Sopranos* who'd desperately wanted to make his show about Madison Avenue in the 1960s for HBO. Not only had the network passed, they hadn't even bothered to respond to the pitch, even though David Chase had tried to get everyone at the network to give it a look.

"It was very disappointing to me, as I pushed the rock up the hill, that they did not notice me," Weiner said of HBO. "Because I was part of the family."

When *Mad Men* subsequently turned into a giant hit for AMC, the story of the brush-off added to a growing narrative that HBO's development team was acting like an ungracious host, leaving the door open for the likes of AMC and Showtime to pick off prestige projects.

"That's been Richard's bugaboo forever," says Strauss, years later, about Plepler and *Mad Men*. "Tell me a programmer who hasn't passed on something. If you want to hold that as my grave, original sin—guilty as charged."

It seemed to be enough to inspire HBO leaders to shift Strauss into a production role and to find someone else to become HBO's primary point of contact with the creative community. In the ten months since Albrecht was forced out, Strauss says she felt an "increasing disconnect" between herself and Plepler and Lombardo. Strauss was used to an enormous amount of autonomy under Albrecht. Plepler and Lombardo, new to programming, were more skeptical of her approach. "They just weren't into the way I was doing it," she says.

Strauss's departure didn't sit well with some HBO contributors. Cynthia Mort, the first woman to create a dramatic series for HBO, *Tell Me You Love Me*, says she was baffled by the decision. Strauss, in her view, had helped usher in the most successful programming run in the network's history. Now she was being forced out by a bunch of guys with no background in creative development. It made no sense. "I was like, look, if I need a plumber am I going to hire a painter?" Mort says. "No, I'm going to hire a plumber. I couldn't believe it."

Months earlier, throughout the fall of 2007, Mort's series, *Tell Me You Love Me*, an emotionally charged portrait of three couples with intimacy problems seeking help from a therapist (Jane Alexander), had aired on HBO. Creating the series under Albrecht and Strauss, Mort says, was the best experience of her career. The notes she got from Strauss were smart and insightful. If she ignored the suggestions, that was okay too. "I got to do really whatever I wanted to do," Mort says. "They were great in that respect."

While the ratings for *Tell Me You Love Me* were relatively modest, the series generated a lot of buzz, and HBO initially renewed it for a second season. But in the tumultuous period of time following Albrecht's departure, says Mort, the creative environment at the network suddenly felt different: more cautious and less self-assured.

At one point, she says, she sat down with Michael Lombardo to discuss the scripts she'd written for the first two episodes of the second season. According to Mort, Lombardo told her that the scripts were beautifully written—but perhaps she could make everything a little bit faster paced, more topical, and more joyful. Mort was displeased. *Tell Me You Love Me* was a dark and intense show. She had zero interest in brightening its tone. Rather than make her therapy show more chipper, she decided to walk away. There would be no second season. "I could tell where they were going, so I bailed," Mort says.

Around the same time, HBO's only other dramatic series from a female creator was also running into problems. The day after removing Strauss, HBO announced it was canceling one of her projects, *12 Miles of Bad Road,* the Dallas-based drama from Linda Bloodworth-Thomason, starring Lily Tomlin as a vituperative real estate broker to the garishly rich. Before the writer's strike halted production, six of the ten episodes had already been shot at an expense of roughly $25 million. Even so, Plepler and Lombardo felt the series' broad humor was off brand and decided to ax it.

Afterward, Bloodworth-Thomason raised a ruckus in the press, sending out copies of the early episodes to critics and trying to pressure HBO's new regime to reverse its decision. While the strategy ultimately failed to revive the series, it did add to the growing sense of dishevelment surrounding the network.

Inside HBO, there were others who were losing faith. Colin Callender, the sagacious British producer who'd first joined HBO in 1987, had seen enough. So much about HBO in recent years felt alien to him. He credited and blamed *The Sopranos*, which he believed was the best thing that had happened to the network, but also maybe the worst. The series had generated an influx of extra revenue from DVDs and foreign sales, and the folks in finance had gotten hooked. Now the big push from the top to replicate the success was shoving aside everything else HBO had long prided itself on.

"It was clear that HBO was trying to find the next *Sopranos*," Callender says. "It was sort of driving in the rearview mirror, looking over its shoulder, worried about people nipping at its heels."

The way Callender saw it, putting Bill Nelson, a money guy, in charge of

HBO was a mistake that would only exacerbate the problem. "He was not a creative executive," Callender says. "He was an administrator. He didn't have the creative vision from a programming standpoint."

Callender was equally perturbed by the appointment of Plepler and Lombardo to oversee programming. The duo had no background in production or development. All of which Callender found alarming. "Programming," he says, "was now in the hands of a PR person and a business affairs person."

Then he watched in disgust as they dumped Carolyn Strauss. "She was unceremoniously fired," he says. "And I thought okay, this is the time to move on."

By the end of the year, he was gone.

CHAPTER 16

Fresh Blood

In early April 2008, HBO announced that Sue Naegle, a thirty-eight-year-old TV agent with United Talent Agency, would be coming on board as the network's new president of entertainment. Moving forward, she would be overseeing series and specials, effectively replacing Strauss.

Naegle grew up in Rockaway, New Jersey, a small town about forty miles west of New York City. After attending college at Indiana University, Naegle moved to Los Angeles and landed an entry-level job in the mailroom at the United Talent Agency. By the time she was twenty-nine, she'd made partner and amassed an eclectic roster of clients, which included the screenwriter Charlie Kaufman (*Being John Malkovich*), Mike White (*School of Rock*), and Alan Ball, the creator of *Six Feet Under*.

"I was less interested in finding someone who could identify hits," Michael Lombardo said. "And more interested in finding someone who could work with writers to embrace shows that they have passion for."

Plepler noted that Naegle had the right temperament to turn down ideas without creating lasting resentment. Because HBO was geared toward programming only a single night each week, the majority of incoming pitches were ultimately destined to be rejected.

"It's important that we say 'no' with respect and that we let people understand that if something isn't right that it's open for later," Plepler said. "The sine qua non of our success and good fortune is that we are the port of first call."

Naegle got to work sifting through the many projects already in development for HBO and the ones just making it on air. A rare bright spot for HBO in 2008, thanks in large part to the departing Colin Callender, was its run of original movies and miniseries, which included *John Adams*, a presidential biopic starring Paul Giamatti; *Generation Kill*, a seven-episode drama from David Simon set during the 2003 invasion of Iraq; and *Recount*, a dramatization of the 2000 presidential election starring Kevin Spacey.

Naegle told reporters that, in terms of upcoming projects, she was particularly excited about the Southern gothic–vampire series *True Blood*, which she'd previously sold to HBO on behalf of Alan Ball, her client. "This is obviously an unusual show, different from what we've done, with the sci-fi and fantasy element," Naegle said. "But there's something about this world and story and voice that's uniquely HBO."

Since the end of *Six Feet Under* in 2005, Ball had been looking around for his next HBO project. One day, while killing time before a dentist appointment, he was browsing the shelves at a Barnes & Noble and picked up a vampire novel called *Dead Until Dark* by Charlaine Harris. "I bought it, and I couldn't put it down," Ball says.

Ball acquired the rights to the series and began adapting it for the small screen. Initially, many at HBO were dubious. "There was a point when people were asking me during pitches, what makes this an HBO show?" Ball says. "I remember thinking, well, that's weirdly corporate. You're more concerned with your corporate identity now? My answer was always like, well, it's good. And it's different."

For months, the project languished. Ball was just about to move on to other ideas when HBO finally decided to move ahead with the series. "It was so different from anything else they had done," Ball says. "It was such a genre show. It didn't feel like '*HBO important*.' By that time, they really liked the mantle of being important."

True Blood was one of the earliest decisions of the Plepler and Lombardo era, and it was a test of their mantra to trust the talent.

"You know, Alan is a brilliant auteur, but when you watched the pilot, you didn't go like, 'Okay, this is the next big thing!'" Plepler says. "It was unusual. I got on the phone with Mike, and we finished each other's sentences. We said, we go with Alan. He's got a vision for this thing. He's got all the talent in the world. We made the bet on Alan."

On November 3, 2008, Barack Obama was elected the forty-fourth president of the United States, the first Black leader to win the country's top office. Inside HBO, the mood was celebratory and hopeful.

That fall, the first twelve-episode season of *True Blood* debuted on HBO on Sunday nights. The series, set in a time of social upheaval, tested the premise of just how far America's experiment with social assimilation could be extended. For the first time in human history, vampires are "coming out of the casket" and integrating into human society, thanks to the Japanese, who have invented a synthetic blood that vampires can drink for nourishment instead of the real thing.

The cultural assimilation of the undead has gotten off to a rocky start. Many humans harbor deep-rooted prejudices against vampires. Others have discovered that drinking vampire blood is a restorative and intoxicating experience—not to mention a powerful aphrodisiac. Some will do anything to get it. To protect themselves against human predation, social bias, and bigoted calls for vampire segregation, vampires are organizing politically and jawing back against conservative pundits on cable news.

The series tells the story of the social unrest through the lens of one sleepy southern town, Bon Temps, Louisiana. There, Sookie Stackhouse (Anna Paquin), a sweet-natured waitress with the thankless supernatural ability to read people's minds, falls in love with Bill Compton (Stephen Moyer), a handsome, 173-year-old vampire whose thoughts she cannot decipher.

Since the end of *Tales from the Crypt* in 1996, HBO had largely stayed clear of fantasy, horror, and science fiction. The arrival of *True Blood* on Sunday nights left critics alternately amused by its campy, unpretentious tone or horrified by its schlocky B-movie titillations. American pop culture was in the midst of one of its periodic vampire crazes, and for some reviewers who felt gung-ho about HBO's edgy social realism, the network's decidedly un-Dickensian dalliance with the undead seemed worrisome.

In interviews, Ball started calling *True Blood* "popcorn TV for smart people."

The initial ratings for the first episode of *True Blood* were not great: 1.4 million viewers, low enough to inspire more headlines about HBO's post-*Sopranos* slump. BLOOD SUCKED, declared the *New York Post*. But as the fall progressed, the show's audience kept growing, and HBO renewed the series.

By the end of its first season, *True Blood* was averaging 6.8 million viewers per week, making it the most popular show on the network since *The Sopranos* and *Sex and the City*. HBO had, at last, scored another pop-culture hit.

"You start worrying," Lombardo admitted. "You see other networks putting on important programs on Sunday nights and you worry, 'Can you bring them back?'"

In the months that followed, the constant chatter in the media about HBO's identity crisis quietly petered out, and Plepler's odds of succeeding Nelson as CEO looked much improved.

While *True Blood* felt different in some ways from traditional HBO fare, it also carried on some of the network's oldest traditions. On *True Blood*, for every pair of bared fangs, there also seemed to be at least one pair of bared breasts. Though the network executives were no longer sending notes asking for more "cable edge," they were not shy about prodding Ball for more bodice-ripping excitement.

An episode in the second season included a scene in which Maryann Forrester (Michelle Forbes), a supernatural Maenad, woos the locals into a Dionysian orgy in the woods. While in production, Ball got a note back from HBO executives offering some critical suggestions on how to improve the debauched scene of writhing Southerners. "They were like, 'Can we see a little more skin?'" Ball said. "'Can it be a little hotter? Right now, it's not quite hot enough.'"

He made the orgy scene hotter.

The success of *True Blood* proved to Plepler and his colleagues that

HBO could make waves in the fantasy genre—an important realization for the network. "It turned into this huge phenomenon, and they were super happy with it," Ball says. "It opened the door for them to do other genre and sci-fi stuff that they might otherwise not have done."

• • •

ENTER THE DRAGONS.

In late 2008, Plepler and Lombardo were weighing whether to order up a pilot of *Game of Thrones*, a fantasy series based on the dragon-laden novels by George R. R. Martin. There were several obstacles. The show would be a big investment for the network. Fantasy shows are the most expensive of any genre, and movies like *Lord of the Rings* set a high bar. Audiences expected lavish special effects.

But the show had a strong advocate: Carolyn Strauss, now championing the show from the sidelines.

Months earlier, when Strauss was negotiating her exit from HBO, she said she wanted to keep a hand in at least one series: a project she had been developing with a pair of young writers named David Benioff and Daniel Brett (D. B.) Weiss.

Benioff and Weiss were novelists by training who had first met while earning master's degrees in Irish literature at Trinity College in Dublin. In the early 2000s, Benioff wrote the screenplay based on his novel *The 25th Hour*, which Spike Lee was adapting into a feature film. Afterward, Benioff became a regular writer and rewriter of Hollywood feature movies.

Strauss first heard of Benioff because of a full-throated endorsement from Steven Spielberg several years earlier. When Spielberg was pitching the network on *The Pacific*, the lavish sequel to *Band of Brothers*, he briefly diverted the conversation to *Troy*, a movie written by Benioff. Spielberg couldn't stop raving about the guy to Strauss. When an agent called Strauss, still in her programming role, sometime later to say Benioff and Weiss wanted to pitch an adaptation of George R. R. Martin's fantasy novels to HBO, she eagerly set up the meeting. The material didn't move her. But Benioff's attachment to the project did.

"I was like, 'Alright, let's see what this kid is all about,'" Strauss recalls.

Even though she had "zero affinity" for the fantasy genre, she says, Benioff and Weiss's pitch blew Strauss away. Along with her deputy, Gina Balian, Strauss made the deal for HBO. And just over a year later, when Strauss found herself packing up her things and walking out the door, she told the network she wanted to be a producer on *Game of Thrones*. She got the deal.

"I just really believed in David and Dan," she says.

Now she had to make the pitch to her former bosses at HBO. Neither Benioff nor Weiss had ever run a production of any size—let alone something massive like a serialized fantasy series. It would be a hard sell.

"She knew that since it was expensive that it would maybe be on the bubble," Plepler says. "And she called me up and said, 'I need you to talk to these guys. I need you to listen to them. It's not just in the script. You have to hear them.' And they came in and had me in about a minute."

HBO would shell out some $10 million, more than double what most networks paid for a drama series. With the network's bountiful support, the showrunners got started in late 2009, shooting elaborate scenes in exotic locations, stretching from Northern Ireland to Morocco. Tom McCarthy, a screenwriter (*The Station Agent*) and actor, who played the crooked *Baltimore Sun* reporter Scott Templeton on the final season of *The Wire*, directed the sprawling affair. All of which seemed promising.

But when the pilot came in, it was terrible—a convoluted, off-putting mess. The costumes looked funny. The hair and makeup looked worse. The relationships between characters were confusing. The tone felt weirdly quaint, like a British period drama. And for a grandiose epic fantasy story, the pilot felt frustratingly claustrophobic. It lacked a sense of grandeur.

Plepler considered pulling the plug. HBO could cut its losses. But the series had strong internal backers. Sue Naegle, the network's newly empowered show picker, was a strong supporter. And Strauss kept pushing.

"When I look at that pilot, I go, 'Okay, there are some definite things that are not working,'" Strauss says, "but there is *clearly* a show here."

For Plepler and Lombardo, there was also an important principle involved. The key to HBO's fortunes, they believed, was identifying talented, singular artists and doing everything you could to support them. They both still believed in the creators of *Game of Thrones*.

They found the vision for the adaptation of George R. R. Martin's Song of Ice and Fire series enthralling. On the surface, it was typical fantasy stuff. Dragons, knights, princes, harlots, and high priests. But on a deeper level, it was all about exploring the dark power dynamics of dueling families, set against a backdrop of looming Armageddon.

If it went forward, George R. R. Martin would serve as a co-executive producer on the series. In many ways, he fit the classic HBO mold. Before sitting down to write his ornately violent fantasy novels, he'd spent a decade toiling unhappily as a broadcast TV writer, working on a pair of CBS series: a show called *Beauty and the Beast* and a reboot of *The Twilight Zone*.

After some consideration, Plepler decided to give Weiss, Benioff, and Martin a second chance. HBO ordered ten episodes, including a reshot pilot. To get started, HBO decided to switch directors, moving on from McCarthy. They needed serious help. It was time to call upon its prized, secret weapon. It was time to call Timmy.

• • •

TIM VAN PATTEN GREW UP in the suburbs of New York City, on Long Island, and started his career in TV as an actor. As a teenager in 1978, he landed his first significant role, playing a high school basketball player on *The White Shadow*, a critically acclaimed CBS drama created by Bruce Paltrow. After spending much of his twenties acting, Van Patten wanted to move behind the camera. "When you're an actor in television, the majority of your time is spent waiting for something to happen," he says. "And for me, I wanted to be in the game. I wanted to be the catcher, not the right fielder. I wanted to see the field. I wanted to be in every play."

In the mid-1990s, he began directing for a handful of broadcast TV dramas, including *Touched by an Angel*, a long-running, intensely saccharine religious series that aired on CBS. The show was everything that HBO at the time was defining itself against: cheerful, uplifting, fuzzily spiritual, and predictably formulaic.

Despite the wildly different styles and target demographic, Van Patten got an interview with David Chase before *The Sopranos* premiered. "David sat me down and we had a talk about everything *but* the show," Van Patten says. They chatted about food, comedies, gangsters, Italy, and Van Patten's upbringing in Massapequa, a town populated by so many Italians and Jews that it was nicknamed Matzoh-Pizza. They hit it off, and—as with Terence Winter and his work on *Flipper: The New Adventures*—Chase didn't seem to mind Van Patten's peculiar credits. Chase welcomed him into the rotation.

In the years that followed, while still doing the occasional episodes of *Touched by an Angel*, Van Patten emerged as a key member of *The Sopranos* team. Once, before the third season, he swung by the show's writers room and told everyone about a dream he had about Paulie and Christopher hunting down a Russian mobster in the snow-covered woods in rural New Jersey. Chase loved it, and the dream ended up inspiring "Pine Barrens," one of the most famous episodes of *The Sopranos*.

Throughout the years, when Chase found himself too busy to direct an episode that he intended to take on, he'd bark out the same instruction to his producers: "Call Timmy." Van Patten ultimately directed more episodes of the series than anyone else, twenty in total, including some of the edgiest, most celebrated, and most violent.

Over time, word spread in the HBO universe of Van Patten's skills, and he started directing key episodes on other HBO series, including *The Wire*, *Rome*, and *Deadwood*. During the high-stakes final season of *Sex and the City*, the network asked Van Patten to come in and help, even if the show's material felt foreign to the director with the heavy Long Island accent.

One day, while on set, Van Patten was instructed to get a wide shot. He asked why.

"We must see the shoes—we must have the Mononcoli Boncoli shoes," Van Patten recalls being told. "Whatever they're called—the Mongoli Bongoli shoes." Even if he was only dimly aware of Manolo Blahniks, Van Patten was a hit among the cast and producers of *Sex and the City*, and he ultimately directed four episodes that season, including the series finale. The regard for

Van Patten's skills was a sentiment shared widely throughout HBO's troupe of auteurs.

"He's an amazing storyteller," says Terence Winter, who worked closely with Van Patten on *The Sopranos*. "He's just got a great visual style. Funny. Adored by crews and casts alike. Really easygoing. Really fun to work with. Just keeps a really fun, light set. And just makes incredible pictures with film."

Now, with HBO making the biggest gamble in the network's history, betting a vast sum on a rejiggered *Game of Thrones*, the network once again turned to Van Patten and asked for help.

Van Patten said no. He was burned out after doing so many seasons of *The Sopranos*, as well as several episodes of *The Pacific* and an upcoming series called *Boardwalk Empire*. Michael Lombardo insisted he read the book. Van Patten got through ten pages of it. "My head exploded," he says. "This was way too much to digest." Then Lombardo showed him the pilot. "This isn't going to make it," Van Patten thought to himself.

But Lombardo was persistent. You're the only one who can do this, Lombardo told him. Van Patten gave it more thought. Van Patten says that unlike in movies—where the director reigns supreme and, for decades, was singularly venerated by aficionados and scholars and video-store clerks—an episodic television director is like being "a substitute teacher" or "a traveling salesman." Now HBO was in a serious jam, and the network had been so good to him over the years. He finally relented.

"As an itinerant director, it can be a fairly lonely life, right?" he says. "It's a little bit of a Willy Loman situation out there. You're just bouncing from show to show, and you have really no skin in the game. But at HBO, you felt you were part of a bigger family, not just the show you were working on. Who the hell doesn't want to be a part of a family?"

After making several tweaks to the cast—most crucially, bringing in the British actor Emilia Clarke to play the key role of Daenerys Targaryen, the series' dragon-riding antiheroine—the creators got started in the summer of 2010. Van Patten directed the newly reshot pilot, as well as the second episode. While on set, to get to the essence of the rambling, complicated epic,

HBO's ace show mechanic would repeatedly ask people nearby a simple, re-ductive question: *Is this a good guy or a bad guy?* "Just boil it down," Van Patten says.

"Shooting a pilot is really hard, and getting into a series is really hard," Strauss says. "If you haven't done it before, it can overwhelm. Timmy had so much series experience, and so much series experience at HBO, they had a lot of trust and faith in him, as did I and Dan and David. What I think works well in television is instinct and taste that's *formed* by experience."

The new pilot impressed everyone at HBO. Following their stay of exe-cution, the *Game of Thrones* team went on to complete the first season. Plep-ler's decision to trust his artists would prove to be one of the best in the network's fifty-year history.

• • •

IN EARLY 2010, the network's long-gestating streaming product HBO GO finally made its public debut. For the past three years, since the furious "sock party" beatdown of the West Coast web agitators, co-president Eric Kessler's team had been cautiously nudging HBO's online video product forward. Consultants from IDEO, the global design firm, had been brought in to cre-ate an extensive study of what HBO online offerings might look like in the future. R/GA, a New York–based innovation consultancy, had been com-missioned to design a snazzy-looking user interface. And in 2008, the prod-uct had been given a small test run among Time Warner Cable subscribers in Wisconsin.

Now it was finally time to enter the streaming universe, albeit tepidly.

On February 17, Kessler announced that HBO's new digital product (tagline: "HBO on your computer") would be launching in partnership with Verizon Fios, allowing Mac and PC users to access a limited amount of HBO programming on-demand via a web browser.

Reporters who covered the launch warned readers that there was a major catch: HBO GO would be available only to customers who already sub-scribed to the premium network as part of a bigger, more expensive cable or satellite bundle of programming. No cable TV? No GO.

The idea, Kessler explained, wasn't to cater to the rapidly growing number of people watching video services like Netflix and Hulu via the internet. The goal was to keep existing cable customers happy. "Ultimately, this is about extending the subscriber life cycle," Kessler said. "This is affiliate friendly."

It was the cable companies—historically famous for their horrid customer service—who would be in charge of authenticating legitimate HBO GO users and resolving any resulting service issues.

Reviewers praised the functionality of the product and its simple, intuitive design. But some were unimpressed with the paltry amount of HBO programming it offered. The whole thing felt decidedly noncommittal.

The headline from TechCrunch: A FIRST LOOK AT HBO GO: CURB YOUR ENTHUSIASM.

Around the same time, in 2010, a young New York filmmaker named Lena Dunham wrote a laconic memo to HBO's programming executives, pitching an idea for a series. It was, in several ways, an odd document. There were no specific characters mentioned, no plot, no setting.

Instead, Dunham devoted her entire proposal to sketching out a stage of womanhood "between adolescence and adulthood," just after college, when the shape of one's life is still raw and nebulous. It's a period of flux, she wrote, that's "heartbreaking and hilarious," "humbling" and "sexy" and "ripe for laughs."

She capped it off by referring to her contemporaries as "the Facebook Generation." "They're beautiful and maddening. They're self-aware and self-obsessed," she wrote. "They're my friends and I've never seen them on TV."

Certainly not on HBO.

In Los Angeles, the members of HBO's development team were impressed. Kathleen McCaffrey, a junior creative staffer just a few years older than Dunham, was particularly enthusiastic. Everyone loved Dunham's recent film *Tiny Furniture*, a fifty-thousand-dollar indie project that she wrote, directed, and starred in, about a listless, postcollege New Yorker living with her artist parents in a gorgeous Tribeca loft.

Still, there were concerns. Dunham hardly fit the template of the typical HBO auteur. She wasn't a middle-aged veteran of network television who'd spent decades banging up against the safety rails of broadcasting. She was only twenty-three years old. And she was a woman—still an exotically rare gender type among HBO creators.

Another potential snag was that Dunham was proposing to plumb the mores and lifestyles of twentysomethings. Historically, HBO hadn't commissioned shows catering to young adults. The belief, strongly held among some HBO Elders, was that it was the head of the family who decided whether a home ought to pay fifteen dollars a month to subscribe to HBO, not their children in high school, college, or fetching coffee in the workforce. The enduring legacy of *the man controls the remote* was hard to shake off. Appealing to a young crowd, some believed, was pointless.

"The conventional wisdom was, 'We don't necessarily do shows with younger protagonists, because it's adults who buy HBO,'" recalls Casey Bloys, the affable development executive who'd joined the network in 2004 and now had a top job in the network's comedy department. "I mean, that was the thinking back then—that it was the adult who set up the subscription in the household, and so a show that skews that young wouldn't be of interest."

But between Bloys's fascination, McCaffrey's zeal, and Naegle's influence, HBO's female-led development crew was able to overcome the internal resistance and buy the project. The next step was to find an experienced showrunner who could be teamed up with Dunham to help turn her spare monograph into a watchable program. Naegle had a hunch on which direction to go: no dudes.

"I felt very strongly that we should try to find Lena a great female mentor and really try to keep the experience in that point of view without the influence of a guy," Naegle would later tell *The Hollywood Reporter*.

So HBO turned to Jenni Konner, the cocreator of two fleeting ABC sitcoms and a former writer on *Undeclared*, a short-lived series on Fox from Judd Apatow. In the dozen years since writing for *The Larry Sanders Show*, Apatow had grown into one of the hottest writers and directors in Hollywood, thanks to hit comedies like *Knocked Up* and *The 40-Year-Old Virgin*. He was also known as a skillful mentor of precocious talent.

As it happened, Apatow had also recently watched Dunham's movie *Tiny Furniture*, on a recommendation from *New York Times* media columnist David Carr. Apatow was dazzled and wanted to work with Dunham on whatever she did next. She was game. At HBO, however, Naegle felt hesitant about bringing Apatow into the mix. She didn't want one of the rare female-driven series at HBO to get bigfooted by some Hollywood hombre, no matter how adept or well connected. But Konner vouched for Apatow, who gave everyone his assurances. He had no intention of bro-jacking the project. Naegle came around, and Apatow joined as an executive producer.

HBO told Dunham and Konner to go ahead and make a pilot for a show called *Girls*.

• • •

IN ADDITION TO *TRUE BLOOD*, HBO's Sunday-night lineup was starting to show more signs of rising from the dead. In the spring of 2010, HBO premiered *Treme*, a new series from David Simon and Eric Overmyer, a former writer on *The Wire*. The show, set in New Orleans, revolves arounds several residents, including an English professor (John Goodman), a trombone player (Wendall Pierce), and a Mardi Gras Indian chief (Clarke Peters), struggling to regroup in the wake of Hurricane Katrina.

Critics were impressed by its authentic New Orleans vibe, if somewhat underwhelmed by its lollygagging pace. Whereas *The Wire* was a deliberate inversion of a popular TV genre, *Treme* was something more amorphous: an attempt to dig into the pluralism of life in an American city without the standard tropes of violence and policing to lean on.

Like *The Wire*, it drew a modest audience. "*Treme* said so much about society," says Simon. "It's just that if you put a trombone in a guy's hand instead of a gun, you're not pulling the same numbers."

There were plenty of guns being fired elsewhere on HBO. In the fall of 2010, HBO rolled out *Boardwalk Empire*, a crackling gangster drama set among the flappers and burlesque shows of Atlantic City in the 1920s during the early days of Prohibition and women's suffrage. Terence Winter, the irascible writer for *The Sopranos*, created the show, based on a nonfiction book by Nelson Johnson. Tim Van Patten, HBO's fix-it man, served as an executive producer and directed four episodes in its inaugural season.

Viewers meet Enoch "Nucky" Thompson (Steve Buscemi), Atlantic City's corrupt, canny treasurer, and his younger brother, Eli (Shea Whigham), the local double-dealing sheriff. With the onset of Prohibition, the value of booze is skyrocketing, and emerging crews of gangsters from New York, Chicago, and Philadelphia are lining up at Nucky's doorstep, hoping to use the city's ports to smuggle in illegal liquor.

Before long, Nucky has a falling out with his protégé, Jimmy Darmody (Michael Pitt), a Princeton dropout and World War I vet whose young mom, Gillian (Gretchen Mol), is a showgirl and prostitute at a local brothel. Soon, various factions of men in well-tailored suits are battling for power amid the gin, the jazz, and the beer.

The first episode of *Boardwalk Empire* was directed by Martin Scorsese, who also served as an executive producer on the series. In recent years, the rise of the cable TV auteur had not gone unnoticed by Scorsese, a leader of Hollywood's previous generation of celebrated rule breakers. "What's happening the past 9 to 10 years, particularly at HBO, is what we had hoped for in the mid-Sixties," Scorsese said.

"Marty basically ran a course on gangster cinema for me and Tim Van Patten," Winter says. "We'd go to Marty's office, where he has a screening room. Every day, we'd watch every gangster movie ever made with Marty Scorsese talking while the movie's on."

One of their big early decisions was who to cast as Nucky Thompson. After batting around some names, Scorsese and Winter quickly settled on Steve Buscemi. It was an unconventional choice. The pallid, bug-eyed, linguine-limbed actor was at the time best known for playing cranky supporting characters in indie films. But Winter had worked with Buscemi throughout the fifth season of *The Sopranos*, on which Buscemi had played Tony's doomed mobster-turned-masseuse cousin.

"Every time I see a movie or a TV show, and it says Steve Buscemi is in it, I'm always like, well, I know that part is going to be good. So I thought, well, if you make him the lead, it'll be great," Winter says. "It was very unscientific."

Everyone at HBO was supportive, he says. "If it were network TV, there's no way Steve would have gotten that role," Winter says. "It would have been some heartthrob, some big, beefy, classically handsome guy."

Habitual HBO fans would eventually be thrilled to see Michael K. Williams—who played stickup man Omar Little on *The Wire*—appear on *Boardwalk Empire* as Albert "Chalky" White, the rakish, racketeering leader of the Black community on Atlantic City's north side.

To Plepler, HBO's lineup looked stable again. *True Blood* was a success. Martin Scorsese was now in the fold. There were numerous promising projects in development. By this point, he and Lombardo had been in their jobs for over three years, and the fallow period of the mid-2000s felt like it was finally coming to an end. "I remember sitting at the *Boardwalk* premiere and just feeling, 'All right, we're on our way,'" Plepler says.

CHAPTER 17

The Albanian Army

By the end of the decade, the movie-rental wars were effectively over. Netflix had won.

In the fall of 2010, teetering under $1 billion of debt, Blockbuster declared bankruptcy. The company's once ubiquitous blue-and-yellow-branded stores were starting to recede from the American landscape on roughly the same trajectory as bison and telephone booths. It was another reminder of what happened to industry front-runners that became so wedded to one era of technology (videocassettes) that they failed to adapt speedily to whatever came next (DVDs and the internet). Basically, extinction.

Subsequent autopsies on Blockbuster would make much of one fateful moment. In 2000, during the doldrums of the dot-com bust, Netflix's cofounders had approached the giant video rental chain and tried to sell their algorithmic, DVD-by-mail business to Blockbuster for $50 million. "We offered to sell a forty-nine percent stake and take the name Blockbuster.com," Hastings later told the *New Yorker*. "We'd be their online service." Unimpressed, Blockbuster turned them down.

Now, ten years later, Blockbuster was going belly-up, and Netflix was thriving on two different fronts: DVD rentals and streaming. In 2010, Netflix made $160.9 million of net income on more than $2.2 billion of revenue.

All told, Netflix could boast of more than 25 million paying monthly subscribers. By the end of the year, Netflix would be valued by investors at more than $9 billion.

Inside Netflix, the next phase of the company's quest to upend the home entertainment industry was getting under way. It was being led by a pair of executives, Ted Sarandos and Cindy Holland, who at first glance seemed like an improbable duo to remake Hollywood.

Sarandos was born in New Jersey in 1964 and moved to Phoenix with his young parents and four siblings when he was in elementary school. His father was an electrician, his mom a housewife. It was an unruly household. The TV was on at all hours, and the Sarandos family got a VCR and HBO well before anyone else in their neighborhood.

"Honestly, in my chaotic world, the people inside the box were living a life that I maybe fantasized about," Sarandos said. "They all had a very structured life."

After high school, Sarandos went to work at a local video store in Phoenix called Arizona Video Cassettes West and dropped out of college. Before long, he moved into sales for a distribution company named East Texas Distributors, which sold movies to video stores. Blockbuster was its biggest client.

In 1999, Sarandos noticed that when a movie was available on both VHS and DVD, customers preferred to rent the disk, not the tape. He threw himself headlong into the emerging new medium, hashing out revenue-sharing agreements between studios and rental stores.

His bullishness on DVDs eventually earned Sarandos a write-up in a trade publication called *Video Business*, which caught the attention of Reed Hastings at Netflix. Hastings proceeded to recruit Sarandos to his two-year-old DVD-by-mail service. At the time, Sarandos knew nothing about the tech world but was impressed by Hastings's unwavering belief that someday soon all entertainment would be distributed over the internet. The "Net" in "Netflix" was prophetic.

"I was blown away by Reed," Sarandos said. "Immediately."

At Netflix, Sarandos got to work managing its DVD inventory, trying to calculate how many copies of each movie and TV show Netflix needed to buy for its ever-expanding library. Once again, it was the rich bank of data from Netflix's website that ultimately helped solve the puzzle.

As Sarandos was building out Netflix's acquisition department, he needed help. In 2003, he made Cindy Holland his first hire in Los Angeles.

Holland grew up in Springfield, Nebraska, about a fifteen-minute drive from Omaha. Her childhood was shaped, in part, by a frustrating sense of cultural scarcity. Beyond broadcast television, access to contemporary filmmaking was in short supply, limited to a handful of VHS rentals at the local Pit Stop gas station and a single art house theater, the Dundee, which was about sixteen miles from her house. "Before I could drive, they might as well have been on the moon," Holland said.

In the 1990s, after graduating from college at Stanford University, Holland went to work for Kozmo.com, a venture-backed start-up that promised free one-hour delivery of everything from magazines to DVDs to Ben & Jerry's ice cream in several cities across the United States. Before the company imploded during the dot-com bust, Holland's job was to hammer out deals with film studios to procure more DVDs—not unlike Sarandos's job at Netflix. "She was the only other person who was doing what I was doing," Sarandos said.

Holland joined Netflix, impressed by the company's rich catalogue of DVDs by mail, which struck her as a great way to provide cultural nourishment to the hinterlands. The advent of streaming distribution would only improve the artistic sowing process.

By 2010, Sarandos and Holland were on the hunt for more TV series to license for its three-year-old streaming service. They were especially interested in premium serialized content, and there was no bigger or better player than HBO.

They saw the evidence in the data from the DVD business. Subscribers would often request the disks for a season of an HBO show, say, *The Sopranos* or *The Wire*, consume it quickly, then request more, finishing every episode of the series before shifting to something else. The serialized storytelling seemed tailor-made for Netflix binging.

Across the market, Netflix was scooping up the streaming rights to TV shows from a range of sources. Many of Showtime's top series, like *Weeds* and *Nurse Jackie*, were not owned by the network but by other studios, which were typically happy to license the streaming rights to Netflix. Disney had just sold the entire back catalogue of *Lost* to Netflix. FX was typically game to take the streamer's money. And AMC series like *Mad Men* and *Breaking Bad* would soon be on the service too.

For years, HBO had happily been selling its famous shows to Netflix on DVD. Each year, Netflix bought tons of DVD units, and HBO considered them a valued customer. But when it came to streaming, things were different. Whenever Netflix executives broached the topic of licensing HBO's programming for the company's streaming service, they got shot down.

"We felt that we had spent a lot of time and money carefully nurturing the HBO brand," recalls Henry McGee. "And to take that IP and allow Netflix to have, essentially, a rival service didn't make financial sense to our company."

Not easily dissuaded, the Netflix execs kept trying. Sarandos, a huge comedy nerd, was a big fan of *Mr. Show*, a sketch comedy series that aired on HBO for three years in the 1990s, hosted by Bob Odenkirk and David Cross. Maybe getting *Mr. Show* for Netflix was worth a shot? It seemed like an easy target. Since going off the air in 1998, the show had been languishing in HBO's vault. Sarandos approached the network's executives. Again, HBO rebuffed the offer.

"The negotiations were painful because Netflix had been such an important customer in terms of physically distributing DVDs through the mail," McGee says. "So it wasn't easy telling them that we weren't interested in using HBO shows to compete with us, delivering directly to the home an electronic version of our programming."

The Netflix team tried yet again. Sarandos approached HBO with an incredibly rich offer for the streaming rights to every season of *Six Feet Under* and *Deadwood*. It was meant to be eye-opening and to provoke Alan Ball's and David Milch's agents into fits, ensuring that they too would put pressure on HBO executives to accept the offer. It was also a test. Sarandos figured that if HBO wouldn't do it at a high price, they were never going to license anything to Netflix, ever.

Again, Bill Nelson, HBO's disciplined chief executive, was unyielding. "Me and my team were not giving one of our up-and-coming competitors, and existing competitors, anything that has an HBO name on it," Nelson says.

"It was a deliberate choice not to sell HBO content to Netflix at the time," Holland recalls.

After Nelson turned down the offer, Sarandos reached a conclusion. HBO wasn't going to budge. Also, it was probably just a matter of time before other networks followed HBO's example and started withholding the streaming rights to their programming. When that happened, Netflix would have to start making its own original shows to fill the gap.

"By the end of 2010, I remember explicit conversations where we're like okay, the more successful we are, the more this model works, yes, the incumbents will be addicted to the money and their quarterly profit cycles, but they're going to say, hey, the drumbeat is getting louder, we're going to have to build these things ourselves, we're going to have our own branded services," Holland says. "So we figured there would be some portion of the market that would start to withhold content."

The time frame, they figured, was about a half decade. "In five years, what will the marketplace look like?" Holland says. "We will probably need to be making our own content."

In spite of the occasional hiccups like HBO's continued intransigence, Netflix was booming. The company was expanding into foreign markets, offering the service for the first time in Canada, Latin America, and the Caribbean. And its technology kept improving. Just the year before, in 2009, Netflix had handed out a $1-million award to an international team of machine-learning experts for developing an algorithm that was able to beat the accuracy of the company's in-house recommendation engine, Cinematch, by 10 percent. Netflix's brand name was growing synonymous with a new, better way of watching commercial-free Hollywood entertainment at home.

Wall Street was smitten. Netflix's stock price was shooting up, and media outlets were fawning over Netflix's future. In the fall of 2010, *Fortune* magazine, which was owned by HBO's parent company Time Warner, named Netflix's CEO Hastings as its Businessperson of the Year.

Jeffrey Bewkes, who in 2008 succeeded Dick Parsons as the chief executive officer of all of Time Warner, was unimpressed. In December, during an interview with the *New York Times*, Bewkes challenged the rosy assessment of Netflix being offered by his top business publication. Just as Hollywood studio bosses in the 1980s had scoffed at the idea of HBO creating original programming, Bewkes now took a contemptuous swipe at Netflix. "It's a little bit like, is the Albanian army going to take over the world?" Bewkes said. "I don't think so."

Back at HBO, some of the younger managers pored over Bewkes's comments with a mix of dread and embarrassment. "As an executive at HBO, I physically cringed when I read that quote," says Jamyn Edis, a former vice president of HBO's consumer technology group. "The sheer level of pride and arrogance that would allow our company's leadership to gracelessly and ignorantly dismiss a competitor out of hand—I knew then that our transformation to a digital company was going to be a bloody campaign."

Others worried that the company's leaders, swaddled in the comfort of their private jets and long accustomed to the trappings of success, just weren't taking the threat from Netflix seriously enough. "It was a very comfortable company," says Allan Wai, a former HBO design and products manager, who was then working on HBO GO. "Everything in the offices is first class. There's a gym. There's a cafeteria. There's an on-site acupuncturist, an on-site tailor, and an on-site masseuse. That creates a certain complacency."

Over at Netflix, Hastings took the Bewkes jab in stride. Weeks after the belittling remark, Hastings gathered his top seventy executives for a regularly scheduled business meeting at the Rosewood Sand Hill, a sumptuous hotel and retreat studded with olive trees, in Menlo Park, California, not far from the Santa Cruz Mountains.

Jonathan Friedland, a former communications executive at Netflix, says that at the meeting, Hastings "kind of made fun of" Bewkes. Like an NFL coach printing out an insulting quote about his team made by a rival player and then hanging it in the locker room during the run-up to a big game,

Hastings used Bewkes's insult as "bulletin board material" for the Netflix pep rally, part inspiration, part rallying cry.

With the quote from Bewkes displayed behind him in a PowerPoint slide, Hastings read off fun facts about the military history of Albania to further fire up the members of his squad. "That's the kind of thing that was super motivating to people," Holland says.

As the meeting wrapped up, Hastings handed out a gift to each of his colleagues: army berets, in camouflage green, stitched with an image of a double-headed eagle from the Albanian national flag.

• • •

ON APRIL 17, 2011, *Game of Thrones* premiered on HBO. It was clear, right away, that Richard Plepler's decision to give the inexperienced showrunners a second shot had been the right one. With Tim Van Patten directing, the many problems of the original pilot had been sorted out, and *Game of Thrones* welcomed viewers into an exotic, alluring, ornately wrought world called Westeros.

In the first episode, bells are ringing, torches are flickering, baths are steaming, horses are snorting, dresses are dropping, and the first severed heads of autumn are starting to roll. A raven arrives in the north with a message. King Robert Baratheon (Mark Addy) is on the march, in need of fresh counsel. Dangerous, power-hungry forces are amassing across the seven kingdoms, plotting to seize power by overthrowing the ruling order.

Amid the growing anxiety, a guard unlawfully deserts his post. When he is captured, he warns that something strange and disruptive is gaining force just beyond their territorial protections. He is handed over to be executed by Lord Ned Stark (Sean Bean), a close, ramrod ally of the king. As a matter of principle, Stark makes his young son Bran (Isaac Hempstead Wright), who soon develops the clairvoyant power of seeing threats to his family well into the future, witness the beheading. The traditional mode of doing things must be upheld, evermore, the patriarch explains. Do you understand? His son nods and responds dutifully, "Our way is the old way."

The first episode of *Game of Thrones* drew a relatively modest audience of 2.2 million viewers. Not terrible, but not a clear-cut success, given its ex-orbitant price tag. In 2003, the series premiere of the similarly extravagant *Carnivàle* had attracted 5.3 million; in 2005, the first episode of *Rome* had been watched by 3.8 million households. But as the season went on, *Game of Thrones* kept pulling in more and more spectators.

By the time Comic-Con, the annual gathering in San Diego of cosplay-ing, autograph-collecting geeks rolled around that summer, avid fans of the show—so-called Throners—came out in force. Among the fantasy fanboy set, *Game of Thrones* was being heralded as the new king.

While most of the reviews were positive, a couple of aspects of *Games of Thrones* drew fire on social media and from critics—particularly the show's rough treatment of female characters and its excessive use of "cable edge."

In July, Mary McNamara, a TV critic for the *Los Angeles Times*, wrote a searing column, calling out the network for its gratuitous use of topless women. HBO's new fantasy series, McNamara noted, routinely featured an "obligatory scattering of reclining females with their blouses open," some-times pawing at each other, to a degree that "isn't just gratuitous and ridicu-lous," but "lazy and sexist."

One character, a political consigliere named Littlefinger (Aidan Gillen), regularly conducts business with other men in his brothels while surrounded by topless women who look more like soft-core lingerie models than hard-ened, medieval sex workers. The phenomenon, she noted, was commonplace across the HBO oeuvre. Perhaps during HBO's early days some men had subscribed to the network because of its rampant nudity. But that was before the internet came along and inundated the world with free porn. Maybe it was time, McNamara advised HBO, to "tone down the tits."

Such notes of criticism, however, were largely drowned out by the fawn-ing praise that grew louder with each episode. The growing success of *Game of Thrones* was a relief for HBO, particularly after a stinging defeat had played out just a couple of months earlier.

In February 2011, members of HBO's development team were consider-ing an idea for a D.C.-based drama series that was making the rounds. Media Rights Capital, an independent production studio, along with David Fincher, one of the top directors in Hollywood (*Fight Club*, *The Social Network*), and the actor Kevin Spacey were pitching a political thriller based on an adaptation of a BBC series called *House of Cards*. Screenwriter Beau Willimon, a former Democratic campaign worker for the likes of Charles Schumer and Howard Dean, was lined up to be its showrunner. The idea—with its blend of D.C. politics, Democratic Party bloodlines, and prestigious Hollywood pedigree—was like something engineered in a lab by scientists to appeal perfectly to Richard Plepler and HBO.

HBO decided to scoop up the series and offered to buy it at a pilot level. But before that could happen, the Albanian Army landed a devastating sneak attack.

In February 2011, Ted Sarandos happened to be sitting down with executives at Media Rights Capital to talk about the rights for *Brüno*, a comedy starring Sacha Baron Cohen. At the end of the meeting, MRC executives let Sarandos know that they had a big project they were taking out to market that weekend. "Would you guys like to look at it?" an MRC executive asked.

Sarandos and Holland looked at all the names attached and came to a swift conclusion. This had to be Netflix's first big splash. Their five-year timeline for jumping into original programming turned out to be more like five weeks. "If we're going to do original content, this is it," Holland said to Sarandos.

By buying *House of Cards*, Netflix would define what content for the internet could be. "Because up until the moment we launched *House of Cards*," Holland recalls, "everything that was made for the internet was webisodes, Funny or Die, people falling off horses or getting kicked in the nuts."

Other streamers like Hulu, says Holland, were making early investments in original programming, but it was what she considered "the Comedy Central space"—in other words, low rent. Netflix, they agreed, ought to begin by aiming high.

"If you have *House of Cards*, then you start *here*, you set the bar *here*," Holland says. "And then you can go anywhere—from a genre perspective, from a brand perspective. But if you start with low-rent stuff, you're always going to be trying to climb out of it."

Because HBO was in hot pursuit, the only way Netflix was going to win was to make an astounding offer. "There's a thousand reasons not to do this at Netflix," Sarandos told Fincher. "I want to give you one reason to say yes."

Sarandos and Holland outlined their plan to Fincher and MRC executives: not only would there be no pilot required, but Netflix would commit to a two-season, twenty-six-episode guarantee, which was unheard of. They also promised Fincher that they would not bog him down with any notes. He could make the show any way he saw fit. And then Netflix offered a staggering amount of money: $100 million for the two-season commitment.

"We made the richest offer that had been seen for something that hadn't been made yet," Holland says.

It worked. Fincher's team chose to go with the streaming newcomer over HBO. Plepler and the programming team were stunned at Netflix's two-year commitment. "We couldn't do that," Plepler says. "We didn't have the financial flexibility to make that commitment."

News of the deal set tongues wagging in Hollywood. It seemed like a hugely risky maneuver. What in the world, everyone wondered, was Netflix up to?

• • •

AROUND THE SAME TIME that Netflix was outmaneuvering HBO for *House of Cards*, Jeffrey Bewkes was tending to other matters. In September 2011, he was preparing to celebrate the nuptials of a good friend. The former chief executive of HBO, Chris Albrecht, at fifty-nine, was getting married.

In the four years since leaving HBO in disgrace following his arrest in Las Vegas, Albrecht had hardly slunk away from the Hollywood spotlight. For a stretch, he'd teamed up with Steve Bing, an ultrawealthy real estate scion and dogged bachelor, to try to buy Playboy Enterprises. Ultimately, their effort to acquire the aging fleshpot magazine and untrousered lifestyle brand fell through, dashing Albrecht's shot at succeeding Hugh Hefner as the pervy paterfamilias of the Playboy mansion. Instead, Albrecht settled into a well-compensated job as the chief executive officer of Starz, a second-tier premium cable channel that competed down-market from HBO.

Albrecht's bride-to-be was Montana Coady, a tall, towheaded twenty-five-year-old equestrian, who had grown up riding horses competitively alongside Kate Albrecht, one of Chris's two daughters.

The puffed-up wedding party, overstuffed with illustrious guests, took place at the Beverly Hills Hotel, a swank temple of Hollywood glamour on Sunset Boulevard, home to a storied red carpet, twelve acres of tropical gardens, and the famed power-lunch spot the Polo Lounge. On the big day, Bewkes, one of the most influential men in the industry, the standard-bearer of a global company with tens of thousands of employees, served as Albrecht's loyal groomsman, presiding over the pageantry at what amounted to a Hollywood state dinner.

Among the multitude of bold names in attendance were Brett Ratner, the feature film director, who in 2017 would be accused by more than a half dozen women of sexual harassment; Leslie Moonves, then head of CBS, who in 2018 would lose his job amid reports of sexual misconduct; and Harvey Weinstein, the prolific producer and sex offender who in 2020 would be convicted on two counts of felony sex crimes.

In just a few years' time, the Hollywood power structure on display that night, its chummy members circling the dance floor, sidling up to the bar, and mingling among the rosebushes and Brazilian pepper trees, would come crashing down, felled by the courageous testimony from numerous women in the TV and film industry. Women who'd been sexually assaulted, or groped, or denigrated by their colleagues or their bosses with impunity. Women who'd been pressured into silence by a co-opted corporate culture. Women who'd watched repeat predators go on to receive promotions and accolades at studios and networks while their own careers languished.

But all of that, the forthcoming justice of the #MeToo movement, was still several years off, and as of yet unimaginable. For now, the self-regarding Hollywood establishment—the executives and producers who determined more than anyone else in American culture what kinds of stories millions of viewers saw on TV and in movie theaters, what women appeared in those productions, how they were depicted on screen, who got promoted, and how much they got paid—still enjoyed an unassailable grip on the industry. Inside the grounds of the Beverly Hills Hotel, they unabashedly joined Jeffrey Bewkes for the occasion, forming in their collective heft a showy phalanx of support for their compatriot Chris Albrecht, the celebrated TV executive and admitted batterer.

Not everyone at Time Warner was amused to see their CEO honoring Albrecht with such a conspicuous act of fealty, even if Bewkes and the groom were longtime buddies. Loyalty, as a palatable defense, has its limits. "Jeff serving in the wedding was in very poor taste," says Shelley Brindle, the former HBO sales and marketing executive. "There are no other factors that could make it okay."

Privately, some uninvited onlookers felt revolted by the ceremonial pomp bestowed upon the May-December romance, which would end in divorce a few years later. One former HBO producer—who says she had enjoyed a long-running affair with Albrecht during the years when he was still married to his first wife and running the network—was taken aback when she first heard about the engagement. Just a few years earlier her daughter had been in high school with Albrecht's new bride-to-be. "I retained a friendship with Chris until he married a girl my daughter's age," she says.

She wasn't the only one who felt perturbed. One person not in attendance at the festivities was Kate Albrecht, who objected to her father's relationship to her younger horse-riding associate. "Due to my disgust and desire to have a functional life, I chose not to attend," she would later write in a book of published essays in a chapter entitled "I Used to Babysit My Stepmom." "You have to protect yourself in life, and if that means not seeing Buzz Aldrin dance at my father's wedding, so be it."

• • •

AFTER BEING STRANGLED BY ALBRECHT and leaving HBO in 1991, Sasha Emerson had spent several productive years developing TV shows at New Line. But ultimately, no matter where she went or what she achieved, people in show business seemed to know her first and foremost as *that woman from the thing at HBO*—it was a kind of scarlet letter, which she had to bear on top of everything else.

Finally she walked away and started building a second career as an interior designer. Emerson was a devoted, lifelong student of art history and design. She was also an avid flea markets visitor, endlessly sifting through the
flotsam of the world and picking out funky, beautiful things. She did the
interior of her own house in Los Angeles. It was elegant and playful, an inviting
style of relaxed modernism, and ended up on the cover of *House & Garden*.
"I was listed as the designer of record," Emerson says. "Then my phone started
to ring."

With a friend, she set up a commercial space, called Orange, located
on lower Robertson Boulevard in Los Angeles, and filled it with interesting
pieces of furniture and found art. From an office in the back, she started an
interiors business. In the years that followed, hundreds of clients signed on
for her services. Many were wealthy actors and screenwriters and producers
whom she'd met, or worked with, or befriended, or gotten jobs for, in her previous line of work. Now, instead of improving their scripts or finding them
a director, she was designing their homes and offices. Gillian Anderson, *The
X-Files* actor, was a client. So, too, was Marcy Carsey, the producer of *The
Cosby Show*.

If it was less lucrative than developing TV shows, in some ways it was
more intimate. Doing interiors was a bit like set design. Every house was a
part of a family's narrative, and Emerson was exceptionally good at helping
people give shape to the stories they would like to tell about themselves.

"There's a playful eccentricity to everything she does, which is incredibly
sophisticated," says Dean Parisot, the director of *Galaxy Quest*. "She is always
repurposing things that you never would have thought would be in your
house. Like a giant clock as a table. Things like that. There's a lot more at play
beyond an aesthetic sensibility. There's also an absurd sense of fun to it."

By the time of Albrecht's wedding, Karla Jensen had also switched professions. Since Albrecht had strangled her in Las Vegas four years earlier,
Jensen had given up her career in front of the camera. Her days reporting
on HBO red-carpet events were over. Due to the intense press coverage surrounding her assault, the lens through which the world saw her had forever
been slanted.

While Albrecht would continue to enjoy a comfortable series of executive entertainment jobs, Jensen faced a more uncertain professional path. Eventually, in 2011, she landed an off-camera position with Films in Motion, a production company based in Baton Rouge, Louisiana. In her spare time, she threw herself into a charitable pastime: taking in, nurturing, and finding new homes for rescued and abused dogs.

Within a few years' time, the public's perception of nonlethal strangulation would start to change dramatically. Strangulation would soon come to be widely seen by prosecutors and social workers as the ultimate red flag in cases of domestic violence, an early warning sign of escalating abuse. Gripping and constricting a person's throat can lead to unconsciousness within seconds and death within minutes. Even if the victim survives with little physical damage, nonlethal strangulation can result in severe, lifelong mental trauma.

In 2009, two years after Albrecht strangled Jensen outside the MGM Grand and was subsequently allowed to plead guilty to a misdemeanor, the state of Nevada would change its criminal laws, making nonlethal strangulation a felony carrying a minimum sentence of one year in prison. Many other states have since followed suit with similar statutes, reflecting the growing awareness among American lawmakers of the seriousness of the crime.

CHAPTER 18

Flying Blind

On the night of October 10, 2011, a crowd of more than a thousand people packed into Alice Tully Hall at Lincoln Center in New York City. They were there to watch a screening of *Paradise Lost 3: Purgatory*, the final film in HBO's documentary trilogy about the awful child murders in Arkansas.

Over the better part of three decades, Sheila Nevins had built the network's documentary division into a juggernaut, surpassing PBS to become the genre's dominant patron. With a budget and platform unmatched by any rivals, Nevins was sending out her squad of verité filmmakers, digging around the margins of modern culture, turning up sensational and socially lacerating works, on everything from AIDS victims (*Common Threads: Stories from the Quilt*) to violent anti-abortion activists (*Soldiers in the Army of God*).

With each passing year, the industry honors kept piling higher inside her corner office at HBO headquarters. Emmys, Oscars, Peabody Awards. "How did I win so many awards?" Nevins says. "Well, there wasn't much competition."

In 2000, HBO aired *Paradise Lost 2: Revelations*, the second film in the true-crime series from Joe Berlinger and Bruce Sinofsky. Therein, the filmmakers delved deeper into the circumstances of the heinous murders and the shoddy police investigation that followed.

Like the original, *Paradise Lost 2* caused an uproar. The three convicted and imprisoned teenagers, Damien Echols, Jason Baldwin, and Jessie Misskelley Jr., came across not only as innocent, but also as victims of a mindlessly stubborn criminal justice system.

Despite the growing outrage, the West Memphis Three remained behind bars. Again, Nevins encouraged Berlinger and Sinofsky to keep filming. They would follow the story to the end.

Now, in the fall of 2011, the crowd inside the New York theater took their seats for the final round in the infuriating saga.

At the start of *Paradise Lost 3: Purgatory*, the gangly, fresh-faced teenagers of the first film are showing signs of middle age. Echols looks gaunt and fragile, the incautious flippancy of his youth long ago drained out of him. Baldwin's voice has coarsened, and his hair is thinning. Misskelley's bald head is adorned with a tattoo of a clock with no arms. In prison, time is broken.

At the law school of the University of Arkansas in Little Rock, lawyers for Echols hold a press conference. Thanks, in part, to money from the Hollywood director Peter Jackson, Echols's defense team has assembled a top-notch crew of forensic experts who have pored over every micrometer of the case. With a large crew of reporters looking on, they lay out significant new evidence in support of their client's innocence.

Even so, the judge in the case remains unmoved and denies their motion for a new trial. The impasse continues.

Berlinger and Sinofsky visit Echols on death row. He tells them that without their films for HBO he would already be dead. "I really do believe these people would have gotten away with murdering me if it would not have been for what you guys did—for being there in the very beginning and getting this whole thing on tape so that the rest of the world sees what was happening," Echols says.

At last, in the fall of 2010, Echols catches a break. The Arkansas Supreme Court grants an evidentiary hearing, which will officially allow lawyers for the West Memphis Three to present their new evidence to the court. With public scrutiny mounting, the prosecutors decide to cut a deal.

On August 19, 2011, the West Memphis Three are summoned to a circuit court hearing. There, they each enter an Alford Plea—an arrangement with prosecutors in which they accept the consequences of a guilty verdict for first-degree murder while continuing to profess their innocence. In exchange, their sentences are reduced to time served. After eighteen years and seventy-eight days of incarceration, they are finally released from prison.

At a press conference afterward, Echols says it had "been an absolute living hell." No real justice has been served, Baldwin says, because the true killers are still at large. With the cameras rolling, the long-separated childhood friends hug and cry.

A couple of months later, at the theater in Manhattan, the screening of *Paradise Lost 3* came to its end, and the lights came up on the mesmerized crowd. Fresh out of prison, Echols, Baldwin, and Misskelley sat in a private box overlooking the theater. As the film credits rolled, the three men rose to their feet. Echols was dressed in black. Baldwin wore a button-down shirt; Misskelley, a sports jacket. Next to them in the box were Sheila Nevins and her unremitting filmmakers, Berlinger and Sinofsky.

From below, there was a rustling in the theater as everyone rose out of their chairs at once, gazed up at the three men, and let out a thunderous roar— a collective venting of joy and sorrow, anger and relief.

"People were in tears," Berlinger says. "It was for what these guys went through. Ten minutes of nonstop ovation."

In the years to come, admiring filmmakers would reference and pay homage to the *Paradise Lost* films countless times. Along the way, the HBO trilogy would help to usher in a sustained and far-reaching boom in commercial, true-crime documentaries. "I can't tell you how many people have come up to me and said, 'Because of *Paradise Lost* I became a filmmaker,'" Berlinger says. "It's taught in law schools. There's an aura around it."

For those who believed in the loftier bits of HBO's mission, it was arguably the biggest night in the network's history: proof that strong patronage of the video arts could amount to something more meaningful than the usual, self-interested focus on ratings and profits and awards. Sometimes, HBO could deliver justice.

"It felt good," Nevins says. "It felt right. I felt that we'd done something important, and that we'd given these kids some kind of life."

It was also a vindication of the HBO method, the one that Nevins had taken from the Maysles Brothers and been refining for decades. Turn the cameras on everyday individuals. Capture their fight to survive whatever ugliness and indignities life has thrown at them. Don't look away from the struggle, even if it takes nearly twenty years to resolve.

"The belief that if you stick to it and sit long enough, that that session with a real person, or a real experience, will produce something very valuable is kind of our motto," Nevins said. "We are very patient for a very impatient medium."

● ● ●

ON MARCH 12, 2012, *Girls* debuted at the South by Southwest festival in Austin, Texas—the first time the gathering of media and film insiders had been used to launch a new TV series. For the occasion, HBO sponsored a free bike share and organized a *Girls*-branded scavenger hunt, directing followers around town via clues on Twitter to collect free tacos and beer.

On a warm Monday afternoon, the young cast of *Girls* strolled down a red carpet leading into Austin's Paramount Theater. Inside, the network played the first three episodes.

Girls is set in contemporary Brooklyn and tells the story of four friends struggling to define themselves in the confusing, exciting, bittersweet aftermath of college, at a time when anxiety is running high for liberal arts majors.

At the outset, an aspiring twentysomething writer named Hannah Horvath (Dunham) is cut off financially by her parents—a cataclysmic moment in the life cycle of a Brooklyn hipster. She is devastated. How will she possibly survive?

Later, she goes to the supervisor of her unpaid internship in book publishing and asks him to start paying her for her labor. But rather than give her a salary, her boss instead sends her packing, further ratcheting up the economic pressure.

Afterward, feeling dispirited, Hannah has rough, awkward sex with Adam, a muscular, underemployed, aspiring actor (Adam Driver). She sits naked in a bathtub and gives romantic counsel to her friend Marnie (Allison Williams). And she awaits a reunion with her friend Jessa (Jemima Kirke), a louche way-farer returning from a stint abroad and moving in with her cousin Shoshanna (Zosia Mamet), who has a *Sex and the City* poster hanging on her apart-ment's wall.

Feeling riddled with anxiety, Hannah starts worrying that she may have AIDS and goes to see her gynecologist. During the examination, Hannah weighs the pros and cons of being infected by HIV in 2012. "If you have AIDS, there's a lot of stuff people *aren't* going to bother you about," Hannah says, during her examination. "For example, no one is going to call you on the phone and say, 'Did you get a job?' Or 'Did you pay your rent?' Or 'Are you taking an HTML course?'"

After the screening in Austin, Judd Apatow joined Dunham and her producing partner Jenni Konner onstage. "I've never been around so many women before," Apatow joked. "It was a new thing."

In the months that followed, the cast members were frequently asked about the show's evolutionary relationship to *Sex and the City*. Dunham explained that whereas the ladies in *Sex and the City* were already well-established professionals with promising careers, *Girls* tackled a different stage of its heroines' lives: their postcollegiate malaise. Whereas *Sex and the City* was explicitly aspirational, *Girls* felt much less self-assured. Also, *Girls* was actually written by a woman, as opposed to its HBO precursor, which was created by Darren Star, and then overseen by Michael Patrick King, two gay men.

"No, it's not *Sex and the City*, where it's a total lie," Kirke told the *New York Times*. "That's four gay men sitting around talking."

When the series started airing on HBO in April 2012, few tuned in. Even so, *Girls* quickly generated a vast amount of attention on social media

and in the press. Dunham emerged as a budding star and irresistible light-
ning rod. There were *Girls* think pieces. Hate pieces. Academic articles. Trend
stories. Manifestos. *New York* magazine put Dunham on its cover: HBO'S
NEW COMEDY 'GIRLS' IS THE BALLSIEST SHOW ON TV, read the headline.
By season three, she was being photographed by Annie Leibovitz for the
cover of *Vogue.*

By now, Casey Bloys—the congenial development executive who upon
his arrival at HBO years earlier had marveled at his colleagues' obsession
with critics—was overseeing all of HBO's comedies. As was the case with a
growing number of successful HBO shows, Bloys had played a key role in
shaping the foundational architecture of *Girls.* Early on, when Dunham was
still sketching out the contours of the series, something felt off. On paper,
Dunham had the four friends embedded in New York and going about their
lives, but there was no sense of momentum, nothing that seemed to set the
series into motion. What it needed was an initial spark, some elemental
stroke of drama to ignite the plot.

It was Bloys who came up with the perfect way to blast off the proceedings. "In the development process, sometimes I'll ask, why are we dropping
in on this story now?" Bloys says. "What dynamics are changing that you
want to watch?"

Bloys had a thought. What if, from the get-go, Dunham's character
learned she was being cut off economically from her parents? That could be
the springboard to drive Hannah's misadventures into high gear.

"That made it feel a little bit more significant," he says. "When your parents say 'no more,' especially for that generation, and especially for that kind
of person trying to work in the arts living in New York, it feels like something that would have been a turning point."

Sure enough, Bloys's idea proved to be the ideal narrative catalyst—and
afterward, the rest fell into place. A first-rate programming executive like,
say, a top-quality magazine or book editor, can steer a project onto a much
better trajectory with a simple, well-timed suggestion, often by bringing a
slightly askew structure into a more harmonious, creative alignment. It was

a crucial skill at HBO for which Bloys clearly possessed a special knack, and Plepler was taking notice. HBO's incisive head of comedy was bound for greater things.

Girls, however, did have one glaring weakness. While many reviewers praised the series for its messy, nuanced depiction of its female characters, *Girls* also drew criticism for the overwhelming whiteness of its cast, an increasingly frequent critique of HBO's slate. "The argument has been made that smart women on screen are already enough of a minority to make up for the lack of women of color," Jenna Wortham wrote about *Girls* in the Hairpin. "Nope. Not good enough."

In response, Dunham said in interviews that the series was largely a reflection of her own personal experience. "I really wrote the show from a gut-level place, and each character was a piece of me and/or based on someone close to me," she told Terry Gross on NPR's *Fresh Air*. "And only later did I realize that it was four white girls."

A few days after the premiere of *Girls* in Austin, HBO executives found themselves struggling with a dilemma, which unlike persistent questions about the network's lack of diversity, was in fact a new one in the network's history.

What to do about a dead horse?

Following the failure of *John from Cincinnati*, HBO had given David Milch, the network's loquacious auteur, another shot. This time around, Milch chose to create a series, entitled *Luck*, set in a world he knew quite well: horse racing. When he was a kid, his father had taken him to the races in Saratoga, New York, and gotten him hooked. As an adult, Milch collected racehorses and tried not to gamble too much.

The series, Milch explained, would explore similar themes as *John from Cincinnati* and *Deadwood*. "The human spirit doesn't have too many variants," Milch said. "It operates in different settings but its truths tend to be universal."

As it came together, *Luck* looked like it couldn't lose. HBO paired Milch with Michael Mann, the producer of the original *Miami Vice* TV series who'd gone on to become an acclaimed moviemaker (*The Last of the Mohicans*, *The Insider*, *Heat*). Mann came on board as an executive producer.

He also directed the pilot, which was set among the gamblers, jockeys, and greedy horse owners at a track in California. Big-screen thoroughbred Dustin Hoffman starred in the leading role, his first significant foray in television—more evidence, critics duly noted, that the industry's top movie talents were increasingly migrating to cable TV. "It was supposed to be *star time*," Milch said.

Despite the impressive pedigree, however, *Luck* limped through HBO's Sunday-night lineup. Only 1.1 million households watched the premiere in January 2012, and subsequent episodes struggled to get a half million viewers. The reviews were largely underwhelming. Even so, HBO renewed the drama for a second season.

With production on new episodes under way in March 2012, an accident happened. A horse was injured on set and had to be euthanized. The mishap drew attention to two other horses who had previously died in service of *Luck*. A spokesperson with People for the Ethical Treatment of Animals was livid. "You put a retired racehorse through a starting gate and run him down a track, it's a race," she said. "He doesn't know he's acting."

Facing a growing outcry, Lombardo and Plepler decided to put *Luck* out of its misery and ended the series. "If you believe the official version it was canceled because three horses died," Milch said.

The truth, Milch would later tell the Television Academy, was that the show was an awful mess long before PETA's hackles were raised. For one thing, *Luck* was way over budget, and Milch was getting along horribly with Mann. "It was not a happy collaboration," Milch said.

During production, Milch had lost forty pounds in six months. Other, long-dormant appetites no longer felt sated. After years of abstinence, Milch had started gambling ravenously on horse races again. As a practical matter, the euthanasia of *Luck* came as a major relief. "I feel like it saved my life," Milch said.

For HBO, the whole messy saga was an early warning sign of a problem that would snowball at the network in the years to come. As much success as the network had with Mike Nichols, Tom Hanks, Steven Spielberg, and Martin Scorsese, it was growing increasingly tempted to sign up eminent film producers and directors to do episodic television. And simply shoehorning big-time movie talent into HBO series was no guarantee for success. Often, it was the opposite.

• • •

HBO WAS HAVING BETTER LUCK with the horse-race politics of Washington, D.C.

In April 2012, HBO began airing *Veep*, the darkly humorous send-up of Washington, D.C., executive produced by Frank Rich and created by Armando Iannucci, a British political satirist with a literary background. Iannucci grew up in Glasgow, studied English literature at Oxford University, and for several years pursued a doctorate focused on John Milton's *Paradise Lost* before eventually dropping out for a career in comedy.

His one previous foray into American broadcast television—a short-lived adaptation of his BBC political sitcom *The Thick of It* for ABC—had not gone well. "There's 15,000 vice presidents of marketing chipping in," he said. "Obviously, you can make good television that way, but it's not how I want to make my stuff." He would enjoy a much better experience at HBO.

"You heard this guy talking about all the things that as a political junkie I was very attentive to: the spectacle, the Kabuki nature of it, the hypocrisy, the disingenuousness," Plepler says. "And, of course, he made it all arch and genius."

Veep stars Julia Louis-Dreyfus, the former *Seinfeld* mainstay, as Selina Meyer, an irascible vice president ruling over a stumbling staff of sycophantic lackeys. In her office, she is the sun, everyone else a lowly succulent. Meyer is driven by an insatiable desire to accrue power, a need that is constantly being undermined by her second-banana status to the unseen president. Among other duties, she is given the societally important—though politically impotent—job of organizing a government task force on obesity. "I'd have more power in my hands if I joined one of those moronic Segway tours of D.C.," she gripes.

"Essentially, every single character only cares about him- or herself—

not just Selina—and is desperate for power," Rich says. "The last people they are thinking about are their constituents."

Before the pilot was shot, Iannucci sent out a production memo about how the show should look. The government offices would be a mess, he wrote. The furniture, crappy. Chairs should be mismatched with desks. There would be detritus everywhere. Unlike *Sex and the City* and the design genius of Patricia Field, all the characters would be dressed in fashions that were a decade behind New York.

Rich, a native of Washington, D.C., says that Iannucci was able to capture "the whole, sort of, provinciality and lack of sophistication" of Washington. "Most portrayals of Washington in pop culture, movies and TV are very romanticized," Rich says. "The standard is *The West Wing*. This could not have been more the un–*West Wing*."

Throughout the series, Meyer's political party is left unclear, and Louis-Dreyfus's performance avoids coming across as a parody of any one politician, say, Sarah Palin or Hillary Clinton. At times, however, there are hints of certain real-world muses. Prior to writing *Veep*, Iannucci had consumed Robert Caro's multivolume series of books about Lyndon Baines Johnson and clearly took much creative inspiration from the thirty-seventh vice president of the United States. Often during *Veep*, Meyer comes across like a female LBJ, if a hapless version. She could be pragmatic, strategically charming, power-obsessed, crass, and conniving.

The mesmerizing performance got critics raving ("Hail to the Veep," declared *The Atlantic*) and solidified HBO's return to the top of cable TV.

In September 2012, HBO's chairman and chief executive officer Bill Nelson announced he was retiring. He was in his sixties, had a big family, and wasn't interested in clinging on to the job forever. No matter what, he'd always planned on a five-year run. "You never know what your health's going to be," Nelson says.

Unlike Michael Fuchs and Chris Albrecht, he was going to leave on his own terms. And he held strong convictions about who should replace him. "It's clearly Richard who should be the successor," Nelson says. "I said that to him."

To the outside world, and even to many people inside of HBO, the power-sharing arrangement looked like a kind of corporate death match. In reality, the fix was in from the start. For nearly five years, Nelson had been quietly grooming Plepler for the top job, even if Plepler didn't know it. In meetings, Nelson walked his protégé through all the crucial aspects of HBO's success beyond programming: the financials, the marketing, the international strategy, the negotiations with studios, the relationships with the cable operators.

Plepler was an eager student. Looking back, he describes his weekly meetings with Nelson as a "master class." "In those four and a half years, every weekly meeting we had, he taught me something," Plepler says.

When Nelson's retirement was announced, Time Warner made it official. Plepler was taking over.

• • •

IN 2012, executives at HBO and Netflix girded to go head-to-head in a streaming battle for the first time—albeit on a distant playing field.

That summer, Netflix announced that it was planning to expand into Norway, Denmark, Sweden, and Finland. Around the same time, HBO revealed that it, too, would be launching a new service in Scandinavia as part of a joint venture with Parsifal International, a European media and technology company.

Both ventures were scheduled to launch that fall.

The effort in Scandinavia, analysts noted, would be a key test for HBO. For the first time, HBO would be selling a streaming product to anyone who wanted it, not just to customers who already paid for a cable or satellite subscription.

"Excited to see HBO join us in offering stand-alone streaming service in Scandinavia . . . what about the USA?" Netflix's Reed Hastings wrote good-naturedly on Facebook. "We thought the first match-up would be in Albania."

Compared to opportunities in Asia and Western Europe, the overall size of the Scandinavian market was relatively small. But for both HBO and Netflix, the territory was appealing for several reasons. Northern Europe offered a relatively wealthy consumer base, lots of high-speed internet, and plenty of young consumers already accustomed to watching programming via computers, tablets, and smartphones.

The local entertainment industry was known for its excellent small-budget TV shows and movies, particularly its dark and stormy Nordic noirs. In HBO's and Netflix's first battle for streaming bragging rights, a discerning audience would decide the winner.

As the fall approached, inside Netflix anxiety ran high. During international expansions, the streaming service was comfortable taking on local incumbents. Clashing simultaneously with such a deep-pocketed U.S. rival was something entirely new and forbidding.

Time Warner revealed that Peter Ekelund, the head of Parsifal, would serve as the chairman of HBO Nordic. Ekelund was largely unknown to HBO's rank and file. That fall, at the Nordic Media Summit in Copenhagen, Denmark, a press release informed curious participants that Ekelund was a graduate of the Stockholm School of Economics, who early in his career helped to develop and launch Absolut Vodka. Ekelund, the conference organizers further noted, was currently living "on a potato and cattle farm at Cape Bjäre" on the west coast of Sweden.

The prospect of a potato-farming Scandinavian vodka baron leading HBO's attempted streaming conquest in the snowy north left industry analysts drooling. One dubbed the fight between HBO and Netflix in the Nordics the "Thiller in the Chiller."

But in the end, the suspense in Scandinavia was short-lived. HBO Nordic couldn't live up to the hype.

During the run-up to launch, according to a former employee, communication with HBO headquarters back in New York was muddled. Nobody seemed on the same page. For a bunch of bureaucratic rather than strategic reasons, the HBO Nordic team ended up building its streaming service on a completely different technology platform than the one being used for HBO GO in the United States. A slew of technology problems cropped up one after another. Initially, HBO had planned to debut in October, but then had to push it back to a later date, allowing Netflix to get to market first.

Netflix, which used the same technology everywhere in the world, suffered no such setbacks. Among online user ratings, HBO Nordic was consistently a poor performer, generally drawing only a couple of stars. By the fall
of 2013, according to the Swedish research firm MMS, Netflix was reaching
on average an estimated 308,000 daily viewers while HBO Nordic was capturing only 17,000.

The first head-to-head battle was a bloodbath. The Albanian Army won
in a rout.

In December 2012, with the threat from Netflix growing more dire by
the day, HBO announced it was appointing a new chief technology officer.
A newcomer named Otto Berkes would take charge of HBO's streaming
future.

Berkes was a Hungarian-born engineer, slight of stature, who had dark
hair, a prominent widow's peak, and glasses. His family had moved to America when he was a kid and had bounced around while his father built up his
medical practice. Growing up, Berkes played the violin, enjoyed building
electronic gadgets like crystal radios, and tended to his extensive collection
of rocks.

He had arrived at HBO the previous year, in 2011, from Microsoft where
he'd spent two decades developing software and hardware products, many
involving the Xbox, Microsoft's successful foray into the video-game console
business. The culture at Microsoft, Berkes sometimes reminded his new colleagues, was different from HBO. Managers had to back up every decision
with quantitative arguments and models of future projections. There was no
such thing as the Microsoft shrug.

Otto Berkes's new job as chief technology officer was to push HBO's
streaming products forward. Since its debut two and a half years earlier, HBO
had extended the streaming service across a range of platforms. There was
now an HBO GO app for the iPad, one for Roku, and ones for tablets and
smartphones using Google's Android software. But across the board, HBO
GO was struggling to keep up with the growing demand for streaming video,
which was accelerating.

At the time, according to internal HBO documents, the peak number of HBO GO users was only about 140,000 concurrent streams, a relatively modest amount. Even so, during prime viewing hours, the service kept breaking down.

"It was a toy app," Berkes recalls. "It fell over when you sneezed."

Every Sunday night at the time, a makeshift team of about twenty HBO employees would hop on a group conference call, set up to monitor the fragile state of the service during HBO's big night. Again and again, with the team looking on anxiously, HBO's servers crashed, sending everyone into a tizzy. "We'd be monitoring it, and the stream would drop," recalls Allan Wai. "We were, like, marketing folks and product design people. What is anyone going to do when a server goes down? It was comical how woefully unprepared we were."

In the face of such struggles, Otto Berkes set out on an ambitious plan to build a more robust streaming technology platform, one that could handle the rapidly growing demand from consumers and the proliferating number of viewing platforms, and that could someday more directly take on Netflix both in the United States and overseas.

In a nine-page white paper, marked "confidential" and entitled "The Future of HBO GO," Berkes noted that the network's streaming service was already "behind the curve" and at an "evolutionary dead end." HBO GO, he wrote, lacked key features like recommendations, deep personalization, social integration, and "watch next episode" buttons. There was no way for users to report issues and no way for HBO to collect, track, or triage the problems that did arise. "We are flying blind," Berkes wrote.

Worse yet, each version of the app was a unique "one-off"—in other words, less like a unified nation-state with one set of rules and more like a series of isolated islands, each governed by its own unique language, bureaucracy, and laws. HBO's streaming apps in the United States ran on different, noncomplementary technology than the ones in Scandinavia and Asia. Implementing any new feature on HBO GO required rebuilding each customized version of the service for each tech platform in each region of the world every time anything needed to be improved—a laborious, costly, and time-consuming process.

What HBO needed to do, Berkes wrote, was to transition to an integrated software-based approach. He recommended that instead of continuing to buy and maintain its own growing number of servers, HBO should commit to a more efficient and scalable model, leasing cloud-based capabilities, as needed, from the likes of Amazon Web Services. As an example of how HBO should proceed, he invoked Netflix, which was an early adopter of Amazon's cloud computing services and used "one code base, one set of product features, one user experience, and one set of apps anywhere in the world." With the right investment, focus, and institutional support, Berkes wrote, HBO could get there in eighteen months.

It was a holistic vision for a service that would be capable of delivering to customers not only HBO's programming but also all of Time Warner's—a vast library of shows from multiple cable TV networks, including TBS, TNT, and CNN.

He dubbed the plan to reinvent HBO GO, Project Halley, after the comet.

To build such a streaming platform from scratch, his team would need hundreds of millions of dollars in new investment. Inside the Michael Fuchs Theater on the fifteenth floor of HBO's Bryant Park headquarters, Otto Berkes began hosting a series of presentations designed to win over various factions at the company. Everyone from Time Warner board members to folks in HBO affiliate relations eventually showed up to listen to his sales pitch.

One of the featured slides reminded everyone what happened to companies that struggled to keep pace with the changes in technology. The image featured a jumbo headline "Failure to Evolve," hanging over a sad gaggle of gravestones, each carved with a company name. Tower Records. IBM. Palm. Myspace. Kodak. BlackBerry. Blockbuster. AOL.

There was no sugarcoating the message. If HBO failed to keep pace with streaming technology it would soon be rendered obsolete.

While Otto Berkes lobbied internally for more resources, his team opened up a new HBO office in Seattle, not far from his old stomping grounds at

Microsoft. There, he began assembling a new team of engineers, product de-signers, and data scientists.

Everybody who came on board knew the ultimate mission. Beat Netflix.

"At the end of the day, I think my story, and the team that I built there, is really about modern tech meets old media," Berkes says. "We think differ-ently. We're data driven. It's not about relationships—couldn't give a shit. It's what you can deliver. Can you bring the goods? Technology doesn't lie."

CHAPTER 19

Send a Raven

Everywhere HBO looked, the Albanian Army was on the march.

In 2012, Netflix premiered *Lilyhammer*, an acquisition from Norway that was technically Netflix's first original series. The show, about a mobster who moves to Scandinavia after being put in the witness protection program, featured a lead actor who would be instantly recognizable to HBO viewers: Steven Van Zandt. His character in *Lilyhammer* is remarkably similar to Silvio Dante, the besuited, frowny mafioso he played in *The Sopranos*.

Netflix acquired the show after Ted Sarandos received a phone call directly from Van Zandt. From there, it quickly shifted into yet another one of the company's closely watched experiments.

"Frankly, it was designed to be the canary in the coal mine because we wanted to launch something quietly and figure out what are all the things that we don't know how to do yet in terms of launching a piece of original content in multiple territories at once," Cindy Holland says. "Multiple language assets, coordinated PR and marketing campaigns: those are things the company hadn't done before. So *Lilyhammer* was our sort of test to see, all right, what do we have to do to get ready for *House of Cards*."

One thing they quickly realized was that nothing Netflix did in original programming would fly under the radar. "What we learned was that the press was really attentive to anything we did in this space," Holland says. "Because we didn't think it was going to get as much attention as it did."

Months later, the media's preoccupation with Netflix's nascent programming slate shot up to a whole other level. On February 1, 2013, Netflix premiered *House of Cards*.

The show is a tale of pork trading and bed-hopping set in the nation's capital. In the first season, Frank Underwood (Kevin Spacey), a canny, venomous congressman from South Carolina and his maleficent, calculating wife, Claire (Robin Wright), scheme to accrue greater political power in the shadow of a new president. They are surrounded by a shifting milieu of lobbyists, sellsword operatives, and meretricious reporters.

Rather than parceling out the first season in chapters, one per week, like a traditional network, Netflix posted the entire first season, all thirteen episodes, at once. All the better, Netflix explained, for the kind of marathon viewing that, according to the company's data, TV consumers increasingly preferred.

The momentousness of the occasion was not lost on critics. "Can you hear the people binge?" Mary McNamara wrote in the *Los Angeles Times*. "Just as *The Sopranos* turned HBO into a game-changer and *Mad Men* reinvented AMC, *House of Cards* makes Netflix an undisputed player in serialized drama."

Sarandos said his final decision to make such a big bet on *House of Cards* was heavily supported by data from the service's website, which suggested there was a large audience for "political thrillers," programming starring Kevin Spacey, and movies directed by Fincher. The fact that the four-part 1990 BBC miniseries *House of Cards* also performed well with Netflix customers only bolstered their conviction.

Sarandos and Hastings had admired HBO's acclaimed programming. They also figured they might have a better way to engineer it.

"We weren't trying to copy HBO," says Jonathan Friedland, the former Netflix communications executive. "We were trying to do it better than them. We were trying to do it with a different approach, a data-driven approach, as opposed to pure touch. That's the fundamental thing to understand about

Netflix: It's a data science and technology company. Every step we took was guided by data. We aspired to the quality level of execution but based on a totally different set of tools."

The data analysis would prove to be spot on. *House of Cards* would go on to air for six seasons, becoming a defining series for the streaming service, proof that Netflix could master the same "It's Not TV" game played by HBO.

"It's sort of like we're the new television series that isn't on television," Kevin Spacey said.

A few months later, in July 2013, taking another page out of the historic HBO playbook, Netflix debuted a series, *Orange Is the New Black*, set in a prison, a la HBO's *Oz*. While *Orange* was much lighter in tone and set in a women's minimum security prison, viewers quickly noticed some thematic overlap. Both shows feature protagonists—*Oz*'s Tobias Beecher (Lee Tergesen) and *Orange*'s Piper Chapman (Taylor Schilling)—who come from white-collar backgrounds, putting them socioeconomically at odds with the majority of their fellow prisoners. Both eventually get branded with swastikas.

During an early episode, *Orange* went so far as to call out its HBO forerunner. "This isn't *Oz*," an inmate counselor tells Chapman on her first day behind bars. "Women fight with gossip and rumors. They might peg you for rich and try to hit you up for a commissary. And there are lesbians. They are not going to bother you. They'll try to be your friend. Just stay away from them. I want you to understand. You do not have to have lesbian sex."

Orange Is the New Black was created by Jenji Kohan, who had previously made *Weeds* on Showtime. Whereas HBO built its slate of original programming by identifying talented writers disgruntled by the rigidity of network television, Netflix was now hiring a veteran of premium cable television who was struggling to find a home for her prison show until she met with the upstart streamer.

"That was a project that everybody passed on," Holland says. "Jenji told me once that HBO was interested in it but only as a half hour. She felt really strongly that it needed to be an hour because of the kind of storytelling she wanted to do—the flashbacks, getting outside of the prison, telling these nuanced stories about these characters. There was something magical about it."

In an interview with *GQ* magazine, Sarandos did little to disguise the state of the streaming network's overarching strategy. He tossed down the gauntlet that would soon become legend in the entertainment business. "The goal is to become HBO faster than HBO can become us," he said.

* * *

BACK AT HBO, Plepler and his chief deputy Michael Lombardo were further consolidating their power. In September 2013, it was announced that Sue Naegle would be leaving her programming position and transitioning, in the short term, into an unspecified producing role for the network. Lombardo would be assuming her duties, effective immediately. It was another reminder that for all the talented female executives who had worked on developing HBO programming over the years—from Bridget Potter, to Sheila Nevins, Betty Bitterman, Sasha Emerson, Susie Fitzgerald, Carolyn Strauss, Gina Balian, and Sue Naegle—one way or another, the promotions always seemed to stall out at a certain level.

"I think you can't help but sort of see the number of people who were fired or not promoted," says Strauss. She noted that when she joined the network in the 1980s, she was amazed by the number of women in positions of real authority at the network. "As I got later in my career, and I got to go to the senior staff meetings in New York, there would be like three women in the room and twenty men—maybe more," she says.

Shelley Brindle, one of the few female executives in HBO history to make it all the way to the network's C-suite, says the challenge for women was deeply embedded in their parent company's culture. "Time Warner was a boys' club," she says.

Ten days after Naegle's departure, the network also announced that Eric Kessler, its chief operating officer, would be leaving HBO. His twenty-seven-year run was over. The network was eliminating his position. In a memo, Plepler praised Kessler's "extraordinary talents" and complimented the job he'd done in recent years overseeing HBO forays into digital distribution.

In reality, the process of distributing HBO digitally was not going smoothly at all. While Netflix was busy mastering HBO's playbook, HBO's quest to become more like Netflix was flailing.

In March 2014, HBO was getting ready to air the final episode of a new, critically acclaimed anthology crime series called *True Detective*. The noirish drama, created by an itinerant, fiction-writing English professor named Nicholas Pizzolatto, had debuted in January and gained a strong following.

The series is set in a mossy, ramshackle, God-fearing stretch of Louisiana. At the start, police find the corpse of a young woman under a tree. Her hands and feet are bound, and she's been strangled and cut with a knife. A crown of deer antlers is attached to her head. The police suspect the occult is involved. Soon, the local, backwoodsy community is in a panic.

A pair of murder police are tasked with investigating. They are an odd couple. Rustin Cohle (Matthew McConaughey) is an ulcerated, cerebral loner, new to the department, who likes to meditate, read books, sketch drawings, and drop mystical pronouncements. Detective Marty Hart (Woody Harrelson) is a faltering family man who is disgusted by his new partner's pessimistic worldview, unkempt appearance, and flights of metaphysical mumbo jumbo. "You get any sleep last night?" Marty asks his colleague early on. "I don't sleep," Rustin replies. "I just dream."

Soon, the detectives are following the corkscrewing trail of a mysterious killer, a scar-faced man cryptically referred to as the "yellow king." Week by week, the suspense ratcheted higher for *True Detective*'s devoted fans.

On the night of Sunday, March 9, HBO subscribers settled in to watch the finale, intent on seeing whether the bickering, nutso, tripped-out detectives would finally catch the elusive killer. Then, at the top of the hour, HBO GO crashed. Many viewers watching online were greeted with a recurring error message, or nothing at all.

By the mid-2010s, the rise of social media networks had ushered in a new type of behavior among TV consumers. During big events like, say, the Super Bowl or the season finale of a popular series like ABC's *Scandal*, many viewers watched the action unfold on their TVs while simultaneously reading and sharing reactions with fellow fans on sites like Twitter. Network executives often hailed "dual-screen" consumption as a boon to the artform, a new impetus for viewers to show up en masse at a particular appointed time rather than recording the program on their DVRs for later consumption. Reliably, word of great TV moments spread quickly through social networks, drawing in additional viewers. The amplification worked both ways. TV train wrecks rapidly pulled in big crowds too.

Now, as the season finale of *True Detective* failed to stream properly, word of HBO's technical incompetence alerted rubberneckers to the scene. Amid the groundswell of attention, prominent writers on Twitter took turns dunking on the network's hapless technology, while HBO offered a plaintive apology. Afterward, the internet was rife with articles, tut-tutting the screw-up.

"If HBO wants to compete with Netflix, they should really revamp their online streaming service as soon as possible," noted a story on Gizmodo. "Otherwise they risk becoming the next Blockbuster Video."

Just a few weeks later, in April 2014, it happened again. During the premiere of the fourth season of *Game of Thrones*, HBO GO stopped working, triggering another round of tooth gnashing on social media. "Having trouble accessing @HBO GO?" the streaming service's official account posted on Twitter during the meltdown. "Send a raven."

Even as the signs mounted that Netflix was bypassing HBO on various fronts, Time Warner CEO Jeffrey Bewkes continued to belittle HBO's rival. When asked by a *Bloomberg Businessweek* reporter about his thoughts on Netflix, Bewkes responded by comparing them to AOL. "AOL's market cap," he said, "was $170 billion five minutes before it became clear it was worth nothing."

While HBO was struggling with its digital products, the nation was once again experiencing a bout of madcap tech euphoria. Every day, another seemingly obscure tech company was going public: FireEye. Cyan. Rocket Fuel. Gogo. Hordes of hopefuls were descending on the Bay Area, renting and living in closets, drinking meal-replacement shakes, hoovering up venture-backed snacks at company "pivot parties," getting autographed by tech titans at product rallies, joining Burning Man camps, and commuting in private buses to carnival-like tech campuses.

The only thing that felt sorely missing was somebody to make fun of it all.

On April 6, 2014, HBO debuted *Silicon Valley*, a timely new comedy from Mike Judge, skewering America's self-congratulatory start-up scene. Judge, the creator of several hit TV shows (*Beavis and Butt-Head*, *King of the Hill*) and movies (*Office Space*, *Idiocracy*) drew inspiration for the series in part from his own brief, lousy experience in the tech industry. In his early twenties, after graduating from the University of California, San Diego, with a major in physics, Judge had worked briefly as an engineer at a couple of tech companies in the Bay Area.

It was not a good professional fit. "I've always had a love-hate relationship with technology that is probably about ninety percent hate," Judge says.

"I mean, I'm addicted to it like everyone else," he adds.

For years, long after Judge left engineering for a career in entertainment, he kept thinking that the world of computer programmers would be a terrific setting for a show or a movie. The family of his then wife was from Palo Alto, so he spent a bunch of time in Northern California. There he marveled at the weird ways in which the aging hippie values of San Francisco were fusing with tech riches, creating an odd culture of enormously wealthy people doing crazy mental contortions to dress up their commercial prosperity in the trappings of ethical righteousness.

By the time the first dot-com boom took off, Judge was a successful animator who found himself being courted by start-ups, including Z.com, a proto YouTube, that were trying to disrupt TV with hubs of cyber entertainment. "It was a crazy feeding frenzy," Judge says. "I got a lot of material from that. It was very funny to watch it all collapse."

In 2012, while researching an idea for a show for HBO, Judge visited a bunch of campuses of tech companies like Google and Facebook and attended sweaty, testosterone-drenched congregations of true believers like TechCrunch Disrupt. "The more we dug into it, the more interesting and hilarious and absurd it was," Judge says.

Based on the research, Judge created a pilot with Dave Krinsky and John Altschuler, who he'd previously worked with on *King of the Hill*. When HBO did not love their first stab at satire, Krinsky and Altschuler stepped aside. Judge reworked the humor with the help of Alec Berg, a former writer on *Seinfeld* and *Curb Your Enthusiasm*, and things fell into place.

Casey Bloys, HBO's genial head of comedy, was a major champion. He felt that *Silicon Valley* had the special ingredient that was baked into most of HBO's successful comedies. "If you look at the history of HBO, in comedy specifically, we've always done really well with writer-performer-directors," Bloys said.

Bloys believed the key was getting at least two of the three categories. Garry Shandling? Writer-performer. Larry David? Writer-performer. Armando Iannucci? Writer-director. Lena Dunham? Writer-performer-director. And Mike Judge? Writer-director.

"With comedies, the tone can be so specific," Bloys said. "When somebody is controlling two of those three things, you can control the tone really well."

Set in contemporary Palo Alto, *Silicon Valley* revolves around a residential tech "incubator," a dormitory like house full of young, male, socially inept software engineers, banging out code, mocking each other, and striving for tech stardom. At the start, Richard Hendricks (Thomas Middleditch), a high-strung computer programmer, is developing Pied Piper, a new app that will allow people to search the universe of recorded music to check for any copyright infringements.

The head of the incubator, a blustery buffoon named Erlich Bachman (T. J. Miller), is not impressed and reminds Richard that "nobody gives a shit about stealing other people's music, okay?" He implores Richard to be more like his housemate, a chipper dimwit named Nelson "Big Head" Bighetti (Josh Brener). Bachman points out that Bighetti is working on a promising start-up called NipAlert, a geolocation app that provides users with "the location of a woman with erect nipples."

"Now that's something people want," Bachman says. "Richard, you need to get in touch with humanity."

Eventually, Richard realizes that while making his app, he has inadvertently created a data-compression algorithm of enormous potential value. A bidding war ensues. Pressed by rapacious, loony tech magnates and their vulturous minions, feeling unsure how to proceed, Richard suffers a panic attack. While seeking medical help, his doctor pitches him on a start-up idea. Everywhere he looks there is a maze of shifting opportunities, hazards, mean-spirited "brogrammers," and greediness masquerading as virtue. It's a world in which his fate—and everybody else's—is at the whim of a few very rich, megalomaniacal, inscrutable men. "Fucking billionaires," says Bighetti.

While critics were generally delighted, not every American tech billionaire was amused by the needling. As part of the show's rollout, HBO held a premiere at the Fox Theatre in Redwood City, California, in the cradle of Silicon Valley. Under dimmed lights, a passel of prominent venture capitalists, cast members, and masters of the tech universe watched the first two episodes. Afterward, Tesla's Elon Musk, well on his way to becoming one of the richest humans on the planet, bristled at HBO's uppity, unflattering depiction of the tech world. It was totally off base, he told Recode.

"I really feel like Mike Judge has never been to Burning Man, which is Silicon Valley," Musk said. "If you haven't been, you just don't get it."

Judge says he later became friends with Musk, but never made it to Burning Man, the annual arts festival and all-hours rave in Nevada's Black Rock Desert. The show's staff, however, did make plenty of other field trips. Between seasons, they would go on safari into the heart of the tech industry, alternately visiting small-time start-ups and enormous tech conglomerates, scooping up fodder for future episodes.

Judge says that at Dropbox one coder told them that the only thing worse than being the sole woman at a tech start-up was "being one of two," because then "everybody thinks you're going to be friends." The insight inspired a recurring joke during the show's second season.

Some critics would later knock *Silicon Valley* for its heavily male-centric cast. But Judge says the gender dynamics on the series reflected the biases of the industry they were ridiculing. "We were taking shots at them for their culture and not having many women around," Judge says. "When you're making fun of something, if anything, you exaggerate it."

Over time, as the series grew into a hit, the tech industry grew more guarded and self-conscious around Judge and his staff. Judge recalls that during a second visit to one of California's big tech giants, his crew received a much different reception. Casually observing brogrammers in the wild was no longer going to be such a breeze. "They put us in a room with nothing but female engineers," Judge recalls.

While Elon Musk was simmering down, HBO had another headstrong tycoon to worry about. In June 2014, just a couple of months after HBO's Sunday night premiere of *Silicon Valley*, Rupert Murdoch, the insatiable media mogul, made an unsolicited $80-billion bid for Time Warner, taking everyone by surprise. Jeffrey Bewkes met with the company's board members, who rejected the offer.

When news of the rebuffed effort broke on July 16, Time Warner's stock price shot up from seventy-one dollars to eighty-three dollars a share by the end of the day. Some onlookers were aghast at the potential impact on the American press. Among other things, if a deal between the two companies was consummated, the conservative owner of Fox News would either be seizing control of CNN or spinning it off to buyers unknown.

Fucking billionaires.

In the weeks that followed, the bid gave something for Time Warner board members to consider—maybe it was time to sell. The competition in media and entertainment was growing more ferocious by the day, and the market might not remain so high forever.

It also increased pressure on the company to convince Wall Street that it had a plan for future growth—a road map for beating Netflix and the giant tech companies like Google and Amazon, who were starting to move into the entertainment industry. "The Fox acquisition attempt changed everything," says one former HBO tech staffer. "They needed something to juice the stock price."

• • •

WHAT TIME WARNER NEEDED was a killer app. But behind the scenes, HBO's plan to build the company a world-beating streaming platform was running into problems. Otto Berkes and his expanding crew in Seattle were increasingly at odds with the rest of the company. The added pressure of the Murdoch bid only made things worse.

Historically, HBO's IT department was a close-knit, collegial group made up of competent, deferential staffers who knew their role in the HBO cosmos. The showrunners and creators were the company's stars, not the folks working on the computers. The tech staff was there to lend support, which they did happily, efficiently, and without great fanfare. Their goal was not to write immaculate, award-winning code, but rather to ensure that everything worked just well enough to support the company's award-winning programming. Meeting deadlines was of the utmost importance, particularly around the premieres of big HBO shows.

Much of the Seattle team, on the other hand, hailed from a different culture with a divergent set of values. Many of the engineers and product managers being recruited by Otto Berkes were accustomed to working at tech and gaming companies in which it is the software makers who are the highly revered talent. The success of such companies rises and falls with the perfection of their products. Charging headlong into the avant garde of computer science is the typical goal, not serving the needs of comedians and ex–English professors.

With time, the confrontations between the two camps grew increasingly personal. Berkes's brusque manner rubbed many of his colleagues the wrong way. Many of the old-timers felt as though the Seattle team treated them like dim-witted troglodytes. As the months passed, many of the folks who'd worked on the early versions of HBO GO were forced out or decided to quit. "They drove out everybody," says Nate Rackiewicz, a former member of HBO's IT team. "It was ugly."

"His plan was sound, but he didn't do the one thing HR told everyone that they needed to do: build relationships," says Allan Wai. "He came from this Microsoft meritocracy and was like eff these guys. No one knows what they are doing. I'm going to do it my way."

While the Seattle staff moved ahead with plans for a new premier streaming platform, the existing HBO GO software continued to struggle— and, on Sunday nights, during peak viewing times, kept crashing. When executives in New York asked when the new platform would be ready, they kept hearing versions of the same answer: you can't rush this thing, give us more time. "*It'll be ready in 18 months!*' became the running joke with HBO executives about the Seattle office," Rackiewicz says. "That's what we constantly heard in terms of when the products would be delivered."

With Wall Street's obsession with Netflix and streaming entertainment companies growing by the day, Richard Plepler, now CEO, decided that despite the internal issues, it was time to make the big move: the moment had finally arrived for HBO to offer a streaming service to anyone in the United States who wanted it, even if they didn't subscribe to a cable or satellite TV bundle.

On the morning of October 15, 2014, at Time Warner's annual investor day gathering in New York, Plepler announced that HBO would release its new over-the-top streaming product, dubbed HBO Now, to the public the following year. "It is time to remove all barriers to those who want HBO," he said. "All in, there are 80 million homes that do not have HBO, and we will use all means at our disposal to go after them."

Following the announcement, a high-pressure deadline hung over the Seattle team. Everyone hustled to get the service ready. But with each passing month, the distance between Otto Berkes's crew in Seattle and Plepler's people in New York seemed to be growing wider. Sometimes it felt like they didn't speak the same language. Berkes tended to communicate with graphs and PowerPoint presentations and analogies drawn from the physical sciences. He dubbed an effort to improve HBO's application architecture "Project Hadron," a reference to a type of subatomic particle made of two or more quarks.

Plepler, on the other hand, preferred to communicate conversationally, sans gadget, and favored military and history analogies. In a strained effort to try to bridge the two worlds, Wai once found himself trying to incorporate a reference to Sherman's March to the Sea into a slide presentation about HBO's streaming future. "We had to research it and come up with a graphic," Wai says. "I was like, I don't know that this translates."

Another part of the problem was a matter of taste and orientation. Plepler was an Apple fan. He had an iPhone, an iPad, and could recount the saga of Steve Jobs, backward and forward. Berkes, on the other hand, was a PC guy. Mr. Microsoft. On paper, they were both committed to ensuring that HBO's streaming future was ecumenical, available to everybody on all devices. But according to former employees, their immediate priorities already seemed to have diverged.

In November 2014, as part of Project Halley, Berkes's team in Seattle released its big new piece of original software into the world. It was a new HBO GO app for the Xbox One, Microsoft's eighth-generation video-game console. By most accounts, it was a well-constructed app and, internally, the Seattleites were pleased.

But others at HBO were baffled. Sure, it worked well—that is, for the small sliver of HBO subscribers who wanted to watch *John Adams* via an Xbox. How long would it take to roll out whatever came next?

With impatience building, HBO executives in New York started considering outside help. That fall, Shelley Brindle, now an executive vice president on HBO's domestic distribution and marketing team, attended Google Zeitgeist, a tech conference in Scottsdale, Arizona. While there, she met Kenny Gersh, an executive with MLB Advanced Media, a limited partnership of Major League Baseball, which had developed an expertise in streaming high-profile TV events. At first, the group just handled baseball games. But with time, their portfolio of clients was expanding to other traditional media companies in need of streaming assistance.

Gersh talked up his colleagues' capabilities. As it turned out, the same Sunday night back in April when HBO GO had melted down during the season premiere of *Game of Thrones*, MLB Advanced Media had successfully streamed WrestleMania, the biggest event of the year for World Wrestling

Entertainment (WWE). There had been no major problems, a fact that Gersh was not shy about contrasting with HBO GO's spasmodic performance.

Brindle returned to New York and told Plepler she might have a solution to their streaming woes. A few days later, Brindle and her colleague Bernadette Aulestia, a top HBO executive in distribution, met with MLB Advanced Media at their offices in Manhattan's Chelsea Market—the former home to HBO's *Oz*, which in recent years had been transformed into a posh hub of New York City's growing tech scene. There, Gersh and CEO Robert Bowman delivered their pitch.

"We walked out and were like, yep, that's our solution," Brindle says.

Meanwhile, Plepler was drifting further away from his Seattle team and into the gravitational pull of the Apple-centric universe, at one point meeting with Eddy Cue, the head of Apple's digital media business. Together, they hatched a dramatic plan for bringing HBO's new direct-to-consumer experience into the world.

In early December, HBO confirmed reports that it was scrapping Project Halley and hiring MLB Advanced Media. The plan was to ensure that HBO Now would be ready to stream the opening day of *Game of Thrones* in the spring.

Otto Berkes promptly resigned. To Berkes, it felt like Jeffrey Bewkes and Time Warner had given up on anything resembling a long-term vision for its future. "There was a dramatic change in people's mindset when the Murdoch thing happened," Berkes says. "You're either going for a win or you're just positioning yourself to be sold and to maximize the transaction value."

"You're not going to be interested in self-disruption or investing in new internal capabilities and assets if you're for sale," he adds. "Those things are not going to be valued in a near-term transaction."

For the time being, rather than building their own proprietary technology from scratch, HBO would rely on the team from MLB Advanced Media to handle its streams. They would rent rather than own.

The decision came at a time in American corporate life when declaring oneself to be a technological disrupter was increasingly en vogue. Across the nation, companies in seemingly every sector of the U.S. economy, from pizza chains to car manufacturers to cigarette makers, were heralding their previously low-fi selves as fundamental, born-again tech businesses. But HBO, for its part, would refocus on what the network did best, not computer programming, not building platforms, but instead, supporting its screenwriters and creating hit shows. "The main thing is to keep the main thing the main thing," Plepler liked to remind his colleagues, echoing the quote by business management guru Stephen Covey.

At that moment, HBO would *not*, as the saying goes, learn to code.

On the morning of March 9, 2015, inside the Yerba Buena Center for the Arts in San Francisco, Apple CEO Tim Cook strode onto the stage. In front of a packed crowd of hooting Apple supporters, he took a moment to praise the cantilevered second floor of a new Apple store in Hangzhou, China. "It's absolutely breathtaking," Cook said. A few minutes later he noted that Apple TV was adding more programming from "all of the leading content providers," including a new channel from HBO.

Plepler walked out onstage. He was wearing a dark suit and crisp white shirt, spread wide open at the neckline. For the next several minutes, he revealed details of the network's plans for its new cable-free streaming app. HBO Now, he said, would be available to consumers the following month, in early April, for the first time. The service would cost $14.99 a month. For the first three months, the app would be available exclusively on Apple devices. "This is a transformative moment for HBO," Plepler said.

The following month, the network got ready to air the first episode of season 5 of *Game of Thrones*. The show was, by now, the most popular in the network's history, topping *The Sopranos* at its peak. And unlike most HBO shows, its popularity extended well beyond the United States.

That spring, HBO announced that it would be simulcasting each episode of the coming fifth season in some 170 countries around the world, turning each new chapter in the *Game of Thrones* saga into a global event.

Even so, in much of the world, few people associated the popular show with HBO. That's because outside of the United States, *Game of Thrones* frequently aired on a cable or satellite channel other than HBO. In Australia, viewers watched it on Rupert Murdoch's Fox Showcase channel; in Germany, Italy, and New Zealand fans saw it on Sky; in France, the dragons flew on OCS; in Iceland, Tyrion Lannister (Peter Dinklage) delivered his fine, jaundiced bon mots on channels operated by 365 media; and on and on.

The reason had to do with the network's global strategy. Whereas in the U.S., HBO was hyperfocused on using its original programming to build up the HBO brand name and amass paying subscribers, internationally the network did the inverse. Overseas, HBO was happy to sacrifice brand recognition for something else: profits.

Sometimes the most efficient way to wring profits out of a particular region was to set up, build, and operate an HBO-branded channel. But often, the opposite was true. It was significantly more lucrative to license HBO's most desirable programming exclusively to the highest local bidder. Incumbent media powerhouses would pay for HBO's library of shows, and then use programs like *Game of Thrones* to promote the desirability of their own channels and networks.

Such deals freed up HBO from the usual obligations and expenses of operating a regional network, such as hiring a local staff, paying for office space, and marketing its new shows. It was a low-risk and high-margin setup. And from a purely bottom-line standpoint, it was an enormously lucrative setup for Time Warner.

But, over time, the strategy also had an obvious downside. Many of the most ardent fans of HBO programming overseas knew nothing about HBO. In large parts of the world, the HBO brand meant nothing to television consumers. As a result, even while enjoying the most popular TV show on the planet, HBO remained largely invisible.

In the years to come, as the streaming wars evolved from a U.S. competition to one increasingly global in scope, HBO's long-running pursuit of profits over brand awareness would come back to haunt it, leaving the door open to rival streaming services. Before long, Netflix would be spreading out across the planet, gobbling up new subscribers and quickly establishing itself as the global leader in advertising-free subscription video-on-demand entertainment.

The blowout in Scandinavia, it turns out, was just a preview. By January 2016, Netflix operated in more than 190 countries, while HBO's hard-earned brand halo, decades in the offing, was essentially stuck at home. HBO would cede the international title without putting up so much as a fight.

Back in the United States, on the night of Sunday, April 12, some 8 million households tuned in to HBO to watch the first episode of season 5 of *Game of Thrones*, by far the most of any show on cable TV that night. Many viewers did so online.

Inside Chelsea Market, the team from MLB Advanced Media prepared to handle the expected surge in viewers watching via HBO Now and HBO GO. To everyone's relief, the night went off smoothly.

"It was an effective short-term Band-Aid," Brindle says.

CHAPTER 20

A Clogged Pipeline

For a certain set of New Yorkers, stepping into Richard Plepler's home on the Upper East Side of Manhattan felt a bit like attending Katharine Graham's cocktail parties in Washington, D.C., in the 1980s. It was an intoxicating intellectual environment, a place where journalists and filmmakers, novelists and politicians could gather over food and wine to discuss politics, mingle with fellow luminaries, and trade interdisciplinary gossip.

Plepler played the ever-attentive host along with his wife, Lisa. He doled out the coveted invitations, oversaw which starlet would sit next to which head of state, and made everybody feel welcome.

HBO's influence under Plepler now reached all the way into the executive residence of the White House. During his presidency, Barack Obama had grown into a loyal *Game of Thrones* fan, who would hit up the network to score early copies of new episodes before they became available to the public.

Once again, HBO felt culturally ascendant.

In September 2015, the network enjoyed the biggest Emmys night in its history. *Game of Thrones* won the Emmy for the Best Drama, the first time HBO had taken the coveted award in eight years. *Veep* won Best Comedy, beating out *Silicon Valley*, which was also nominated as a finalist. *Olive Kitteridge*, a four-part limited series set in Maine, starring Frances McDormand as a cantankerous schoolteacher, nearly swept every major miniseries award. Julia Louis-Dreyfus of *Veep* won for Lead Actress in a Comedy Series.

All told, HBO took home forty-three Emmys, the biggest haul in its history, and just one shy of the record set by CBS in 1974, when the only competition was the other two broadcast networks and PBS. Most important, for all the fawning over Netflix, HBO had routed the streaming upstart, which took home a single award.

Afterward, HBO hosted a sweaty, swaggering party at the Pacific Design Center in West Hollywood. The mood among HBO creators was triumphant. Amid a swirl of goblet-hoisting merrymakers, George R. R. Martin, the big-bearded fantasy novelist, sat at a table across from the comedian John Hodgman, with his *Thrones* Emmy planted on the table like a golden amulet. "I lost this six times, and the seventh is the lucky charm," Martin said. "Between *Thrones*, *Veep*, and *Olive Kitteridge*, we crushed the competition."

Throughout the bustling courtyard, HBO executives accepted congratulations from throngs of Hollywood kingfish and tuxedoed well-wishers. "It's a once-in-a-lifetime moment," Michael Lombardo said, in a joyous daze.

Back in New York, things were also clicking for HBO on the stand-up front. Chris Rock, long the face of HBO stage comedy, hadn't done a new special for the network in seven years, but he was finding other ways to contribute. Rock directed a stand-up special for HBO entitled *Amy Schumer: Live at the Apollo*, which aired in October 2015 and got rave reviews from fans. Over the course of an hour, Schumer, a Rabelaisian, cringe-zilla comic who'd grown up in the Long Island suburbs of New York, delved into topics like sketchy massage parlors, dirty underwear, movie theater popcorn, buttered saltines, scones, khakis, urinary tract infections, and gender double standards in comedy.

"I'm labeled a sex comic," Schumer said. "Like, that's in interviews. People are always like, 'So you're—you keep talking about sex.' I'm like, I think it's because I'm a girl. I feel like a guy could get up here and literally pull his dick out and everybody would be like, 'He's a thinker!'"

HBO had never won more awards and never been more profitable. But television development is a cyclical process, and all the accolades were papering over a growing problem. Aside from *Game of Thrones*, the network was struggling to find another hit drama series.

True Blood, Boardwalk Empire, and *Treme* had all wrapped up. The second season of *True Detective* was an embarrassing mess. *The Newsroom*, a drama from Aaron Sorkin, the creator of *The West Wing*, had come and gone, its three plodding, pedantic seasons underwhelming critics and never quite living up to its great expectations.

The rut came at a time when other cable networks seemed to have loads of popular dramas. Showtime had *Homeland*. FX had *The Americans*. Netflix had *House of Cards*. AMC had *The Walking Dead*.

HBO executives were beginning to confront a sort of psychic blow—they were far from being the only game in town.

"HBO understood that in most open market situations—meaning any bidding situation—if it wanted something more than others, and if the financials were equivalent, or better, HBO would win," says Michael Ellenberg, who was then running the drama department. "And then at some point, it was clear that can no longer be assumed. That shift was difficult."

To try to give the network a jolt, Plepler and Lombardo started to pour money into unscripted programming. They made a deal with *Vice*, the hipster Brooklyn brand, to make a daily newscast that would, in Plepler's words, become a "millennial missile" and reinvent how news could be told on television. They recruited Bill Simmons, the ESPN sports and culture columnist, to host a talk show. And they signed deals with a pair of Comedy Central stars: John Oliver, to serve as host of a weekly topical late-night show; and Jon Stewart, fresh off his enormously successful run from *The Daily Show*, to make a daily animated series that would riff off the news.

HBO executives believed the plan would give them an instrument that Netflix did not have: topical relevance. If Netflix's surging popularity was based on bingeable content that had an endless shelf life, HBO would pivot to something that played in its favor—it was still a cable channel that could offer fresh commentary daily.

The drama situation could hopefully be sorted out. Part of the problem was that the network's development pipeline had become overgrown and clogged with big-name producers and overly rich ideas. HBO would sign them up and then not make their programs. David Fincher, the producer of *House of Cards*, had two projects in the works that HBO put to a halt. A Lewis and Clark miniseries being produced by Tom Hanks and Brad Pitt was scrapped after weeks of shooting. A limited series from *12 Years a Slave* director Steve McQueen was dropped.

Casey Bloys believed his peers in drama had grown so worried that hit shows were appearing on other networks that they began falling victim to "defensive buying."

"The drama department had, for years, notoriously just been buying and developing, buying and developing," Bloys says. "I think partly because there was a little bit of an existential, like, 'What is an HBO show? What should we be doing?' There was fear of letting things go to other places."

Even HBO's bullpen of established auteurs was growing restless. Mike White, the creator of *Enlightened*, the critically adored but low-rated HBO series starring Laura Dern that was canceled after two seasons in 2013, was one of the frustrated veterans. He'd written a script about a hard-charging drag queen who becomes a nanny for the three children of a conservative Texas family. White was passionate about it. But after committing to a pilot, HBO ultimately balked at making it into a series.

"They had all of these deals with all of these fancy people, and they were just notorious for never letting things go or coming to a decision," White says. "They're so much about artist relationships, but it ended up being—and I felt this—you want to keep me on the hook but you don't actually want to make my shit. Like, leave me alone. Stop calling me! This is not working. I have other places to go and do things."

Following *The Wire*, *Generation Kill*, and *Treme*, David Simon was also looking to get his next opus under way. He pitched the network on doing an international espionage series revolving around the CIA, based on the book *Legacy of Ashes*, a detailed history of the spy agency by Tim Weiner. HBO passed.

Simon also proposed doing a series, called *The Deuce*, that would be set in New York City in the 1970s and would delve into the origins of the American pornography industry. Again, HBO turned him down. The problem, Simon was told, was that HBO was already committed to making an opulent rock-and-roll drama series called *Vinyl*, from Martin Scorsese, Mick Jagger, Terence Winter, and journalist Rich Cohen, set in 1970s New York. There was too much overlap.

Instead, HBO gave Simon the go-ahead on his idea for a miniseries, much smaller in scope, called *Show Me a Hero*, about a racially charged political dispute over the development of a housing project in Yonkers, New York.

Simon was upset. He had a lucrative deal with HBO, and yet over the next two years, he would only be making six hours of TV for the network. "I felt like they wanted me in the brand," says Simon. "I get them on the op-ed pages. To lose me would say something they don't want to say. But they really don't want to make that much TV with me. Because they know I don't really have an audience. That's how I felt."

Simon began shopping *The Deuce* around to other networks. "I got two kinds of meetings," he says. "One was, *No. That doesn't work for us*. Or, *Yeeaah, porn! Oh boy!* . . . Wrong reaction."

Eventually, Simon heard secondhand that there were problems with the scripts for *Vinyl*. He went back to HBO and proposed teaming up with Scorsese and combining the two projects. According to Simon, Lombardo told him that *Vinyl* had too much momentum behind it and too many big names to shelve it, but encouraged Simon to proceed with his similar project.

In the summer of 2015, HBO gave Simon the go-ahead to shoot a pilot for *The Deuce*. If *Vinyl* didn't work out, Lombardo promised, HBO would be willing to try a second show about New York in the 1970s. "He said, 'You're going to have to trust me,'" recalls Simon. "And I did."

•   •   •

IN FEBRUARY 2016, HBO began airing *Vinyl* on Sunday nights. The series begins in 1973 and tells the story of Richie Finestra (Bobby Cannavale), a burned-out, benumbed owner of a music label called the American Century, which is in decline. He has a private plane and a chauffeured Mercedes, but he's lost touch with the creative pulse of the music world. "I had a golden ear, a silver tongue, and a pair of brass balls," Finestra says. "But the problem became my nose, and everything I put up it."

His wife, Devon (Olivia Wilde), an alumna of Andy Warhol's Factory scene, is likewise unhappy and grasping for whatever comes next. All around, New York City is in seizures. Disco, rap, and punk rock are erupting from the grimy streets. Deals, buildings, and marriages wobble on the brink of collapse.

The pilot episode, directed by Scorsese, stretched out for nearly two hours. Armed with $100 million from HBO, the *Vinyl* team made sure every period-specific pixel of New York was pumped up for maximum tooth-grinding, graffitied glitz. Get off my lawn, *Mad Men*, it practically screamed.

"I've said kiddingly that I want this show to do for cocaine what *Mad Men* did for cigarette smoking," Winter said.

The ratings were dismal, and the reviews weren't much better.

Writing in *The New Yorker*, Emily Nussbaum called it "a preachy mess" that "never sheds its air of leaden nostalgia" and is "so bombastic on the topic of mind-blowing art that *won't sell out, man*, that it grinds you down, as if you were standing way too close to some guy in a club who keeps screaming about how high he is."

Initially, HBO committed to making a second season. But then, in April 2016, amid reports of tension among the creators, HBO confirmed that the network would be replacing Terence Winter as its showrunner.

Winter says that, in retrospect, *Vinyl* was hampered by creative differences, particularly between him and Mick Jagger. "I thought I was getting into business with the guy from 1972, the poster boy for sex, drugs, and rock and roll," Winter says. "Which is what I wanted the show to be. But Mick Jagger from 2010 is Sir Mick Jagger. He's a very proper British gentleman."

According to Winter, Jagger strongly objected to the show's many depictions of drug abuse, nudity, and sexism in the record industry, and argued that *Vinyl*'s female characters should be more empowered in the workplace. "I was like, 'Mick it's 1973, they'd be fired,'" Winter says. "My mother got her ass pinched every day as a secretary in New York in the 1970s. I said, 'I'm not going to do a disservice to the women who went through this shit by pretending that that didn't exist. I want to depict reality. We're not saying it's right. We're saying this is how it was.'"

As the disagreements and infighting continued, Winter says he was shocked by HBO's reaction. "Suddenly, HBO was pushing back and siding with Mick on that stuff," Winter says. When HBO eventually asked him to fire all his writing staff and start over with a new team for the second season, Winter refused. "When we finally had it out, I was like, what happened to you guys?" Winter says.

In May, several weeks after HBO aired the final episode of *Vinyl*, Michael Lombardo lost his job too. Plepler announced that the HBO veteran, less than a year removed from his ecstatic moment at the Emmys, would be leaving his position and, per tradition, segueing into an unspecified producing role.

• • •

THE FOLLOWING WEEK, in May 2016, HBO named Casey Bloys as the network's new president of programming, its top creative slot. Bloys, who was forty-four, had narrow blue eyes and short brown hair. He was extremely well liked in the industry. He was the father of two children with his husband, lawyer Alonzo Wickers.

Bloys grew up in Bethlehem, Pennsylvania, the youngest of three brothers. He went to the same public high school as Dwayne "The Rock" Johnson, graduating a year apart, but knew him only by reputation: the son of a professional wrestler, already high school famous. Later, when Johnson was starring in the HBO series *Ballers*, Bloys would joke around on set with the muscular leading man, reminiscing about their adolescent years, enjoying the fruits of Lehigh Valley, drinking in cornfields and searching for house parties.

Throughout his childhood, Bloys was also a fairly obsessive TV viewer. He spent hours after school watching reruns of older shows like *Leave It to Beaver*, *Bewitched*, *The Munsters*, *The Jeffersons*, *Laverne & Shirley*, and *What's Happening!!* At night, he consumed countless hours of *Family Ties*, *Hill Street Blues*, and *L.A. Law*.

"Now that I have kids, I am shocked at the amount of television I was allowed to watch," Bloys said.

Bloys always knew he wanted to work in television, but after graduating from Northwestern with a degree in economics, he was unsure what would be the best way in. He worked a stint in advertising, then moved to Los Angeles, where he got hired in marketing at Paramount. But he soon realized that if he wanted to get a job in programming, he would have to start at a lower level. He took a job as an assistant to a creative executive at CBS, Laurie Zaks, answering her phone and fetching her egg-white omelets.

After a couple of years, Bloys went to work in development at a production company that had a deal with Disney and was pumping out possible series ideas for ABC. In 2004, Bloys left for a job at HBO Independent Productions, where he was blown away by the difference in culture. By 2006, he was working in HBO's comedy department and quickly moving up the chain of command, eventually overseeing series like *Girls*, *Veep*, *Silicon Valley*, *Eastbound & Down*, and *Flight of the Conchords*.

When it came time to cast Selina Meyer, the lead character in *Veep*, some HBO executives were dreaming of a movie star: Sigourney Weaver was raised as a possibility. But Bloys thought it would be more interesting to pair Armando Iannucci's sophisticated, BBC wit with an accomplished network TV performer. At the time, he knew Julia Louis-Dreyfus, the former *Seinfeld* star, was available, having just finished a five-season run on the NBC comedy *The New Adventures of Old Christine*. Bloys faced some resistance internally to casting her—"From people who thought she was, you know, *network*," he says—but he was confident he was right. He prevailed.

"It was Casey's idea to get Julia," Plepler says.

Following his promotion, Bloys would be in charge of overseeing all of HBO's dramas, documentaries, films, miniseries, sports, and Cinemax programming—a big leap in power.

When Bloys took charge of the drama department, one of his first moves was to clear out the development pipeline. He polled colleagues and raised a question: What are we actually going to make? Talent relations had been fraying because of HBO's recent habit of defensive buying, and he thought it would be best to let writers and producers take their scripts back.

"When you have to wait around and find out if you're going to get picked up or not, it just wasn't healthy," Bloys says. "It wasn't good for writers. It wasn't good for the work level for the drama executives, which was very high because we expect that everybody gets thoughtful and thorough notes and a good experience. It wasn't good for business because we got a reputation for 'they buy things and don't make anything.' So you got to keep that ratio down."

Bloys released hundreds of scripts out of development purgatory, much to the delight of writers, producers, and agents. Next, he diagnosed a problem with the network's lineup. In addition to being gummed up with half-digested ideas, it was also too "hardcore male," he told his colleagues. In the two decades since *If These Walls Could Talk* first clued in HBO leaders to the network's dire need for more female perspectives, having shed top female development executives like Carolyn Strauss and Sue Naegle, HBO's retinue of male executives had somehow managed to unlearn the crucial lesson. It was time, Bloys told his associates, for HBO to broaden the lens. Both personally and professionally, Bloys's taste in TV tended to be soapy and female-centric.

"What I would like to see is more diversity in the drama slate," Bloys said shortly after taking over. "And by diversity, I don't mean just ethnic diversity but diversity in terms of scale, scope, location, tone."

And then, just a few weeks into the job, Bloys made an emphatic programming decision: he was canceling *Vinyl*. There would be no second season. "Quite frankly, if I've got limited resources, there's other things I want to do," he told reporters.

With *Vinyl* dead, the network was free to move on to their plan B for 1970s New York dramas. David Simon and his team would get their shot to make *The Deuce*. "We ended up raiding all of *Vinyl*'s props and sets and taking it over to our warehouse," Simon recalls.

Given the subject matter—prostitution and pornography—there was every reason for critics to suspect that *The Deuce* would carry on HBO's kneejerk tradition of using gratuitous female nudity as a cheap ploy to entice male viewers. But Simon and his cocreator George Pelecanos were adamant that they weren't interested in making "the boys' version of the sex industry."

The goal of the series, they explained, was to explore America's evolving sex economy in the 1970s through a wide cast of characters, ranging from pimps and prostitutes, to police officers and politicians, to media entrepreneurs and gangsters. Nothing about the series would make sex work seem easy or trivial. "It's about sexual commodification, misogyny, and exploitation," says Simon.

The series would go on to star Maggie Gyllenhaal in a leading role as Candy, an independent sex worker, in grimy midtown Manhattan. Later as pornography is legalized and the industry takes off, Candy becomes a respected director of literary-inspired erotica.

Before joining *The Deuce*, which would premiere the following year, in 2017, and end up running on HBO for three seasons, Gyllenhaal insisted that, due to the potentially hazardous subject matter, she would only sign on if HBO made her a producer. "I wanted some kind of guarantee that they wanted not just my body but also my mind," Gyllenhaal later explained. "I want to be part of the storytelling and the conversation about what happens to this woman." The results would be instructive. With Gyllenhaal providing notes; and Nina Noble, Simon's longtime collaborator, serving as executive producer; and esteemed TV veteran Michelle MacLaren directing the pilot and the finale of the first season, the series would go on to generate many positive write-ups. For once, an HBO series would receive plaudits for its depiction of female sex workers, instead of groans of embarrassment.

"By the way, if you were watching *The Deuce* as a man thinking, 'I'm going to get off on some porn,' we hope we ruined it for you," says Simon.

CHAPTER 21

AOL Déjà Vu

In the summer of 2016, HBO executives were grappling with a growing concern. Other than John Oliver's talk show, the network's strategic advance into topical programming was stumbling. In June, HBO aired the first episode of *Any Given Wednesday*, a weekly half-hour talk show hosted by Bill Simmons, a former ESPN blogger, podcaster, and founder of *Grantland*, who'd departed the Disney-owned cable-sports network following a bitter falling out with its leadership.

Michael Lombardo, who recruited Simmons to HBO, was convinced he'd thrive in the network's more freewheeling on-air culture. Get psyched, HBO's promos suggested, to see Simmons unchained.

Instead, Simmons came across in his HBO debut as hobbled and tongue-tied, a talent still struggling to transform from a writer into a TV host. In *Time*, critic Daniel D'Addario noted that Simmons seemed "overmatched by the most basic aspects of TV talk."

After a single, disappointing season, HBO canceled the series.

Other attempts at topical relevance were likewise sputtering. HBO's nightly *Vice* newscast was formally inventive, visually gripping, and broke plenty of news. Yet it drew a tiny audience. There was no tradition of viewers tuning in to HBO each night to learn about what was happening in the world that day. The habit didn't exist, not for millennials, not for anyone. And HBO's rudimentary streaming apps, which lacked a simple, functional way for producers to alert subscribers to new episodes, were ill-suited to the task of promoting fresh daily content.

Around the same time, technological hurdles dashed the plans for Jon Stewart's animated program, which was shut down before a single episode aired. Instead, HBO promised there would be two comedy stand-up specials from Stewart. "I'm really thrilled to be able to return to stand-up on HBO," Stewart said. But the performances never materialized. In the end, Stewart's four-year contract with HBO amounted to little more than hosting a charity special, a total bust.

By comparison, things at Netflix were going swimmingly. That fall, *The Crown* premiered on Netflix, a period drama about the royal family created by British screenwriter Peter Morgan. It was the first of a planned six-season series that would rotate casts every two years and chronicle Queen Elizabeth II's life from when she ascended to the throne in the 1950s to the present day. Critics raved over the first season and were especially blown away by the show's palatial sets and costumes.

The Crown was expensive to make, and it also cost a fortune to acquire from Sony, the studio that produced it. But Netflix was now reaching a league of its own in terms of what it was willing to spend. "They just overwhelmed us with sort of shock-and-awe levels of money and commitment," said John Landgraf, the CEO of FX, about losing out on the bidding on *The Crown*.

By 2016, FX was no slouch, spending about $1 billion a year in programming compared to HBO's $2 billion. But Netflix was already pushing well past that level. Ted Sarandos announced that Netflix would spend $5 billion on content alone in 2016.

Outspending rivals by a dramatic amount was once a familiar tactic at HBO. In fact, it was something of an inspiration to Sarandos. Back in early 2007, when HBO started shooting *The Pacific*, the lush World War II follow-up to *Band of Brothers*, the network had to earmark a jaw-dropping $200 million for the Tom Hanks, Steven Spielberg miniseries. Sarandos was confounded by the economics of such a deal. It was industry legend by that point that *Band of Brothers* had managed to recoup its $100 million–plus budget thanks to its enormous DVD sales. But by 2007, the DVD market was flattening, and the chances of earning back the costs of *The Pacific* seemed highly improbable.

Sarandos found a moment one day over lunch in Beverly Hills to ask Albrecht point-blank why on earth he would do such a deal.

"Because we can," Albrecht replied nonchalantly, introducing Sarandos for the first time to the HBO shrug. At first, Sarandos thought such a mindset was reckless. But he eventually came around and saw its value. If a network is large enough and willing to spend aggressively, it can make things that its competitors cannot afford. Such one-of-a-kind spectacles can be used to lure in more curious customers, which, in turn, can be used to fuel even greater spending. Ideally, it's a positive feedback loop that drives one's rivals bonkers—and can even chase them away from competing in certain genres.

Nearly a decade later, Netflix's rivals, including HBO, were growing incensed by the tech arriviste's free-spending ways. Also, because there were no Nielsen ratings for streaming shows, Netflix was under much less scrutiny on a show-by-show basis. Viewers and critics drooled over their apparent hits while overlooking their costly flops like *The Get Down* or *Marco Polo*.

In October 2016, the situation grew worse. News broke that Chris Rock was decamping to Netflix, a major coup for the streamer. The Albanian Army had struck again. To win Rock over, Netflix had agreed to pay the comic $20 million per special, a staggering sum.

Sarandos, a devout fan of stand-up comedy, orchestrated the whole thing. For years, the Netflix programmer had been an unabashed admirer of HBO's comedy legacy. He never missed an episode of comedian Bill Maher's weekly talk show on HBO, and his personal connection to the brand went back much further. Each year, from 1995 to 2008, starting in the Albrecht era, HBO had sponsored the U.S. Comedy Arts Festival in Aspen, Colorado. Among other highlights, the event featured reunions of the casts of Monty Python and *Saturday Night Live*, tributes to Steve Martin and Goldie Hawn, and memorable performances by up-and-comers like Sarah Silverman and Jack Black. Nearly every year, Sarandos happily attended as a paying fan.

Sarandos loved HBO's rich tradition of stand-up comedy, and now he was perfectly positioned to usurp it.

Since Netflix's initial public offering on the Nasdaq exchange in May 2002, the company's valuation had soared from roughly $300 million to nearly $50 billion at the start of 2016. The monstrous growth was due not just to Netflix's performance but also to the prevailing mood on Wall Street. Watching Amazon and Facebook put up huge returns, investors had grown deliriously hungry for superfast-growing tech companies.

In search of the next big thing, both public and private investors were more than happy to pump money into unprofitable tech ventures like the ride-hailing service Uber, or the office subleasing company WeWork, or the home-sharing app Airbnb, so long as they were expanding wildly and gobbling up market share. The most important thing, according to the new paradigm of tech investing, was to crush the incumbents. Wooing new customers with ludicrous prices that made no long-term economic sense beyond undermining competitors was not only tolerated, it was expected and rewarded.

Netflix was happy to oblige. In the increasingly asymmetrical war between Netflix and HBO, stand-up comedy emerged as the leading front.

Over the next several months, Netflix went on a stand-up comic buying spree, virtually knocking HBO out of the business it had helped to recreate in the 1970s and '80s. The streamer struck mega-deals with Jerry Seinfeld, Louis C.K., Jim Gaffigan, and Dave Chappelle. It packed its streaming platform with top-rated comics, second-tier comics, no-name comics, and local comics who would specifically appeal to international regions where Netflix was trying to lure more subscribers.

Months later, admitting defeat to reporters, Casey Bloys told them that stand-up specials generated little viewing on HBO Now and HBO GO, and the $20 million price tag Netflix was putting on the specials was preposterous. "It's hard for me to justify paying exorbitant prices," he said. "So, when prices come back down or when it makes sense, when it's a relatively easy entry point, we'll get back in."

In the years to come, Sarandos would go about creating his own version of HBO's Aspen comedy festival, assembling an all-star lineup of heavyweight comedians scattered across two dozen venues in Los Angeles. It was called "Netflix Is a Joke: The Festival."

• • •

IN AUGUST 2016, Gary Ginsberg, a top communications executive at Time Warner, was in Martha's Vineyard expecting to catch up with his friend Peter Chernin. For years, Ginsberg and Chernin worked side by side at Rupert Murdoch's News Corporation. After leaving Murdoch's empire, Chernin had grown into a successful media mogul in his own right. In 2014, he started a joint venture with AT&T called Otter Media, gradually developing a good relationship with Randall Stephenson, the telecom's chief executive.

Ginsberg was expecting to go on a bike ride with his old pal when Chernin changed the plan. He suggested meeting for an early breakfast instead. There was something important to discuss.

Over bagels at a small outdoor café in Menemsha, Chernin posed a fateful question: "Would you guys ever consider selling the company to AT&T?"

From there, the two former Murdoch lieutenants excitedly skittered back and forth over the parameters of a potential deal. Chernin asked Ginsberg to see if Jeffrey Bewkes would sit down with Stephenson.

"Call Chernin and tell him it's a go," Bewkes told Ginsberg several hours later.

The next week, AT&T's Stephenson met with Time Warner's Bewkes. Over a salmon lunch in the tenth-floor dining room at the Time Warner Center, it became clear to everyone that they were seeing eye to eye on price. From there, they quickly reached a handshake agreement.

A short while later, in early October, Bewkes got a surprise message from Bob Iger, the head of Disney. He, too, was interested in discussing a possible deal to acquire Time Warner. Like everyone else in the home-entertainment business, Disney was girding itself for the transition from the cable-and-satellite era to the streaming age and was looking for ways to bulk up its portfolio of entertainment brands. But he was too late, Bewkes realized. The talks with AT&T were already too far along to entertain an offer from Disney.

Perhaps if Bewkes had been just a bit more patient, or a bit more diligent at identifying potential buyers, HBO and their colleagues at Time Warner might have found a new and inviting home as part of one of the biggest, most experienced media companies on the planet. But instead of Disney, Bewkes was forging ahead along a different route, selling the proud media conglomerate to a telephone company almost entirely inexperienced in the entertainment industry.

Bewkes sidestepped Iger and pulled the trigger. Just two years after rejecting Rupert Murdoch's bid for $85 a share, he'd found a suitor, a Hollywood naïf, willing to pay significantly more. Time Warner announced it was selling itself to AT&T, the heavily indebted telecom behemoth, for $107.50 a share in cash and stock, in a deal worth upward of $85 billion.

On October 22, in a conference call with reporters, Bewkes said that he and AT&T's Stephenson saw the evolution of their industries similarly. Everybody wanted more premium content on their tablets, TVs, and mobile phones. Advertisers wanted more precise, data-savvy ways to target consumers. Between AT&T's 100 million television, mobile, and broadband subscribers and Time Warner's enormous stock of programming, their combined prowess in distribution plus content would be unstoppable. "We think what this is going to do is supercharge our creative abilities," Bewkes said.

He acknowledged that Time Warner's history with similar mergers was lamentable. He called the AOL deal, which sixteen years earlier had been sold on a similar rationale, a "misstep." This time would be different. Time Warner and AT&T, Bewkes said, "fit together very well culturally."

Watching from the sidelines, Steve Case, the architect of AOL's calamitous purchase of Time Warner, assessed the situation more succinctly. "Déjà vu," he wrote on Twitter.

Before completion, the deal would have to pass regulatory scrutiny in Washington, which at the moment was consumed with the hectic, final weeks of a wild presidential campaign. On the eve of the announcement, when word of the acquisition leaked, Republican presidential candidate Donald Trump wasted no time in expressing his opposition, telling a crowd of frenzied supporters in Gettysburg, Pennsylvania, that "deals like this destroy democracy."

Time Warner executives were incredulous. "We were like what the fuck?" Ginsberg recalls.

Many in Hollywood greeted the news with concern. In the past, similar mergers had proved disastrous. For years, Universal Pictures had suffered through a prolonged slump as it rotated through a series of owners, including bankers, a liquor company, a cable company, and General Electric. When Coca-Cola purchased Columbia Pictures in the 1980s, the culture clash was immediate and damaging.

In the days after the sale's announcement, Richard Plepler delivered a message to AT&T via the *New York Times*: Leave HBO alone. Sitting at his preferred corner table at the Lambs Club, a power restaurant just around the corner from the network's Bryant Park offices, Plepler said that "the last thing they have any interest in doing is messing with a winning game," and urging AT&T executives to maintain a "Chinese wall" between its Dallas operations and HBO's properties in New York and California.

When they read Plepler's comments, some HBO executives privately bristled. Did he really think poking the bear was a good strategy?

A few days later, they had another big and disheartening development to worry about. On November 3, Donald Trump defeated Hillary Clinton to become the forty-fifth president of the United States. Throughout the campaign, Trump had repeatedly lashed out at HBO's sibling network, Time Warner's CNN, calling it "fake news," "fraud news," "garbage journalism," "dishonest," "unwatchable," "distorted," "sick," "a great danger to our country," and "the enemy of the American people."

"We knew during the transition there were going to be problems," Ginsberg says. "We were hearing from Trump's people that he was going to come after us. The source of the ire was CNN."

To try to mollify the incoming president, AT&T's CEO Randall Stephenson cozied up to the new regime. Stephenson met with the president-elect at Trump Tower, praised him to investors, and described himself as one of Trump's "biggest defenders on public policy." Behind the scenes, AT&T made four separate payments of fifty thousand dollars to an obscure limited liability company founded by Trump's personal lawyer, Michael Cohen.

All of which would prove fruitless. Trump refused to be pacified.

• • •

ISSA RAE WAS FRUSTRATED.

It had been over a year since Rae, a digital video wunderkind, had struck a deal with HBO, and yet she still had not gotten a green light from the network to make a show. Draft after draft, her ideas remained stuck in development.

Rae, a Stanford graduate who grew up in Maryland and Los Angeles, got her first exposure to fame when she created and starred in the online series *The Misadventures of Awkward Black Girl*, which debuted in 2011. The series quickly captivated a devoted following, and critics warmly compared it to *Curb Your Enthusiasm*. "Much of the humor is conveyed through Ms. Rae's face: She's quick with a furrowed brow or with a wide-eyed look of incredulity," Jon Caramanica wrote in the *New York Times* in 2012. "Her brand of comedy is small, anecdotal, experiential."

By 2015, she had released a bestselling memoir, observing her growing disillusionment with the portrayal of Black women in entertainment.

"How hard is it to portray a three-dimensional woman of color on television or in film?" she wrote. "I'm surrounded by them. They're my friends. I talk to them every day. How come Hollywood won't acknowledge us?"

At HBO, she began to get impatient with the protracted development process. Rae went through multiple rewrites, and it wasn't really jelling.

"I just remember being really impatient because I had come from the internet and I was like, why is this taking so long?" Rae told *Vanity Fair*. "Like I could create this in two minutes and it'll be out there."

Initially, the show was going to be a traditional workplace comedy, similar to *The Misadventures of Awkward Black Girl*. In the drafts and outlines that she prepared for HBO's programming team, Rae's friends existed only on the periphery.

But in one meeting, Bloys and his team perked up when Rae started talking about her real-life best friend. In response, Rae showed them text-message exchanges with her pal. Bloys had a thought. Why not reorient the show around Issa and the relationship with her best friend and the world surrounding them? Bloys, dipping back into his deep vault of childhood TV memories, asked what would it look like if Rae did her version of *Laverne & Shirley*, the *Happy Days* spin-off about two friends living and working in Milwaukee?

The suggestion from Bloys helped unlock something for Rae. She loved telling that part of the story. "That opened my eyes," she said.

"I got to rewriting, and then I was also like, oh, fuck it," Rae said. "Like, I'm putting all elements of my life in here, so I can say this is rooted in authenticity. This is a real story. And that's when they were like, 'OK! Green light.'"

In October 2016, HBO broadcast the first episode of *Insecure*, which finds Issa, a Stanford graduate living in southern Los Angeles, stuck in an uninspiring nonprofit job and weighing whether to end a five-year relationship with her boyfriend. Meanwhile, Molly, Issa's best friend, is thriving in her career as a corporate lawyer, but her dating life is a disaster. Throughout the first season, Issa and Molly lean on each other for support, even when they get on each other's nerves.

"It was really exploring Molly's life as fully as you're exploring Issa's," Bloys says. "That kind of opened it up."

To Rae, it felt like she was finally able to accomplish what she had originally set out to do: portray two Black women in a friendship who aren't "pitted against one another."

Like David Chase before her, Rae was passionate about where the show was shot. It had been suggested that the show could save some money if they filmed in the Valley and just pretended it was southern Los Angeles. Not a chance, said Rae. It was vital to her to shoot in neighborhoods like Inglewood and Baldwin Hills.

"You can't fake these locations," Rae said. "There's something about being there that feels real. The entire point was to showcase those particular neighborhoods."

At first, Bloys and his colleagues wanted a big-name director for the pilot. Instead, Rae requested they go with Melina Matsoukas, who had no TV or movie credits except music videos for superstars like Rihanna and Beyoncé. HBO acquiesced.

As it took off with fans, *Insecure* marked an important breakthrough for HBO. The network, like much of Hollywood, had a hideous track record in making shows with Black creators.

Critics adored it. "In the years before *Insecure* and a handful of other shows debuted in 2016, viewers were unaccustomed to seeing the mundanities of Black life depicted on television; with some notable exceptions, many Black people on TV at the time were either minor characters on white-led series or reality-TV personalities," Hannah Giorgis wrote in *The Atlantic*. "By filling that void, *Insecure* became a Black popular-culture phenomenon."

Still, the release of a single beloved show hardly fixed HBO's broader diversity issues overnight. Months after *Insecure* premiered, with *Game of Thrones* at the zenith of its popularity, the creators of HBO's hit sci-fi series were contemplating their next move. In July 2017, the network announced that Benioff and Weiss would be making a new drama for HBO, entitled *Confederate*. The alt-history series would be set in a reimagined America in which instead of losing the Civil War, the Southern states have seceded from the union, slavery has evolved into a "modern institution," and hostilities are rising on both sides of the "Mason-Dixon Demilitarized Zone."

Benioff and Weiss would be teaming up on the project with two Black screenwriters, a husband-and-wife team, Nichelle Tramble Spellman (*Justified*, *The Good Wife*) and Malcolm Spellman (*Empire*).

With Trump in the White House and white nationalists across the country feeling increasingly emboldened, the premise of the HBO show was greeted with widespread trepidation and disgust. On social media, prominent writers and critics rebuked the project, suggesting it was "slavery fan fiction," a fantasy series for the hood-wearing, cross-burning set.

In *The Atlantic*, Ta-Nehisi Coates argued that *Confederate* would continue in a lamentable decades-old tradition in Hollywood of pumping out revisionist narratives about post–Civil War America, collectively sanitizing the heinousness of slavery. "*Confederate* is a shockingly unoriginal idea, especially for the allegedly avant garde HBO," he wrote. "'What if the white South had won?' may well be the most trod-upon terrain in the field of American alternative history."

The network sprang into damage-control mode. In an interview with *New York* magazine, Benioff, Weiss, and the Spellmans decried the history of American slavery and asked people to reserve judgment until they saw the actual show. "You know, we might fuck it up," Benioff said. "But we haven't yet."

Whatever its potential merits, HBO had botched the initial rollout so thoroughly that the project was unsalvageable. For Casey Bloys's internal push for more diversity in HBO programming, the screw-up was a painful setback—though, as it would turn out, not a fatal one.

It also signaled the beginning of the end of Benioff's and Weiss's time with the network. Two years later, following the conclusion of *Game of Thrones*, they would depart for Netflix.

• • •

WITH THE MIGRATION from cable TV to streaming video accelerating, major changes were sweeping through the industry. In August 2017, Disney revealed that it was ending its deals to license its famous catalogue of kids and Pixar movies to Netflix. Just as Sarandos and Cindy Holland had anticipated, major media companies were starting to claw back their best programming from Netflix in preparation for new streaming services of their own.

Days later, Netflix announced that it was poaching one of Disney's most successful showrunners, Shonda Rhimes, the creator of the popular ABC dramas *Grey's Anatomy* and *Scandal*, in a massive nine-figure deal. Like Netflix's huge payout to Chris Rock, the giant contract for Rhimes was just the opening salvo. In the months and years that followed, Netflix would corral more and more top TV writers with enormous paydays.

With the entertainment business evolving rapidly, HBO and Time Warner executives found themselves stuck on the sidelines, as their regulatory problems in Washington, D.C., continued to mount. In November 2017, the U.S. Department of Justice filed an antitrust suit seeking to block AT&T's acquisition, alleging that the deal would hurt competition and lead to higher prices. Lawyers for AT&T retorted that the government's true motivation was Trump's personal grudge against CNN. Neither side backed down, and the case slowly ground its way toward trial in the U.S. District Court.

While Netflix was busy gobbling up industry talent, HBO was losing one of its core players. In December 2017, Sheila Nevins announced that after thirty-eight years and twelve hundred documentaries, she was leaving the network. Many other HBO folks would soon follow her out the door.

For Nevins it was a bittersweet moment, one that she couldn't quite believe was happening. "I thought I would die there," Nevins says. "We used to have three-quarter-inch video boxes. I thought, oh god, one day they will probably put my ashes in a three-quarter box and put it on a shelf in some memorial closet at HBO."

Her colleagues, however, weren't entirely surprised. In recent years, a rift of sorts had opened up between Nevins and Richard Plepler. Whereas Nevins's previous bosses had shown little interest in making documentaries, Plepler was a lifelong devotee of nonfiction. He had lots of ideas about documentaries that HBO should pursue, and his taste in subjects was different. From her earliest days at HBO, Nevins said she didn't like *famous*. She liked *everyday*. Real-people stories.

"Richard changed my world because he was very political and I was not," Nevins says. "He was very aware of editorials in the *Times* and celebrity and things that I didn't really get as much as he did. We sort of worked side by side."

"Mine were more colloquial," she adds. "The paths didn't really cross. But docus started to become a more political entity and closer to the times— more friendly to the commercial biggies and the political biggies. Sometimes I found it interesting. But as long as I could keep doing my thing, I didn't look in there much. Maybe I should have, but I didn't. I worked on some of Richard's. But I didn't really lose sleep over them."

It was all fine. Until, eventually, it wasn't.

"She is unquestionably one of the singular talents in her field," Plepler says. "Even when we sparred occasionally, I had nothing but the highest respect and adoration for her, and I loved working with her."

Across the industry, documentary makers lamented the news of Nevins's resignation.

Liz Garbus, one of the most celebrated documentarians of the last twenty-five years, who has made films like *The Execution of Wanda Jean* and *Bobby Fischer Against the World*, credited Nevins with giving her a career. When she first met with Nevins in the late 1990s, she said it felt like "gaining access to the holy house of saints." And if you worked with her, she explained, you were a *documentarian*—there were no side hustles necessary.

"People talk about the Golden Age of documentaries now—with streaming and all the wonderful outlets and eyeballs out there—and it is," she says. "But the Golden Age began if you were making a documentary with Sheila Nevins back at that time. You had financing, you had an audience, you had someone who creatively would support your mission. You could make a *film*."

"Sheila was renowned for being, yes, idiosyncratic," she continues, "but also being quite visionary and helping filmmakers make the film they wanted by means of both creative and financial support. And that was the only place."

The *Paradise Lost* filmmaker Joe Berlinger put it simply: "If I had to pick one individual who has the greatest impact on the modern documentary as an executive, she would be it."

For decades, says Berlinger, it was Nevins who financially supported the American documentary community with a level of resources unmatched by anyone else. "Documentaries were considered the bastard stepchildren of the entertainment industry," he says. "Agents didn't pay attention to it. Studios didn't pay attention. Sheila and that department have played a large role in the explosion that we see today."

Now, the boom in documentaries that Nevins had helped to ignite at HBO would be carried on by others. Netflix was at the front of the pack. By 2017, under the guidance of Netflix executive Lisa Nishimura, the streaming platform was routinely making "quality noise," with multiepisode documentary series on far-flung topics, ranging from true crime, to politics, to sports.

"The baton was handed off," Berlinger says. "Lisa Nishimura and all the good folks at Netflix have figured out how to brilliantly push the genre even further, how to turn it into a global franchise. They, more than anybody, are responsible for creating the concept of the doc series as a bingeable event."

In the end, of all the hundreds of buzzy, award-winning films that Nevins had commissioned over the years, her favorite, she says, was one that almost nobody saw. One day in 2010, she was watching CNN's coverage of an industrial disaster, the Deepwater Horizon oil spill in the Gulf of Mexico, when some birds caught her attention. The forlorn, grounded pelicans were covered in oil, and a group of naturalists was trying to save them. Nevins was intrigued.

Years earlier in the aftermath of Hurricane Katrina, during HBO's rollout of Spike Lee's documentary *When the Levees Broke*, Nevins had visited New Orleans. She adored the city's food and music, its waterfront and waterfowl. For whatever reason, Nevins had a thing for stories about survivors. Even pelicans. She gave the assignment to filmmaker Irene Taylor Brodsky.

The resulting documentary, *Saving Pelican 895*, told the story of one wounded bird's struggle to live. Conservationists at the Fort Jackson Wildlife Rehabilitation Center in Louisiana are shown bathing the pelican by hand, training him to eat, protecting him from an incoming storm, and then encouraging him to fly.

"He doesn't go right away," Nevins says. "I thought, well, this is going to have a sad ending. You can't fix a pelican. That's the moral, here. Once a broken pelican, always a broken pelican. But then, this fucking little bird, he flew."

It was the kind of thing that, in another HBO context, might have made Mike Tyson momentarily unclench his fists or Tony Soprano pass out in his pile of duck feed. Nevins felt elated.

In many ways, it was the same approach she had first experienced decades earlier, interviewing passersby on the sidewalks of Manhattan, the method she had been encouraging from her repertory of filmmakers ever since. The documentary, so narrow in scope, managed to grapple with something much larger. How an individual can survive in such a harsh and dirty world; and whether, in spite of all the trauma, you can restore someone's sense of self and nurse them back to flight.

"I don't even like pelicans particularly," Nevins says. "But I like this one."

PART V

HBO TO THE MAX

(2018–2022)

CHAPTER 22

Dawn of the Bell Heads

Richard Plepler stood onstage at the front of the Michael Fuchs Theater and gazed around the bustling room. Dozens of HBO employees were taking their seats. It was midday on a Tuesday in June 2018. Only five days earlier, a federal judge had ruled in AT&T's favor over the Justice Department, paving the way for the phone company to complete its $85.4 billion acquisition of HBO's parent company, Time Warner.

After twenty months stuck in perilous limbo, HBO staffers were finally ready to meet the new owners.

Plepler, in a blue sport coat with a bright white pocket square, welcomed everyone to the town hall meeting. For the next hour, he explained, he'd be discussing the future with his new boss, John Stankey, a top AT&T executive who was leading the telephone company's charge into the programming business. There would be time for questions. But first, said Plepler, it was time to hear from the talent.

Plepler stepped aside and a video played on the theater's large screen. For the next several minutes, a parade of actors from HBO shows, including Tony Hale (*Veep*), Jeffrey Wright (*Westworld*), Bill Maher (*Real Time with Bill Maher*), and Danny McBride (*Eastbound and Down*) welcomed their new owners.

"Hello, John. It is fantastic to be a part of the AT&T family, really," said Bill Hader, the star of HBO's comedy *Barry*. "It's every actor's dream to work for the phone company."

The circus-like theme music from *Curb Your Enthusiasm* blared through the theater's speakers. "From this day forward, you shall be known as Sir John Stankey," said Emilia Clarke, the British actress who plays Queen Daenerys Targaryen, the mother of dragons, on *Game of Thrones*. "All shall bend the knee to Lord Stankey."

When the waggish video was over, Stankey, a bald-headed, broad-shouldered Texan, climbed onstage and folded his sturdy six-foot-five-inch frame into a seat next to Plepler. Stankey was wearing oval glasses, a drab sports jacket, and pleated, brown dress pants.

Born in 1962, he grew up in Los Angeles and went to college at Loyola Marymount University, where he studied finance, and graduate school at the University of California, Los Angeles, where he earned a master's in business administration.

In 1985, Stankey joined Pacific Bell. In the years that followed, as the telecom industry consolidated and his company got swallowed up by AT&T, known uneasily in the industry by its nickname, the "Death Star," Stankey kept climbing the corporate ranks, eventually ascending to the upper echelons of the Dallas-based company. Just recently, he had completed stints as AT&T's chief technology officer and as the head of its struggling DirecTV unit. In front of the HBO crowd, Stankey referred to himself as a "Bell head," aka a telecom lifer. It was a term that sounded altogether alien to the HBO crew.

In nearly every way, Stankey and Plepler came across as opposites. Plepler was on the board of the Council on Foreign Relations; Stankey sat on the board of UPS. Plepler was a creature of New York and Connecticut who played tennis; Stankey lived in Dallas and enjoyed the occasional bird-hunting or fly-fishing expedition. Plepler was a cultural omnivore; Stankey watched college football and little else. Plepler was an avowed Democrat; Stankey was a longtime donor to Republican campaigns.

Looking out over the room of progressive New Yorkers, with his big hands occasionally chopping the air in front of him for emphasis, Stankey spoke about corporate culture and compensation and potential human resource redundancies. In a deep baritone voice, he invoked "efficiencies," "marginal cost structures," and "binomial distributions."

With a note of chagrin, Stankey grumbled about how newspapers were suddenly so interested in his personal life. "You're now in the entertainment business, John," Plepler interjected. "There are no secrets."

Stankey went on to explain AT&T's broader rationale for buying Time Warner. The telecom business, he said, was on the verge of rolling out its next generation of wireless network technology, known as 5G. Mobile upload and download speeds were poised to get much faster. Soon, wireless networks would be behaving more like the seamless internet connections inside office buildings. Everything would be instantaneous, no delays. Stankey said that 5G was on the verge of ushering in a wave of new mobile technologies. For example, autonomous self-driving cars.

It wouldn't be long before commuters in a city like Los Angeles would be sitting in the backseat of their cars watching premium video on the way to work instead of driving, he said. Over the next four years, individuals would be consuming, on average, an additional hour to an hour and a half of video each day. "We need to get our share of that space," Stankey said. "We don't want them just putting likes on Facebook."

Together, HBO and AT&T could conquer this brave new world, he continued. But to succeed, the network needed to reach more customers: 35 to 40 percent of the U.S. market was no longer enough. HBO would need to transform its premium brand into something more broadly appealing. And it would need to make a lot more programming. The era of ruling Sunday nights had passed. One night a week would no longer cut it. "We need hours a day," Stankey said. "It's not hours a week, and it's not hours a month. We need hours a day. You are competing with devices that sit in people's hands that capture their attention every fifteen minutes."

Plepler noted that, in recent years, the network had done the best job it could with the hand he was dealt. At times, he said, the network had been outbid for programming, which was frustrating. He cited *House of Cards* as

an example. "I don't need to tell you what Netflix is spending internationally," Plepler said.

Stankey appeared sympathetic, to a point. Yes, Plepler was right. To
compete on a global level in the new streaming era of home entertainment,
AT&T would need to step up investment in the network. "We've also got to
make money at the end of the day, right?" Stankey said.

"We do that," Plepler responded.

"Yes, you do," Stankey said. "Just not enough."

"Oh no," Plepler said. "Be careful."

As the tension in the room simmered, both men kept fidgeting, speaking with their hands and recrossing their legs. There was little eye contact.
The next year, Stankey told the crowd, would be a difficult one for HBO.
The old way of doing business wouldn't cut it anymore. The industry was
being disrupted by Silicon Valley. He didn't mention Netflix by name. But
he didn't have to. "You will work very hard, and this next year will—my wife
hates it when I say this—feel like childbirth," he said.

Translation: There would be lots of pain and blood and screaming. "You'll
look back on it and be very fond of it," he said. "But it's not going to feel great
while you're in the middle of it."

HBO would be reborn according to the vicarious needs of its new, har-
ried parents in Dallas. "It's going to be a tough year," Stankey said.

Afterward, some HBO staffers walked out of the room in a bit of a daze.
If Stankey and Plepler were an odd couple, a buddy comedy did not appear
to be in the offing.

• • •

ON SUNDAY NIGHTS IN JUNE 2018, HBO began airing *Succession*—a show
about an aging billionaire and his retinue of suck-ups, yes men, and bum-
bling courtiers that seemed perfectly tailored to the preoccupations of liberal viewers, spellbound by the daily indignities and nepotistic excesses of
the Trump presidency.

At the outset, Logan Roy (Brian Cox), the founder and chief executive
officer of Waystar Royco—a global entertainment conglomerate with cruise

ships, a movie studio, and a right-leaning cable TV news network, reminiscent of Rupert Murdoch's media empire—is turning eighty and seemingly on the brink of retirement.

His pending abdication has set up a dynastic power struggle among his jaded, emotionally stunted adult children. There is Kendall (Jeremy Strong), a spineless, coke-snorting, jargon-spewing wannabe business titan; Roman (Kieran Culkin), a foul-mouthed smart-aleck; Connor (Alan Ruck), a libertarian flaneur; and Siobhan (Sarah Snook), a shrewd political operative.

Logan, the gruff, all-powerful patriarch, disdains them all.

Despite a previous stint in rehab, Kendall is the scion initially poised to take over. But then he gets pushed around during negotiations to buy a media start-up, and Logan informs his family that there's been a change of plans. He is staying in command.

Badly rattled, Kendall implores his father to cede power. The media world is changing, he mewls. The old days of magazines and movies and cable TV are over. "Where's the growth?" he asks his dad. "All our graphs go down. . . . The world is changing."

"Yeah, yeah, yeah," says his father. "Everything changes. The studio was going to tank when I bought it. Everyone was going to stay home with videotape. But guess what? No. They want to go out."

He looks hard at his son. "You make your own reality."

Kendall is flummoxed. What to do about rich, unscrupulous men clinging to old ideas who are capable of creating their own reality? By the second year of the Trump administration, it was a question of growing national concern.

Jesse Armstrong, the show's creator, was a British screenwriter who got his start in TV making sketch comedy programs and children's sitcoms. In 2003, Armstrong cocreated the long-running, darkly humorous sitcom *Peep Show* for Channel 4. Later, he worked with Armando Iannucci—the creator of HBO's *Veep*—as a writer on the British government satire *The Thick of It*, and its 2009 spin-off movie, *In the Loop*. The following year, at the Academy Awards, Armstrong was one of four writers nominated for Best Adapted Screenplay.

In 2010, Armstrong penned a biopic about Rupert Murdoch, which later made its way onto Hollywood's "Black List," an annual survey of the best scripts that haven't yet been made into movies. There, it caught the attention of Adam McKay, a writer, producer, and former collaborator with comedian Will Ferrell. McKay commissioned Armstrong to write a movie about Lee Atwater, the hard-edged Republican strategist who, in 1988, helped George H. W. Bush win the presidency.

One day, while reviewing a stack of submissions as part of his consultant duties for HBO, Frank Rich came across Armstrong's two unmade scripts.

"I thought they were brilliant and mordantly funny," Rich says. "I was knocked out in the case of the Lee Atwater script that this guy who was a British writer could have such a command of American politics."

A short while later, Armando Iannucci brought in Armstrong to write the final episode of the first season of *Veep*. Armstrong and Rich, an executive producer of *Veep*, met and became fast friends.

Soon, Rich and Armstrong were teaming up to develop a project, commissioned by HBO, titled *The Imperialists*. The series centered around two American guys, just a few years out of college, who buy a coffee-bean farm in Africa. They plan to manufacture artisanal chocolate and coffee, and make a killing selling it to hipsters back in Williamsburg and Silver Lake. But complications ensue, and the bros get entangled in the geopolitical turmoil of the region.

"It touched on a bunch of things like the Chinese 'Belt and Road Initiative' and this sort of new, slightly Cold War-ish thing going on in developing countries, between the U.S., the E.U., and China," Armstrong says. "It was sort of a buddy comedy with some geopolitics going on beneath it."

Armstrong and Rich loved the project, and McKay was set to direct the first episode. But HBO's drama department—then mired in the depths of its *Vinyl*-era development logjam—seemed to lose interest. "It was not a priority, we came to realize," Rich says. "The process was sluggish and frustrating."

With the series going nowhere, McKay went off to direct *The Big Short*, and Armstrong turned his interest elsewhere. In 2015, he enthusiastically consumed *The Jinx*, HBO's multipart documentary series about Robert

Durst, the accused murderer and bizarre scion of an uberrich New York real estate family.

Afterward, Armstrong buried himself in a stack of books about business leaders and media tycoons. He read biographies of Conrad Black, Tiny Rowland, Lord Rothermere, and William Randolph Hearst. He breezed through *Disney War* by James B. Stewart about the stormy tenure of Michael Eisner and his friendship-turned-rivalry with Jeffrey Katzenberg. By the time Armstrong picked up the autobiography of Sumner Redstone, the powerful and sex-crazed head of Viacom, he saw the similarities among tycoons piling up.

They all seemed to have such a paucity of self-reflection. "It's almost like a superpower," Armstrong says.

Constructing a project based on a multimogul composite rather than tethered to a single actual person, Armstrong felt liberated. "It's just fun to be completely freed from any sense of responsibility to portray real people realistically," he says.

Initially, his agents wanted to avoid repeating the lousy experience of *The Imperialists* and were wary of selling it to HBO. His agent called Rich and explained why they would be taking the project elsewhere. Armstrong was set to meet with other networks.

The next day, Rich and his wife, Alex Witchel, dined with Richard and Lisa Plepler at the HBO chief's house in Greenwich. "You're about to lose Jesse Armstrong," Rich told Plepler over dinner. At the table, Plepler called his programming team. Bloys hastily arranged a meeting with Armstrong.

In person, Armstrong told Bloys, tongue in cheek, that his show would combine the elements of the low-budget Danish cult classic *Festen*, with the rah-rah 1980s network drama *Dallas*. On a more serious note, he explained that his show would be tonally similar to *The Sopranos* and *Six Feet Under*, the two series that he admired most.

At the time, NBC was airing *This Is Us*, a popular, heart-jerking family drama. Bloys was on the lookout for something in a similar vein only with a vicious HBO spin.

Armstrong proceeded to write a script. HBO picked it up for a series, and Rich joined as an executive producer.

With HBO's early programming successes in mind, Bloys wanted a cast that was not overflowing with stars. Just as *Sex and the City* took B-actors and made them famous, *Succession* would do the same.

"Unless you were working in Hollywood, you wouldn't know any of the actors," Bloys said. "We specifically didn't want to put feature actors in it. I believe that TV historically has made stars. We're good at scouting talent, finding talent, and putting it out there."

HBO's initial expectations for the series were modest. As the network had gleaned repeatedly, series focused on the media tend to be a niche interest. In the run-up to the premiere of *Succession*, one high-ranking HBO executive likened it to a "utility player." It would fill the gap between the second season of *Westworld*—HBO's sci-fi western starring Evan Rachel Wood as a self-conscious, AI-powered android—and the hotly anticipated limited series *Sharp Objects*.

In the end, *Succession* would wind up becoming HBO's most successful drama since *Game of Thrones*.

In the fall of 2018, a few months after the debut of *Succession*, HBO announced it was getting out of the boxing business. Over the past forty-five years, HBO had aired more than a thousand fights, from the Thrilla in Manila to Buster Douglas's improbable victory over Tyson in Japan, to Mayweather's defeat of De La Hoya at the MGM Grand. But in recent years, fewer and fewer customers were watching. By 2018, only 2 percent of HBO subscribers were tuning in to the network's biggest fights.

The sport had struggled for decades to find a follow-up act equal to the theatrics of Mike Tyson. Over the years, viewers had migrated to UFC fights on ESPN and WWE matches on the USA Network. For years, there'd been little to justify HBO's continued investment in the sport other than the tradition of the network and the renown of HBO's boxing team. But the days of HBO passion projects, and the HBO shrug that enabled them, were coming to an end.

"This is not a subjective decision," said Peter Nelson, the head of HBO Sports. "Our audience research informs us that boxing is no longer a determinant factor for subscribing to HBO."

• • •

NOT LONG after taking over, John Stankey sent out a memo to top executives, including to Richard Plepler, describing the ways he preferred to interact with staff. The memo was awkwardly titled "Operating Cadence and Style." "I am not a big fan of meetings," wrote Stankey.

Entertainment executives often preferred to convene at a relaxed pace over lunch or dinner. At HBO, executives prided themselves on a culture in which they could freely circulate in and out of each other's offices. Stankey did not work that way, he now made clear. Instead, he liked to keep meetings short, thirty minutes at most because of the "discipline it drives for individuals to pre-mediate their points and get to the crux of the issue." In other words: Please skip the personal talk.

Texts would not be a good way to get in touch with him. "I try to segment text messages to my personal life," he explained. "Use it sparingly when you really need my attention on something short fused." Other written communications would be difficult too. "I am not a prolific e-mailer . . . go figure," he said.

As the memo circulated among company executives, it was met with grumbles. It struck some as oddly condescending, imperious, and impersonal. Trying to get to know Stankey in a professional setting was like trying to free climb Yosemite's El Capitan. There was nothing easy to latch on to.

Stankey, it seemed, was not the only AT&T executive who preferred to avoid meetings. During AT&T's courtship of the company and afterward, Randall Stephenson, the company's chief executive, failed to invite Plepler to lunch, dinner, or coffee. HBO's convivial leader told several friends that the snub surprised and hurt him.

There were other sources of growing tension. Plepler and his closest associates were beginning to suspect that for a group of newly empowered cultural gatekeepers, the AT&T folks were nothing more than a bunch of Philistines. "They didn't regard television as art," says one former HBO executive.

The misgivings were mutual. "These guys back in New York, they think they're ball players," Stephenson said at one point, referring to Plepler and CNN chief Jeff Zucker, according to the *New York Times*. "They're not ball players. They're executives."

According to a person close to Stankey, the towering Texan thought that many of the executives he inherited in New York and Los Angeles had been managing the company on autopilot for years. Due to perversely engineered financial incentives and perks, they'd been maintaining the status quo in order to pump up their bonuses and pad their gluttonous expense accounts off the backs of shareholders, while shirking the gnarly task of reinvention that needed to get done, pronto. Suggestions to put aside their bitter, internecine rivalries and to work together collaboratively with an eye on the streaming future, they resisted. On top of that, Stankey didn't even know if he could trust them. He felt that anything he put in email could be leaked to the press and twisted into a maddening narrative about AT&T's numbskullery. Caricature, not facts.

In the coming months, the "Chinese wall" that Plepler had hoped to keep between AT&T and HBO crumbled. Piece by piece, with Stankey's blessing, AT&T was beginning to muck with the business functions under Plepler's purview, ranging from distribution to data analysis to finance.

With their expanding control, AT&T executives set about installing their plan. If Time Warner had historically been a holding company for a bunch of independent entities that each had distinct cultures and identities, those days were over. AT&T decided Time Warner would get a name change and would now be known as WarnerMedia—one word. The balkanized divisions inside the company would now be required to work cooperatively toward a single goal. It was essentially the same task that had tempted and frustrated company executives all the way back to the early days of the AOL merger.

Often, Plepler would sit at his corner booth at the Lambs Club and engulf that day's guest with a circular screed about how the AT&T guys—Stankey, in particular—just did not get it. "Richard was incensed," says one lunch companion. "And he was just on a loop. On a loop!"

"You could easily see Richard was distracted," says Quentin Schaffer. "Clearly there was a different mindset uptown with John Stankey. And

Richard was telling John where he disagreed with him, where he felt he was wrong: 'John, that's not going to work.' And I could see Richard's frustration that he wasn't being listened to. It just kept building."

Money was a frequent source of irritation. Among other disagreements, Plepler and Stankey did not see eye to eye on the company's plans for a direct-to-consumer streaming service. Stankey was intent on building a Netflix-like competitor. Plepler told associates that he felt that AT&T had nowhere close to the resources or money needed for it. Instead, Plepler wanted AT&T to make improvements to HBO and let it broaden out its programming slate.

"When Richard and John were having conversations, John would make some proposal of what he wanted to do, Richard would say, 'Okay, John, but where's the money?'" Schaffer says.

In October 2018, with such disputes still largely out of the public's sight, AT&T announced that it would be launching a new giant streaming service. It would be bigger and broader than HBO Now and HBO GO, and designed to better take on the likes of Netflix, Hulu, Amazon Prime Video, and the forthcoming one from Disney. It was still at least a year away. There was a lot to work out. Stankey was unperturbed.

"The bundle will be compelling," Stankey told investors. "It will be a great value. It will be desirable content. And it will have brand character."

Stankey started assembling a team to lead the new service. Kevin Reilly, the former Brillstein executive who worked on *The Sopranos*, and later at FX, NBC, and Fox, would be the chief content officer, and in charge of picking new shows and library acquisitions. A cast of AT&T functionaries, newly arrived at WarnerMedia, set about concocting a convoluted, tortuous multi-tiered pricing model for the new streaming service, which left many people inside and outside of the company scratching their heads. Months later, the pricing plan would have to be scrapped for something simpler.

From the sidelines, Plepler took it all in with growing dissatisfaction. By early 2019, just a few months after the town hall debacle, Plepler decided it was time to bring his twenty-seven-year run at the network to a close.

On February 26, 2019, *The Hollywood Reporter* broke the news that WarnerMedia was considering Bob Greenblatt, the former Showtime and NBC executive, for a major new role. Two days later, Plepler announced his departure. Late in the afternoon on the last day of February, Plepler sent a note to HBO staffers. "Hard as it is to think about leaving the company I love, and the people I love in it, it is the right time for me to do so," Plepler wrote.

The news tore through the industry. Plepler would later tell people it was apparent to him at the first, fraught town hall meeting with Stankey that it was not going to work out for him.

"Essentially, he was disgusted by them and wanted out," says Frank Rich of Plepler and AT&T. "And those of us who were left were extremely worried about what would happen to the HBO culture under these guys."

Only a few hours after Plepler's announcement, the network held a screening of a new HBO documentary by Alex Gibney called *The Inventor*, chronicling the Icarus-like rise and fall of Elizabeth Holmes and her blood-testing start-up Theranos. It was followed by a dinner party at Porter House, a steakhouse with a view of Central Park.

Around 9:30 p.m., about two hundred screenwriters, filmmakers, journalists, and HBO employees filed into the restaurant. As they made their way to their seats, they passed by a table in the front of the room, set with glowing candles, bouquets of yellow roses, and a name card that read RICHARD PLEPLER. The power table was desolate. Every seat was empty.

Events like these, designed to get their filmmakers noticed, had been a hallmark of Plepler's HBO. The network was dropping a hundred thousand dollars on the party just to promote the relatively small project. Plepler liked to say that HBO got a "halo" from such gatherings.

Now it felt more like a pall.

"How do you trumpet the horn in a way that lets people know that this is important, that you should watch, and attention must be paid?" said Gibney at the party, lamenting the loss of Plepler, whom he described as his "impresario." "That's what Richard was great at. He was also great at nurturing talent. I mean, I loved him for that."

He was hardly alone. Under Plepler, HBO's generosity to its favored artists felt boundless and unconditional. When HBO made Larry David's 2013 feature film *Clear History*, the comedian requested that the network add a few million dollars to the budget. Plepler gave it to him. When David asked if the movie could be shot on Martha's Vineyard, where he owned a home, the network acquiesced. Plepler believed in indulging the needs of the talent, and they, in turn, loved Plepler's attentive bedside manner.

Occasionally, they even name-checked him in their work. In *The Sopranos*, David Chase named a doctor who attends to Tony Soprano's gunshot wound "Dr. Lior Plepler." Likewise, Larry David's character in *Clear History* would go on to invoke his benefactor's name when referring to an expensive painting on his wall. "It's a Plepler!" he says.

After a couple of hours of commiserating over sixty-dollar steaks and three-berry shortcake desserts, the room at the Porter House began to empty out. Just after 11:30, a waiter in a white jacket approached an empty table, leaned down, and swiped away Plepler's name card, barely breaking stride.

CHAPTER 23

It's Just TV

On March 4, days after Plepler's last dinner party, AT&T made it official. Moving forward, Bob Greenblatt, the fifty-eight-year-old former head of entertainment at Showtime and NBC, would be the new chairman of WarnerMedia Entertainment, giving him direct oversight of HBO.

Nobody could mistake Greenblatt for yet another telecom putz. Raised in the cornfields of Rockford, Illinois, Greenblatt grew up avidly watching "That's Entertainment!," a 1974 highlight reel of classic MGM musicals. He was a theater junkie and an early investor in *Hamilton*. He proudly kept an 1898 Steinway grand piano, with ivory keys, in his office. Dolly Parton was a good friend. "He's definitely got to be the only Catholic Robert Greenblatt in the world," she once said.

In his new role, Greenblatt would oversee the company's forthcoming launch of its direct-to-consumer streaming service, which would debut in May 2020. The service, WarnerMedia executives figured, would likely cost fifteen dollars a month, the same price as HBO on cable, which would make it more expensive than Netflix, Disney+, and Hulu. The next question was what to name it.

The new WarnerMedia team wanted something that sounded big. "Warner" was briefly bandied about. For decades, moviegoers had seen the "WB" shield at the beginning of motion pictures. Then again, it wasn't quite a consumer-facing brand. "It's never been Disney," says one WarnerMedia executive. "You've never gone to Warner Land."

HBO was the next best thing. But there were drawbacks. HBO was known as an adult service, not particularly suited for the whole family. After decades of hype, advertising, and direct mail, HBO was stuck in the neighborhood of thirty-five million subscriptions. "The dirty little secret is that HBO has hit a ceiling," Greenblatt said in an interview that year. "It can't grow. In a world where there's Netflix and Amazon, the only way to grow, I guarantee you, is to bundle it with something else that's going to lift it."

To name the bigger bundle, HBO+ was ruled out almost immediately; the + signal was already overplayed in the market. Other names were considered: including HBO Ultra and HBO Verse, which was nixed since it might be confused with U-verse TV, an offshoot of AT&T's DirecTV. And then there was HBO Max. It suggested something large. And it also had a human quality to it. Max was a person's name. Max could be your friend. A consensus soon emerged: HBO Max was the best way to go.

The rebranded HBO also needed a new hue, ideally some flash of color that would stand out from all the other noisy apps competing for attention on smartphone and smart-TV menus. After commissioning and scrutinizing much market research, the executives made up their minds. Max would be purple. It was more festive than old-school HBO's somber black and white, more royal than Netflix's garish red.

WarnerMedia executives also wanted other ways to contrast HBO Max with the new slate of competitors from Silicon Valley. With that goal in mind, the network debuted a website, highlighting recommendations of HBO shows made by fellow fans—and, pointedly, not by algorithms. Its name, "Recommended by Humans," was a none-too-subtle dig at Netflix.

With AT&T firmly in charge, institutional changes came fast. In March 2019, HBO executives told its staff that its satellite communications center in Hauppauge, New York, the once state-of-the-art facility that had been operating since 1983, would be shutting down. AT&T put the property up for sale. The two hundred employees who worked there would be given a chance to transfer to other offices. Many, however, would be losing their jobs. The symbolism was hard to miss. With the Thrilla in Manila, HBO had kicked off TV's satellite age. Now, HBO was saying goodbye to yesterday's future.

In May, HBO staffers in Manhattan were preparing to move out of the glassy green cube that had served as the network's headquarters since 1984. Bank of America was set to move into HBO's longtime home.

The final weeks in the office were chaotic. WarnerMedia leadership informed staffers that space at their new facilities in Hudson Yards on the far West Side of Manhattan would be smaller. For the first time since the early days inside the Time-Life Building, the network's employees would be working under the same roof as their corporate siblings, like CNN and Turner Broadcasting. The days of HBO's prized independence were over.

Those who previously had offices at Bryant Park would either be getting smaller ones or would be tossed in an open-seating floor plan, cheek by jowl with everyone else. There was a strict limit, staffers were told, on what they could bring with them. As a result, decades' worth of HBO documents, keepsakes, and tchotchkes would have to be thrown out.

Garbage bins arrived in the hallways. Soon they were overflowing with mountains of DVDs, action figures, *Sopranos* T-shirts, and internal HBO documents. It all got tossed.

"It was sad, because I think there was a lot of history from HBO that got put in the dumpster because we had a limited amount of time to pack up," Quentin Schaffer says.

With the move, HBO's center of gravity rapidly shifted westward, moving from Plepler's base of operations in New York to Greenblatt's in Los Angeles. Many longtime HBO employees took buyouts.

"It almost got to the point where every week or two weeks, you'd hear another name," Schaffer says. "And these were all substantial names—people who had been running businesses, who had been doing this for a long time and had this great institutional knowledge of what had worked and what hadn't."

The brain drain was disconcerting, says Schaffer, "because you had a very healthy culture with open dissent," and then all of a sudden it felt like "all of these strong voices" were gone.

Schaffer would soon be one of them. In August 2019, he left the company, ending thirty-nine sparkling years at the network, nearly four decades of building relationships with reporters and helping to burnish HBO's invaluable brand. Nancy Lesser, the network's West Coast communications maestro and a master awards campaigner, would leave a few months later, bringing to a halt her thirty-five-year run of tirelessly networking in Hollywood on HBO's behalf.

Meanwhile, with its massive debt piling up, AT&T was confronted with a major nuisance on Wall Street. Elliott Management, a hedge fund led by the fearsome activist investor Paul Singer, was quietly amassing a $3.2 billion stake in AT&T.

In September 2019, Elliott Management went public with a scathing letter, eviscerating AT&T's management and, in particular, its handling of the Time Warner acquisition. The letter highlighted the high rate of leadership turnover at HBO and other WarnerMedia assets, which it called "alarming," given AT&T's lack of experience in entertainment. Step one to reviving shareholder value, the hedge fund argued, was to sell DirecTV, which AT&T had purchased in 2015 for $49 billion, a deal that was looking worse by the day. Step two: get rid of Stankey.

The letter caused a massive commotion among AT&T investors and ratcheted up the pressure on the company to prove its managerial competence. Everything was riding on HBO Max.

Throughout the fall of 2019, WarnerMedia hastily shoveled together large tranches of programming designed to broaden the service's appeal. The bric-a-brac slate of acquisitions included various reruns of popular sitcoms from the 1990s and 2000s such as *The Fresh Prince of Bel-Air*, *The Big Bang Theory*, and *Friends*.

HBO Max's big hot-ticket item at launch would be a *Friends* reunion that would bring together the six original cast members, as well as its creators Marta Kauffman and David Crane. The special would combine a cannonade of old clips with new interviews with the stars, each of whom would receive upwards of $2.25 million for their trouble.

The company also revealed that HBO Max would feature a bunch of new reality-show competitions. In one, called *The Greatest Space*, teams of interior designers would compete to see who could make an empty room look the most appealing. For some of the network's longtime employees, it was hard to imagine a show that sounded less like HBO. It was so off brand, it felt almost hostile.

The network's talent was growing uneasy.

In recent years, of all the attempts to add topical relevance to HBO's lineup, *Last Week Tonight with John Oliver* was by far the most successful. Oliver was a British stand-up comic with an impish manner and a face like a muppet. From 2006 to 2013, he served as the "senior British correspondent" and occasional guest host on Comedy Central's *The Daily Show with Jon Stewart*.

In 2014, he joined HBO and began hosting *Last Week*, a half-hour program taped in front of a studio audience. In each episode, Oliver would acidly dismember, at length, a particularly appalling stupidity in the news, ranging from capital punishment to net neutrality to payday loans. Critics heaped praise on the show, and it would go on to win the Variety Talk Series Emmy for six consecutive years.

One Sunday night in October 2019, Oliver found a worthy target of his mockery close to home.

"Have you heard about HBO Max?" Oliver said. "Looking to add another app and monthly charge to watch things? HBO Max has you covered. It's gonna have all your favorites. Reruns of *The Big Bang Theory*, reruns of *Friends*, reruns of *The Fresh Prince of Bel-Air*. You can pay for all of those through HBO Max."

Oliver stared sourly into the camera and concluded his deadpan sales pitch: "HBO Max: It's not HBO. It's just TV."

• • •

TO THE CREATIVE TEAM, Stankey's day-to-day presence often felt less destructive than, basically, nonexistent. People who worked closely with him said his interest was almost exclusively in the tech side of things. Programming was of no consequence to him. Short of an emergency, emails were frequently ignored. When he did respond, the reply would usually amount to nothing more than a few words.

In an ideal world, that sort of autonomy would empower WarnerMedia executives to make decisions on their own. But because so many things had to be tackled at once, it created a sense of chaos, they said. At Stankey's request, the entire company was being reorganized on the fly. Managers were tasked with tearing down old departments and divisions and building new ones while delicately attempting to knit together utterly distinct workplace cultures. "It was just pandemonium," says one former executive.

When Stankey did communicate, it was often difficult to follow his jargon-rich dialect. One of Stankey's go-to metaphors was the "flywheel." In a mechanical system, such as a tractor or a locomotive, a flywheel is a device that helps store rotational energy, smoothing out any yips in the system. Somewhere in the annals of mansplaining, however, pundits and corporate CEOs had latched on to the flywheel as a versatile figure of speech to describe more or less any business cycle that is chugging forward, gaining momentum. It had a nice mouth feel.

When Stankey deployed it, he would often lift a hand in the air, pressing his index and ring fingers together to form a makeshift axis, which he would roll forward emphatically. If the metaphor needed an extra beat of embellishment, he might add a word or two about the "virtuous cycles" of streaming content creation, customer acquisition, and earned media.

None of it made much sense.

"We would joke about it. He would say something like: 'The functionality of the flywheel in the system . . .' and you're just like, What are you talking about?" said one staffer. "I really think it's an engineer's brain. It was always this obtuse, officious language."

Stankey's conviction, firmly held, was that HBO's prestigious library of programming combined with Warner Bros.' massive vault was going to be a home run, no matter what. When colleagues insisted that new, original programming would be necessary to gin up excitement at the time of the launch, Stankey was unmoved.

"His back of the envelope plan at first was no originals for launch, and then a small smattering for 2021," said one staffer.

Eventually, Stankey softened his stance. But for the creative team working on HBO Max, trying to catch up with Netflix, the promise of additional resources seemed frustratingly beyond reach. Netflix was on pace to spend roughly $17 billion on programming in 2020, up from about $15 billion the year before. It felt like the entire HBO Max game was riding on convincing AT&T to cough up additional funding for an expansion in programming. It was a game they were on the verge of losing.

Part of the problem was that Stankey had plenty of other mouths to feed.

Every year since 1985, AT&T had annually increased the size of its dividend payout to investors, making it a so-called Dividend Aristocrat and a favorite with investors and wealth managers. Among this crowd, AT&T's ongoing adventure in Hollywood was a growing cause for concern. Between the DirecTV and Time Warner acquisitions, the company had borrowed a massive amount of money. At the end of 2019, it carried roughly $150 billion in debt. And for what?

With each passing month, the company's diversification strategy was looking less self-assured. The DirecTV unit was hemorrhaging customers while, at the same time, AT&T's core business in wireless communication was facing heightened competition. T-Mobile, which was in the process of acquiring rival Sprint, was on its way to passing AT&T as the number two wireless carrier in the United States. To keep pace with T-Mobile and Verizon, AT&T would need to spend heavily on building out its 5G infrastructure, a huge capital-intensive undertaking.

Amid all the simultaneous needs for cash, the investment community offered dire warnings of what might happen to AT&T's share price if the company were to cut back on their cherished dividend. Stankey was under tremendous pressure not to waver.

Something would have to give.

• • •

IN THE FALL OF 2019, HBO began airing *Watchmen*, a limited series based on the 1980s comics series by Alan Moore and Dave Gibbons. Whereas the original comics unfurled a fantastical, alternative history of the United States during the Cold War, the HBO series delivered a remix of the source material, applying a similar tone, style, and sensibility to another vexing fissure in American life—the nation's history of race relations.

At the start, the show plunges viewers into the carnage of a real event from American history: the Tulsa Race Massacre of 1921. A mob of white Americans rampages across the screen, feverishly destroying a bastion of Black wealth, killing its residents, looting their stores, and setting their homes on fire.

From there, the series jumps forward in time to the contemporary United States. Robert Redford is president and has rolled out a far-reaching liberal agenda, including strict gun control measures and reparations for the descendants of slavery. The right wing is violently inflamed.

In Tulsa, a gang of white supremacists, known as the Seventh Kavalry, goes on the attack. With their faces hidden behind spooky inkblot masks—inspired by Rorschach, the reactionary antihero of the original comic—they anonymously wage a terrorist campaign against the government. The cops, in turn, have taken to shielding their identities with masks in order to protect their families.

The show was created by Damon Lindelof, an American screenwriter whose previous credits included *Lost*, a Delphic, sci-fi thriller that ran with great fanfare for 121 episodes on ABC, and *The Leftovers*, a suspenseful supernatural drama that aired on HBO to tempered acclaim from 2014 to 2017.

During the rollout, Lindelof explained that he'd come up with the idea for his adaptation of *Watchmen* while reading "The Case for Reparations," an essay by Ta-Nehisi Coates, which appeared in *The Atlantic* in 2014. Previously, Lindelof, who is white, had never heard of the Tulsa Race Massacre. Initially, he said, he was unsure if it was a story he should be telling. But he figured he'd spent much of his career making shows that predominantly made white actors famous and was ready to try something different.

Watchmen starred a diverse cast, which included Regina King, Yahya Abdul-Mateen II, Louis Gossett Jr., and Hong Chau, that was much less white than HBO's typical dramas. Of the twelve people in the writers room, Lindelof said, only four were white men.

Cord Jefferson, a Black writer on the series, says that initially there was a lot of back and forth about how prominently the series would lean into the Tulsa massacre. Should it appear in the middle of the season, they debated, or perhaps somewhere in the pilot? After weeks of conversation, they agreed to open the series with the wrenching eight-minute scene.

"The more we discussed it, the more you realized, 'Oh, this is going to be a show about the original sin of the Tulsa massacre and the violence that was inflicted upon this community,'" Jefferson says. "And then we realized we're going to show the repercussions and the cascading effects of that a century later, and how it's still affecting people nowadays."

In the hours after its premiere, #BlackWallStreet and the Tulsa massacre began trending on Twitter, helping grow awareness to an American catastrophe. Another HBO series, *Lovecraft Country*, would revisit the Tulsa massacre the following year.

Watchmen arrived at a time in American life when the forces of white supremacy were feeling rejuvenated. President Trump had recently offered a mealymouthed condemnation of the Unite the Right rally, a violent gathering of neo-Nazis, neo-Confederates, and members of the alt-right that raged through Charlottesville, Virginia, in 2017.

During early conversations about the series, Jefferson says that he and Lindelof talked about what would happen in certain corners of America if reparations for slavery were to be paid. How would white people on the right react? "We had just seen Charlottesville, where a bunch of young white men in polo shirts were carrying tiki torches," Jefferson says. "So what does our version of that kind of group look like? From there, the Seventh Kavalry was born."

Watchmen attracted a sizable, passionate following. Critics were likewise impressed. For many reviewers, the series felt like a vital allegory, laying bare the obstinacy of racial resentment and the metaphysical nature of resistance.

Just a few short years after being castigated for its racial blind spots during the *Confederate* mess, HBO found itself applauded for the series' incisive exploration of America's racial antipathies. Bloys's effort to diversify HBO's slate was showing results.

Watchmen would go on to win the Emmy for Outstanding Limited Series, and Lindelof and Jefferson would take home Emmys for Outstanding Writing. It was a particularly impressive feat for Jefferson, considering how new he was to the industry.

Several years earlier, Jefferson was a journalist who worked as a staffer at Gawker and The Root and freelanced for publications like the *New York Times* and *Bookforum*. He switched to television in 2014 and eventually landed jobs writing for Larry Wilmore's late-night show on Comedy Central, *Master of None* on Netflix, and *The Good Place* on NBC. In 2017, he met Lindelof at a dinner party. Within months, he'd signed on to write for *Watchmen*.

Among New York creative professionals, Jefferson was hardly the only one being drawn into a second career in television. By the late 2010s, the TV industry was neck-deep into a new era of superabundance, often referred to as Peak TV. With Netflix and other well-funded streaming services pouring billions of dollars into original programming—and traditional networks like HBO trying to keep up—the amount of TV being made was shooting up like never before.

With each passing year, the TV industry was spitting out more comedies, cop shows, sci-fi thrillers, miniseries, game shows, cartoons, fishing adventures, interior decorating competitions, and lavish period dramas. According to one estimate, between 2002, the year *The Wire* first arrived on HBO, and 2019, when *Watchmen* made its debut, the total number of adult scripted series airing in the United States had nearly tripled, soaring from 182 to 532.

To fuel the expansion, the TV industry was ravenously gobbling up bodies from adjacent creative professions. In New York, where many of the plump magazine and newspaper empires of the twentieth century were desperately cutting weight, a steady migration of talent was being steered into the welcoming arms of Peak TV.

Just two decades after *Sex and the City* author Candace Bushnell had greeted her small-screen suitors with indifference, the TV industry was now a primary destination for highly educated liberal arts majors aspiring to earn a sustainable living. Retraining programs proliferated, practically medevacing MFAs and the like to Hollywood. In 2021, Jefferson would start a new fellowship aiming to "help unemployed or underemployed journalists get into film and television."

The same economic forces were at work on another staple of New York's creative class: the theater. One of the writers working alongside Cord Jefferson in the *Watchmen* writers room was Branden Jacobs-Jenkins, one of the most electric playwrights living in New York. Though only in his midthirties, Jacobs-Jenkins had already earned a MacArthur genius grant, and two of his plays, *Gloria* and *Everybody*, were finalists for the Pulitzer Prize in Drama. Even so, *Watchmen* brought him a whole new level of exposure.

"I mean, even my name on the title card for *Watchmen*, I got more texts about that than anything I've done in the last five, ten years," Jacobs-Jenkins says.

Thanks to his membership in the Writers Guild, it also got him health insurance.

By 2021, Jacobs-Jenkins would have an overall deal with FX and would be at work creating a new series for the basic-cable network. "You could suddenly make a living doing the thing you like to do," Jacobs-Jenkins says. "If you compare the tax return of a playwright to the tax return of a TV writer, it's going to be a joke."

• • •

WITH THE PROSPECT of serious competition looming, Netflix suddenly seemed less self-assured. That fall, for once, Netflix's endless tinkering with

TV technology misfired. In recent years, a number of efficiency-minded consumers had taken to listening to podcasts at revved-up tempos. In late October, Netflix confirmed reports that it was testing out a new feature that would allow viewers to watch movies and TV shows at 150 percent speed.

The news was not welcome in Hollywood. "Don't make me have to call every director and show creator on earth to fight you on this," Judd Apatow observed. "Save me the time. I will win, but it will take a ton of time. Don't fuck with our timing. We give you nice things. Leave them as they were intended to be seen."

Even amid the warbles of displeasure, Netflix was broadening its influence over the industry. The days of wanting to become HBO were long gone. With hundreds of original TV series, including reality shows, animated programs, children's entertainment, movies, and local language productions, Netflix was emerging as something far bigger and broader than a premium cable channel. Few disagreed when AT&T's Randall Stephenson said he thought of Netflix as "the Walmart" of streaming services.

Even as the streamer grew its global subscriber base, many television critics wondered why so many Netflix series seemingly petered out in quality. Not long after signing a mega-deal with Netflix in 2018, Kenya Barris, the creator of the ABC comedy *black-ish*, soon negotiated an exit, noting that his voice didn't mesh with "Netflix's voice."

"The stuff I want to do is a little bit more edgy, a little more highbrow, a little more heady, and I think Netflix wants down the middle," he told *The Hollywood Reporter*. "Netflix became CBS."

For years, Netflix executives had gone out of their way to play up the company's competition with HBO. Between 2012 and 2014, in communiqués to shareholders, Reed Hastings often drew specific comparisons between Netflix and HBO. But in recent years, Netflix had largely moved on, inviting comparisons to other ascendant cultural forces, such as the hugely popular video game *Fortnite*. "We compete with (and lose to) *Fortnite* more than HBO," Hastings told shareholders in 2019.

There was another aspect of HBO's history that Netflix showed no inclination to repeat. From its early days, HBO's leaders, from Michael Fuchs to Richard Plepler, had always seen the network as a powerful vortex of progressive values. From AIDS to abortion to gun control to the environment, HBO was ever-eager to throw itself into controversial political subjects and to score points on behalf of their liberal beliefs.

Netflix, by contrast, reflexively shied away from such difficult political stands.

In November 2019, Reed Hastings appeared onstage at the *New York Times*'s DealBook conference in New York to talk about the state of Netflix.

The previous fall, Hasan Minhaj, the brainy progressive host of a topical news-comedy show on Netflix, had produced a segment lambasting Saudi crown prince Mohammed bin Salman for the killing of journalist Jamal Khashoggi. The Netflix host also criticized Saudi Arabia for its alleged war atrocities in Yemen. Afterward, the Saudi government complained to Netflix that the piece violated its anticybercrime law and asked the company to prevent the episode from streaming in Saudi Arabia, effectively hiding it from the local populace.

Just as CBS had pulled its Reagan biopic years earlier in the face of unwarranted conservative ire, Netflix now did the same in the Middle East. Netflix folded.

When news of the self-censorship became public, it did not go over well. PEN America said the decision "legitimizes repression." "Every artist whose work appears on Netflix should be outraged," said a spokesperson for Human Rights Watch.

Onstage in New York, *New York Times* reporter Andrew Ross Sorkin pressed Hastings about the decision. Whereas an HBO executive might have licked his or her chops at the opportunity to stand up for an artist in the face of such state-sponsored oppression, Hastings took a different tack. He told the audience that Netflix executives didn't feel bad about their capitulation at all.

"We're not in the news business," Hastings said. "We're not trying to do 'truth to power.' We're trying to entertain."

• • •

IN APRIL 2020, AT&T announced that John Stankey would be replacing Randall Stephenson as the telecom company's next chief executive. To fill the resulting vacancy at the top of WarnerMedia, Stankey decided to bring in an outsider. Starting the following month, Jason Kilar, a zealous technology executive with jet-black hair, dark eyes, and the enthusiastic mien of a motivational speaker, would be taking over.

Early in his career, Kilar had cut his teeth at Amazon.com, where he learned to embrace the customer-first, data-observant ways of Jeff Bezos. Later, he served as the first CEO of Hulu.com, a streaming service supported by NBC Universal, 21st Century Fox, and Disney.

Eventually, Kilar clashed with the service's media-establishment backers and in 2011 let loose with an impassioned blog post on the Hulu website detailing his team's view on the changing state of home entertainment. He argued that traditional TV had too many commercials, consumers expected viewing shows to be "more convenient," and social media was an important marketing tool. The ideas expressed in Kilar's post were hardly new or radical at the time. Still, the breathless, contrarian tone of his writing conveyed a sense of momentousness—as if he were Martin Luther nailing his 95 Theses to the door of the Wittenberg Castle Church.

Reporters at Hollywood trade publications started calling Kilar's blog post the "bad boy memo," and a streaming star was born.

The news that Kilar would be taking over WarnerMedia was greeted by titters of excitement from Wall Street to Silicon Valley. It was further validation that in the new streaming era of Hollywood, experience reading data points was considered more valuable than experience reading scripts. Fellow members of the tribe offered their congratulations. "Scary for us to have you there," Netflix's Hastings wrote on Twitter. "But great for the world that HBO will be strong."

On May 1, 2020, Kilar took the reins of WarnerMedia at a particularly challenging time. Much of the country was in pandemic lockdown, hoping to slow the spread of COVID-19. Most of WarnerMedia's thirty thousand–plus employees were working from home. Movie theaters were shuttered. Production of films and TV shows were at a standstill. Sports leagues were on hiatus. And HBO Max was set to debut before the end of the month.

That spring, WarnerMedia launched a new advertising campaign to try to clarify the coming changes to the reformulated, hypermaximized HBO. The ads, which ran on TV and the internet, mixed and matched recognizable figures from classic HBO shows with new arrivals to the platform, presenting them all as one big, eccentric, harmonious TV family. "Where Lions and Tigers and Bears meet Friends and Heroes and Princes," explained one of the ads, followed by the HBO Max tagline: "Where HBO meets so much more."

"We didn't feel like we needed to beat our chest about quality because it's right there on the screen," said Chris Spadaccini, the chief marketing officer for WarnerMedia Entertainment. "What we did have to do is explain that HBO Max is more *than* HBO. It's not more *of* HBO."

As AT&T hastily attempted to reposition HBO's brand, folks in the advertising industry watched closely. It was hardly the first time someone had tried to pull off such a maneuver. Plenty of retailers had previously attempted to take high-end prestige brands intentionally down-market in order to sell a broader array of more cheaply produced goods to a mass audience while maintaining an elevated price point. The tactic was common enough to have earned its own portmanteau.

HBO was on the verge of its new life as a "masstige" brand.

"There's a great tradition of using class to get to mass," said Andrew Essex, the cofounder of the marketing services company Plan A. "This idea of HBO launching a mass-prestige platform has plenty of precedent. Think about premium fashion brands like Ralph Lauren and Prada. A strong brand does have equity to be stretched in search of higher margins."

The strategy came with plenty of potential for AT&T, but also plenty of long-term risk.

The history of retail, marketing experts point out, is littered with cautionary tales of formerly best-in-class premium brands like Cadillac and

Calvin Klein that lost their cachet after wandering too far down-market. If things went awry, the same fate could happen to HBO.

"The risk they're taking is that instead of giving you more HBO, more award-winning un-TV, they're throwing the kitchen sink at it and putting everything under the one brand," says Allen Adamson, the cofounder of Metaforce, a marketing strategy company. "The more you stretch a brand, the more dilutive and confusing it becomes. Once you start taking a brand from premium to mass, it's often a downward spiral. It could do phenomenal damage to what HBO has spent decades building."

Inside of WarnerMedia, things were growing more tense.

Weeks before the debut of HBO Max, top executives from across WarnerMedia got together in a virtual meeting to provide their "launch status" updates. Pretty soon, it became clear, according to a source familiar with the discussions, that there was a serious problem facing HBO Max. Consumers didn't know how to access it. A plethora of internal research suggested that potential subscribers of all stripes, particularly existing HBO subscribers, had no clear idea how exactly they would go about activating HBO Max on their phones, tablets, and smart TVs once it became available. What steps were needed, and how many, varied considerably depending on what device customers were using and what distributor they were trying to access it through.

Making matters worse, WarnerMedia had so far failed to reach an agreement with Roku, the dominant maker of smart TVs and streaming-entertainment boxes in the United States. As a result, any HBO fans among Roku's nearly forty million customers would have no easy way to access HBO Max at the time of its launch. WarnerMedia was facing a similar situation with Amazon, the other top maker of streaming-TV devices, also with roughly forty million users.

Stankey, for one, did not seem concerned that things could go sideways. Perfect is the enemy of good, he liked to say. Thanks to the Department of Justice, HBO Max was already behind schedule. Getting to market as fast as possible was the key. When real customers came aboard, it would sharpen everyone's focus. He continued to believe that the appeal of HBO Max was easy enough to understand. The flywheel would smooth out any bumpiness in the system.

On May 27, 2020, HBO Max finally launched, joining an increasingly crowded field of new services, which now included Disney+, Apple TV+, Peacock, and Quibi, and incumbents like Netflix, Hulu, and Amazon Prime Video.

Much as the insiders had feared, HBO Max landed with a thud.

Six months earlier, when Disney had uncorked its long-awaited streaming service Disney+, the new entrant enticed subscribers with an original new big-budget sci-fi series called *The Mandalorian*, which was yet another spin-off from the beloved *Star Wars* franchise. Right out of the gate, subscriptions to Disney+ soared.

For the past year, WarnerMedia executives had been pinning their hopes on the *Friends* reunion special. But then COVID-19 disrupted the production, and it wasn't ready to go. Without it, there wasn't any major new attraction to woo curious customers to check out the service.

With HBO Max's lack of "quality noise," sign-ups were sluggish, confusion about how to sign up ran rampant, and market watchers were underwhelmed.

In a conference call with reporters two days after the launch, influential analyst Michael Nathanson called HBO Max's debut a missed opportunity. "Pricing is high, the buzz is not there," he said. He noted that his own children—every parent's ultimate focus group—were entirely uninterested. "Nobody came to me yesterday and said, 'We should get HBO Max now, Dad.'"

CHAPTER 24

The Traumatic Arts

While HBO Max was struggling, the original-formula HBO was also evolving. In June 2020, HBO began airing a coproduction with the BBC entitled *I May Destroy You*, a half-hour comedy-drama set in London.

Arabella (Michaela Coel) is an up-and-coming writer whose first self-published book has led to a contract with a major publisher. On deadline, Arabella holes up in an office, vowing to pull an all-nighter.

Struggling to get words on the page, she gives herself an hour-long break and meets up with some friends. They sing karaoke then head to a bar, Ego Death, where they take shots of tequila. On the dance floor, Arabella feels wobbly. Suddenly, she's on her knees, crawling toward the exit.

The next morning, she comes to her senses with a cut on her forehead. The screen on her phone is smashed. Before long, she figures out that somebody must have slipped something in her drink, then sexually assaulted her. She goes to the police.

Afterward, Arabella struggles to piece together what happened. Her best friends Terry (Weruche Opia) and Kwame (Paapa Essiedu) try to help her deal with the trauma while processing troubling sexual encounters of their own. Arabella sees a psychologist, does yoga, and goes to art therapy. But she is suffering from involuntary flashbacks and having trouble focusing. Her relationships fray. Her book falls apart. She turns compulsively to the netherworld of social media for validation and vengeance.

"Sometimes when we try our best to see the big picture, we lose sight of the little one altogether," a therapist tells her. "The little detail here is you."

As Arabella recuperates, her imagination is reinvigorated, and *I May Destroy You* takes off into a flighty telling and retelling of how Arabella will revitalize her art—and potentially confront her assailant. The result is a vivid journey along the zagging fault lines of sexual experimentation, abuse, and recovery.

I May Destroy You landed in a world awash in grief. In the summer of 2020, countless families were mourning the loss of loved ones to COVID-19 and struggling with the continuing uncertainty of the pandemic. At the same time, protests were proliferating across the United States, venting anger, frustration, and sorrow over the murder of George Floyd, an unarmed forty-six-year-old Black man killed by police officers in Minneapolis.

Amid the pain and reckoning, *I May Destroy You* resonated widely. Its central preoccupations felt in sync with the state of the world: How does an individual, or a society, manage to come back from a deeply wounding trauma? What does justice look like? How do we heal?

Michaela Coel, the creator, writer, codirector, and star of the series, was born in 1987 and grew up in a public-housing project in London, one of a handful of Black families. Her parents were immigrants from Ghana. Her mom was a nurse.

I May Destroy You, Coel revealed, was based on her own recent experience of being drugged at a bar and sexually assaulted.

The reviews were rapturous. *Vanity Fair* called it the show of the summer. NPR's Linda Holmes described *I May Destroy You* as an "unforgettable, unmissable drama" and noted the significance of HBO having put it on the air in the United States, given the network's "dismal record" in the past of finding and empowering diverse auteurs.

The critical response drew attention to something else, a broader shift that was already well under way in the HBO universe. HBO was leaning into a new favorite archetype. By the early 2020s, many of HBO's most critically acclaimed series revolved around imperfect heroines acting daringly to shed light on the misdeeds of powerful, dangerous, entitled men.

In addition to *I May Destroy You*, the newly ascendant type of HBO character was on display in a string of the network's most critically celebrated shows, including *Sharp Objects*, a 2018 miniseries starring Amy Adams as a self-harming newspaper reporter who returns to her hometown in Missouri to look into the murders of two young girls; *The Undoing*, a 2020 mystery thriller featuring Nicole Kidman as a psychologist in Manhattan struggling to discern whether her husband has murdered a young woman with whom he was having an affair; and *Mare of Easttown*, a 2021 miniseries starring Kate Winslet as a depressed female police detective investigating the murder of a young teenage mother.

HBO was zeroing in on a burgeoning genre of programming, which was taking off in Hollywood during the years of the Trump administration, and becoming a driving force in what you might call the "traumatic arts."

The new focus wasn't limited to HBO dramas. A similar trend could be seen in HBO's nonfiction programming as well, which increasingly featured central female subjects uncovering or escaping the abuse of powerful men.

In the summer of 2020, HBO premiered *I'll Be Gone in the Dark*, a true-crime docuseries about reporter Michelle McNamara's effort to write a book unmasking the identity of the Golden State Killer, a notorious rapist and murderer who terrorized California in the 1970s and '80s.

The series was directed and produced by the documentarian Liz Garbus, a longtime member of HBO's repertory of filmmakers. McNamara's effort to track down the killer was called to Garbus's attention by Nancy Abraham and Lisa Heller, a pair of executives who had taken over HBO's documentary department following Sheila Nevins's exit. Initially, like many other documentarians, Garbus felt unnerved by Nevins's departure.

"To have her gone from HBO felt scary," Garbus says. "But when they made the decision of leaving her job to her top deputies, Nancy and Lisa, that gave a lot of people a sense of security."

Abraham and Heller sent Garbus the galleys of McNamara's book, which her husband, comedian Patton Oswalt, had helped finish after she died of an accidental drug overdose. Garbus and Abraham met with Oswalt and secured the rights.

When the documentary series debuted, it received raves. "In *I'll Be Gone in the Dark*, the protagonist is McNamara, and she serves a multilayered, simultaneous role as detective, victim, and, as a self-declared true-crime aficionado, a proxy for everyone watching this show and others like it," Jen Chaney wrote in *Vulture*. "That last factor enables *I'll Be Gone in the Dark* to interrogate the reasons why this genre is so enticing, especially to women, something that other TV true crime has rarely, if ever, done."

In the months that followed, HBO would go on to air documentaries investigating the alleged misdeeds of director Woody Allen, the music manager Ike Turner, and the NXIVM multilevel marketer and convicted sex trafficker Keith Raniere.

• • •

THE ON-AIR SHIFT toward more female protagonists could be traced back, in part, to the directive made in 2016 by Casey Bloys to diversify HBO's lineup. In the years since, HBO had ushered in the most female-centric stretch of programming in the network's history.

By the end of the decade, HBO began airing *Euphoria*, a teenage drama about the intoxicated misadventures of Rue Bennett (Zendaya) and her pack of synapse-burning friends; *Divorce*, a breakup comedy starring Sarah Jessica Parker; *A Black Lady Sketch Show* from comedian Robin Thede; and *My Brilliant Friend*, the adaptation of the Elena Ferrante novels about female friendship.

HBO's leadership by this point was also decidedly less male-centric. Under Bloys, nearly every key power position was occupied by a woman. Amy Gravitt ran the network's comedy department. Nina Rosenstein oversaw talk shows and specials. Francesca Orsi was in charge of HBO's drama department, with Nora Skinner and Kathleen McCaffrey serving as her key lieutenants.

In the fall of 2021, while accepting the Emmy Award for Outstanding Actress in a Limited Series for her role on *Mare of Easttown*, Kate Winslet would thank the show's creator, Brad Ingelsby, for "creating a middle-aged, imperfect, flawed mother," and then would give a shoutout to Orsi and Skinner. "Frannie and Nora, two *women* at HBO—I learned so much from you," she said.

Behind the scenes, HBO was also revamping how the network manufactured its "cable edge." By the late 2010s, HBO was requiring every new production to employ an "intimacy coordinator" on set—that is, a person specifically responsible for ensuring the physical and emotional well-being of the actors participating in any sex scene. The relatively new role, which was like a stunt coordinator, only for sex, was growing increasingly common on TV and movie sets in the wake of Hollywood's #MeToo reckonings.

At HBO, the safe-TV-sex mission was overseen by Alicia Rodis, a former stage actor and fight choreographer. Rodis started on the second season of *The Deuce*, and from there, went on to work for a string of other HBO shows, including *Watchmen* and *Succession*. Eventually, HBO hired her as an exclusive consultant, responsible for designing, improving, and enforcing the network's evolving protocols and for training additional frontline intimacy coordinators.

While everyone at HBO's corporate level was supportive of the changes, Rodis says, she still occasionally runs into recalcitrant directors who are worried she is there to police them or to interfere with their artistic vision. In such situations, she typically explains that if the director is just telling his actors to roll around and get off on each other, he's basically asking them to do sex work, which is not what they signed up for. "It's a simulation. Let's specify what the choreography is," she says. "When you know you're not going to mistakenly assault your partner, the product ends up being a lot better."

Rodis credits HBO for being the first network to publicly mandate intimacy coordinators, a decision, she says, that has rippled out across the industry. HBO's far-reaching influence on issues of sex and gender dynamics is something, Rodis says, that she knows from personal experience. "I think I first learned about sex by watching HBO as a kid," she says.

Despite the various progressive changes at HBO, certain gender inequities persisted. Institutions, particularly rich and venerated ones, don't morph entirely overnight. Despite all the badass women tearing it up onscreen at HBO, female creators of dramas and limited series were still few and far between.

In the HBO pantheon, there was now a well-established slot for female writer-performers like Lena Dunham, Issa Rae, and Michaela Coel. But when it came to selecting the visionary HBO creator—the impassioned, literary writer of a big sweeping drama for which HBO had become celebrated—the role was still largely reserved for men. Even, in many cases, on shows about women.

Big Little Lies, HBO's successful adaptation of a novel by Liane Moriarty, starring Reese Witherspoon, Nicole Kidman, Shailene Woodley, Laura Dern, and Zoë Kravitz, about a group of Californian women who get caught up in a murder investigation, was created by David E. Kelley and directed by Jean-Marc Vallée. HBO's adaptation of *My Brilliant Friend* also came from a male creator, Saverio Costanzo. Ditto, *Mare of Easttown*.

For the most part, full membership in HBO's most prestigious club remained limited to men. Its enviable benefits—the famously generous HBO support, the institutional tolerance for risk-taking, the willingness to overlook initial missteps—sometimes felt like it applied to only one gender.

To wit: In 2018, HBO commissioned a pilot for a new *Game of Thrones* series to be helmed by the British writer Jane Goldman, directed by female British screen veteran S. J. Clarkson, and starring Naomi Watts. That HBO would entrust its biggest franchise to a team of women was big news at the time. When the pilot came in, HBO executives were not thrilled—a replay, it seemed, of what had happened years earlier with David Benioff and D. B. Weiss. Only this time, there was no second chance, no multimillion-dollar rescue plan, no talk of believing in the artists' vision. HBO shelved the project and moved forward with an alternate *Game of Thrones* spin-off, helmed by a male creator, Ryan Condal.

Cynthia Mort, the creator of HBO's 2007 *Tell Me You Love Me*—and to this date, still one of the few women to create an HBO drama—notes that even as shows with female protagonists have proliferated on the network, often in series created by men, there continues to be an enormous amount of graphic violence against women on screen. She pointed to painful scenes of domestic violence from *Mare of Easttown* and *Big Little Lies* as examples. "Why did they have to show us that stuff? I don't get it," she says. "But of course it's male showrunners and male directors. So there you go."

"As much as we all want to believe it's changing, if you really look underneath, it's not," Mort says. "It's just been spruced up."

Mort recalls that, years earlier, while still on an overall production deal with HBO, she teamed up with the writer and producer Bill Condon (*Gods and Monsters, Dreamgirls*) to create a series called *Tilda*, about a reclusive, sharp-elbowed Hollywood blogger, reminiscent of the real-life Nikki Finke. Diane Keaton signed on in the starring role, and in 2010 HBO ordered a pilot.

During production, however, Mort and Condon got into a creative dispute. In 2011, amid public reports of the behind-the-scenes rancor, HBO passed on the project. Looking back, Mort says, she is disappointed in how the network handled the situation and feels like nobody at HBO stood up for her. "It was very fraught," she says. "In the end, they supported him. They stick with the guy, whether it's right or wrong."

It's a reputation that continues to impact HBO's business, even years after the network's executives stopped talking in meetings about men controlling the remote controls or paying the cable bills. "When I went shopping for an overall development deal, I didn't even want to take a meeting at HBO," says an experienced writer-producer who has worked on several HBO series. "Over the years, I'd watched HBO buy up many of the most talented female writers in Hollywood, only to use them as babysitters for their stable of male 'auteurs.' If you're a woman who writes drama, taking a deal at HBO is the best way to ensure you'll never make your own show."

• • •

JASON KILAR, WarnerMedia's new CEO, was bursting with enthusiasm, a reassuring contrast from his phlegmatic predecessor, John Stankey. But at times Kilar's exuberant stabs at humor struck some of his colleagues as odd.

Not long after joining the company, Kilar popped up on an internal companywide video call wearing a purple wig and a pair of giant orange novelty sunglasses. A stuffed white owl sat on his shoulder. He looked like a rich guy visiting Burning Man for the first time.

Then there was his preoccupation with TikTok. The short-form video-sharing site, owned by the Chinese company ByteDance, was exploding in popularity, particularly with young people. There were viral dancing videos. Acting lessons. Fashion tutorials. Recipes. Pranks.

Above all else, Kilar wanted HBO Max to have an impressive presence on TikTok. He convened one meeting after the next to discuss the topic. His idea was to hire a group of young interns to make their own videos inspired by HBO and Warner Bros. programming.

Facing a nearly endless list of emergencies—COVID, Black Lives Matter, programming and technical upgrades to HBO Max—Kilar devoted many hours on the initiative. "It just depends on do you think the internet is a big deal or not?" Kilar says. "I think it distills to that."

Finally, a handful of paid college interns got HBO Max up and running on TikTok. By the end of the summer, they were making videos riffing on the makeup styles of HBO's teen drama *Euphoria* and getting ready for a big Halloween marketing push for the coming fall.

To several staffers at WarnerMedia, the whole thing seemed like an odd priority. "We were running around saying, 'Oh my god, there are so many things going wrong,'" said one staffer. "We said to each other: 'Why are we wasting so much time on this?'"

Under Kilar, much to the dismay of already dizzy staffers, more corporate shake-ups followed. In August 2020, Kilar announced he was ousting top executives Bob Greenblatt and Kevin Reilly as part of yet another round of corporate restructuring. Casey Bloys, the head of programming for HBO, would be bumped up yet again, becoming the chief content officer for HBO and HBO Max. In the two months since HBO Max's debut, the streaming service was struggling to sign up customers. And as part of the corporate shake-up, numerous employees were being let go.

For the past two years under AT&T, WarnerMedia employees had been watching the wrecking balls swing back and forth, knocking down the walls between all their historically detached divisions and brands. No more silos, no more fiefdoms, they were told. Everyone is part of the same team now.

Which made it all the more bewildering, sources say, as they watched Kilar and his inner circle—which included several former Hulu executives— turn HBO Max into its own quasi distinct vertical. With each passing month, the Kilar crew felt increasingly separate from everyone else. "We can barely even get them to take meetings," says one WarnerMedia staffer.

With AT&T's ongoing crush of obligations—the dividend, its debt, its promises of a 5G revolution—the company eventually found a quick way to pump some high-cost programming into HBO Max without building up any additional development capacity or siphoning much extra money from its other pressing needs.

On December 3, 2020, in a brief, buoyant note on the website Medium, Kilar revealed that the following year, the company would be changing how it released Warner Bros.' entire slate of feature movies. In 2021, all seventeen of the films, ranging from the giant CGI-blockbuster *Godzilla vs. Kong* to the critically anticipated musical drama *In the Heights* from Lin-Manuel Miranda to the sci-fi adaptation *Dune*, would be released simultaneously in theaters *and* on HBO Max in the United States. As a result, Kilar noted, roughly every three weeks, HBO Max subscribers would get to see "a huge motion picture" at home at no additional cost.

Kilar explained that the move, dubbed "Project Popcorn," was inspired in part by the ongoing challenges of visiting movie theaters during the COVID-19 pandemic, and in part to better cater to the desires of fans. "We so thoroughly believe in this mission," he wrote.

The decision, which threatened to undermine the way major Hollywood studios had been releasing movies for decades, caused an immediate uproar. Movie-theater owners, already suffering through the worst stretch in the industry's history, were livid. Vaccines, they pointed out, were just around the corner.

Kilar's announcement took large numbers of his colleagues and partners by surprise. Several of Warner Bros.' top moviemakers, including Christopher Nolan, were incensed. "Some of our industry's biggest filmmakers and most important movie stars went to bed the night before thinking they were working for the greatest movie studio," Nolan told *The Hollywood Reporter*, "and woke up to find out they were working for the worst streaming service."

Kilar would later concede that he had errantly rushed the decision, and in the months ahead WarnerMedia would have to pay out significant fees to mollify its angry film partners.

But in the short term, Project Popcorn did draw rapturous applause from streaming boosters and analysts. What mattered in the streaming era, according to the prevailing mindset on Wall Street, was devotion to the customer, not to movie-theater operators and not to the artist. If anything, their unhappiness was a good sign for HBO Max. "We suspect Nolan simply does not understand subscription economics," Richard Greenfield, a media analyst and prominent streaming advocate, noted.

"We are accountable to the customer directly, each and every hour of the day," Kilar says. "And it's a tremendous pressure on this organization but it's a healthy pressure."

Other observers saw the move not as some bold stroke of disruption but as a hasty act of desperation by AT&T to boost HBO Max's growth: a Hail Mary pass, burning countless creative relationships to give a short-term advantage to their struggling streaming service, knowing Wall Street stock pickers would react approvingly.

"It might not just be about building up one division at the expense of another, but rather it might be about building up one division at any cost so you can quickly boost its value, sell it, and wash your hands of this whole nightmare," Richard Rushfield wrote in *The Ankler*, an incisive newsletter about the entertainment industry. "Pump and Dump, I believe, is the term of art."

One of the upset filmmakers was David Chase. After many years in development, Chase's long-anticipated, pandemic-delayed prequel to *The Sopranos*, a feature film entitled *The Many Saints of Newark*, was scheduled to premiere in the fall of 2021. Among other enticements, the movie would feature Michael Gandolfini playing a teenage version of Tony Soprano, the character made famous by his father. After decades of trying to escape the confines of TV, Chase was poised to make a splash on the grand big screen.

Then Kilar repurposed Chase's work as part of Project Popcorn without so much as a heads-up phone call. There'd been time for TikTok, but no time for Chase.

The *Sopranos* creator felt angry and burned. What he wanted was for ticket-paying customers to experience the film communally in a hushed and darkened theater. "Movie magic," he says. "It's that simple."

Now, AT&T has gone and jammed the return of the outsize Soprano clan back into home television sets. Just when Chase thought he was out of TV, they pulled him back in.

· · ·

WHILE FLAWED, heroic female protagonists were taking center stage on HBO, certain well-known characters from the network's recent past were being hurriedly rounded up and ushered out HBO's back door—Ideally, never to be heard from again.

Not all art ages well. But in the entire stretch of *Homo sapiens'* run on Earth, dating back to cave drawings, few artistic ventures have seen their reputation plummet as far and as fast as the HBO series *Entourage*.

The series, which originally aired on HBO from 2004 to 2011, was a ditzy, testosterone-doused celebration of the Hollywood highlife. The show revolved around the sybaritic escapades of budding movie star Vincent Chase (Adrian Grenier) and his plundering pack of randy, coattail-riding buddies from Queens. There was Turtle (Jerry Ferrara), a slow-minded simpleton, Eric "E" Murphy (Kevin Connolly), a pragmatic spoilsport, and Johnny "Drama" Chase (Kevin Dillon), a dim-witted sorehead.

Together, the guys cruise around Los Angeles in sports cars and Hummers, marauding for models and comparing notes on their conquests. It was based, in part, on the behavior of the real-life friends of movie star Mark Wahlberg, who served as an executive producer on the show.

Despite some initial grumblings from critics, *Entourage* turned into a reliable hit for HBO, running for ninety-six episodes across eight seasons and earning a slew of industry awards. In 2007, it was nominated for an Emmy for Outstanding Comedy Series. Prior to his arrest in Las Vegas for strangling his girlfriend, HBO's chief executive Chris Albrecht regularly praised *Entourage* as an unflinching portrait of what life is really like in Hollywood. "I love it," Albrecht said.

In the years that followed, however, as the status quo in Hollywood came under increasing scrutiny, the reputation of *Entourage* started to nosedive. It began in 2015, when Warner Bros. released a theatrical spin-off. The *Entourage* movie was written by Doug Ellin, the creator of the original series, and produced by Steven Mnuchin, the future Secretary of the Treasury under President Trump.

The feature-length movie revived the show's frolicking foursome at an increasingly awkward moment for sympathetic depictions of entitled misogynists. The movie put up lousy numbers at the box office and ran into a firing squad of critics who were suddenly and fiercely unamused by the many sordid ways in which Ellin tended to write about women.

A sample line of dialogue from the movie: "Fun is when you forget a girl's name while you're fucking her," Johnny Drama says.

In *The Observer*, Mark Kermode called the *Entourage* movie a "hatefully unfunny" spin-off, "napalming the screen with waves of pornographic consumerist vulgarity—cars, asses, cars, tits, boats, asses, cars—dredged directly from Tinseltown's festering scrotum."

From there, things went downhill for *Entourage* defenders. In June 2017, at the ATX Television Festival in Austin, Texas, during a panel event promoting the new Netflix series *GLOW*, actor Alison Brie told her own *Entourage* gross-out story. "Early in my career, I auditioned for three lines on an episode of *Entourage* that I had to go on in a bikini!" she said. "Or like . . . the tiniest shorts. And they were like, 'Okay, can you take your top off now?'"

Later, Brie clarified on Twitter that she had a bikini on underneath her top at the time of her disrobing. Even so, her remarks set off a vigorous round of *Entourage* bashing.

Then a few months later, in the fall of 2017, actor Ariane Bellamar, who

worked as an extra on the show, accused *Entourage* cast member Jeremy Piven
of sexually harassing her on set. Piven denied the allegations.

Later, several more women came forward accusing Piven of prior sexual
misconduct unrelated to his work on *Entourage*—allegations that Piven again
denied. By 2019, Piven was blaming his growing reputational problems not
on his own misdeeds but rather on the fictional behavior of Ari Gold, the
boorish, unlikeable agent who Piven had played on *Entourage*. Piven argued
that people were unfairly conflating him with the loathsome character he
brought to life for the increasingly toxic show.

As the #MeToo movement spread through Hollywood, a new genre of
Entourage criticism blossomed online, where writers took turns hate-watching
the HBO series and excavating its many scabrous moments for reexamina-
tion. Quickly, a new consensus emerged: *Entourage* was not just some silly,
skin-deep look at life in Hollywood but rather a pernicious example of the
industry whitewashing its own sins behind a glittering barrage of aspirational
status symbols and jocular "boys will be boys" platitudes.

"Most women on this show are objectified to the point of absurdity,"
Anne Cohen wrote for *Refinery29*. "They are ogled, demeaned, talked down
to, and generally reduced to the status of sex dolls that happen to walk
and talk."

"Given the current deluge of women outing predators, harassers, and rap-
ists, it felt especially harrowing to watch our four 'lovable' dudes freely co-
erce women into performing sexual favors that they don't feel comfortable
doing," Jill Gutowitz wrote in *Vice*.

By 2021, in large progressive swaths of America, publicly confessing a
love of *Entourage* would be akin to unironically wearing a MAGA hat or supporting Rush Limbaugh's Medal of Freedom.

Creator Doug Ellin continued to defend his show, exasperatingly pointing back to positive reviews and the awards it accumulated. *Entourage* was a
piece of art, he argued, that was devoted to skewering the banalities of American show business, not reveling in them. Satire, in other words, not guileless
adulation.

In April 2021, Ellin accused HBO of trying to hide *Entourage* from viewers. In an interview with Yahoo News, he complained that despite being one of the longest-running comedies in HBO's history, *Entourage* was all but invisible on HBO Max.

"It would be nice if HBO was like, 'We have this great 96 episodes of content and we should let our audience know it was there,'" he said. "I would type in 'E-N-T-O' into HBO Max and *Curb Your Enthusiasm* would come up! What the hell was this?"

He went on to allege that HBO was snubbing *Entourage* as a direct result of the "wave of righteous PC culture" sweeping through Hollywood. "I resent it tremendously."

CHAPTER 25

Crimes of the Past

On a cold afternoon in mid-February 2021, David Zaslav, the chief executive of Discovery—a publicly traded media company founded in Maryland—set off a chain of events that would get AT&T out of the entertainment business.

Zaslav was at his beachfront mansion in East Hampton watching the Pebble Beach Pro-Am Tournament on the Golf Channel. If not for the pandemic, he would have been on the Monterey Peninsula watching the golfers in person. Instead, he was at home, in private. The perfect environment to make a clandestine serenade. At 2:57 p.m. on February 13, Zaslav tapped out an emoji-speckled email to John Stankey, the AT&T leader.

Subject line: Watchin AT&T Pebble.... 🏌️ 🏌️ 🕶️

Body: ... you around ... i've been thinking.... Sent from my iPhone

A few minutes later, Zaslav's phone lit up with a response. "Always scares me when you do that:)." Stankey replied. "Would you like to chat?"

They hopped on the phone, and Zaslav evoked a metaphor for Stankey. Most media companies were stuck on the edge of a roiling lake and gazing to the other side, where Netflix and Disney were already successfully pitching tents and erecting houses. Discovery and AT&T were marooned on the wrong side. Most of the players around them would drown or be devoured trying to cross the treacherous waters. But if the two companies combined forces and swam together, he argued, they'd surely make it to the far shore safely and thrive.

The conversation went on for hours. At the end, they agreed to meet in person in the coming weeks.

At sixty-two, Zaslav was one of the highest paid executives in the TV industry. In 2021 alone, he received a compensation package worth $246.6 million. With all the money, Zaslav had amassed an immodest, sprawling portfolio of high-end real estate. Every day, he showed up at work in blue jeans and a vest, a uniform familiar to anyone who has ever traveled to Sun Valley for its annual media mogul confab.

Zaslav grew up in Rockland County, New York, graduated from college at SUNY Binghamton, and from law school at Boston University. After an unsatisfying stint in corporate law, he got his first job in television with NBC in 1989, and for the next seventeen years helped launch a flock of new cable TV networks, including the business-news channel CNBC.

He jumped to Discovery in 2006. In the years that followed, he helped build the company into a cultural and economic force with a mix of nature shows, as well as cheap, lowbrow reality television, including series like *Here Comes Honey Boo Boo*, *Sex Sent Me to the ER*, *Naked and Afraid*, *Dr. Pimple Popper,* and *Wives with Knives*. It may not have been the most illustrious portfolio of cable networks, but revenues soared under his watch.

By 2019, Zaslav could see that the world was changing. Streaming was the future. It was a land of giants, and Zaslav knew Discovery, already the owner of HGTV, the Food Network, and Animal Planet, still needed to gain size. He scoured the entertainment landscape, looking for the right partner.

In April 2019, Zaslav visited the Time Warner Center, armed with a PowerPoint presentation, highlighting Discovery's hulking stockpile of unscripted shows. WarnerMedia, he argued, should team up with Discovery on a streaming platform. "We have all the reality shows," he told the team at WarnerMedia. "You have all the scripted shows. We combine these assets, come up with a joint venture, and go to market together."

Stankey wasn't interested. The idea of going into business together seemed too complicated. He was confident that HBO Max had more than enough schlock to gain subscribers, to achieve masstige lift-off, on its own.

WarnerMedia was not the only company Zaslav spoke with, but he eventually decided, at least for the moment, Discovery would go it alone. About a year and a half later, in late 2020, Zaslav announced that Discovery+ would be launching in the early months of 2021 for five dollars a month with commercials and seven dollars without. The proposition, Zaslav explained, would be different from Netflix, Apple TV+, or HBO Max.

Discovery+ would aim to be an ambient TV experience, something viewers could turn on when they didn't have anything particularly in mind—background noise while folding the laundry or doing the bills. And he'd do it without expensive stars.

"Almost all of the players in the business moved toward scripted series and scripted movies," Zaslav said right before the debut of the service. "They went to the big stars and the red carpet. The big shiny object."

"We're not as shiny," he continued, "and we don't have a lot of red carpets."

In January 2021, in one of the darkest months of the pandemic, Discovery+ launched in the United States and quickly caught on, beating its initial modest expectations.

But Zaslav hadn't forgotten about his earlier pitch to Stankey. He still believed that Discovery and WarnerMedia would be better off together. As AT&T's challenges mounted, Zaslav waited for the right moment to rekindle the conversation. Then he turned on the golf tournament and took his best swing.

The red carpets of HBO beckoned.

• • •

THAT SPRING, Zaslav's primary Manhattan townhouse was undergoing an extensive renovation. So in the predawn hours of April 1, Zaslav and a pair of his advisers met at Zaslav's backup Manhattan townhouse, a well-appointed rental nearby.

Zaslav's assistant picked up a dozen donuts at the Donut Pub, a twenty-four-hour bakery on Fourteenth Street, and a couple of cardboard containers of coffee from Dunkin' Donuts. A few minutes before their 8:00 a.m appointment, Stankey arrived with Starbucks in hand, along with a couple of top AT&T executives.

The conversation stretched out over five and a half hours. Around them, the townhouse was decorated with vintage photos of Bob Dylan, the Rat Pack, and a 1960s photo of the actor Steve McQueen wielding a revolver.

"That photo," said Discovery's Bruce Campbell, "became a totem, or sort of the mascot, of the deal to me."

For his part, John Stankey kept silent on the secret proceedings. HBO's Casey Bloys and, more critically, WarnerMedia's CEO Jason Kilar, were both in the dark.

With AT&T ready to move forward, both sides called in the bankers to hammer out the details. The resulting transaction, which would again require approval from federal regulators, would not be a typical acquisition. It would require AT&T to spin off WarnerMedia, which would then merge with Discovery. It would alleviate some of AT&T's debt and allow the company to get back to its core business.

Code names were used to ensure secrecy. Among the AT&T crew, WarnerMedia became "Magellan" and Discovery was "Drake." The Discovery side had its own cryptic handles, calling the deal "Project Home Run," with each company referred to by the name of a baseball great: WarnerMedia was "Williams," AT&T was "Aaron," and "Discovery" was "DiMaggio."

Stankey also pushed for the new company to have just one class of shares, which, he believed, would make it simpler to run and easier to sell if a giant suitor became interested in swallowing it whole. With such a setup, the new company and HBO could be back on the market, yet again, within a few years.

On the morning of May 17, the companies trotted out the deal. Stankey and Zaslav appeared together at a Zoom press conference. Stankey spoke in the same dense businessspeak as always, twice referring to himself as "the capital allocator-in-chief." Zaslav let loose excitedly, promising to empower talent and spend more on programming. "We're going to be starting with twenty billion dollars, and we want to invest in more," he said.

Analysts and reporters took it all in. Five years after jumping into Hollywood with huge, splashy ambitions, AT&T was bowing out with little to show for it beyond a long line of laid-off workers, bitter former executives, and angry filmmakers. In the end, all of Stankey's big hires came and went in a flash. Jason Kilar was a lame duck.

By giving away Warner Bros.' 2021 slate of movies, they were managing to get a decent bump in HBO Max's subscriber numbers. From AT&T's perspective, the company had achieved what Time Warner had failed to do under Jeffrey Bewkes—build a streaming platform able to compete directly with Netflix, Disney, and Amazon.

What AT&T did for HBO, Stankey says, is take a "respected but static" content provider and transform it into a much larger global business. "HBO Max would not be where it is today if not for the AT&T and Time Warner merger," Stankey says. "Prior to the combination of the two companies, Time Warner did not have the strategic bandwidth, cash, or the technology operations to take HBO beyond a wholesale product that could compete and transform into the global direct-to-consumer streaming service that it is today."

"I can tell you that the last two years, I think are probably the most consequential creatively, economically, and audience-wise in the history of HBO," Kilar says.

Still, the streaming service was nowhere near catching up to Netflix or Disney+. HBO Max's international rollout was off to a sluggish start. Even among its fans, HBO Max was gaining a reputation for being the buggiest, most glitchy of the major video-streaming services.

"What a dismal failure, and what an embarrassing chapter for what was once one of America's most storied companies," said Craig Moffett, an industry analyst.

AT&T had gone through all the pain of reorganizing WarnerMedia's assets without sticking around long enough to see if any of the changes would end up working. In truth, AT&T didn't have the resources to stay in the game.

"We were at a point where we needed to continue to step up our investment," Pascal Desroches, AT&T's chief financial officer, explained to dazed WarnerMedia employees the day after the merger was announced. "Given where we are in terms of our balance sheet, and also the need to invest in other parts of the business, if we didn't provide the necessary capital—let's just say we stayed the course—WarnerMedia would have been at a competitive disadvantage. And what does that do? We all know a bit of a death spiral starts."

With the deal, Zaslav and his management team would take control of the combined company. Stankey would exit, as would Kilar after the deal closed, ending a stormy, short-lived tenure. "I see nothing but a bright future as the collective capabilities of the combined companies are unleashed!" Stankey wrote to WarnerMedia employees.

Zaslav, meanwhile, took up every chance he could get to talk up the network he long admired. "My gosh, HBO," he says. "Our ambition is that those three letters, everywhere in the world, people are going to say that's the place to go to see great stories, great talent, and just have some fun."

In the coming months, Zaslav repeatedly paid homage to HBO's history, a stark contrast from Stankey in his early days. As an early proponent of cable TV, Zaslav revered HBO as the trailblazing network that started it all. "To me, HBO was like the gravitational pull into this industry," he says. "Because a lot of people thought all of us that got into the business were crazy."

Anyone who doubted HBO's viability in the future was wrong. "Not only do I love it, but I think it's gonna make it," Zaslav says. "It was the lead horse for the industry for a long, long time."

If Zaslav had tried to make a deal for HBO and Warner Bros. just a few years earlier, there would likely have been shrieks of horror throughout Hollywood. Zaslav? The guy behind a biblical plague of lobotomized reality shows? Who famously cuts corners and skimps on budgets? But compared to the Bell heads Zaslav looked downright enlightened.

"It's certainly in better hands," media macher Barry Diller said on CNBC after the deal was made. "How could it ever have been in worse hands?"

Zaslav would spend much of the coming summer getting ready for the takeover. Out on the East End of Long Island, he met for dinner with Jeffrey Bewkes and Richard Plepler.

One day, several weeks after the deal was announced, Zaslav showed up at Warner Bros.' Steven J. Ross Theater in Burbank to introduce himself to his new colleagues. Despite being a cable industry warhorse, Zaslav remained mostly unknown to HBO veterans. At one point, he rattled off a list of HBO shows that he had watched recently, including *Band of Brothers* and *The Pacific*.

Then he name-checked another series that he'd happily binged on during the pandemic. Of all the myriad attempts by HBO to peel back the curtain on life in Hollywood and show it for what it really is, there was one that had apparently captured Zaslav's imagination as he prepared for his own big leap into Tinseltown.

"I rewatched *Entourage*," Zaslav told the crowd. "We were pretty bummed when we finished."

• • •

OVER THE SUMMER OF 2021, Jesse Armstrong spent several weeks in Tuscany, shooting the final episodes of the third season of *Succession*.

Since its premiere three years earlier, the show had grown in both popularity and critical acclaim. In 2020, the second season won the Emmy for Best Drama Series, joining *Game of Thrones* and *The Sopranos* as the third series in HBO's history to win the most prestigious prize in television.

At the start of the second season of *Succession*, the Roy family business is under duress. Too many internal squabbles and too much debt has left it vulnerable to a hostile takeover. Logan Roy presses his lead banker for a candid assessment of the media conglomerate's standing in the market. "There's blood in the water. Your price is edging down. Tech is coming. Tech is here. Tech has its hand around your throat," the banker tells him. "There's maybe one, two legacy media operations that will make themselves big enough to survive."

There is another festering problem. For years, Logan's company has been covering up a series of sexual assaults stemming from its cruise line. Now reporters are on the verge of exposing the past misdeeds, including secret hush payments to victims. It's yet another challenge hounding the grizzled, lumbering media conglomerates of the twentieth century as they try to reinvent themselves for the new era. Their pasts are riddled with half-buried, half-forgotten episodes of misogyny, racism, and abuse that look ghastly when examined in the light of the present day. Nobody at Waystar Royco—or at WarnerMedia or HBO, for that matter—seems to know how to address their corporate crimes of the past. Meanwhile, unburdened by history, their new competitors in streaming tech are skating along conscience-free.

In order to protect and expand his empire, Logan Roy wants to buy a rival, PGM, a left-leaning and journalistically rigorous media company. Nearly everyone thinks it's a cockeyed plan, but the patriarchal tycoon plows ahead anyway.

Caving to Logan's desire, the caterwauling Roy clan visits the palatial estate of the Pierces, the Waspy, moralistic family that owns PGM. They are warned ahead of time to avoid any mention of certain fraught topics such as Israeli politics or their profitable right-wing cable news network. "Steer onto gossip, investments, art, movies, tittle-tattle," advises Frank Vernon (Peter Friedman), Logan's consigliere. "Wider cultural interests."

The Roys do their best to charm the Pierces and convince them that they will be good and worthy stewards. Mostly, they fail. But then Kendall Roy spends a night drinking vodka and snorting cocaine with a key member of the Pierce family, winning over her support in the process. The $25 billion deal is on, at least temporarily.

For all the complexities of the acquisition, and all the bankers and lawyers it requires, Armstrong's storyline suggested that such deals between big media companies really boil down to money, personality, and ego.

"Once you read enough of those books, you realize the boundaries are very strict on what's possible," Armstrong says. "But within what's possible, anything is possible—as long as the money makes sense."

The stated business explanations are often little more than masks, rationalizing the deeper psychological impulses and egotistical needs of the central players. "Even with HBO and Time Warner, and AT&T and Discovery, whenever the new deal is being sold to the shareholders and to the world, the logic, we are told, is completely compelling," Armstrong says. "And then, when these deals unwind a few years hence, suddenly everyone's telling you why the logic wasn't so compelling, and why the new deal is."

The market, he says, may be a rigorous tool for finding value. "But the humans involved in it are also extraordinary machines for vanity and telling stories and making new shapes out of the world, which don't turn into anything," Armstrong says. "AOL is going to be the behemoth to which Time Warner clings, and then AOL is gone in a puff of smoke and these things that were everything become nothing."

At the time, *Succession* wasn't the only project under way at HBO aiming to vivisect the machinations, excesses, and evolving mores of globe-trotting rich people.

In the summer of 2020, five months into the pandemic, with productions across the industry hobbled by the virus, HBO executives were desperate for series that could be shot under tight COVID-19 protocols. In August, Francesca Orsi, the head of HBO's drama department, reached out to Mike White, the creator of HBO's *Enlightened*, to see if he had any ideas.

White was feeling listless. "I was just so bored, and kind of depressed at the time," White says.

White got the impression that if he came up with an idea about a couple of people communicating over Zoom, HBO would be into it. They had a handful of similar series in the works. But he also knew he wanted to do something more than a Zoom show.

"I was like, anything sounds better than just sitting around my house and watching CNN," White says. "And so I was like, what could get me out of L.A.? Then I had this idea. Maybe we do it at a hotel."

Over the next several weeks, typing furiously, White banged out six scripts and a fully fleshed-out idea for a limited series with an ensemble cast, which would take place solely at a Hawaiian resort. White says that by the time HBO executives read it in September, they realized it was maybe "worthy of giving it a little bit more resources." Even so, the budget would be small, and the schedule insanely tight. The six-episode limited series would need to be wrapped within a few months.

Less than a year later, in July 2021, *The White Lotus* premiered on HBO. In the first scene, a handsome, frustrated guy named Shane (Jake Lacy) is standing at a window in a Hawaiian airport, looking outside where a casket is being loaded onto a plane.

Another HBO whodunit, it appears. But unlike, say, *The Undoing* or *Mare of Easttown*, White introduced the corpse as a send-up. "It's such a trope at this point," White told *The New Yorker* shortly after the show premiered. "All of these limited series where there's a dead body at the beginning. I was, like, 'You want your dead body? Here's your dead body.'"

Instead of yet another true-crime mystery, *The White Lotus* is an upstairs-downstairs drama revolving around the dynamics between a group of well-to-do vacationers, mostly white, and the diverse, socioeconomically challenged hotel workers who tend to their many needs.

Like the androids in HBO's *Westworld* who are suddenly and painfully gaining a conscience, the wealthy vacationers of *The White Lotus* are struggling through the first unsettling flickers of self-awareness. They know that the history of the past several centuries has dealt them an unfair advantage. But they feel unsure about what to make of their privilege. What responsibility do they have for the crimes of their ancestors? How are they to play their winning hand?

One evening, Nicole (Connie Britton), a Sheryl Sandberg–like executive, asks her daughter's friend Paula (Brittany O'Grady) a question. Why, she wants to know, did Paula leave dinner so abruptly the previous night?

Before Paula can answer, Nicole's daughter, Olivia (Sydney Sweeney), jumps in. Olivia explains that her friend, who is one of the only vacationers of color, was "disturbed" by the resort's hula-dancing ceremony.

"It bothers her to watch Hawaiians dance for a bunch of white people," Olivia says.

Her mom objects. The dancers, she argues, seemed to be having a good time, honoring their culture.

Then Olivia's father, Mark (Steve Zahn), jumps in with a life lesson. Yes, killing people and stealing their land is bad, he says. But that's the reality of imperialism and American history and human nature. Everyone is out for their own good. Nobody cedes their own privilege willingly. What's done is done.

"How are we gonna make it right? Should we give away all our money?" he says. "Maybe we should just feel shitty about ourselves all the time for crimes of the past?"

Mike White says he wanted the show to explore the corrosive effects of too much wealth on humanity, but also to ground it in something recognizable to viewers. To him, *Succession* felt like "a king's court," a series about a class of billionaires so beyond reach that they can easily be otherized. By contrast, he says, *The White Lotus* is more focused on "the millionaire next door."

Over the course of its six-week run, *The White Lotus* grew in popularity with an audience that swelled to roughly three and a half times its size of its premiere. Critics responded with delight. *The New Yorker*'s Naomi Fry called it a "near-note-perfect tragicomedy."

It was also a reminder of many of the things that HBO continued to do well. White was both the sole writer and director of the series, bringing together two of the three elements in the writer/director/performer formula that Bloys identified as being a key to HBO success. The cast was filled with character actors or unknowns, and wound up minting stars, including Sweeney as the acid-tongued daughter, and Murray Bartlett as the hotel's unctuous, bitter, blottoed manager.

Once again, HBO was notching a victory by listening not to the customer, not to the data, but to one of their trusted, in-house artists.

"I have a relationship with them, as much as it was fraught at times," White says. "When you can hit it with HBO, I just think that's just the A+ version of this kind of rollout."

White says that at HBO, which has been his TV home since making *Enlightened*, everyone cares about the project as much as he does. "The people who cut your trailers do a good job, they're responsive," White says. "They hire good people in different departments—press, marketing."

Over the years, White says, Netflix executives had been in touch with him to make a show for the streaming service. But he never seriously considered leaving HBO in favor of the algorithmic streamer. Netflix just wasn't for him. "I've had meetings at Netflix and I really felt like I was in a Mike Judge satire of the modern television industrial complex or something," White says.

• • •

ONE AFTERNOON IN MARCH 2021, Sasha Emerson joined a Zoom call to do something she'd first learned decades earlier. Helping a young writer pitch a TV show to a network. This time, to Netflix. The artist was David Zheng, a Chinese American playwright who grew up working behind the bulletproof glass in his parents' Chinese takeout restaurant in the Bronx. The series, *KetchupBBQHotSauce*, would be set in a takeout joint called Bamboo Garden.

The nerves never get old, Emerson thought before the call.

Since signing a nondisclosure agreement and leaving HBO in 1991, her career had taken several sharp turns and somehow ended up right back where she'd once imagined it would be during her first exhilarating days of graduate school: shepherding new voices toward greater creative fulfillment and cultural recognition.

She was still running her interior design business, and the commissions were still rolling in. But as the years passed, and Emerson's kids grew up, she had moved back to New York and did more dramaturg work on the side. She joined the staff of the Ojai Playwrights Conference, a workshop held annually in the foothills of the Topatopa Mountains of Southern California, where Emerson helped to recognize and champion new plays from diverse American writers.

She joined the board of advisers for the Yale School of Drama. And in 2017, she started a part-time job as a "new writers and theatrical consultant" for AMC Networks, discovering, evaluating, and harvesting talent from the theatrical world for the New York–based entertainment company behind such cable TV hits as *Mad Men* and *The Walking Dead*.

Emerson mentored countless young playwrights, directors, and actors.

As the competition between streaming services escalated and the demand for new original programming ratcheted up, she watched as her protégés landed roles or sold shows to Netflix and the like. "That's the part I just love," Emerson says. "Working with creative, marginalized voices and watching them get power and success and artistic achievement. What could be better than that?"

A few years ago, the Ojai Playwrights Conference organized a night of celebration to honor her. At one point, a musician and writer named Chris Gabo bounded up onstage and took the microphone. As a teenager, Gabo had participated in Ojai's youth workshop, and later Emerson had helped him get into the Yale School of Drama on a full scholarship for playwriting.

"Being a young artist can often feel like traversing a great desert with no knowledge of the stars, no wisdom with which to read the shifting of the sands. . . . The word 'unmoored' comes to mind," he said. "That's why elders in this thing we do, people who really honestly take an interest in young artists, are invaluable beacons in the night. And Sasha Emerson is truly the brightest light that has ever shone in my path. Now, I don't know what I did to merit the support I have personally received from her. But goddamn, I feel quite lucky."

A few years later, after graduating from Yale, Gabo landed an overall deal to write for HBO. Somehow, decades after being unceremoniously cast aside from the network, Emerson was still feeding HBO new voices, even if nobody there knew it.

"She is an extremely passionate advocate for playwrights," says Kate Cortesi, whose play about a sexual-misconduct reckoning between a boss and his mentee, entitled *Love*, was selected as part of the Ojai festival in 2019. "Getting to know Sasha made me realize that she had been hustling for me even before she met me because she liked the work. That was really wonderful. I see her doing it for other people. I consider her a real friend and mentor and advocate."

"It's amazing what a good studio executive she would have been," Cortesi adds. "She's effective and quick on her feet. She understands how relationships make things happen."

These days, if they are asked, Emerson's friends will marvel at her resilience and ability to get over the injustice done to her by HBO and keep going in life with a sense of humor and without self-pity or complaint; and her willingness to nurture the careers of so many young talented people even after her onetime boss had used his position of power in the industry to ruin hers. But typically, her friends don't think too much anymore about how Emerson managed to cope with what was stolen from her so long ago. To them, that was just Sasha, an indomitable spirit.

Still, the scars of the trauma persisted, if you looked carefully. Emerson spent much of the pandemic of 2020 pedaling around the empty streets of Brooklyn on a beat-up bike, gazing at the architecture and the parks and the brownstones, never wearing a helmet. Strangers would look up, see her exposed noggin, and yell a few words of warning in her direction. She would ignore them. All these years later, she still couldn't bear to feel anything constricting her throat, not even the spindly strap of a bike helmet. And so she rode on without protection.

* * *

ON A WARM NIGHT IN OCTOBER 2021, HBO welcomed a group of actors, executives, producers, and journalists into the marbled, echoing halls of the American Museum of Natural History. It was time to celebrate the upcoming third season of *Succession*.

With COVID cases down, boosted antibodies up, masks off, and the bar open, the mood was jubilant. Never mind that the show was about the excruciating collapse of a New York media empire—or that they were surrounded on all sides by reminders of the cruelty of evolution, the taxidermied and fossilized specimens of once-fearsome apex predators, now long extinct.

HBO and HBO Max chief content officer Casey Bloys took it all in. He had every reason to feel positive about the network's future. Despite everything—the virus, the variants, the insurrectionists, the phone guys— HBO had enjoyed one of its best years. Between *The White Lotus, Mare of Easttown, Succession*, and the final celebrated season of *Insecure*, HBO would finish 2021 once again basking in critical and popular acclaim.

Additionally, HBO Max, after its initial bumbles, felt like it was settling more comfortably into its masstige, middlebrow identity. Project Popcorn, the strategy to put an entire year of Warner Bros. movies on HBO Max the same day as their theatrical releases, may have infuriated artists like David Chase, but it proved to be quite popular with virus-wary consumers. Crucial carriage agreements had been hammered out with Amazon and Roku, and the early reports of HBO Max's glitchiness were gradually subsiding. Even Netflix wasn't looking quite so invincible: in the coming months, the streaming front-runner would lose subscribers for the first time in a decade, sending its share price into a tailspin and raising questions about the quality of its programming slate.

Together, HBO Max and HBO would end 2021 with 73.8 million global subscribers, an increase of 13 million from the year prior. It was still a far cry from Netflix's 221.8 million customers, but better than management had forecasted.

HBO was not Blockbuster, not yet. Over five decades, it had proven remarkably resilient, surviving the Premiere attack, the *Ghostbusters* fiasco, the rise of VCRs, the spread of DVDs, the indignities of AOL, the end of *The Sopranos*, the attacks from the Albanian Army, the *Entourage* movie, and AT&T.

Through it all, HBO kept turning out unexpected hits.

Frank Rich, the executive producer on *Succession*, credited Bloys for carrying on HBO's traditions even after Richard Plepler got plunked and AT&T had their run of the place. "They never got it, and they were gone," Rich says of AT&T. "Thank God. But it could have gone on much longer. And then, who knows?"

Unlike many of its new rivals, such as Netflix and Amazon and Apple, HBO's culture had never been driven by a single, visionary founder. Over the past fifty years, its success had always been a collective effort, dependent not on the genius of any particular individual, but rather on a progression of newcomers who devoted years to mastering the HBO playbook, then pushing it forward under a series of different executives. For the time being, it was Bloys who would be carrying on the historic HBO bloodline.

"While there hasn't been a single leader, there are these overlaps of tenures where people who were trained in a certain way and trained to care about certain things remain," says Carolyn Strauss, the former HBO executive who was there from its go-go *Sopranos* and *The Wire* era. "You can trace Casey's lineage all the way back."

The same holds true, Strauss points out, of Nancy Abraham and Lisa Heller in documentaries; Nina Rosenstein in talk shows and specials; Francesca Orsi in drama; and Amy Gravitt in comedy. They all came up through the ranks, put in their time, strengthened their creative instincts through years of experience and repetition. When it came to programming development, HBO was well buttressed for the future, particularly if the network would someday consider finally elevating a woman to the top job.

"When I was at HBO, I lived through the Warner thing, I lived through the Turner thing, I lived through the AOL thing," Strauss says. "And each step took you in a more corporatized direction. And each step made programming decisions a little more complicated, threw a few more factors in. I do feel that there was clearly a sea change in the AT&T one, in terms of culture and everything else."

"However," she continues, "programming-wise, there are still people there, like Casey and Amy and Frannie, who have their roots in a different HBO and are still shaped by that. While they may not have been there in the beginning, they were often trained by the people who were."

As a producer for more than a decade, Strauss continued to supply series for HBO, even after she was pushed out. There was *Game of Thrones*, of course, but also *Chernobyl*, a surprise hit about the 1980s nuclear reactor disaster that would take the Outstanding Limited Series Emmy in 2020. Now when she talks to screenwriters trying to figure out the ideal home for their projects, the answer, almost surprisingly, remains the same.

"HBO still is the one they want to go to," Strauss says. "There is still a way that they look at things and a process that they go through, which is a cut above."

As the cable era drew to a close, Bloys recognized that the streamniks were right about one thing, data science was immensely useful for certain tasks like marketing, customer retention, and optimization of budgets on a broad scale. But great television, he also knew, would never come from listening to the customers or mining their preferences on the internet.

"People don't know they need the Roys until they meet the Roys," he says of *Succession*. "If you ask a group of people, do you want to see a show about selfish, venal billionaires in New York? They'd say no. Same for *The Sopranos*."

Great television came only from one place. From listening to artists and supporting their instincts and visions zealously. "The thing about testing is it tells you about the past, not what the future is," Bloys says.

Not that HBO was immune from trying to mine its own past for future profit. In October 2021, on the day *The Sopranos* prequel landed in theaters and on HBO Max amid ambivalent reviews, WarnerMedia announced it had signed David Chase to a five-year deal, giving the company the first look at anything new he came up with, including *Sopranos* spin-offs. In December, HBO Max began streaming *And Just Like That*, a critically gnawed-on and much-watched sequel to *Sex and the City*. In January, Lena Dunham told *The Hollywood Reporter* that she would like to someday make a *Girls* sequel. Meanwhile, HBO has a *Six Feet Under* follow-up in the protozoan stages of development. And much more *Game of Thrones* programming is, as they say, *coming*.

Even so, it's unlikely that HBO will ever become fully Disneyfied, endlessly recycling, revamping, reengineering the characters of its past for future generations of viewers. HBO might tolerate the era of the reboot, but it will not define it. The Larry Sanders Cinematic Universe will never throw a scare into Marvel.

What HBO knew how to do was to find the thing nobody was looking for and turn it into something everybody thought they wanted all along. And there was still a lot of value in that. "I think people get caught up with 'What's the next . . . ?'" Bloys says. "As Carolyn used to say, when the question was, 'What's the next *Sopranos*,' it's not what's going to be the next *Sopranos*. It's what is the next great show. And you don't know what it's going to be."

Someday soon, he notes, people would start saying, "'*Succession* is going away. What's the next *Succession*?' It probably will not be another show about a billionaire family in New York," Bloys says. "It will be something else that comes out of left field."

Inside the American Museum of Natural History, the party for *Succession* pushed deeper into the night. Bloys circulated through the crowd, warmly greeting colleagues and cast members. David Zaslav, the media tycoon months away from becoming the latest HBO overseer, swanned about, looking on approvingly. For now, everything felt okay. You could squint and it almost felt like a classic HBO premiere party from the heady zenith of cable TV—prepandemic, pre-AT&T. For now, no one was obsessing about what came next. For now, everyone was just happy to get another drink with the museum's magnificent, life-size model of a blue whale hanging benignly over their heads.

ACKNOWLEDGMENTS

It's Not TV is the result of hundreds of original interviews with current and former HBO staffers, executives, show creators, and rivals. Our gratitude goes out to everyone who spoke with us. We couldn't have done this without your generosity of time and the acuity of your insights

Our book also synthesizes a significant amount of historical material. Thank you to Jordan Mitchell at the Annenberg School for Communication Library for helping us access the HBO Oral History Project; to Brian Kenny of the Cable Center's Barco Library; and to everyone at the Television Academy, whose interviews with various HBO creators and former executives proved vital.

We also salute all the great beat reporters, feature writers, and television critics from newspapers, magazines, and websites who have done a terrific job over the years dissecting HBO's myriad shows, often on tight deadlines.

Our team at Viking has been incredible. Our amazing editor, Allison Lorentzen, sharpened every page through multiple drafts with her erudition and wit. Dan Novack provided us with helpful legal counsel. Thanks also to Camille LeBlanc, Mary Stone, Julia Rickard, and Kristina Fazzalaro for all the help with everything.

Our exacting researcher and fact-checker Gabriel Baumgaertner proved to be an invaluable reader and skillful excavator of interesting historical nuggets.

We might never have written this book—and possibly never met and become such close friends—if it were not for the influence of the late Peter Kaplan, our former editor and mentor at the *Observer*, who brought us and so many others together in the madcap pursuit of great storytelling with a strong point of view.

And a special high five to Sara Vilkomerson, our pal and go-to fixer in all things, who several times rescued us in a pinch.

From Felix:

Among others at Bloomberg News, I'm beholden to Mike Bloomberg, John Micklethwait, Reto Gregori, Brian Bremner, and Crayton Harrison for their strong institutional leadership and passion for great business journalism without which none of this would be possible.

I'm proud to be part of Bloomberg's media, entertainment, and telecom team with my excellent crewmates Lucas Shaw, Gerry Smith, Kelly Gilblom, Ashley Carman, Scott Moritz, Chris Palmeri, Rob Golum, and (emeritus) Nick Turner.

At *Bloomberg Businessweek*, I've long benefited from the guidance and editing of Joel Weber, Jim Aley, Kristin Powers, and Max Chafkin. I'm also appreciative of my wildly talented book-writing colleagues Brad Stone, Sarah Frier, Ashlee Vance, Joshua Green, and Emily Chang.

Much gratitude to my agent, Ethan Bassoff at Ross Yoon, who provided sage counsel, good humor, and smart feedback throughout this entire process.

It was my acerbic, exacting former editors across a range of publications who taught me how to report and write. Many thanks to all of you, especially Howard Witt, Erik Wemple, Tom Scocca, Josh Tyrangiel, Sheelah Kolhatkar, and Bryant Urstadt.

Thank you also to my author friends Andrew Rice, Josh Levin, Devin Leonard, Alexandra Jacobs, David Randall, Garth Hallberg, Sridhar Pappu, and Tom Lucas for your encouragement and insights into the publishing process.

Lots of love to my wonderful stepfather Peter Walker, to my marvelous stepmother Margaret Marsh, and to my lovely parents-in-law Pat and Philip Gelber.

I'd be nowhere and nothing in life without my big brother, Ellery Gillette, who has never once wavered as my number one fan, booster, and hype man; my dad, Howard Gillette, who instilled in me a love of history, team sports, and newspaper clips; and my mom, Jane Gillette, from whom I inherited a love of literature, sharp language, and my genetic predisposition for needling powerful people in story form.

Most of all, I am forever grateful to my wife, Jenny, and my sons Hugo and Dexter, who rode out the book-writing process with me during a pandemic, keeping me mostly sane with bountiful wilderness hikes, board games, read alouds, fishing trips, Nintendo sessions, and paddle sports. I love you like Taco loves bird-watching and Solich loves eating plants.

From John:

I've had the amazing privilege of reporting on HBO and the television industry since 2015. Thank you to all the editors at the *Times* who have been my champions, particularly Jim Windolf, Ellen Pollock, Carolyn Ryan, Bill Brink, and Connor Ennis. And thank you to all the phenomenal editors who have mentored, guided, and protected me through the years, especially Tom McGeveran, Josh Benson, Tommy Craggs, and Stuart Emmrich.

This project would have gone nowhere without my fantastic agent, Elias Altman, who helped steer an idea into a proposal and then, miraculously, a finished product.

A big shout-out to my entire family, including my brothers James and Jason, as well as Lucy, Devon, Dawn, Lori, Olivia, Rob, and Ian. And thank you to Dad and Dee for putting a TV in my room before I could read.

This project would have been truly impossible without my incredible friends: Zack Woolfe, for getting me through the pandemic; James Doty, for deeply considered thoughts; Fred Martin, for the summer Exley sessions; Michael Grynbaum and Brooks Barnes, for daily serenity; James Dreiss, Matt Lynch, Alexandra Jacobs, Matthew Schneier, Irina Aleksander, and Dan Palmer, for the entertainment; James Freedland, Erik Maza, Buck Ellison, and Katherine Taylor, for shelter.

And, finally, thank you to my best friend, Bennett Madison, for virtually everything. I love you the most.

NOTES

PROLOGUE: TAKING FLIGHT

2 **"In my mind, the transmission"**: Kara Swisher, *There Must Be a Pony in Here Somewhere* (New York: Three Rivers Press, 2003), 68.

2 **The operation was hemorrhaging money**: Brian Winston, *Media, Technology and Society: A History: From the Telegraph to the Internet* (London: Routledge, 1998), 287–91.

2 **Levin came on board**: *HBO, The First Ten Years* (New York: Home Box Office, Inc., 1982), 13.

2 **Dolan's idea—conceived**: "The Reminiscences of Charles F. Dolan," Annenberg School for Communication HBO Oral History Project, University of Pennsylvania, interview by Howard Burkat, December 20, 2013, 6–7.

4 **"Very demoralizing," Levin said**: "The Reminiscences of Gerald M. Levin," Annenberg School for Communication HBO Oral History Project, University of Pennsylvania, interview by Howard Burkat, January 8, 2014, 17.

4 **"All of a sudden, these locavores"**: "The Reminiscences of Gerald M. Levin," 25.

5 **"It was crystal sharp"**: "The Reminiscences of William G. Hooks," Annenberg School for Communication HBO Oral History Project, University of Pennsylvania, interview by Howard Burkat, January 13, 2015, 37.

5 **"On came the fight"**: "Robert Rosencrans," Hauser Oral History Collection, Cable Center, interview by Jim Keller, November 17, 2000.

6 **"We had climbed"**: "Nick Nicholas," Hauser Oral History Collection, Cable Center, interview by Steve Nelson, June 11, 2002.

6 **"When they installed"**: Thomas P. Southwick, *Distant Signals* (Overland Park, KS: Intertec, 1999), 120.

7 **prayer of gratitude**: "25th Anniversary of Satellite Launch Panel" (Jack Cole, Jerry Levin, Monty Rifkin, Bob Rosencrans, Hub Schlafly, Sid Topol), Cable Center, interview by Brian Lamb, November 25, 2000.

7 **"We didn't just build HBO"**: "Michael Fuchs," The Interviews, Television Academy Foundation, interview by Karen Herman, July 21, 2010.

CHAPTER 1: SURVIVING THE PREMIERE

11 **"Is it a dirty channel?"**: "Sheila Nevins," The Interviews, Television Academy Foundation, interview by Karen Herman, May 2, 2006.

11 **Then she returned:** "Sheila Nevins," Hauser Oral History Collection, Cable Center, interview by Steve Nelson, July 31, 2001.

12 **Inside, there was:** David W. Dunlap, "Press 'L' for Landmark: Time & life Lobby, a 50's Gem, Awaits Recognition," *New York Times*, June 17, 2002.

13 **"I was very, very uncomfortable":** "Sheila Nevins."

14 **Premiere was dead:** David Crook, "Cable TV Network Premiere Folds," *Los Angeles Times*, June 5, 1981.

14 **Growing up, he loved sports:** "Michael Fuchs," The Interviews, Television Academy Foundation, interview by Karen Herman. July 21, 2010.

15 **By his late twenties:** "Michael Fuchs," Hauser Oral History Collection, Cable Center, interview by Joel Fleming, June 3, 1999.

15 **One study found:** Ken Auletta, *Three Blind Mice* (New York: Vintage Books, 1992), 24.

15 **"It was canned entertainment":** "Michael Fuchs," Hauser Oral History Collection, Cable Center.

15 **"to establish a character":** Tom Jory, "TV Talk: Michael Fuchs Programming for HBO," Associated Press, April 16, 1981.

16 **the campus included:** Eileen Carstairs, "There's No Place Like HBO," *Corporate Design & Realty Magazine,* January–February 1985.

16 **"go on unchecked":** Robert Lindsey, "Home Box Office Moves into Hollywood," *New York Times,* June 12, 1983.

19 **"It was a huge boondoggle":** "The Reminiscences of Linda Frankenbach," Annenberg School for Communication HBO Oral History Project, University of Pennsylvania, interview by Howard Burkat, November 14, 2014, 50.

20 **In exchange for providing:** Kathryn Harris, "HBO Plans Sale of Film Partnerships: Project Would Aid Pay-TV Service's Move into Hollywood," *Los Angeles Times*, February 19, 1983.

20 **"a love-hate relationship":** "The Reminiscences of Gerald M. Levin," Annenberg School for Communication HBO Oral History Project, University of Pennsylvania, interview by Howard Burkat, January 8, 2014, 47.

21 **To try to parse out:** "David Baldwin," Hauser Oral History Collection, Cable Center, interview by Steve Nelson, December 6, 2007.

22 **"the man in the household":** "Michael Fuchs," The Interviews, Television Academy Foundation.

22 **"It was an education":** "Sheila Nevins," The Interviews, Television Academy Foundation.

CHAPTER 2: PUNCH LINES

24 **for roughly $40 million:** Bill Mesce, Jr., *Inside the Rise of HBO* (Jefferson, NC: McFarland & Company, Inc., 2015), 103.

24 **"I went about my business":** "Michael Fuchs," The Interviews, Television Academy Foundation, interview by Karen Herman. July 21, 2010.

24 **campaigning for Bobby Kennedy:** Bill Carter, "No Laughing Matter," *New York Times*, November 5, 1989.

25 **"I love Michael":** "Sheila Nevins," The Interviews, Television Academy Foundation, interview by Karen Herman, May 2, 2006.

25 **less than a year old:** "Chris Albrecht," Hauser Oral History Collection, Cable Center, interview by John Higgins, October 22, 2003.

26 **buy 25 percent:** Budd Friedman, *The Improv* (Dallas: BenBella Books Inc., 2017), 193.

26 **"used to be a slogan":** Friedman, *The Improv*, 255.

27 **Showtime was broadcasting:** Steve Schneider, "Cable TV Notes: Those Fillers Are Doing Double Duty," *New York Times*, September 2, 1984.

27 **his first comedy special:** Tom Jory, "Garry Shandling, Alone in Vegas on Showtime," Associated Press, August 9, 1984.

27 **Showtime swooped in:** "Chris Albrecht," Hauser Oral History Collection, Cable Center.

28 **a boss 2,450 miles away:** "Chris Albrecht," The Interviews, Television Academy Foundation, interview by Stephen J. Abramson, October 7, 2013.

28 **He told one coworker:** Through his lawyer, Albrecht says he cannot recall telling anyone that he slept with more than a thousand women but if he "made a comment like this, it was facetious and joking, and could never have been understood by any rational listener as an assertion of fact."

29 **roughly $35 million:** "Chris Albrecht," Hauser Oral History Collection, Cable Center.

30 **"gave us a jolt":** "Chris Albrecht," Hauser Oral History Collection, Cable Center.

CHAPTER 3: THE UNSWEET SCIENCE

34 **free ride was over:** Iver Peterson, "Scrambling of Signals Today Thwarts TV Dish Antennas," *New York Times*, January 15, 1986.

35 **"the wrong time to get out":** "Ross Greenburg," Hauser Oral History Collection, Cable Center, interview by Tom Umstead, May 15, 2003.

37 **the Heavyweight World Series:** Gerald Eskenazi, "Unification Fight Lures Holmes Back," *New York Times*, March 4, 1986.

37 **"I did evil things":** Gary Smith, "Tyson the Timid, Tyson the Terrible," *Sports Illustrated*, March 21, 1988.

38 **"my brothers and babies":** William Nack, "Ready to Soar to the Very Top," *Sports Illustrated*, January 6, 1986.

38 **"our Arnold Schwarzenegger":** Skip Myslenski, "Tyson Puts Punch in HBO's Ratings," *Chicago Tribune*, January 22, 1988.

39 **"All these stories":** John Flinn, "On Location with Pay TV," *Channels*, November 1988.

39 **"a repertoire of fictional characters":** Newhouse News Service, "Trudeau's Man for the '88 Race," *Newsday*, February 13, 1988.

40 **ended the series:** Kathryn Baker, "'Tanner' Fades on HBO and Hopes to Jump to PBS," Associated Press, August 24, 1988.

40 **"The fact is":** Kathryn Harris and Paul Richter, "Time Warner: Merger Creates a World Power," *Los Angeles Times*, March 5, 1989.

41 **"take it personally":** Carter, "No Laughing Matter," *New York Times*, November 5, 1989.

42 **"ghoulish, nightmarish, perverse stories":** Frank Di Matteo, "A Comic Nightmare Returns," *Newsday*, June 4, 1989.

42 **attention of critics:** Kathryn Baker, "Comic-Book Scary 'Tales,' Not for Kids," Associated Press, June 2, 1989.

42 **"whores like queens":** John O'Connor, "A Summer Cycle of Horror Shows on HBO," *New York Times*, June 5, 1989.

43 **"We strive to bring":** Jack Mathews, "Crypt Disinterred for HBO," *Los Angeles Times*, June 8, 1989.

CHAPTER 4: THAT "CABLE EDGE"

46 **At the time, she also:** John O'Connor, "Review/Television; 3 Films About Women Behind Bars," *New York Times*, January 26, 1991.

47 **While incarcerated, he discovered:** Ray Loynd, "Charles Dutton Not Prisoner of His Past," *Los Angeles Times*, January 20, 1990.

48 **The lavish bungalow:** "John Landis," Directors Guild of America, interview by Jeremy Kagan, June 11, 2013.

48 **little choice but to say yes:** Daniel Cerone, "Landis' Lucky Lot: Rare TV Clips Have a Major Role in New HBO Series," *Los Angeles Times*, July 8, 1990.

48 **shown three minutes:** Richard Sandomir, "His Dreams Are Always in Black and White," *New York Times*, January 17, 1993.

51 **"what's so bad about that":** Benjamin Svetkey, "HBO's 'Dream On' Is the Sauciest Show on Television," *Entertainment Weekly*, June 19, 1992.

51 **lapped it up:** Bill Carter, "HBO Finds Hits the Networks Miss," *New York Times*, July 15, 1991.

51 **a brief engagement:** Bill Carter, "No Laughing Matter," *New York Times*, November 5, 1989.

52 **"a male-dominated culture":** "The Reminiscences of Gerald M. Levin," Annenberg School for Communication HBO Oral History Project, University of Pennsylvania, interview by Howard Burkat, January 8, 2014, 59.

53 **"more fun than college":** "The Reminiscences of Linda Frankenbach," Annenberg School for Communication HBO Oral History Project, University of Pennsylvania, interview by Howard Burkat, November 14, 2014, 7.

54 **the dismissive reply:** Through his lawyer, Albrecht denies that he told Susie Fitzgerald he was resistant to female comedians starring in HBO sitcoms because "they're not going to take their tops off."

54 **"The danger," Givens said:** Laura B. Randolph, "Robin Givens: Life After Tyson," *Ebony*, March 1990.

55 **re-airing Tyson's defeat:** Larry Stewart, "HBO Deal with Tyson Still Good; Douglas Fight Replay Friday," *Los Angeles Times*, February 13, 1990.

55 **grabbed Bewkes by his lapels:** Bewkes says that regarding the Tyson incident—as well as his reaction to the Nielsen ratings from *If These Walls Could Talk*—he either "doesn't remember the exchange" or has a "different recollection" but "doesn't want to quibble or counter anybody's recollections" and is "happy to let everybody's version stand."

56 **Tyson announced he was jumping:** Thomas Tyrer, "Tyson Chasing Pact at Showtime," *Electronics Media*, December 17, 1990.

56 **"I love animals," she testified:** Joe Treen and Bill Shaw Bill, "Judgment Day," *People*, February 24, 1992.

56 **Donald Trump loudly defended Tyson:** David Shortell and Miguel Marquez, "When Mike Tyson Was Convicted of Rape, Donald Trump Came to His Defense," CNN, October 28, 2016.

58 **Albrecht was allowed to stay:** Bewkes declined to comment on his role in the aftermath of Albrecht's attack on Emerson. He also declined to answer whether, in retrospect, he thinks that the way HBO responded to the incident was conducted fairly. He also declined to comment on why HBO never reported the incident, or the resulting settlement, to shareholders.

58 **an unsourced item:** Paula Parisi, "Sr. Vice President Emerson Out at HBO Prods.," *Hollywood Reporter*, November 11, 1991.

58 **It would not be the last:** Amy Wallace, "Violence, Nudity, Adult Content," *GQ*, November 5, 2010.

CHAPTER 5: QUALITY NOISE

59 **"ran out of heroes":** "Michael Fuchs," The Interviews, Television Academy Foundation, interview by Karen Herman, July 21, 2010.

60 **"we can be offensive":** Dennis McDougal, "When Miss Sheri Got an Abortion," *Los Angeles Times*, January 3, 1992.

60 **several well-known Hollywood actors:** Bernard Weinraub, "Stars Flock to Be in HBO Film About the Early Years of AIDS," *New York Times*, January 11, 1993.

61 **Cooper got into a spat:** Leonard Klady, "HBO's 'Band' Hits Sour Note," *Daily Variety*, April 23, 1993.

61 **"most made-for-TV movies":** Richard Zoglin, "Fighting the Good Fight," *Time*, September 13, 1993.

61 **"primary part of our decision":** Wayne Walley and Diane Joy Moca, "HBO Originals Take Center Stage," *Electronics Media*, September 13, 1993.

61 **"no modern Dickens":** Daniel Cerone, "Plugging into Hollywood," *Los Angeles Times*, November 23, 1993.

62 **"The value of quality noise":** Eric Mink, "Quality Noise Lets HBO Take Chances," *Chicago Tribune*, August 28, 1992.

63 **"It worked," said Quentin Schaffer:** "Quentin Schaffer," Hauser Oral History Collection, Cable Center, interview by Steve Nelson, December 6, 2007.

63 **a new comedy pipeline:** Connie Bruck, *Master of the Game* (New York: Penguin Books, 1994), 278–79.

63 **shot down that idea too:** Bruck, *Master of the Game*, 284–85.

64 **Kauffman and Crane walked away:** Lisa de Moraes, "Lor Gets Bright, Crane, Kauffman," *Hollywood Reporter*, April 20, 1992.

65 **"The show is a metaphor":** Lawrence Christon, "Heeeere's Larry," *Los Angeles Times*, August 12, 1992.

65 **he vowed to begin:** Lynn Hirschberg, "Gary Shandling Goes Dark," *New York Times*, May 31, 1998.

67 **"*Larry Sanders* taught me":** Todd Holland, *Not Just the Best of the Larry Sanders Show* (Sony Pictures, 1997), disc 2.

68 **Nielsen introduced a new way:** Randall Rothenberg, "Black Hole in Television," *New York Times*, October 8, 1990.

68 **"Suddenly, Black viewership":** "The Reminiscences of Donald E. Anderson," Annenberg School for Communication HBO Oral History Project, University of Pennsylvania, interview by Howard Burkat, December 6, 2015, 19.

69 **pointed and profane:** Greg Braxton, "Laughz n the Hood," *Los Angeles Times*, August 6, 1992.

69 **an angry crowd:** "Teens Charged in Boys' Death," Associated Press, June 5, 1993.

72 **a big promotion:** Robin Schatz, "Home Box Office Boss Is New Warner Music Maestro," *Newsday*, May 4, 1995.

73 **"It's a sad day":** Chuck Philips, "Time Warner to Abandon Gangster Rap," *Los Angeles Times*, September 28, 1995.

74 **"arrogant and vindictive":** Sallie Hofmeister and Chuck Philips, "Fuchs' Fall Is as Dramatic as His Rise Was Meteoric," *Los Angeles Times*, November 17, 1995.

74 **"an extraordinary talent":** Chuck Philips, "Shake-up at Time Warner," *Los Angeles Times*, November 17, 1995.

CHAPTER 6: THE LAND OF OZ

78 **"I'm in trouble":** "The Reminiscences of Jeffrey Bewkes," Annenberg School for Communication HBO Oral History Project, University of Pennsylvania, interview by Howard Burkat, November 19, 2014, 9.

78 **into the laps of HBO:** Geraldine Fabrikant, "As the Competition Intensifies, HBO Chief Has Impressive Start," *New York Times*, December 30, 1996.

78 **2.3 million subscribers:** Skip Wollenberg, "Time Warner Replaces Music Boss with HBO Chief," Associated Press, May 3, 1995.

85 **HBO steered some $60 million:** Dottie Enrico, "HBO Ads Tickle Primal Funny Bone," *USA Today*, January 13, 1997.

86 **struck a deal:** Doris Toumarkine, "Moore, TNT in Abortion 'Talk,'" *Hollywood Reporter*, December 10, 1992.

86 **Moore called them "restrictive":** Claudia Dreifus, "A Case for Abortion Rights. No Apologies," *New York Times*, October 13, 1996.

86 **"We had to beg":** Merle Ginsberg, "Demi Inc: From Sweaty Star to Movie Mogul," *Buffalo News*, May 26, 1996.

86 **"was beautifully written":** Dreifus, "A Case for Abortion Rights. No Apologies."

87 **twenty million people:** "Sopranos Hits Ratings High as It Closes Shop Until March," *Seattle Post-Intelligencer*, April 13, 2000.

CHAPTER 7: A GLAMOROUS PLAYGROUND

89 **blared the cover:** Lisa Birnback, "Good-bye, L.A. Hello, N.Y.C.," *New York*, February 20, 1995.

89 **"sort of flipped":** "Darren Star Interview," Television Academy Foundation, interview by Adrienne Faillace, October 6, 2015.

90 **"Welcome to the age":** Candace Bushnell, *Sex and the City* (New York: Grand Central Publishing, 1996), 2.

91 **"a traumatic experience":** "Darren Star," The Interviews, Television Academy Foundation, interview by Adrienne Faillace, October 6, 2015.

91 **felt it was preposterous:** "Darren Star," The Interviews, Television Academy Foundation.

92 **Eight weeks after:** "HBO to Explore Upscale Sex In New York City," Reuters, December 24, 1996.

93 **high strung and dramatic:** Peter Biskind, "An American Family," *Vanity Fair*, April 4, 2007.

93 **Chase was entranced:** *Baer v. Chase*, Rule 56.1 statement, United States District Court, D. New Jersey, April 29, 2005.

93 **gave a presentation:** *Baer v. Chase*.

94 **several scripts for feature films:** David Chase interview, *The Sopranos—The Complete First Season* (HBO, 1999), DVD, interview by Peter Bogdanovich.

95 **an inferior version:** "David Chase," The Interviews, Television Academy Foundation, interviews by Karen Herman, December 11, 2008, and April 29, 2009.

95 **it would never sell:** David Chase interview, *The Sopranos*.

95 **he could create:** "David Chase," The Interviews, Television Academy Foundation.

97 **In February 1997:** *Baer v. Chase*.

97 **they loved the therapy angle:** *Baer v. Chase*.

99 **When he was young:** Brett Martin, *Difficult Men* (New York: Penguin Books, 2014), 35.

100 **sifting through the ranks:** Brett Martin, *The Sopranos: The Book* (New York: Time Home Entertainment, Inc., 2007), 11.

101 **"I knew this character":** "Edie Falco on Sobriety, The Sopranos, and Nurse Jackie's Self-Medication," interview by Terry Gross, *Fresh Air*, NPR, April 9, 2014.

101 **offered the job:** *Talking Sopranos with Michael Imperioli and Steve Schirripa*, episode 13, "I Dream of Jeannie Cusamano," with Edie Falco, June 22, 2020.

CHAPTER 8: SHOOTING THE MOON

103 **sadistic white supremacist:** David Zurawik, "We're Not in Kansas Anymore," *Baltimore Sun*, July 7, 1997.

104 **"blew the doors off":** "Chris Albrecht," The Interviews, Television Academy Foundation, interview by Stephen J. Abramson, October 7, 2013.

105 **"The only difference":** "Oral History with Chris Albrecht," Hauser Oral History Collection, Cable Center, interview by John Higgins, October 22, 2003.

107 **massive marketing campaign:** Brian Lowry, "Miniseries or Not? A Serious Question on 'Earth to Moon,'" *Los Angeles Times*, April 4, 1998.

108 **Following a screening:** Army Archerd, "White House Moons over HBO Mini," *Variety*, March 5, 1998.

108 **"Thank you, Jeff Bewkes":** William Jefferson Clinton, "Remarks at a Screening of 'From the Earth to the Moon,'" March 5, 1998, American Presidency Project, https://www.presidency.ucsb.edu/documents /remarks-screening-from-the-earth-the-moon.

108 **A lawyer for Grey responded:** Lynette Rice, "Shandling, Grey in $100 Mil Suit," *Hollywood Reporter*, January 16, 1998.

108 **$10 million countersuit:** Jonathan Davies, "Grey Files Shandling Countersuit," *Hollywood Reporter*, March 10, 1998.

109 **told a producer:** Lynn Hirschberg, "Garry Shandling Goes Dark," *New York Times Magazine*, May 31, 1998.

110 **"In terms of the writing":** "Judd Apatow: Lessons From Garry Shandling," interview, *In Depth with Graham Bensinger*, November 2, 2016.

CHAPTER 9: THE GROUND FLOOR

114 **the guests descended:** "From Russia, with Love, to Leo," *New York Post*, June 4, 1998.

114 **a screening of *The Sopranos*:** Matt Zoller Seitz, "Born in Jersey, E Streeters Take Manhattan. Springs-teen Turns Out for Pal's TV Premiere," *Star-Ledger* (Newark), January 8, 1999.

114 **the four-hundred-seat basement theater:** Lorraine Bracco, *On the Couch* (New York: G. P. Putnam's Sons, 2006).

115 **"You are safe":** Irene Lacher, "A 'Bright Shining' Dilemma," *Los Angeles Times*, May 24, 1998.

115 **Pressed for his reaction:** Rick Lyman, "HBO's 'Shining Lie' Draws Early Complaints," *New York Times*, May 20, 1998.

116 **The series treated New York:** Emily Nussbaum, "Sarah Jessica Parker Would Like a Few Words with Carrie Bradshaw," *New York*, May 12, 2008.

117 **The sensibility earned:** Nancy Hass, "Sex Sells in the City and Elsewhere," *New York Times*, July 11, 1999.

117 **"Worse still, they're sexual bores":** Mark Lorando, "Babes in Boyland," *Times-Picayune* (New Orleans), June 4, 1998.

118 **HBO was boasting:** Veronica Chambers, "Sex and the Single Girl," *Newsweek*, August 2, 1999.

118 **HBO started throwing:** Hass, "Sex Sells in the City and Elsewhere."

118 **The finale, though largely panned:** John Carmody, "A Whole Lotta Yadda: 76.3 Million Viewers Make 'Seinfeld' Finale the No. 6 Show In History," *Washington Post*, May 16, 1998.

121 **getting more expensive:** Jeff Goodman, "HBO Won't Renew Contract to Cover Wimbledon," Associated Press, June 28, 1999.

124 **While CEO pay was skyrocketing:** Lawrence Mishel, Jared Bernstein, and John Schmitt, *The State of Working America, 1998–1999* (Ithaca, NY: Cornell University Press, 1999).

125 **"the advent of e-commerce":** "1998 Record Year for Layoffs," CNNMoney, January 7, 1999, https:// money.cnn.com/1999/01/07/economy/challenger/.

125 **"more than any American television":** Stephen Holden, "Sympathetic Brutes in a Pop Masterpiece," *New York Times*, June 6, 1999.

125 **"I get more":** "Shrink Rap: A Rapid-Fire Conversation with Lorraine Bracco, Mob Psychiatrist in 'The Sopranos,'" *Buffalo News*, March 16, 1999.

126 **The Sopranos was the talk:** Bill Carter, "A Cable Show Networks Truly Watch," *New York Times*, March 25, 1999.

127 **"A movie comes and goes":** Paula Bernstein, "HBO Paying to Make a Big Hit," *Hollywood Reporter*, January 7, 1999.

CHAPTER 10: SUNDAY IS HBO

131 **They considered selling:** Marc Randolph, *That Will Never Work* (New York: Little, Brown and Co., 2019), 11–17.

131 **"Amazon was having":** Reed Hastings and Erin Meyer, *No Rules Rules* (New York: Penguin Press, 2020), 3.

132 **slow to adapt:** Eileen Fitzpatrick, "Blockbuster Will Maintain Limited Rollout of DVD," *Billboard*, November 22, 1997.

133 **prepared to open:** Randolph, *That Will Never Work*, 228–30.

134 **While many Time Warner:** Nina Munk, *Fools Rush In* (New York: HarperBusiness, 2004), 199–200.

135 **They were deep:** Amy Wallace, "Violence, Nudity, Adult Content," *GQ*, November 5, 2010.

135 **"the HBO Shrug":** Wallace, "Violence, Nudity, Adult Content."

136 **Critics tended to focus:** Charlie McCollum, "A Comedy More Caustic Than Seinfeld," *San Jose Mercury News*, October 14, 2000.

137 **In high school:** "Mamaroneck Softball Comeback Fails Against Scarsdale," *Daily Times* (Mamaroneck, NY), May 28, 1981.

139 **"In the funeral home":** Jessica Mitford, *The American Way of Death* (New York: Vintage Books, 1963), 25–45.

139 **Make everybody nicer:** "Alan Ball," The Interviews, Television Academy Foundation, interview by Nancy Harrington, August 25, 2011.

140 **"People were calling me":** "Alan Ball," The Interviews, Television Academy Foundation.

140 **He would later describe:** Brett Martin, *Difficult Men* (New York: Penguin Books, 2014), 99.

140 **"Their notes were":** "Alan Ball," The Interviews, Television Academy Foundation.

144 **"The TV part here":** Tad Friend, "The Next Big Bet," *New Yorker*, May 14, 2001.

144 **"There's a beautiful, beautiful essay":** "Alan Ball," The Interviews, Television Academy Foundation.

CHAPTER 11: CABLE ENVY

147 **"Just as soldiers":** Gary Levin, "'Brothers' Invades Fall Lineup HBO's WWII Miniseries Battles Network Premieres," *USA Today*, January 9, 2001.

147 **He made a couple hundred copies:** Brian Lowry, "NBC's President Takes a Potshot at 'The Sopranos,'" *Los Angeles Times*, May 2, 2001.

149 **"I don't think most people realize":** "Terence Winter," The Interviews, Television Academy Foundation, interview by Karen Herman, June 18, 2013.

151 **"All you have to do":** Mike Reynolds, "A Highly Original Interview with HBO's Albrecht," *Multichannel News*, June 11, 2001.

151 **Brad Grey told:** Bill Carter, "NBC Searching for Lessons in 'Sopranos,'" *New York Times*, May 2, 2001.

151 **"A company that uses the slogan":** Tad Friend, "The Next Big Bet," *New Yorker*, May 14, 2001.

152 **wrote a lengthy memo:** Rafael Alvarez with David Simon, *The Wire: Truth Be Told* (New York: Grove Press, 2009), 32–36.

153 **Ads for the series:** Monica Hogan, "HBO Unleashes 'Brothers' Marketing Assault," *Multichannel News*, August 6, 2001.

153 **"It was always":** Brian Lowry, "HBO Assesses Impact of 'Brothers' Campaign," *Los Angeles Times*, November 14, 2001.

154 **"in a family newspaper":** David Zurawik, "Vision Cloudy on HBO show," *Baltimore Sun*, September 11, 2001.

155 **"reclaim my identity":** Sallie Hofmeister and Edmund Sanders, "AOL Chief Announces Retirement," *Los Angeles Times*, December 6, 2001.

155 **"Instead of a male hierarchy":** Seth Stevenson, "The Believer," *New York*, July 6, 2007.

158 **But before that could happen:** Jonathan Abrams, *All the Pieces Matter* (New York: Three Rivers Press, 2018), 30–31.

159 **HBO's box set retailed:** John Higgins and Allison Romano, "The Family Business: It Became a Cultural Phenomenon, but Now The Sopranos Is a Money-Making Machine Beyond Tony's Wildest Dreams," *Broadcasting & Cable*, March 1, 2004.

160 **As a parting gift:** Michael Ciepley and Edmund Sanders, "The Very Model of a Modern Media Manager," *Los Angeles Times*, May 6, 2003.

160 **"really grown toward Chris":** Cynthia Littleton, "Move to CEO a Natural for HBO's Albrecht," *Hollywood Reporter*, July 22, 2002.

161 **Executives at HBO were floored:** Bill Carter, "Sopranos Star Files Lawsuit Against HBO," *New York Times*, March 8, 2003.

162 **It was a messy split:** Gary Susman, "Gandolfini's Divorce Unearths His Drug Past," *Entertainment Weekly*, October 17, 2002.

162 **disappeared with no warning:** Brett Martin, "The Night Tony Soprano Disappeared," *GQ*, June 19, 2013.

162 **Gandolfini backed down:** Bill Carter, "Sopranos Star Drops Suit and Will Return to Series," *New York Times*, March 19, 2003.

CHAPTER 12: NOVEL RECKONINGS

163 **Much litigation, backstabbing:** Mark Davis, "Steve Wynn Bid for A.C. Site: His Hotel-Gaming-Shopping Plan Topped Donald Trump's Bid for a Golf Course. Next the City Will Vote," *Philadelphia Inquirer*, August 19, 1995.

163 **Danny DeVito signed on:** Stephen Lynch, "Fight Night! Trump vs. Wynn Brawl Coming to HBO," *New York Post*, December 6, 2003.

164 **Never happened, the conservatives hollered:** Jim Rutenberg, "Some See Peril to Presidential Legacy from TV Movie Coming Next Month," *New York Times*, October 21, 2003.

165 **The entertainment industry watched:** John Consoli, "Buyers Worry a Precedent Is Set as CBS Dumps 'Reagans,'" *Adweek*, November 10, 2003.

165 **"How much of this really happened":** Frank Rich, "Angels, Reagan, and AIDS in America," *New York Times*, November 6, 2003.

168 **Some 10.6 million people:** David Bauder, "Sex and the City Lures Best Audience," Associated Press, February 25, 2004.

168 **"the show ultimately betrayed":** David Blum, "Darren Star: The Kindle Singles Interview," Amazon Kindle Singles, January 6, 2016.

170 **its prevailing epithet:** Rob Thomas, "'The Wire' Resembles a Novel by Dickens," *Capital Times* (Madison, WI), June 10, 2003.

170 **"It's like them never giving":** "The Wire Receives One Last Emmy Snub," Associated Press, July 17, 2008.

171 **"It's the network version":** Lynn Elber, "Soapy 'Desperate Housewives,' Washes Out Reality," Associated Press, December 8, 2004.

171 **"I have received a telegram":** Denise Martin, "HBO Decision Going Down to the Wire," *Daily Variety*, January 14, 2005.

173 **"The whole overwrought montage":** Virginia Heffernan, "And They All Died Happily Ever After, Sort Of," *New York Times*, August 22, 2005.

173 **conducted a study:** Maureen Ryan, "Who Creates Drama at HBO?," *Huffington Post*, March 6, 2014.

174 **"'don't go anywhere'":** "David Milch," The Interviews, Television Academy Foundation, interview by Stephen J. Abramson, December 27, 2012.

174 **"Oftentimes profanity is used":** "David Milch," The Interviews, Television Academy Foundation.

175 **Milch told reporters:** Rich Kushman, "Deadwood Continues HBO's Streak of Terrific Dramas," *Sacramento Bee*, March 19, 2004.

175 **"Even a shitbird":** "David Milch," The Interviews, Television Academy Foundation.

176 **with the estate of William Faulkner:** Carolyn Kellogg, "Q&A: David Milch Talks William Faulkner and His New HBO Deal," *Los Angeles Times*, November 30, 2011.

176 **Inside a trailer:** Mark Singer, "The Misfit," *New Yorker*, February 6, 2005.

CHAPTER 13: INTERNET PTSD

179 **more than $12 billion:** Jill Goldsmith, "DVDs Spin Respect on Street," *Variety*, December 15, 2003.

179 **The company ended 2005:** Gina Keating, *Netflixed* (New York: Portfolio/Penguin, 2012), 163–64.

180 **companies including Amazon:** Elizabeth M. Gillespie, "Amazon.com Launches Long-Awaited TV, Movie Download Service," Associated Press, September 8, 2006.

180 **and Apple preparing:** Byron Acohido, "Apple Beats Amazon to Punch with Movie Downloads," *USA Today*, September 6, 2006.

180 **Netflix looked vulnerable:** Michael Liedtke, "Netflix Lowers Its Online Video Rental Fees," Associated Press, July 22, 2007.

183 **By any measure, Comcast:** The Lazard Report, Time Warner Inc., February 1, 2006.

186 **the article reported:** Ron Grover, "HBO's Bold Broadband Plans," *Businessweek*, November 2, 2006.

186 **"a big moment for us":** Michael Liedtke, "Coming to a Computer Near You, Netflix Delivered on the Internet," Associated Press, January 15, 2007.

188 **"It's people hating the Yankees":** Michael Malone, "Strauss' Big Dig; HBO Prez Searches for the Network's Next Hit," *Broadcasting & Cable*, April 2, 2007.

189 **"I've had seven angioplasties":** Alan Pergament, "Milch Keeps the Critics Amused," *Buffalo News*, January 17, 2007.

CHAPTER 14: A DESERT GALE

190 **When tickets first:** Steve Springer, "Oscar De La Hoya vs. Floyd Mayweather Jr: Backed into a Corner," *Los Angeles Times*, May 4, 2007.

193 **"It's Mayweather's relationship":** Tim Dahlberg, "Mayweathers Make for Must-See Reality TV," Associated Press, April 18, 2007.

193 **The seats closest:** Bernard Fernandez, "Hopkins Close to Hiring Roach as Trainer," *Philadelphia Inquirer*, May 8, 2007.

194 **filled the arena:** Bill Dwyre, "De La Hoya Showed Heart of a People's Champ," *Los Angeles Times*, May 6, 2007.

194 **Some 2.4 million:** Mark Kriegel, "How Floyd Mayweather Turned Cinco de Mayo into Boxing's Super Bowl," ESPN.com, May 5, 2020.

194 **an all-time record:** Dan Rafael, "TV Heavyweights," *USA Today*, May 30, 2002.

194 **She "pissed me off":** "HBO Chief's Two-Fisted Fury," TheSmokingGun.com, May 10, 2007.

194 **Clark County Detention Center:** Nikki Finke, "Chris Albrecht Blames Alcohol & Takes Leave from HBO After Las Vegas Arrest," *Deadline*, May 8, 2007.

195 **Thanks to posts:** "HBO Boss in Domestic Violence Bust," TheSmokingGun.com, May 7, 2007.

196 **convinced to look past another:** Amy Wallace, "Violence, Nudity, and Adult Content," *GQ*, November 5, 2010.

196 **"a wakeup call to me":** George Rush and Joanna Rush Molloy, "HBO's Chief Down & Out After Night at the Fights," *New York Daily News*, May 9, 2007.

197 **set off a tabloid frenzy:** Angela Montefinise, "I'm Doing 'Time': Sex Babe; 'Madam' & Exec," *New York Post*, June 17, 2006.

197 **HBO CHIEF ACCUSED:** Claudia Eller, "HBO Chief Accused of Assault in 1991," *Los Angeles Times*, May 9, 2007.

199 **An anonymous source:** "Why HBO Boss Got the Boot," *New York Post*, May 10, 2007.

199 **"a blatant abuse":** Claudia Eller, "Exec Faces Fallout from HBO Payout," *Los Angeles Times*, May 18, 2007.

199 **Albrecht released a statement:** "Ex-HBO Chief Pleads No Contest to Battery," Associated Press, May 12, 2007.

CHAPTER 15: HBOVER

203 **In June, they announced:** Jon Lafayette, "HBO Looks at Life After 'Sopranos'; Internal Promotions Signal Stability in Post-Albrecht Era," *Television Week*, June 11, 2007.

205 **Scanlon seemed to know:** Benjamin Reeves, "The Man Behind the Thrones," Worth.com, December 22, 2016.

206 **its sole employee:** Jason Klinger, "Commencement Remarks: Richard L. Plepler," Franklin & Marshall College, fandm.edu, May 9, 2015, https://www.fandm.edu/commencement/commencement-archive/commencement-2015/commencement-2015-citations-and-remarks/2015/05/09/commencement-remarks-richard-l-plepler.

206 **raised money for and produced:** Peter Johnson, "New View of Clash in Gaza," *USA Today*, January 16, 1990.

208 **wrote Peter Kaplan:** Peter Kaplan, "Tony's Blackout," *New York Observer*, June 12, 2007.

209 **an ill-fated real-estate boondoggle:** Andrew Gomes, "HBO Chief's Big Isle Project Bankrupt," *Honolulu Star-Advertiser*, January 7, 2011.

210 **"a great roast-master":** "Theatrical Attack on Old Boss," Page Six, *New York Post*, June 21, 2007.

211 **"We have the best":** Mike Reynolds, "AMC Goes 'Mad'—But Is Not; Original Series Push Is 'New Beginning,'" *Multichannel News*, July 16, 2007.

211 **"AMC said they wanted":** Mike Hughes, "AMC's 'Mad Men' Delves into the Cutthroat World of 50s Advertising," *USA Today*, July 3, 2007.

211 **"What they were":** Bill Carter, "HBO's Rivals Say It Has Stumbled, Though Catching Up Is Tough," *New York Times*, August 23, 2007.

211 **on the verge of shutting down:** Dave McNary, "Scribes Beating the War Drums," *Variety*, September 3, 2007.

212 **announced his first deal:** "Showtime Networks Acquires British Hit Series Secret Diary of a Call Girl," PR Newswire, December 17, 2007.

212 **He'd long wanted:** "A Fresh Tart at Showtime," *Variety*, December 17, 2007.

213 **"If I collide":** Felix Gillette, "The Hire," *New York Observer*, May 27, 2008.

214 **"I love this"**: Gillette, "The Hire."

215 **"It was very disappointing"**: Alex Witchel, "Mad Men Has Its Moment," *New York Times*, June 22, 2008.

217 **roughly $25 million**: Aaron Barnhart, "HBO Faces Stagnation," *Ventura County Star*, April 5, 2008.

217 **raised a ruckus**: Lisa de Moraes, "'Bad Road' Tries to Survive a Bad Break," *Washington Post*, March 21, 2008.

CHAPTER 16: FRESH BLOOD

219 **"I was less interested"**: Felix Gillette, "HBO, The Writer's Network," *New York Observer*, September 15, 2009.

220 **"It's important that we"**: Gillette, "HBO, The Writer's Network."

220 **"This is obviously"**: Bill Keveney, "Blood Could Pump Life into HBO," *USA Today*, September 4, 2008.

222 **BLOOD SUCKED, declared**: Post Staff, "Blood Sucked," *New York Post*, September 11, 2008.

222 **averaging 6.8 million viewers per week**: Gary Levin, "Fans Drink Up 'True Blood,'" *USA Today*, November 21, 2008.

222 **"You start worrying"**: David Bauder, "Fascination with Blood-Suckers Helps HBO to Well-Timed Hit 'True Blood,'" Associated Press, November 17, 2008.

222 **Ball got a note back:** "Alan Ball," The Interviews, Television Academy Foundation, interview by Nancy Harrington, August 25, 2011.

224 **would shell out**: Dave Itzkoff, "A Heroic Fantasy for Skeptics," *New York Times*, April 10, 2011.

225 **Before sitting down**: Joy Press, "A Dark World, a Blinding Vision; It Required Big Thinking to Re-Create George R. R. Martin's 'Game of Thrones' for HBO," *Los Angeles Times*, March 20, 2011.

225 **As a teenager:** "Tim Van Patten," The Interviews, Television Academy Foundation, interview by Ron Simon, June 26, 2009.

228 **be available only to customers**: Rob Pegoraro, "HBO Go Site Offers Online Video to Existing Subscribers Only," *Washington Post*, February 17, 2010.

229 **"Ultimately, this is"**: Todd Spangler, "Fios Rides HBO's 'Ferrari,'" *Multichannel News*, February 22, 2010.

229 **The headline from TechCrunch**: Erick Schonfeld, "A First Look at HBO Go: Curb Your Enthusiasm," TechCrunch, February 17, 2010.

229 **Instead, Dunham devoted**: Lacey Rose, "It's Goodbye 'Girls' as Lena Dunham, Cast, Execs Overshare in Show Oral History," *Hollywood Reporter*, February 1, 2007.

230 **"I felt very strongly"**: Rose, "It's Goodbye 'Girls' as Lena Dunham, Cast, Execs Overshare in Show Oral History."

231 **on a recommendation**: John Koblin, "How David Carr Became the Daddy of *Girls*," Gawker, March 18, 2013.

231 **a modest audience**: Tom Jicha, "Treme Gets Second Season Despite Weak Debut," *South Florida Sun-Sentinel*, April 14, 2010.

232 **not gone unnoticed by Scorsese**: Nikki Finke, "TCA: Why Martin Scorsese Is Now Doing TV," Deadline, August 7, 2010.

CHAPTER 17: THE ALBANIAN ARMY

234 **"We offered to sell"**: Ken Auletta, "Outside the Box," *New Yorker*, January 26, 2014.

235 **"Honestly, in my chaotic world":** "Ted Sarandos," The Interviews, Television Academy Foundation, interview by Jenni Matz, August 13, 2019.

235 **Blockbuster was its biggest**: Eileen Fitzpatrick, "Indram's Reorganization; Talking Shelf Talkers," *Billboard*, February 19, 1994.

235 **His bullishness on DVDs**: Joan Villa, "Video City Is Using Revenue-Sharing to Achieve Depth," Video Business, October 4, 1999.

235 **"I was blown away":** "Ted Sarandos," The Interviews, Television Academy Foundation.

236 **In 2003, he made Cindy Holland**: "Netflix Adds Depth to Content Acquisition Team," PR Newswire, January 13, 2003.

236 **"Before I could drive"**: Rob Owen, "Netflix Wants to Rule the World," *Pittsburgh Post-Gazette*, November 21, 2018.

236 **"the only other person":** "Ted Sarandos," The Interviews, Television Academy Foundation.

238 **a $1-million award**: Steve Lohr, "Netflix Awards $1 Million Prize and Starts a New Contest," *New York Times*, Sept. 21, 2009.

239 **named Netflix's CEO Hastings:** Michael V. Copeland, "Reed Hastings: Leader of the Pack," *Fortune*, November 18, 2010.

239 **In December, during an interview:** Tim Arango, "Time Warner Views Netflix as Fading Star," *New York Times*, December 12, 2010.

240 **a relatively modest audience:** James Hibberd; "'Game of Thrones' Premiere Ratings Are In," *Entertainment Weekly*, April 19, 2011.

241 **had attracted 5.3 million:** Allison Romano, "Best Sex Ever Helps Carnivale, K Street," *Broadcasting & Cable*, September 21, 2003.

241 **the first episode of *Rome*:** Aimee Deeken, "Rome Conquers for HBO," *Mediaweek*, September 5, 2005.

241 **By the time Comic-Con:** James Wolcott, "Where the Fanboys Are," *Vanity Fair*, October 2011.

241 **wrote a searing column:** Mary McNamara, "HBO, You're Busted," *Los Angeles Times*, July 3, 2011.

243 **teamed up with Steve Bing:** Michael O'Keeffe and Nathaniel Vinton, "Tommy Constantine, One of Two Defendants in NHL Con Case, Had Talks with Playboy About 'Potential Acquisition': Lawyer," *New York Daily News*, May 31, 2015.

245 **end in divorce:** Ian Mohr, "Starz CEO Splits from Much Younger Wife," *New York Post*, April 14, 2015.

245 **"Due to my disgust":** Mr. Kate [Kate Albrecht], *A Hot Glue Gun Mess* (New York: William Morrow, 2015), 92–94.

247 **While Albrecht would continue:** Cynthia Littleton, "Chris Albrecht Teams with Legendary for International TV Production Venture," *Variety*, December 18, 2019.

247 **an off-camera position:** Karla Jensen Mathews, LinkedIn profile, https://www.linkedin.com/in/karlajensen1/.

247 **rescued and abused dogs:** Karla Jensen @karlitasway22 Twitter.

247 **an early warning sign:** Nancy Glass et al., "Non-Fatal Strangulation Is an Important Risk Factor for Homicide of Women," *Journal of Emergency Medicine* 25, no. 3 (October 2008): 329–35.

247 **nonlethal strangulation a felony:** Jaclyn O'Malley, "Strangulation Attacks Now Carry Year in Jail," *Reno Gazette-Journal*, October 25, 2009.

247 **Many other states:** Harmeet Kaur, "In a Few Places in the US, Strangling Someone Is Only a Misdemeanor. Lawmakers Want to Change That," CNN.com, January 23, 2020.

CHAPTER 18: FLYING BLIND

251 **"The belief that":** "Sheila Nevins," Hauser Oral History Collection, Cable Center, interview by Steve Nelson, July 31, 2001.

251 ***Girls* debuted at the:** Emily Nussbaum, "It's Different for 'Girls'; Lena Dunham's New Show Is Like Nothing Else on TV," *New York*, April 2, 2012.

252 **After the screening:** Christopher Rosen, "SXSW 2012: Lena Dunham's 'Girls' Debuts with Help from Apatow," *Huffington Post*, March 3, 2012.

252 **"where it's a total lie":** Dave Itzkoff, "Cable's New Pack of Girls, Trying on the Woman Thing," *New York Times*, March 2, 2012.

252 **few tuned in:** Scott Collins, "Slow Start for HBO's 'Girls,'" *Los Angeles Times*, April 17, 2012.

253 **By season three:** Nathan Heller, "Lena Dunham: The New Queen of Comedy's First Vogue Cover," *Vogue*, January 15, 2014.

254 **"The argument has been made":** Jenna Wortham, "Where (My) Girls At?" TheHairpin.com, April 16, 2012.

254 **"I really wrote the show":** "Lena Dunham Addresses Criticism Aimed at 'Girls,'" interview by Terry Gross, *Fresh Air*, NPR, January 11, 2013.

254 **When he was a kid:** Scott Timberg, "HBO Letting It Ride on 'Luck,'" *Los Angeles Times*, January 22, 2012.

254 **"The human spirit":** "David Milch," The Interviews, Television Academy Foundation, interview by Stephen J. Abramson, December 27, 2012.

255 **Only 1.1 million households:** Scott Collins and Patrick Kevin Day, "HBO Cancels 'Luck' After Third Horse Death," *Los Angeles Times*, March 15, 2012.

255 **"You put a retired racehorse":** Dave Itzkoff, "After 'Luck' a Post-Mortem Debate," *New York Times*, March 16, 2012.

255 **"If you believe the official version":** "David Milch," The Interviews, Television Academy Foundation.

256 **Iannucci grew up:** Ian Parker, "Expletives Not Deleted," *New Yorker*, March 19, 2012.

256 **"There's 15,000 vice presidents":** Meredith Blake, "The Man Behind the New 'Veep'; Armando Iannucci Has Satirized U.K. Politics. Now Playing: The U.S.," *Los Angeles Times*, April 30, 2012.

257 **Iannucci had consumed:** Mike Ayers, "F That POTUS: Dissecting VEEP Season One, with Creator Armando Iannucci," *GQ*, June 11, 2012.

257 **In September 2012:** Sharon Waxman, "HBO Promotes Richard Plepler CEO as Bill Nelson Retires," The Wrap, September 20, 2012.

258 **That summer, Netflix announced:** Scott Roxborough and Georg Szalai, "Netflix to Enter Sophisticated, Competitive Market with Scandinavia Launch," *Hollywood Reporter*, August 15, 2012.

258 **Around the same time:** Jason Gilbert, "HBO Goes Online—Only in Scandinavia, Giving Americans Hope of a Netflix-Like Future," *Huffington Post*, August 31, 2012.

258 **"Excited to see HBO join us":** Reed Hastings, Facebook post, August 30, 2012, https://www.face book.com/reed1960/posts/277406729031341.

259 **Time Warner revealed that:** Georg Szalai, "HBO Unveils Scandinavian Joint Venture as Netflix Also Plans Nordic Launch," *Hollywood Reporter*, August 15, 2012.

259 **the conference organizers further noted:** "HBO Nordic—Joining In on the Battle of the Nordic VOD Market," Xstream A/S, September, 13, 2012.

259 **One dubbed the fight:** Colin Nixon, "HBO Nordic Stumbles, Netflix Soars in Scandinavia," nScreen-Media; April 10, 2013.

260 **By the fall of 2013:** Tero Kuittinen, "Netflix Is Crushing HBO in Europe," Yahoo News, November 21, 2013.

260 **Growing up, Berkes:** Daniel Joseph Harvey, "Alumni Corner: Otto Berkes," University of Vermont, February 27, 2020.

CHAPTER 19: SEND A RAVEN

265 **The momentousness of the occasion:** Mary McNamara, "'House of Cards' Is Deliciously Spiteful," *Los Angeles Times*, February 1, 2013.

265 **heavily supported by data:** Jake Coyle, "Netflix Show House of Cards, Is a Big Gamble," Associated Press, January 24, 2013.

266 **"we're the new television":** Coyle, "Netflix Show House of Cards, Is a Big Gamble.".

267 **tossed down the gauntlet:** Nancy Hass, "And the Award for the Next HBO Goes to . . . ," *GQ*, January 29, 2013.

267 **In September 2013:** A. J. Marechal, "HBO President Sue Naegle to Exit for Production Deal," *Variety*, September 23, 2013.

267 **Ten days after Naegle's departure:** Tim Molloy, "HBO Cuts 27-Year Vet Eric Kessler's Job 9 Months into COO Role," The Wrap, October 4, 2013.

269 **"If HBO wants to compete with Netflix":** Jesus Diaz, "True Detective Finale Crashes HBO Go," Gizmodo, March 9, 2014.

269 **Just a few weeks later:** Charlie Campbell, "HBO Go Crashes During *Game of Thrones* Season 4 Premiere," *Time*, April 7, 2014.

269 **When asked by:** Diane Brady, "Time Warner Makes Strides in Digital Media," *Bloomberg Businessweek*, February 14, 2013.

270 **drew inspiration for the series:** "'Silicon Valley' Asks: Is Your Startup Really Making the World Better?" Mike Judge interview by Dave Davies, *Fresh Air*, NPR, April 17, 2014.

271 **Judge reworked the humor:** Lacey Rose, "'Silicon Valley,' Confronts a Darker Side of Tech Culture," *Hollywood Reporter*, March 17, 2018.

271 **"If you look at the history":** "Comedy Master Class with Casey Bloys and Jenni Konner," Banff World Media Festival, June 27, 2016, https://www.youtube.com/watch?v=7jVOLp_DRtY.

272 **Afterward, Tesla's Elon Musk:** Nellie Bowles, "At HBO's *Silicon Valley* Premiere, Elon Musk Has Some Notes," Recode, *Vox*, April, 3, 2014.

272 **Some critics would:** Esther Breger, "The Boring Sexism of HBO's 'Silicon Valley,'" *New Republic*, May 30, 2014.

273 **In June 2014:** Hadas Gold, "Rupert Murdoch's Failed $80B Bid for Time Warner," *Politico*, July 16, 2014.

273 **When news of the rebuffed effort:** Andrew Ross Sorkin and Michael J. de la Merced, "Murdoch Puts Time Warner on His Wish List," Dealbook, *New York Times*, July 16, 2014.

275 **"remove all barriers":** Kelsey McKinney, "HBO Will Let You Watch Their Shows Online—Without Having to Buy Cable," *Vox*, October 15, 2014.

276 **It was a new HBO Go app:** Natalie Jarvey, "HBO Go Arrives on Xbox One," *Hollywood Reporter*, November 20, 2014.

277 **Meanwhile, Plepler was drifting:** Nicole Laporte, "HBO to Netflix: Bring It On," *Fast Company*, April 7, 2015.

277 **In early December, HBO confirmed:** Keach Hagey and Amol Sharma, "HBO to Use MLB Advanced Media for Stand-Alone Streaming Product," *Wall Street Journal*, December 9, 2014.

277 **Otto Berkes promptly resigned:** Todd Spangler, "HBO CTO Otto Berkes Resigns After Network Enlists MLB to Build OTT Platform," *Variety*, December 9, 2014.

278 **most popular in the network's history:** Sam Thielman, "Game of Thrones Is the Most Popular Show Ever on HBO," *Adweek*, June 5, 2014.

278 **simulcasting each episode:** Aaron Couch, "Game of Thrones Season 5 Set for Global Day-Date Release," *Hollywood Reporter*, March 10, 2015.

280 **By January 2016, Netflix:** Ezequiel Minaya and Amol Sharma, "Netflix Expands to 190 Countries," *Wall Street Journal*, January 6, 2016.

280 **Back in the United States:** Emily Steel, "'Game of Thrones' Season 5 Premiere Draws 8 Million Viewers," *New York Times*, April 14, 2015.

CHAPTER 20: A CLOGGED PIPELINE

281 **During his presidency:** Lauren Said-Moorhouse, "Obama Gets New 'Game Of Thrones' Before You as 'Leader of the Free World,'" CNN, April 14, 2016.

282 **a sweaty, swaggering party:** John Koblin, "HBO, Longtime Emmy Favorite, Reigns Supreme," *New York Times*, September 21, 2015.

283 **had become overgrown:** Kim Masters, "HBO High-Class Problems, $100M 'Vinyl' Disappoints Amid 'Westworld,' David Fincher Woes," *Hollywood Reporter*, February 24, 2016.

286 **"I've said kiddingly":** "Terence Winter," The Interviews, Television Academy Foundation, interview by Karen Herman, June 18, 2013.

286 **"a preachy mess":** Emily Nussbaum, "Waiting on the Man," *New Yorker*, February 14, 2016.

286 **amid reports of tension:** Elizabeth Wagmeister, "'Terence Winter Out as 'Vinyl' Showrunner Following Creative Differences," *Variety*, April 8, 2016.

287 **In May, several weeks:** Emily Steel, "Michael Lombardo, HBO Programming Chief, Is Stepping Down," *New York Times*, May 20, 2016.

288 **"Now that I have kids":** "HBO's Casey Bloys at Moravian College," interview by Joel Nathan Rosen, September 6, 2017, https://www.youtube.com/watch?v=cx19Qky26uA.

288 **He took a job:** "HBO's Casey Bloys at Moravian College."

290 **adamant that they weren't interested:** Dan Barry, "'The Deuce' Recalls Sex and Sleaze in 1970s Times Square," *New York Times*, August 24, 2017.

290 **"I wanted some kind of guarantee":** Amy Zimmerman, "HBO's New '70s Porn Drama 'The Deuce' Casts a Female Gaze on Sex," *Daily Beast*, June 6, 2017.

CHAPTER 21: AOL DÉJÀ VU

291 **"overmatched by the most basic aspects":** Daniel D'Addario, "HBO's Any Given Sunday Brings Out the Worst in Bill Simmons," *Time*, June 23, 2016.

292 **"I'm really thrilled":** Althea Legaspi, "Jon Stewart to Return to Stand-Up for HBO Specials," *Rolling Stone*, July 27, 2017.

292 **"They just overwhelmed us":** Michael Schneider, "FX's John Landgraf on the State of Peak TV, and the Network 'Arms Race,'" TV Insider, January 16, 2016.

292 **Back in early 2007:** Alex Ben Block, "How HBO Spent $200 Million on 'The Pacific,'" Associated Press, August 26, 2010.

292 **It was industry legend:** Mike Snider, "Are We Our DVD Collections? Even If We Don't Watch?," *USA Today*, August 26, 2004.

293 **News broke that Chris Rock:** Elizabeth Wagmeister, "Netflix Nabs Chris Rock for Two Comedy Specials in $40 Million Deal," *Variety*, October 13, 2016.

293 **the event featured reunions:** Stewart Oksenhorn, "HBO Pulls US Comedy Arts Festival," *Aspen Times*, May 12, 2007.

294 **Sarandos would go about creating:** James Hibberd, "Netflix Announces Stand-Up Festival with 130 Comics, Including Dave Chappelle," *Hollywood Reporter*, December 6, 2021.

295 **Over a salmon lunch:** Gerry Smith and Scott Moritz and Jeffrey McCracken, "Dinner at Martha's Vineyard Sparked AT&T's Time Warner Deal," *Bloomberg*, October 24, 2016.

295 **Bewkes got a surprise message:** Edmund Lee and Andrew Ross Sorkin, "The WarnerMedia-Discovery Deal Could Have Gone Very Differently," *New York Times*, May 24, 2021.

296 **expressing his opposition:** Andrew Wallenstein, "Donald Trump: Deals Like AT&T-Time Warner Merger 'Destroy Democracy,'" *Variety*, October 22, 2016.

297 **delivered a message:** John Koblin, "Media's Odd Couple: Proudly Freewheeling HBO and Buttoned-Up AT&T," *New York Times*, October 30, 2016.

297 **repeatedly lashed out:** Felix Gillette, "Get Ready for Big Media to Get Bigger After AT&T Victory," *Bloomberg Businessweek*, June 12, 2018.

297 **described himself as:** Scott Moritz, "AT&T CEO, Among Trump's 'Defenders,' Felt Blindsided by DOJ Suit," *Bloomberg*, November 29, 2017.

298 **Behind the scenes:** Brian Stelter and Hadas Gold, "AT&T Confirms It Paid Trump Lawyer Michael Cohen's Company," CNN, May 9, 2018.

298 **Draft after draft:** "Issa Rae Re-Answers Old Interview Questions," *Vanity Fair*, May 17, 2021.

298 **"Much of the humor":** Jon Caramanica, "Life's Hard, Web Series Gracefully Illustrates," *New York Times*, July 13, 2012.

298 **"How hard is it":** Issa Rae, *The Misadventures of Awkward Black Girl* (New York: Simon & Schuster, 2015), 45.

298 **"I just remember":** "Issa Rae Re-Answers Old Interview Questions."

299 **Rae showed them:** James Bland, *Insecure: The End* (HBO, 2021).

299 **Why not reorient the show:** "Issa Rae Re-Answers Old Interview Questions."

299 **"That opened my eyes":** "Casey Bloys in Conversation with Issa Rae," Paley Center for Media, April 25, 2017.

299 **"I got to rewriting":** *Insecure: The End*.

299 **"You can't fake these locations":** "Issa Rae Re-Answers Old Interview Questions."

301 ***Confederate* is a shockingly unoriginal idea":** Ta-Nehisi Coates, "The Lost Cause Rides Again," *Atlantic*, August 4, 2017.

301 **decried the history:** Josef Adalian, "HBO's 'Confederate' Producers Respond to the Backlash," Vulture .com, July 20, 2017.

301 **In August 2017, Disney revealed:** Natalie Robehmed, "Disney to End Distribution Agreement with Netflix, Launch Streaming Service," *Forbes*, August 8, 2017.

301 **Days later, Netflix announced:** Andrew Wallenstein, "Netflix Lures Shonda Rhimes Away from ABC Studios," *Variety*, August 13, 2017.

302 **after thirty-eight years and twelve hundred documentaries:** Maureen Dowd, "The Grande Dame of Documentary Is Leaving Her Home at HBO," *New York Times*, December 16, 2017.

CHAPTER 22: DAWN OF THE BELL HEADS

310 **went to college:** Aaron Pressman, "Who Is New AT&T CEO John Stankey?," *Fortune*, April 24, 2020.

310 **college football and little else:** Kim Masters, "Meet Time Warner's New Boss: A Hollywood Outsider with a Grand Plan," *Hollywood Reporter*, August 9, 2017.

316 **"Unless you were working in Hollywood":** "HBO's Casey Bloys at Moravian College," interview by Joel Nathan Rosen, September 6, 2017, https://www.youtube.com/watch?v=cxT9Qkyz6uA.

316 **In the end, *Succession* would:** Kate Arthur, "'Succession' Renewed for Season 4 By HBO," *Variety*, October 26, 2001.

316 **"This is not a subjective decision":** Wallace Matthews, "HBO Says It Is Leaving the Boxing Business," *New York Times*, September 27, 2018.

317 **The misgivings were mutual:** Edmund Lee and Lauren Hirsch, "After Media Detour, AT&T Confronts Old Problems," *New York Times*, May 18, 2021.

319 **Stankey told investors:** AT&T Inc. Analyst Meeting, November 29, 2018.

319 **Kevin Reilly, the former:** Meg James, "Turner's Kevin Reilly Joins Team Developing Planned Warner-Media Streaming Service," *Los Angeles Times*, December 14, 2018.

319 **multitiered pricing model:** Etan Vlessing, "WarnerMedia's Tiered Streaming Plan Takes Shape," *Hollywood Reporter*, December 5, 2018.

319 **Months later, the pricing plan:** Lillian Rizzo and Joe Flint, "AT&T Eyes $16- to $17-a-Month Streaming Service in Strategy Shift," *Wall Street Journal*, June 6, 2019.

320 **WarnerMedia was considering Bob Greenblatt:** Kim Masters, "WarnerMedia Eyes Bob Greenblatt for Major New Role," *Hollywood Reporter*, February 26, 2019.

320 **The power table was desolate:** John Koblin and Edmund Lee, "At an HBO Premiere Party, the C.E.O.'s Seat Was Empty," *New York Times*, March 1, 2019.

CHAPTER 23: IT'S JUST TV

322 **Moving forward, Bob Greenblatt:** Edmund Lee and John Koblin, "AT&T Assembles a Media Team, Joining a Battle with Giants," *New York Times*, March 4, 2019.

322 **Nobody could mistake Greenblatt:** John Koblin, "New HBO Boss Excelled at Broadcast TV. Will He Succeed in Cable's Next Era?," *New York Times*, March 4, 2019.

323 **"The dirty little secret":** Lacey Rose, "'HBO Has Hit a Ceiling': Bob Greenblatt Details Growth Strategy for HBO Max and the Streamer He Pitched NBC," *Hollywood Reporter*, December 20, 2019.

323 **the network debuted a website:** Julia Alexander, "HBO Launches 'Recommended by Humans' Tool to Help You Escape Algorithm Nightmares," *The Verge*, August 6, 2019.

323 **HBO executives told:** Felix Gillette, "HBO Is Closing Long Island Facility as Part of Reorganization," *Bloomberg*, March 13, 2019.

325 **Elliott Management, a hedge fund:** Michael J. de la Merced and Edmund Lee, "A Hedge Fund Becomes a Very Noisy Stakeholder in AT&T," *New York Times*, September 9, 2019.

326 **each of whom would receive:** Joe Flint, "WarnerMedia Nears Deal with 'Friends' Cast for Reunion Special," *Wall Street Journal*, February 6, 2020.

328 **Netflix was on pace:** Todd Spangler, "Netflix Projected to Spend More Than $17 Billion on Content," *Variety*, January 6, 2020.

328 **Every year since 1985:** "AT&T: This Dividend Aristocrat Offers 13–14% Total Returns over the Next 10 Years," Seeking Alpha, February 4, 2019.

328 **the company had borrowed:** Karl Bode, "AT&T Tried to Buy Out the Streaming Wars—And Customers Are Paying for It," *The Verge*, January 30, 2020.

328 **on its way to passing AT&T:** Drew FitzGerald, "T-Mobile Overtakes AT&T to Become No. 2 Carrier," *Wall Street Journal*, August 6, 2020.

328 **offered dire warnings:** Will Healy, "How Safe Are AT&T Stock and Its Dividend?," *Motley Fool*, February 6, 2020.

329 **During the rollout:** Jeremy Egner, "The Story's Heart? Race and Masks," *New York Times*, October 20, 2019.

330 **Of the twelve people:** Egner, "The Story's Heart? Race and Masks."

330 **Another HBO series, *Lovecraft Country*:** Mara Bachman, "Lovecraft Country: The True Story of the Tulsa Race Massacre Explained," ScreenRant, October 17, 2020.

331 **Just a few short years:** Troy Patterson, "The Time-Bomb Tension and Thrilling Surreality of HBO's 'Watchmen,'" *New Yorker*, October 18, 2019.

331 **According to one estimate:** Michael Schneider, "Peak TV Tally, According to FX Research," *Variety*, January 12, 2022.

332 **Though only in his midthirties:** Lucy Feldman, "Playwright Branden Jacobs-Jenkins on the MacArthur 'Genius' Grant," *Wall Street Journal*, September 22, 2016.

333 **Netflix confirmed reports:** Janko Roettgers, "Netflix Is Testing Variable Playback Speeds," *Variety*, October 25, 2019.

333 **when AT&T's Randall Stephenson:** Sara Salinas, "AT&T CEO Takes a Swipe at New Rival Netflix and Calls It the 'Walmart' of Video Streaming," CNBC, September 12, 2018.

333 **"The stuff I want to do":** Lacey Rose, "'I Want to Do In-Your-Face S***': Kenya Barris on Why He Left His $100M Netflix Deal to Launch BET Studios," *Hollywood Reporter*, June 23, 2021.

334 **"Every artist whose work appears":** Mattha Busby, "Outrage After Netflix Pulls Comedy Show Criticising Saudi Arabia," *Guardian*, January 1, 2019.

335 **In April 2020, AT&T announced:** Tony Maglio, "John Stankey to Replace Randall Stephenson as AT&T CEO," The Wrap, April 24, 2020.

335 **Eventually, Kilar clashed:** Henry Blodget, "Jason Kilar: Here Are My Thoughts on Hulu and the Future of TV," *Business Insider*, February 5, 2011.

335 **Reporters at Hollywood trade publications:** Tim Appelo, "The Aftermath of Hulu CEO's Bad Boy Memo," *Hollywood Reporter*, February 18, 2011.

336 **said Chris Spadaccini:** Felix Gillette, "The HBO Name, TV's Classiest Brand, Tries to Prove It Can Be Everything to Everyone," *Bloomberg*, May 26, 2020.

337 **Making matters worse:** Travis Clark, "HBO Max's Lack of Roku and Amazon Support Casts a Big Shadow over Its Launch Day," *Business Insider*, May 27, 2020.

337 **WarnerMedia was facing:** Todd Spangler, "HBO Max's 80 Million Household Dead Spot: Why Streamer Isn't on Roku or Amazon Fire TV," *Variety*, May 27, 2020.

338 **In a conference call:** Dade Hayes, "HBO Max So Far Generates a Grade of C+ as 'An Opportunity Lost,'" Deadline, May 29, 2020.

CHAPTER 24: THE TRAUMATIC ARTS

340 **Michaela Coel, the creator:** E. Alex Jung, "Michaela the Destroyer," *Vulture*, July 6, 2020.

340 **NPR's Linda Holmes:** Linda Holmes, "'I May Destroy You' Is HBO's New Unforgettable, Unmissable Drama," NPR, June 7, 2020.

341 **had helped finish:** Temi Adebowale, "How Patton Oswalt Helped Finish Michelle McNamara's I'll Be Gone in the Dark Book," *Men's Health*, June 29, 2020.

342 **"the protagonist is McNamara":** Jen Chaney, "*I'll Be Gone in the Dark* Makes Us Ponder Our Own True-Crime Fixation," *Vulture*, July 27, 2020.

343 **At HBO, the safe-TV-sex mission:** Breena Kerr, "How HBO Is Changing Sex Scenes Forever," *Rolling Stone*, October 24, 2018.

344 **HBO shelved the project:** Dominic Patten and Nellie Andreeva, "'Game of Thrones' Prequel Pilot Starring Naomi Watts Not Going Forward at HBO," *Deadline*, October 29, 2019.

345 **Diane Keaton signed on:** Nellie Andreeva, "Diane Keaton & Ellen Page in HBO's 'Tilda,'" *Deadline*, May 26, 2010.

345 **During production, however:** "HBO's 'Tilda' Removes Showrunner Mort," *Hollywood Reporter*, August 24, 2010.

345 **In 2011, amid public reports:** Nellie Andreeva, "HBO Not Going Ahead with 'Tilda' Comedy," *Deadline*, February 25, 2011.

346 **a handful of paid college interns:** Kelsey Sutton, "HBO Max's Secret to Viral TikToks: Letting Their Interns Run the Account," Adweek.com, October 12, 2020.

346 **Kilar announced he was:** Nellie Andreeva, "WarnerMedia Shakeup: Bob Greenblatt, Kevin Reilly & Keith Cocozza Out, Ann Sarnoff & Casey Bloys Upped," *Deadline*, August 7, 2020.

347 **in a brief, buoyant note:** Jason Kilar, "Some Big 2021 News For Fans," Medium, December 3, 2020.

347 **Movie-theater owners:** Anthony D'Alessandro, "AMC Boss Adam Aron Slams Warner Bros HBO Max 2021 Theatrical Window Concept: Studio Sacrificing 'Considerable' Profit," *Deadline*, December 3, 2020.

348 **Nolan told *The Hollywood Reporter*:** Kim Masters, "Christopher Nolan Rips HBO Max as 'Worst Streaming Service,' Denounces Warner Bros.' Plan," *Hollywood Reporter*, December 7, 2020.

348 **Kilar would later concede:** J. Clara Chan, "WarnerMedia CEO Concedes Rushed Rollout of HBO Max Day-and-Date Plan," *Hollywood Reporter*, September 28, 2021.

348 **pay out significant fees:** Lucas Shaw and Kelly Gilblom, "Warner Bros. Guarantees Filmmakers a Payday for HBO Max Movies," *Bloomberg*, January 9, 2021.

348 **"We suspect Nolan":** Richard Greenfield, "Dear Chris Nolan," LightShed Ventures, December 8, 2020.

348 **wrote in *The Ankler*:** Richard Rushfield, "Special Dispatch: Mad Max," *The Ankler*, December 4, 2020.

349 **The *Sopranos* creator felt angry:** Zach Sharf, "'Sopranos' Creator 'Extremely Angry' Prequel Film Streaming on HBO Max: I Wouldn't Have Made It," *IndieWire*, September 14, 2021.

349 **It was based:** Mark Yarm, "The Real-Life Bros of 'Entourage,'" *Rolling Stone*, June 4, 2015.

350 **"I love it":** Preston Turegano, "Showtime Updates Its Slogan from 'No Limits' to a 'New Face,'" *San Diego Union-Tribune*, July 23, 2004.

350 **a "hatefully unfunny" spin-off:** Mark Kermode, "Entourage Review—Hatefully Unfunny," *Guardian*, June 21, 2015.

350 **during a panel event:** Francesca Bacardi, "Alison Brie Was Asked to Audition Topless for 'Entourage,'" *New York Post*, June 12, 2017.

350 **Brie clarified on Twitter:** Stephanie Marcus, "Alison Brie Clarifies Entourage Audition Story," *Huffington Post*, June 12, 2017.

350 **actor Ariane Bellamar:** Zach Sharf, "CBS 'Looking Into' Claims That Jeremy Piven Groped Reality Star Ariane Bellamar on 'Entourage' Set," *IndieWire*, October 31, 2017.

351 **Piven denied the allegations:** Erin Nyren, "Jeremy Piven Unequivocally Denies Groping Allegations," *Variety*, October 31, 2017.

351 **By 2019, Piven was blaming:** Charles Trepany, "Jeremy Piven Sounds Off on MeToo Movement," *USA Today*, July 3, 2019.

351 **"Most women on this show":** Anne Cohen, "I Watched 11 Hours of *Entourage* & This Is What It Taught Me About Harvey Weinstein," *Refinery29*, November 1, 2017.

351 **"Given the current deluge":** Jill Gutowitz, "Does the Pilot of 'Entourage' Actually Suck?" *Vice*, January 4, 2018.

352 **Ellin accused HBO:** Ethan Alter, "Entourage Creator Doug Ellin on How 'Wave of Righteous PC Culture,' Impacted HBO Show's Legacy," Yahoo News, April 27, 2021.

CHAPTER 25: CRIMES OF THE PAST

353 **a clandestine serenade:** Edmund Lee and John Koblin, "In a Deal with Discovery Hatched in Secret, AT&T Sheds Its Media Business," *New York Times*, May 17, 2021.

354 **In 2021 alone:** Tim Baysinger, "Discovery CEO David Zaslav's Pay Sinks 65% to $48.5 Million," The Wrap, April 29, 2020.

354 **After an unsatisfying stint:** Richard Siklos, "New Chief at Discovery Is 2nd Senior Executive to Leave NBC This Week," *New York Times*, November 17, 2006.

355 **Zaslav said right before the debut:** John Koblin, "Will You Pay to Stream Comfort Shows? Discovery Is About to Find Out," *New York Times*, January 3, 2021.

357 **Even among its fans:** Gerry Smith, "HBO Max Frustrates Subscribers with Glitchy Streaming Tech," *Bloomberg*, July 26, 2021.

357 **"What a dismal failure":** Meg James and Stephen Battaglio, "AT&T Plans to Spinoff WarnerMedia in a Huge Deal with Discovery. What Went Wrong?," *Los Angeles Times*, May 16, 2021.

358 **Barry Diller said on CNBC:** Nicholas Jasinski, "Media Mogul Barry Diller Criticizes AT&T's M&A History," *Barron's*, May 21, 2021.

362 **"It's such a trope":** Carrie Battan, "Mike White on Money, Status, and Appearing on 'Survivor,'" *New Yorker*, July 18, 2021.

363 **grew in popularity:** Denise Petski, "'The White Lotus' Season Finale Draws 1.9M Multiplatform Viewers for Series High," *Deadline*, August 17, 2021.

365 **A few years later:** Marilyn Reles, "HBO Writer & Latinx Rapper Chris Gabo Drops an Anthem for the Misunderstood: 'One of Those,'" TheHypeMagazine.com, October 8, 2021.

367 **Project Popcorn, the strategy:** Travis Clark, "Warner Bros.' Strategy of Releasing Movies to Theaters and HBO Max on the Same Day Is Very Popular with Consumers, According to a New Survey," *Business Insider*, May 10, 2021.

367 **Together, HBO Max and HBO:** Mollie Cahillane, "HBO Max Grows to 73.8 Million Global Subscribers Ahead of Pending Merger," *Adweek*, January 26, 2022.

367 **a far cry from Netflix's:** Tim Peterson, "The Rundown: Netflix's Subscriber Growth Sped Up in Q4 2021 but Fell Short of Expectations," DigiDay, January 21, 2022.

369 **a five-year deal:** Peter White, "David Chase Strikes Five-Year First-Look TV & Film Deal with WarnerMedia," *Deadline*, October 1, 2021.

369 **gnawed-on and much-watched sequel:** Alexandra Del Rosario and Nellie Andreeva, "'And Just Like That . . .' Delivers HBO Max's Strongest Series Debut," Deadline, December 10, 2021.

369 **In January, Lena Dunham:** Seth Abramovitch, "Lena Dunham on Her First Film in a Decade, Youthful Blind Spots and Hope to Reboot 'Girls,'" *Hollywood Reporter*, January 19, 2022.

369 **a *Six Feet Under* follow-up:** Joe Otterson, "'Six Feet Under' Follow-Up in Early Development at HBO," *Variety*, December 10, 2021.